Contents

THE
DRAMATIC WORKS
OF
DENIS JOHNSTON

Volume 1

COLIN SMYTHE LIMITED
Gerrards, Cross, 1977

The Dramatic Works of Denis Johnston first published as a complete collection in 1977 by Colin Smythe Ltd, P.O. Box 6, Gerrards Cross, Bucks, SL9 7AE.

Standard Edition ISBN 0–901072–52–4

Limited Signed Edition ISBN 0–901072–71–0

These plays are intended for the stage and the writer is pleased to have them performed as often as possible. There is, however, a fee payable for any public use, which can usually be negotiated with the author, care of the publishers, Colin Smythe Ltd.

Produced in Great Britain
Typeset by Watford Typesetters Limited,
and printed and bound by Billing & Sons Limited,
Guildford, Oxford and Worcester

To
my dear
BETTY
who can't abide
some of the parts
I write for women.

Acknowledgements

The author wishes to thank the following for permission to reprint copyright material:

Macmillan & Company, Ltd, and Michael and Anne Yeats for the stanzas from *Cathleen ni Houlihan* from *The Collected Plays* and *Into the Twilight* from Yeats's *Collected Poems*.

Introduction

NEARLY everybody I know seems at one time or another to have written a play. Even my Auntie Sadie, a most amiable and well balanced woman in her day, responded to my juvenile request to provide a drama for production in a toy theatre. The resulting script conformed strictly to the available cast of cardboard figures to most of whom she gave names taken from the suburbs of Belfast – Lord Knock, Bally McCarrot, Sandy Row and so on. And it had as its title 'The Mystery of the Blackstaff' – also a matter of local interest. All of this assured an early production by the satisfied Management although it only had a brief run, and as far as I can remember no Notices appeared in any of the local papers. However, it was as good in its way as are most first plays, and as is usual with its genre, the manuscript has not survived.

The general tendency to write plays rather than novels or gossipy biographies is probably due to a certain glamour that clings around the Theatre, and to the fact that in this particular field of literary endeavour the work consists mainly of dialogue, in the composition of which there seems to be no need for either research or grammar. In my own first ventures the urge was partly as above, but to an even greater extent it was rooted in the fact that I liked the company and conversation of actors and actresses – particularly the latter, two of whom I married, although not at the same time. I might have been classified as a hanger-on in Greenrooms, especially that of the Abbey Theatre, which was quite accessible to people of that class in those days.

Being a very bad actor myself, temperamentally averse to being looked at by people I could not see, it was inevitable, I suppose, that I would gravitate sooner or later into the role of a Director rather than that of a Performer. And it was equally likely that in the course of time I would find it harder and harder to find the kind of plays that I enjoyed handling. So in the end I started writing them myself.

In the tradition learnt from my Aunt, it is hardly surprising that my earlier work should conform to the peculiarities of a ready-made cast, with so many of my closest friends in the Abbey and later in the Gate Companies of the middle thirties, and that their entrances and exits should as a rule take place from the side of the stage on which their dressing rooms happened to be. This is an aspect of play-construction for the Abbey in its hey-day that has not yet come to the notice of many writers of doctorial theses, although it has been noticed by some of the more persistent students that very little action of importance was usually planned to take place up-stage right, for the simple reason that the proscenium arch of the old Theatre was not even remotely opposite the centre of the stage, leaving that particular area out of sight for about a third of the Audience. More important still for a Dramatist to keep in mind was the hazard that once the curtain was up exposing the rear wall of the stage itself (as was frequently the case), a character requiring to get to the other side in preparation for his next entrance had to leave the theatre by the scene-dock door, hurry down a Lane and ring a bell to get in by another door at the corner of the street. No harm was done if in the meantime there were sufficient lines in the play to keep things going during any delay caused by conversations with casual acquaintances whom one usually met in the Lane. Otherwise there could be a nasty hold-up. More subtle still was the point frequently overlooked by beginners that for a play to be popular with the stage staff it should conclude in the same set in which it opened, so that the crew did not have to strike the scenery after the final curtain, but could leave it up for another opening on the following night. At those salaries a happy crew was something to be desired.

Keeping these technical points in mind, it is hard to see how any thoughtfully written play could be turned down by the Management, however bad it might be in other ways. And its observance by me may well account for the acceptance of several plays of my own that in other respects were clearly out of line with Abbey traditions. In those days for a play to be recognised as being genuinely 'Irish' it should take place in a rural setting, and should have 'PQ' rather than metropolitan dialect. (PQ stands for 'Peasant Quality' and does not cover the Dublinese popularised by Sean O'Casey.) As regards subject matter, they should centre around people who are either in or escaping from jail, or about the problems of enlightened Priests or of delinquent children. Or, if comedies, they should begin with a funny Will, or Returned

Americans, or simply the question as to who will marry who and get the farm. It is true that some people such as Lennox Robinson did manage to touch on such subjects as upper-class poverty, abortion, and even incest. But then he was in a position to accept his own plays, while O'Casey had not only a new vocabulary to exploit but also a set of splendid characters known to him from his Citizen Army days, whom he put on the stage for as long as they lasted, sometimes without even bothering to change their names. But then Sean, thanks to a sound political and industrial background was licensed to cause Riots, which is not everybody's privilege.

At that time, if in the mainstream of Irish playwriting (and in this I do not include the work of either Synge or Shaw) one did not venture to question or even to imply any mockery of religious or moral convictions, and certainly no dirty words were ever heard, apart from an occasional 'bloody'. Nowadays the most successful Irish plays tend to be openly anti-clerical, while the most popular jokes are about birth control, the Holy Ghost and menstruation. All of this is happily accepted by an intimidated corps of critics who do not wish it to be thought that they are not 'up' in these subjects. In those days I once had a line queried in a radio script that raised the suspicion that it might be a bit questionable. Ahem. If you will forgive me, the line was: 'This silken girl with sable hair.' I must say however that when I offered to still these fears by altering the word 'silken' into 'woollen' the conference dissolved into laughter, and I got away with the phrase. Laughter is always a safe catalyst for our country's problems.

Anyhow, the only dramatic morceau of my own that ever raised a public protest on the stage was a small, pastoral Ballet about a shepherd with a flock of sheep that happened to include a goat. (The danger of this can be seen.) After the second night all theological overtones were eliminated by the Management. But it was too late. For the rest of the run half the audience who knew the point were explaining it to the other half.

It will be fairly clear from the present collection that I have not moved with the times so far as Dublin's Theatre is concerned. Indeed, having been somewhat out of step at both ends of my career, it might well be questioned as to whether any of my plays can be classified as 'Irish' at all. Maybe they belong to some unclassified underworld in which problems are presented from which there is no solution and questions are asked that had better be ignored. At any rate this must have been the impression in the minds of most of the original cast of *The Moon in the Yellow*

River, some of whom went off to the National Library to look up the words of St Thomas Aquinas. They came back with amendments to some of my lines that dimmed his nimbus even further than I would have wished to do. As they were all players of considerable experience they managed to perform the play with that subtle air of not being in any way responsible for its sentiments, but this, of course was only to begin with. At the last production at which I was present, all the parts were approximated to with considerable verve, and the final curtain was omitted altogether, whether by design or by accident I have never found out. It may be that Agnes had to catch a last bus.

If you – my reader – have ever been puzzled by the universal problem of ever getting a first play put on, let me say before we part that as a rule the difficulty is not necessarily one of merits, but one of how to get it read at all. The talents that make a great Theatrical Impresario do not usually extend to an ability to read. He can usually recognise what he likes when he sees what may even be a bad performance, but scripts have got a way of piling up in a front office where they never get read except by a young lady inhabiting a desk. And when she is told to weed them out it will be understood that she has a vested interest in finding some good reason for saying 'No' before the third page. These plays come in all sizes and shapes including one that I remember arriving at the Abbey with a covering note which said: Enclosed Short Play. Actually the most unusual thing about it was that it was written on the back of a roll of wall paper, and so far from being 'short' it was about twenty feet long, and had to be read down on the floor.

So if I may presume to give some advice about this impasse it is this: Capitalise on another special feature of the Stage which is that almost as many people feel in their hearts that they can act as those who are certain that they can write plays – if only etc. etc. So start a small repertory movement of your own with private membership to begin with for economy's sake, and open up with *Peer Gynt*, or *Waiting for Godot* if scenery raises too much of a problem. This should set the tone, and if not, follow it up with Pinter. You should have no trouble in persuading some local Name to lend his title to the Presidency, while a capable, frustrated wife of somebody else will usually make a fine unpaid Secretary. Your own play then comes on at about third or fourth in the list – you not having been able to resist persuasion, and, after all, as Organiser you can hardly say No. What is more – it may turn out to be good, in which case it will be revived with Notices in the Papers, and then

– Presto – it gets around that some Manager is dropping in to take a look at it. Whether he does or not is of no importance. It just has to be thought that some possible competitor is after it, and out it comes from all those piles of scripts. If it is no good it will save you a lot of further trouble, but if it's worth trying, you're on your way. And good luck to you.

This is the way the Abbey started – and the Gate – and the Provincetown Playhouse on the Cape. Eugene O'Neill – R. C. Sheriff – James Bridie – and even Shaw himself (who did better still and got himself banned.) It all goes to show that on the Stage as in all the Arts, self-help is the best way in.

A more serious question may be how and when to get out. The last of these plays of mine to be written was completed over twenty years ago and I am sometimes asked by friendly busybodies why I have not written any more since then. Indeed the late Bernard Shaw, above mentioned, who could be a King Busybody if he chose, once wrote to me on a postcard: Why don't you write more plays? I suppose the answer is that there comes a point after which nobody ought to write more plays – a phenomenon that applied to Shaw as pertinently as to all of us. And if you are kind enough to ask me how to recognise when that point has come, I would say that it is when one notices that what one has written lightheartedly in the twenties turns out to be only too horribly true in the seventies.

In the meantime, let us continue to read and enjoy and respect everything that that great old Dubliner has had to say.

And then, do the opposite.

THE OLD LADY
SAYS 'NO!'

*A Romantic Play in Two Parts
with Choral Interludes*

OPUS ONE

ONE of the best loved figures of Irish romantic literature is Robert Emmet. The story of his rebellion of 1803 has all of the elements that make for magic. It was very high-minded, and completely unsuccessful. It was picturesquely costumed and insufficiently organized. Its leader – a young protestant university man of excellent social background – having failed to achieve anything more than an armed street riot, remained behind to bid goodbye to his forbidden sweetheart, instead of taking flight as any sensible rebel should do. In consequence of this, he was captured by an ogre of melodrama called Major Sirr, and was hanged after making one of the finest speeches from the dock in the annals of the criminal courts – and we have had some pretty good ones in Ireland.

So we all love Robert Emmet. Yeats and De Valera loved him, each in his own fashion. I do too; and so did Sarah Curran. Even the hoardings along the Canal have been known to display a chalked inscription, 'UP EMMET'. We all agree that it was a pity that some of his supporters had to murder one of the most liberal judges on the bench, Lord Kilwarden, and that the only practical outcome of his affray was to confirm the Union with England for about a hundred and twenty years. Our affection is not affected by these details.

The tragedy of his love has been immortalized by Tom Moore in one of his finest ballads:

> She is far from the land
> Where her young hero sleeps,
> And lovers around her are sighing.
> But coldly she turns from their gaze, and weeps,
> For her heart in his grave is lying.

Who cares that this reason for her absence from the land is the fact that she subsequently married an English officer, and ended her days happily with him elsewhere? For us, her heart will always be lying in Robert's grave. And lying is the operative word.

15

The whole episode has got that delightful quality of story-book unreality that creates a glow of satisfaction without any particular reference to the facts of life. To put it into conflict with those facts ought to be an easy proposition in the theatre, and particularly so back in 1926, when several years of intermittent and unromantic civil war had soured us all a little towards the woes of Cathleen ni Houlihan. It was inevitable that such a play would be written in Ireland by someone or other at about that time.

Although it is by no means my favourite play, and is my only work that might fairly be described as anti-Irish, it is by far the best spoken-of in its native habitat. In Dublin it is now generally regarded as a strongly nationalistic piece, full of sound popular sentiments and provided with a title calculated to annoy Lady Gregory and the Abbey Theatre. It is true that on the occasion of its first production at the Gate, some tentative efforts were made to have me prosecuted – for what, I cannot at present remember. But those days are long past, and the only acrimony that the play evokes today is among the cast, the older members of which argue strongly during rehearsals over business and movements that were used on previous occasions, and must not now be altered.

As for the title, I cannot be held responsible for this. It was written by somebody on a sheet of paper attached to the front of the first version, when it came back to me from the Abbey. Whether it was intended to inform me that the play had been rejected, or whether it was being offered as an alternative to my own coy little name for the play – *Shadowdance* – is a question that I never liked to ask. So it remained, thereafter, as the title of the work – a definite improvement for which I have always been grateful. Lennox Robinson used to complain bitterly about any suggestion that Lady G. was against the play, but all I know of the matter is the distaste she expressed to me in the back sitting-room of her hotel in Harcourt Street. I was never invited to Gort.

It is, of course, a director's play, written very much in the spirit of 'Let's see what would happen' if we did this or that. We were tired of the conventional three-act shape, of conversational dialogue, and of listening to the tendentious social sentiments of the stage of the 'twenties, and we wanted to know whether the emotional appeal of music could be made use of in terms of theatrical prose, and an opera constructed that did not have to be sung. Could dialogue be used in lieu of some of the scenery, or as a shorthand form of character-delineation? Could the associations and thought-patterns already connected with the songs and slogans of our city be used deliberately to evoke a planned reaction from a known audience?

The opening playlet – which was felt by Lady G. to be an all-too-brief preliminary to a vein of "coarseness" that was to follow – is made up almost entirely from lines by Mangan, Moore, Ferguson, Kickham, Todhunter, and the romantic school of nineteenth-century Irish poets, still well known to everybody although no longer imitated. So too, the final speech of the play contains some easily recognizable sections of Pearse's funeral oration for O'Dono-van Rossa, together with a large portion of Emmet's actual speech from the dock, which concludes:

'When my country takes her place amongst the nations of the earth, then, and not till then, let my epitaph be written.'

There are both handicaps and benefits to be derived from writing for so specialized an audience. A phrase such as 'When in the course of human events' will spontaneously call up an association-pattern when uttered in the United States, where it belongs. An Englishman, prodded with the expression 'Kiss me, Hardy', may react in a variety of ways, but some response is usually noticeable. On the other hand, outside Ireland, a reference to 'my four beauti-ful green fields' will not wring any withers, but becomes instead a mere literary reference that may or may not be recognized as an echo from Yeats.

Thus, although written in a language common to all three coun-tries, *The Old Lady* is not quite the same play in London or New York as it is in Dublin. Across the sea its intentional clichés are no longer clichés, and the various daggers concealed within its lacy sentiments find no flesh into which to probe. For this reason, apart from one production in New York, a couple in London, and a few presentations in colleges with *avant garde* theatre departments, it has never been performed outside Ireland. There the pattern devised by Hilton Edwards and Micheál MacLiammóir for its first production in 1929 has become as much an integral part of the play as is the text.

Although many of its expressionist tricks are now commonplace, especially in radio production, it was, at the time of writing, a fairly original type of play, and technically it owes less to other dramatists than anything that I have written since. The play's actual foster parents are neither Evreinov, O'Neill nor Georg Kaiser. Nor has Joyce got much to do with it, although I gratefully acknow-ledge the presence of his finger in the stirring of some of my later pies. I have once or twice been written to by students of the drama who feel that they can trace the influence of *Finnegans Wake* upon *The Old Lady*. This is a book that I first attempted to read through about ten years ago, and the only part of it that has got into my play did so by a most circuitous route. This is the *Thuartpeatrick* phrase, misspelled *St Peetrick* by me in the party scene. Its presence there is a surprising reminder that Tuohy, the artist who painted both Joyce and his old father, had sentences from Joyce's own lips that he was bandying around Dublin as early as the Nine Arts Ball of 1925. In this very second-hand condition the expression has found its way into my text, as a quotation from a section of a book that had then hardly been begun. There are, of course, two short quotes from *Ulysses* in *The Old Lady*, together with a phrase or two, such as 'Jacobs Vobiscuits'. But any resemblances to the *Wake* have nothing to do with me.

The two plays to which this experiment does owe something are, firstly, Kaufman and Connelly's *Beggar on Horseback* – a superb piece of American expressionism that I have always admired – and secondly, a Continental satire called *The Land of Many Names* that I once saw in the 'twenties. Who wrote it, and where it came from, I have often since wondered. I think it may have been one of the Capeks.

The Old Lady Says 'No!'

This play was first produced by the Dublin Gate Theatre Studio at the Peacock Theatre on July 3rd, 1929, with the following cast:

The Speaker (Robert Emmet)
MICHEÁL MACLIAMMÓIR

Sarah Curran   MERIEL MOORE

Major Sirr   HILTON EDWARDS

First Redcoat   JOHANN MANNING

Second Redcoat   MITCHEL COGLEY

The Other Ones:

GEARÓID O'LOCHLAIN   CORALIE CARMICHAEL

MICHAEL SCOTT   DOROTHY CASEY

FRED JOHNSON   HAZEL ELLIS

DUDLEY WALSH   FLORENCE LYNCH

ART. O'MURNAGHAN   IDA MOORE

DOM. BOWE   KAY SCANNELL

PAULINE BESSON   SUSAN HUNT

SHEILA CAREY

The play produced and lit by Hilton Edwards; the settings designed and executed by Micheál MacLiammóir; costumes designed by Micheál MacLiammóir and made up by Bougwaine Wilson.

The action of the play opens in the garden of The Priory, the home of John Philpot Curran, close to Rathfarnham, on the night of August 25th, 1803.

PART ONE

To the left the dark gable of a building can be seen with a light burning behind the blind in the first-floor window. It is the house of John Philpot Curran, The Priory, close to Rathfarnham, a village outside Dublin. To the centre and to the right are the trees of the garden, and behind them the profile of Kilmashogue and the hills beyond. It is the night of August 25th in the year 1803, and the sound of men's voices is dying away into the distance as the Curtain rises.

VOICES.

> With their pikes in good repair,
> > Says the Shan Van Vocht,
> To the Curragh of Kildare
> The boys they will repair,
> And Lord Edward will be there,
> > Says the Shan Van Vocht.

(The window opens and SARAH CURRAN *gazes out towards the mountains.)*

SARAH.

The air is rich and soft – the air is mild and bland.
Her woods are tall and straight, grove rising over grove.
Trees flourish in her glens below and on her heights above,
Oh, the fair hills of Eire, oh.
Down from the high cliffs the rivulet is teeming
To wind around the willow banks that lure him from above.
Ah, where the woodbines with sleepy arms have wound him . . .
(She starts.)
Who is there? I heard a rustling in the trees!
Who is there, I say?

(The SPEAKER *emerges from among the trees. He is dressed as Robert Emmet in a green tunic, white-plumed hat, white*

21

*breeches and Wellington boots with gold tassels. At his side
hangs a large cavalry sword.)*

SPEAKER (*with an appropriate gesture*). Hush beloved, it is I.

SARAH. Robert! I think, oh my love, 'tis thy voice from the kingdom of souls!

SPEAKER. Was ever light of beauty shed on loveliness like thine!

SARAH. Oh, Robert, Robert, why have you ventured down? You
are in danger.

SPEAKER. My bed was the ground, my roof the greenwood above:
and the wealth that I sought, one far, kind glance from my love.

SARAH. My love, for a vision of fanciful bliss to barter thy calm life
of labour and peace!

SPEAKER. What matters life! Deirdre is mine: she is my queen, and
no man now can rob me!

SARAH. The redcoats are everywhere. Last night they were around
the house and they will come again.

SPEAKER. Let them come! A million a decade! Let me be persuaded
that my springing soul may meet the eagle on the hills, and I am
free.

SARAH. Ah, go, forget me. Why should sorrow o'er that brow a
shadow fling?

SPEAKER. My strong ones have fallen from the bright eye of day.
Their graves are red, but their souls are with God in glory.

SARAH. Ah, love, love! Where is thy throne? It is gone in the wind!

SPEAKER. A dark chain of silence is thrown o'er the deep. No streak
of dawning is in the sky. It is still unriven, that clanking chain.
Yet, am I the slave they say?

SARAH. A lost dream to us now in our home! Ullagone! Gall to our
heart!

SPEAKER. But there is lightning in my blood – red lightning tightening in my blood! Oh, if there was a sword in every Irish hand!
If there was a flame in every Irish heart to put an end to slavery
and shame! Oh, I would end these things!

SARAH. It is too late! Large, large affliction unto me and mine, that
one of his majestic bearing, his fair and stately form, should
thus be tortured and o'erborne – that this unsparing storm
should wreak its wrath on head like this!

SPEAKER (*softly*). My earthly comforter, whose love so indefeasible
might be! Your holy, delicate, white hands shall girdle me with
steel. You'll pray for me, my flower of flowers! You'll think of
me through daylight hours, my virgin flower!

SARAH. At least I'll love thee till I die.

SPEAKER. How long, ah, Sarah, can I say how long my life will last?

SARAH. Cease boding doubt, my gentlest love; be hushed that struggling sigh.

SPEAKER. When he who adores thee has left but a name, ah say, wilt thou weep?

SARAH. I shall not weep. I shall not breathe his name. For my heart in his grave will be lying. I shall sing a lament for the Sons of Usnach.

SPEAKER. But see, she smiles, she smiles! Her rosy mouth dimples with hope and joy; her dewy eyes are full of pity!

SARAH. Ah, Robert, Robert, come to me.

SPEAKER (*climbing up*). I have written my name in letters of fire across the page of history. I have unfurled the green flag in the streets and cried aloud from the high places to all the people of the Five Kingdoms: 'Men of Eire, awake to be blest! Rise, Arch of the Ocean and Queen of the West!' I have dared all for Ireland and I will dare all again for Sarah Curran. Ah, it is a glorious thing to dare!

(*He is about to touch her outstretched hand when –*)

A VOICE. Halt! Who goes there?

SARAH. Ah God! The yeomen!

VOICES. The countersign.
    Stand.
    Front point.
    Advance.

SPEAKER. The flint-hearted Saxon!

(*He makes a gesture to her. She disappears and the light goes out.*)

SARAH. . . . in their fearful red array!

FIRST REDCOAT (*rushing forward*). Hold! Surrender or I fire!

SECOND REDCOAT. We hold this house for our lord the King.

FIRST REDCOAT. Amen, says I. May all traitors swing.

SPEAKER. (*springing down and folding his arms*). Slaves and dastards, stand aside!

(MAJOR SIRR enters.)

SIRR. Spawn of treason, bow down thy humbled head to him, the King!

SPEAKER. A nation's voice, a nation's voice, 'tis stronger than the King.

SIRR. Silence rebel! Do you not know who I am?

SPEAKER. A jackal of the Pale.

23

SIRR. Major Sirr.

SPEAKER. Who trapped Lord Edward?

SIRR. The same.

SPEAKER (*drawing his sword*). I am honoured. Ireland will remember. Look well to your soul, Major Sirr, for the dawn of the Gael is still to break; when they that are up will be down and they that are down will be up. I tell you, Major Sirr, we'll be a glorious nation yet – redeemed, erect, alone!

> (*He leaps upon them. One of the* REDCOATS *clubs his musket and strikes him a resounding blow upon the head. The lights flicker momentarily and he lies still.* SARAH CURRAN *appears once more at the window.*)

SARAH. A star is gone! There is a blank in heaven. The last great tribune of the world is dead.

SIRR (*seemingly a little surprised*).

> The sport of fools – the scoff of knaves,
> Dead ere they blossomed, barren, blighted.
> They came, whose counsels wrapped the land in foul rebellion's flame,
> Their hearts unchastened by remorse, their cheeks untinged by shame,
> To sue for a pity they shall not – shall not –
> Er –

> (*One of the* REDCOATS *kneels beside the* SPEAKER *and shakes him by the shoulder.* SIRR *looks helplessly into the wings from which he receives a whispered prompt.*)

PROMPT. Find.

FIRST REDCOAT. Ay!

SECOND REDCOAT. What's up?

SIRR (*to the wings*). Curtain ... curtain ... I say.

STAGE HAND. Is he hurted?

VOICES. He's hurt. Hurt. He's hurt. Hurted.

FIRST REDCOAT. It wasn't my fault. I only ...

SIRR. Curtain, please. Do stand back for a moment and give him a chance.

VOICES. Loosen his collar. What do you think you're doing? How did it happen? What's the matter? He'll be all right. Give him brandy. Take those boots off. Stand back, please. Did you see the skelp he gave him? Can I help?

> (*The Curtain comes jerkily down and there is a heavy tramping behind upon the stage. Presently* SIRR *comes through the Curtain. House lights up.*)

24

SIRR (*beckoning to someone in the audience*). Is there a doctor in
... I say ... can you?

DOCTOR. Me?

SIRR. Just come through for a minute. I think he'll be all right.

DOCTOR. It looked a heavy enough ...

SIRR. I don't think it is ...

DOCTOR. ... blow from the front.

SIRR. ... very serious, really.

DOCTOR. I hope not. Anyhow you had better see whether you
can't ...

(*They disappear through the Curtain, talking. Presently* SIRR
re-appears.)

SIRR. Ladies and gentlemen ... he ... er ... the doctor would like
the curtain up again ... the draught blows through from the
scene dock when it's across. We're really very sorry that the
performance should be held up ... but you see ... it's nothing
really ... He ... er ... says he will be all right in a moment if
he's kept quiet and not moved ... if you would only be so good
as to keep your seats and stay perfectly quiet for a few moments
... just a few moments ... while the doctor is ... er ... busy
... I'm sure we'll be able to go on ... if you don't mind ...
curtain please ... quite quiet please ... just for a few minutes
... thank you so much.

(*He hurries off. The Curtain is slowly drawn again, disclosing
the* SPEAKER *where we left him, now attended by the* DOCTOR,
the STAGE HAND *and one of the* REDCOATS. *A black gauze
curtain has been drawn behind him through which we can
see dim figures moving about and hear the thumping of heavy
weights.*)

DOCTOR. That's better now. Can you get them off?

STAGE HAND. Yes, sir. They're coming now.

(*He draws off one of the* SPEAKER'S *boots.*)

REDCOAT. How could I know anyway? It wasn't my fault. I tell you
I only ...

DOCTOR. That's all right. Hold up his head a little. That's better.
Oh, they've got it up.

(*He refers to the Curtain.*)

REDCOAT. Ah, God, isn't it awful!

DOCTOR. Ask those people to keep quiet there while he's coming
round.

STAGE HAND. Ay, Barnie, tell them to shut up! Give us a hand with
this boot. I can't get a grip on it at all.

REDCOAT. I don't know how it could have happened at all. You pull now.

STAGE HAND. Ah, will you hold on? How the hell . . .

DOCTOR. Sssssssh!

STAGE HAND. There she comes.

DOCTOR. See if you can get something to cover his legs with. He must be kept warm. And ask them to turn down that light a bit. He'll be all right soon if he's kept quiet and allowed to come round.

(*The* STAGE HAND *goes out obligingly.*)

REDCOAT. I swear to God I hit him no harder than I was shown yesterday. I only . . . look . . .

DOCTOR. Ah, be quiet you, and be off. You're more of a hindrance than a help.

REDCOAT. It's all very well blaming me, but I only did what I was shown bef . . .

DOCTOR. Ssssssh!

(*The* REDCOAT *goes off muttering protestations. The lights are dimmed, making the forms behind the gauze clearer still. Presently the* STAGE HAND *enters with a pair of gaudy carpet slippers.*)

STAGE HAND. Would these be any use? They were all I could find. They belong to Mr . . . er . . .

DOCTOR. He's stirring a little.

(*He examines the* SPEAKER *while the* STAGE HAND *puts the slippers on his feet.*)

STAGE HAND. Is the lights O.K. now?

DOCTOR. What's that? Oh, fine. You'd better . . .

STAGE HAND. I brought a sup of brandy.

DOCTOR. Brandy! Good heavens, no! He has a slight concussion.

STAGE HAND. Is that a fact? A what?

DOCTOR. But I tell you what. Go and see if you can manage to get a little ice.

STAGE HAND (*dubiously*). An ice?

DOCTOR. Yes. You know. In a basin of cold water. For a compress.

STAGE HAND. Oh, for a . . . Oh I see.

(*He goes out slowly.*)

DOCTOR. And . . . (*He notices the slippers.*) My God, what are those? I told you to bring something for his legs. Do you hear? A rug. (*He rises and crosses*). Has anybody got a rug? (*He goes off and his voice is heard faintly.*) A rug for his legs. Ah, thanks so much. That will . . .

26

(Silence. The figures behind the Curtain have ceased to move and are clustered in a silent group peering through towards the spot where the SPEAKER *is lying. Presently the latter stirs and his lips begin to move. There is a dim and distant boom-boom-boom as of someone tapping on a big drum. The lights pulse.)*

SPEAKER. Redeemious . . . Oh . . . be a redeemious . . . re . . . warmest core I said . . . we'll *(He opens his eyes and stares weakly ahead.)* . . . I love thee . . . love thee bosom my head bosom my head's all . . . Oh, God! *(There is a pause while he stares out into the auditorium.)* They that are down will be down . . . down . . . up . . . erect . . . redeemiable . . . love thee, Sarah . . . redeemiablecurran . . . I see you. *(Pause – then with a great effort)* I am the Speaker . . . Deadbosom I see you.

THE FORMS *(answering on behalf of the audience with unctuous friendliness).*

A.	Quirke	present
B.	Quinn	present
C.	Foley	present
D.	Byrne	present
E.	Ryan	present
F.	Carrol	present
G.	Lynch	present
H.	Dwyer	present
I.	Burke	present
J.	Farrell	present
K.	Gleeson	present
L.	Mooney	present
M.	Quigley	present

SPEAKER *(holding up his hand peremptorily).* Stop! *(Pause. He bows solemnly.)* Thank you.

THE FORMS *(whispering in rhythm).*

> Poor poor poor poor
> Hit him hit him
> With a gun
> Butt end butt end
> Dirty dirty
> Give him water
> For a compress
> Calf's foot jelly
> Fever fever
> Ninety-nine point ninety ninety

> Fahrenheit Centigrade
> Centigrade Fahrenheit
> Very unsettled unsettled unsettled
> Take his boots off
> Milk and soda
> Patrick Dun's and
> Cork Street Mater
> Adelaide and
> Vincent's Elpis
> Baggot Street and
> Mercer's Meath and
> Is he better?
> How's the headache?
> Ambulance ambulance
> S.O.S.
> S.O.S. S.O.S.
> Tut tut tut tut
> Tut tut tut tut
> Poor poor poor poor ...

SPEAKER (*with an impatient flap of his hand*). Slaves and dastards stand aside, a nation's voice ... nation's voice is stronger than a Speaker ... I am an honoured gloriable nationvoice your Sirrflinthearted Saxons ... Oh! ... if it would only stop going round ... round ... round ... up ... down ...up will be down ... O God, I am the Unspeakerable.

THE FORMS (*relentlessly*).

> On with the performance
> Programmes Tenpence
> No Smoking
> Spitting Coughing
> Nobody admitted
> Till after the Performance
> After nine
> Point ninety ninety
> For further particulars
> Apply to the Manager
> N. Moore
> O. Callan
> Q. O'Reilly
> R. Donovan
> S. Muldoon

SPEAKER (*with the rhythm*). Yes ... yes ... yes ... yes ...

THE FORMS.

    T. Cosgrave
    U. O'Toole
    V. Kelly
    W. Fogarty

SPEAKER.

Red lightning tightening through my blood
Red tightening lightning tightening through my blood
My tightening blood . . .

(*The voices are merged in a clanking, shrieking concatenation that swells up . . . the throb of petrol engines, the hoot of motor horns, the rattle and pounding of lorries, and, above all, the cry of the newsboys.*)

NEWSBOYS.

    Hegler Press
    Late Buff Hegler Press
    Weekly Honesty
    Hegler Press

SPEAKER. (*commencing to act again, at the top of his voice*). Their graves are red but their souls are with God in glory. A dark chain of silence is thrown o'er the deep. Silence . . . silence I say. O Ireland, Ireland, it is still unriven, that clanking chain . . . still unriven. O Ireland, Ireland, no streak of dawning is in the sky.

(*As he has been declaiming the crowd breaks up and passes to and fro as in the street. The gauze parts. Headlights of motor cars. A policeman with a white baton is directing the traffic, while behind him upon a pedestal stands* GRATTAN *with arm outstretched. He has the face of* MAJOR SIRR.)

SPEAKER (*now in the midst of the traffic.*) Men of Eire, awake to be blest! Do you hear? (*He fiercely accosts a* PASSER-BY.) Do you hear? Awake!

PASSER-BY (*politely disengaging himself*). Sorry. The banks close at half two.

SPEAKER. At the loud call of freedom why don't they awake? Come back! . . . Rise Arch of the Ocean . . . Let me be persuaded that my springing soul may meet the eagle on the hills . . . the hills . . . the hills . . . I say . . . (*He shouts.*) I say! Look here!

(*The* STAGE HAND *enters with the script.*)

STAGE HAND. What's the trouble?

SPEAKER. The hills!

STAGE HAND. What hills?

SPEAKER. Yes, what hills? Where?

STAGE HAND. Where's which?

SPEAKER. Don't be so stupid. You know I must have them. The eagle on the . . .

STAGE HAND. Did the Artistic Director say you were to have hills?

SPEAKER. I don't know what you mean. I can't go on like this. This is not right.

STAGE HAND. Well it's the first I heard of it. Wait now till I get the place.

SPEAKER. Down from the high cliff the rivulet is teeming. Go away! Be off!

STAGE HAND. Where had you got to?

SPEAKER. Not very far. I was with Sarah. She was up there. I was talking to her.

STAGE HAND (*producing a dirty programme*). Scene One. Wait now till I see. Who did you say you were?

SPEAKER. Robert Emmet. See there.

STAGE HAND. Oh is that you? I thought I rekernized the unyform.

SPEAKER. 'The action of the play opens in the garden of "The Priory", the home of John Philpot Curran close to Rathfarnham.' You see. This is not Rathfarnham.

STAGE HAND. No. I suppose not.

SPEAKER. I can't go on here. Can't you stop this noise?

STAGE HAND. Well you know I'd be glad to do all I can, but . . . well, you see, it's all very well telling me now.

SPEAKER. The air is rich and soft, the air is mild and bland, her woods are tall and straight, grove rising over grove . . .

STAGE HAND. Yes, I know, but I don't know what I can do. You should have told me sooner. You see the shops is all shut now . . .

SPEAKER. And Sarah . . . Sarah Curran is gone too. Clear all this away!

STAGE HAND. Ay, you can't touch that! That's wanted for the dancing class.

SPEAKER. Stop them! My play! Rathfarnham!

STAGE HAND. Ah you know I'm doing my best for you. But as a matter of fact I have to be off now.

SPEAKER. Off where?

STAGE HAND. I'm due at my Irish class this half hour.

SPEAKER. And what am I to do?

STAGE HAND. Ah sure aren't you doing well enough. You're very particular all of a sudden.

SPEAKER. Come back, damn you!

STAGE HAND. Ah, they won't know the difference. It's good enough for that gang. Ta-ta now or I'll be late.

SPEAKER. Stop! You must tell me . . .

STAGE HAND. You'll get a Rathfarnham bus over there at the corner. Goodbye-ee!

(*He goes.*)

SPEAKER. Here! Oh my head! At the corner where? Rathfarnham.

BUS MAN. Rathfarnham bus. No. 17 Rathfarnham. Step along now please.

SPEAKER. Are you going to Rathfarnham?

BUS MAN. This bus's full. Full, I tell ya. You'll have to wait for the next.

SPEAKER. Nonsense . . . there's lots of room. See . . .

BUS MAN. The bus's full. D'ye want to get me into trouble? Let go the bar now there's room for no more here. There'll be another along behind.

SPEAKER. I tell you there's nobody there.

(*Ding Ding Ding.*)

BUS MAN. Fares please. (*And he moves off mysteriously*).

SPEAKER. There's nobody there! Liar! Cheat! You're all a lot of . . . a lot of . . . I shall speak to the stage manager about . . . (*His voice breaks.*) Oh my head! I wish I wasn't so tired. I wish I wasn't so terribly tired!

(*He sinks down upon something in the centre of the stage. The passers-by thin out and the noise dies away, first into a low hum and then into complete silence. There is nobody left but the figure of* GRATTAN *and an old tattered* FLOWER WOMAN *in a black straw hat who sits crouching at the base of the pedestal.*)

SPEAKER (*mumbling*). My bed was the ground – my way the green-wood above, and the wealth I sought . . . I sought . . . the wealth . . . Oh, what is it?

GRATTAN. How long, O Lord, how long?

(*Pause.*)

SPEAKER (*without looking round*). What was that?

GRATTAN. This place stifles me. The thick, sententious atmosphere of this little hell of babbling torment! Sometimes the very breath seems to congeal in my throat and I can scarce keep from choking.

SPEAKER (*nodding gravely*). I might have known it.

WOMAN. Penny a bunch th' violets.

31

GRATTAN. God forgive me, but it is hard sometimes. Very hard.

SPEAKER. All the same I will not allow this. It is the voice of Major Sirr. It is not my part.

GRATTAN. Your part? Ah yes! More play-acting. Go on, go on.

SPEAKER. I am Robert Emmet and I . . .

GRATTAN. A young man playing Robert Emmet! Yes, yes, they all come here.

SPEAKER. I am Robert Emmet. I have written my name in letters of fire across the page of history. I have unfurled the green flag . . .

GRATTAN. Letters of fire?

SPEAKER. Their graves are red but their souls . . .

GRATTAN. Ah yes, the graves are red . . . the grave of one poor help-less old man, the justest judge in Ireland . . . dragged from his coach by the mob and slaughtered in the road.

SPEAKER. Kilwarden!

GRATTAN. Kilwarden's grave is red.

SPEAKER. Who said that? I did my best to save him, but the people were mad . . .

GRATTAN. 'Let no man perish in consequence of my death,' he cried, as his lifeblood stained the cobbles crimson . . .

SPEAKER. . . . maddened by long centuries of oppression and injustice. I did my best to save him. What more could I do?

GRATTAN. 'Let no man perish, save by the regular operation of the laws.' And with that, pierced by a dozen patriot pikes, he died, at the feet of his gallant countrymen.

SPEAKER. It was horrible. But it was war.

GRATTAN. Eighty tattered turncocks from the Coombe; a plumed hat, and a silver sword. War, for the liberation of Erin!

WOMAN. Me four bewtyful gre-in fields. Me four bewtyful gre-in fields.

SPEAKER. Men of Eire, awake to be blest!

GRATTAN. The full long years of my life I gave for her, with the harness weighing on my shoulders and my heart bleeding for my country's woes.

SPEAKER. Rise, Arch of the Ocean!

GRATTAN. Full fifty years I worked and waited, only to see my country's new-found glory melt away at the bidding of the omniscient young Messiahs with neither the ability to work nor the courage to wait.

SPEAKER. I have the courage to go on.

GRATTAN. Oh, it is an easy thing to draw a sword and raise a barricade. It saves working, it saves waiting. It saves everything but blood! And blood is the cheapest thing the good God has made.

WOMAN. Two apples a penny. Penny a bunch th' gre-in fields.

SPEAKER. Listen! Something is telling me that I must go on. I must march proudly through to the final act. Look! (*Pointing.*) The people are waiting for me, watching me.

GRATTAN. Fool, fool, strutting upon the stage! Go out, into the cold night air, before you crucify yourself in the blind folly of your eternal play-acting.

SPEAKER (*to the audience*). He is an old man. He does not understand the way we do. He can only doubt ... while we believe ... believe with heart and soul and every fibre of our tired bodies. Therefore I am not afraid to go on. I will kiss my wounds in the last act. I will march proudly through, head high, even if it must be to my grave. That is the only test.

GRATTAN. Ah, the love of death, creeping like a mist at the heels of my countrymen! Death is the only art in which we own no masters. Death is the only voice that can be heard in this distressful land where no man's word is taken, no man's message heeded, no man's prayer answered except it be his epitaph. Out into every quarter of the globe we go, seeking for a service in which to die: saving the world by dying for a good cause just as readily as we will damn it utterly by dying for a bad one. It is all the same to us. It is the only thing that we can understand.

(*The* WOMAN *laughs shortly and shrilly and breaks into a wheezy cough.*)

SPEAKER. What is that woman doing here?

WOMAN. God bless ye, lovely gentleman, spare a copper for a cuppa tea. Spare a copper for yer owin old lady, for when th' trouble is on me I must be talkin' te me friends.

GRATTAN. A copper, lovely gentleman, for your own old lady.

SPEAKER. Go away! There is something horrible about your voice.

GRATTAN.

Young she is, and fair she is
And would be crowned a Queen.

SPEAKER. What can I do in this place? I can't even remember my lines!

WOMAN. Yer lines, ducky. Ay Jack, pull them up on ye!

SPEAKER. I must go back to Rathfarnham. They will understand there.

GRATTAN. A shadowy land has appeared.

SPEAKER. Sally!

GRATTAN.
> Men thought it a region of Sunshine and Rest,
> And they called it 'Rathfarnham', the Land of the Blest.

SPEAKER. Oh if the will had wings, how fast I'd fly to the home of my heart!

GRATTAN. Poor weary footsore fool. And we are all the same, every one of us, whether we look to the foreigner for our sovereign or for our salvation. All of us fit to lead, and none of us fit to serve.

SPEAKER.
> If wishes were power, if words were spells,
> I'd be this hour where my true love dwells!

GRATTAN. Driven blindly on by the fury of our spurious moral courage! Is there to be no rest for Ireland from her soul? What monstrous blasphemy has she committed to be condemned to drift for ever like the wandering Jew after a Heaven that can never be?

WOMAN (*crooning softly to herself*).
> She's a darlin', she's a daisy,
> She has all the neighbours crazy,
> And she's arrums an' legs upon her like a man.
> But no matter where she goes,
> Sure everybody knows
> That she's Mick Magilligan's daughter, Mary Ann.

GRATTAN. In my day Dublin was the second city of a mighty Empire. What is she now?

SPEAKER. No! No!

GRATTAN (*with unutterable scorn*). Free!

(*He bursts into a wild peal of laughter.*)

SPEAKER. You are lying! It is the voice of Major Sirr! You are trying to torment me ... torture me ... Ghosts out of Hell, that's what you are.

(*The figures are blotted out by black curtains which sweep across behind the SPEAKER, entrapping him in their folds.*)

SPEAKER. But I'm not afraid! Heads up! One allegiance only! Robert Emmet is not afraid! I know what I want and I'm going on. (*Feverishly fumbling with the folds.*)

> God save Ireland cried the heroes,
> God save Ireland cry we all,
> Whether on the scaffold high –
> Whether on the scaffold high
> The scaffold high ... !

Come out! Come out! Where are you? Oh, where am I? Come

out! I . . . can't . . . remember . . . my lines . . . !

(*An old blind man, tap-tapping with his stick, passes slowly across the stage, a mug outstretched and a fiddle under his arm.*)

SPEAKER. If only I could get through. Where's the way through?

(*A* FLAPPER *and a* TRINITY MEDICAL *appear.*)

FLAPPER. No, I don't like the floor there, the Metropole's much better. As for that Buttery basement up and down and down and up Grafton Street. Tea for two and two for tea on one enchanted evening in the Dewdrop Inn. Do you like my nails this shade? Heart's Despair it's called.

MEDICAL. Play wing three for Monkstown. Four caps in the last couple of seasons. Pity they've put those glass doors in the Capitol boxes.

FLAPPER. Brown Thomas for panty-bras and Elizabeth Arden to rebuild drooping tissues. Max Factor, Chanel Number Five and Mum's the Word. Has your car got a strap round the bonnet?

MEDICAL. Well let's go up to Mother Mason's and hold hands. She needs decarbonizing probably. Botany Bay, you can be sure. Number twenty-one is my number.

SPEAKER. Can I get through here?

FLAPPER. Brittas Bay in a yellow M.G.

SPEAKER. I beg your pardon.

MEDICAL. Would you like a part in the Trinity Players?

SPEAKER. What?

FLAPPER. Tennis at Fitzwilliam all through the summer. We all go to Alexandra where the Lady Ardilaun lectures on Gilbert and Sullivan are quite indescribable. See you at the Carrickmines Mixed Singles. The Aga Khan is playing.

MEDICAL. Tyson's ties tie tightly. Going to crew next week for Dr Snufflebottom. Coming in left, Wanderers. Use your feet!

BOTH (*singing as they disappear*).

Kitty she was witty, Kitty she was pretty,
Down in the valley where they tried to pull her leg.
One of the committee thought he would be witty,
So he hit her on the titty with a hard boiled egg.

SPEAKER. What was that?

(*A* WELL-DRESSED WOMAN *and a* BUSINESSMAN *appear.*)

WELL-DRESSED WOMAN. This is the way to the Ringsend Baby Club. Double three Clubs. You are requested to attend a meeting of the Peamount After-care Committee. Ballsbridge, at 11.30 a.m. (*She yawns loudly.*)

BUSINESSMAN. Dame Street to Clarinda Park East Kingstown not Dun Laoghaire. Second National Loan Deferred Preference is now at thirty under proof. And only last Saturday I went round the Island in twenty-five and a bisque. Service not self I always say. Telegrams: 'Stability' Dublin. Have you got a *Herald*?

SPEAKER. Please . . . please! Can't you tell me the way out of here?

WELL-DRESSED WOMAN. Cover the milk. Do keep the milk covered, there's a good man.

(*Goes.*)

BUSINESSMAN (*making a secret sign*). Past Grand High Deacon for the Fitzwilliam Lodge. Honorary Treasurer of the Sandycove and District Philatelic Society. House Committee, Royal St George. Assistant District Commissioner, South County Dublin Boy Scouts. Achievement. (*Goes.*)

(TWO YOUNG THINGS *from somewhere up Phibsboro' way appear.*)

CARMEL. Down at the Girls' Club a Parnell Square. Janey Mac, such gas as we had!

BERNADETTE. Ah God, if I'd only a known! I couldn't get out a Tuesday. Were the fellas in?

CARMEL. They were. The Grocers' and Vintners' Assistants Association. D'ye know?

BERNADETTE. An' I suppose you had the Wet Dreams to play?

CARMEL. We had. The Gorgeous Wrecks were on in the Banba Hall. But listen. D'ye know the fella out a Cusack's a Dorset Street?

BERNADETTE. Is it that awful-lookin' iabeck with the red hair?

CARMEL. He ain't an awful lookin' iabeck, Bernadette, an' his hair's auburrin.

BERNADETTE. Yer taste's in yer mouth, duckie. Anyway . . . eyes off. He's walkin' out with Sarah Morrissy for I seen them meself last Sunday week a-clickin' on the Cab-ar-a Road.

CARMEL. Well wait now till I tell ya. He asked me for an A.P. at the Depot next Sunday an' he said to bring a pal an' he'll get her a fella, will ye come?

BERNADETTE. Will I come? Te th' Depot? Looka Carmel, I'll be there in me best Viyella.

CARMEL. Looka I'm off up to meet him a half five a Doyle's. He said th' Phib, but I think he has one eye on the Courtin' Park if I know that laddo. Do ye know?

36

BERNADETTE (*giggling*). Ah such gas! Sarah'll be wild when I tell her.

CARMEL. That one! You'd think she was someone.

SPEAKER (*politely*). I beg your pardon.

(BERNADETTE *nudges* CARMEL.)

SPEAKER. Did I hear you mention Sarah?

BERNADETTE. There's a fella tryin' to click.

CARMEL. Where? What sort of a fella?

BERNADETTE. Behind you. A queer-lookin' skin.

SPEAKER. If you would be so good? I'd be very much obliged.

(CARMEL *queries* BERNADETTE *with her eyebrows. The latter thinks not.*)

BERNADETTE. Give him the back of yer hand, Carmel. I'm not on.

SPEAKER. Could you tell me . . . ?

CARMEL (*turning with great dignity*). Chase yerself Jiggs or I'll call the Guards.

SPEAKER. Please don't misunderstand me. I only want to make an inquiry.

(*The two girls look knowingly at one another.*)

BERNADETTE (*in a hoarse whisper*). One of the Foresters.

CARMEL. Aw yes, well ye didn't meet me in Bray last summer. So goodbye-ee.

SPEAKER. In Bray? I said . . .

(BERNADETTE *giggles hysterically.*)

CARMEL (*to* BERNADETTE). That's th' stuff to give th' trupes. Well, I'll have to be off now or I'll be late. He'll be wild as it is. So long love.

BERNADETTE. Corner a Prussia Street a Sunday?

CARMEL. Mind yer there a half seven. Ta-ta so.

SPEAKER. Listen . . . I must speak. I will not have this!

CARMEL. Egs-scuse me! But may I ask who you're addressin' in that tone a voice?

BERNADETTE (*fluttering*). Ay – ay!

SPEAKER. I can't have this.

(*He tries to restrain her with a hand.*)

BERNADETTE. Ay, give us a hand someone!

CARMEL. Oh ye can't have this so ye can't, then listen to me, me Mountjoy Masher, ye'll have the flat of me fist across yer puss if ye can't conduct yerself when addressin' a lady, an' I'll thank ye to take that big slab from fingerin' me bawneen before I have ye run in the way God knows ye ought to be pesterin' an' pursuin' a pair a decent girls in th' public thoroughfare!

SPEAKER. Stop! For God's sake!

BERNADETTE. Ay-ay! Help! Help!

CARMEL. It's not safe for a respectable woman to leave th' shadda of her own door, so it's not, for the dirty gowgers that would be after them like . . . (*He tries to place his hand over her mouth. She bites him.* BERNADETTE *screams.*) Looka, I suppose you think yer face is yer fortune, but God knows at that rate some of us should be on the dole!

VOICES. Ay, what's up? What's the matter?

CARMEL. I declare to God I'd be ashamed of meself. A big lowsey yuck the like of you, why can't ye get a job a honest work and not be annoyin' young girls in th' street. It's lucky for your skin me fella's on th' far side of the Tolka River this minnit d'ye hear that now!

VOICES.
What did he do?
Is that him?
What's up?
Ay, can't ye leave the girl alone?
(*Rows of heads, hatted and becapped. The Curtains part again, disclosing a street.*)

BERNADETTE (*breathlessly*). Laida – laid aholt of us he did . . . an' says he, didn't I meet you in Bray last summer? says he, didn't I meet you in Bray? . . . An' then he takes her by the arm and says he . . .

SPEAKER. I did nothing of the sort!

VOICES.
Hold that fella.
Disgusting.
Put him out.

SPEAKER. I was only asking the way.

CARMEL (*choking*). Askin' th' way! Now d'ye hear that? . . . only askin' th' – looka what sort of a brass neck has that one got at all!

BERNADETTE. Look at what wants to ask th' way!

VOICES (*raucously – laughing*). To ask the way! 'Will any lady show a gentleman how who doesn't know the way?'

AN OLDER MAN. Ay, see here now. You ought to know better at your age. You'd better leave the girls alone or maybe some of these days you'll be finding your way where you least expect. This is a decent country.

VOICES.
>Still dear. No longer dirty.
>
>Keep to the right.
>
>Does your mother know yer out?

SPEAKER.
>How shall I reach the land that I love?
>
>Through the way of the wind, the high hills above?
>
>Down by the blue wide ways of the sea?
>
>(*Pause.*)

OLDER MAN. What's that?

CARMEL. God blessus, he's up the spout!

SPEAKER. That this unsparing storm should wreak its wrath . . .

OLDER MAN. Ay, give over. What's up with ye?

CARMEL. Well ye won't see me in his bewty chorus!

>(*General laughter.*)

OLDER MAN. Be quiet youse! I'm lookin' after this. What's yer name?

SPEAKER. I am Robert Emmet.

A VOICE. Robert Emmet?

A VOICE. Who?

A VOICE. Any relation to Paddy Emmet of Clonakilty?

OLDER MAN. Ssssh!

VOICES. Ssssh!

SPEAKER. I could explain it all in a moment if only you thought it worth while to give me a chance.

OLDER MAN. Oh if you're Robert Emmet you'll get every chance you want here. This is a free country. Is this true what you say?

SPEAKER. It is.

BERNADETTE. Well, d'ye hear that?

CARMEL. Who did he say?

BERNADETTE. Emmet. D'ye know. That fella.

A VOICE (*as fingers point*). That's Robert Emmet.

VOICES.
>Emmet.
>
>Emmet.
>
>That's him.
>
>Ay, d'ye know.

OLDER MAN. If yer Robert Emmet it must be all right.

SPEAKER. Won't you let me explain?

OLDER MAN. You can speak yer mind here without fear or favour.

VOICES.
>Nor sex, nor creed, nor class.

One for all and all for one.
Can laws forbid the blades of grass
From growing as they grow?
That's right.
A iree country.
Up freedom!

SPEAKER. I knew it would be all right when I told you. And it will be so much better for all of us.

OLDER MAN. Let him have his way. I'll see that justice is done.

VOICES.
Without fear or favour.
That's right.
It's Robert Emmet.
Fair play for all.
Let him have his way.
He's all right.
Be reasonable.
Justice.
Free speech.
All right. All right.

OLDER MAN (*fussing round as if putting everybody into their seats*). Sit down now all. Be easy. I'll look after this. I'll see you through. Leave it all to me now an' we'll fix it all up for you in half a jiffy. Isn't that right?

(*General clapping. The* OLDER MAN *assumes an air of platform importance, coughs, and comes forward to address the audience.*)

OLDER MAN. Ladies and gents . . . we are very fortunate . . . in having with us tonight . . . one, who . . . I am sure . . . will need no introduction from me to a Dublin audience . . . His fair fame . . . his manly bearing . . . his zeal in the cause of the Gael . . . his upright character . . . his unbounded enthusiasm for the old cause . . . whatever it may or may not have been . . . his Christian charity . . . his wide experience . . . his indefatigable courage . . . his spotless reputation . . . and his kindness to the poor of the city . . . have made his name a household word wherever th' ole flag flies.

CARMEL (*shrilly*). Who wounded Maud McCutcheon?

OLDER MAN (*tolerantly*). Now, now, we mustn't touch on controversial matters . . . In introducing him to you this evening . . . I can say with confidence . . . that you will one and all listen to what he has to say . . . whatever it may be . . . and I am sure we

40

are all looking forward to it very much indeed . . . with the
greatest interest and with the deepest respect . . . The views
which he has at heart . . . are also very near to the hearts of
every one of us in this hall . . . and before calling upon him to
address you I would just like to say that the committee will be
glad to see any or all of you at the Central Branch Whist Drive
in Ierne Hall next Friday and the treasurer will be waiting in the
passage as you pass out for those members who have not yet
paid their subs. Ladies and gents, Mr — er – er –

A VOICE. Emmet.

OLDER MAN. Mr Robert Ellis.

(*Applause.*)

SPEAKER. Don't gape at me like that. It is you who are confused
– not I. It is only in this place that I am mocked. But I will
carry you away to where the spirit is triumphant . . . where the
streets have no terrors and the darkness no babbling torment of
voices . . . where all will be plain . . . clear and simple . . . as
God's sky above, and the chains will fall from your souls at the
first sound of her voice from the lighted window. Which of you
would not be free?

BERNADETTE. Up the Repubbelick!

SPEAKER. We know only one definition of freedom. It is Tone's
definition; it is Mitchell's definition; it is Rossa's definition. Let
no man blaspheme the cause that the dead generations of
Ireland served, by giving it any other name and definition than
their name and their definition. Life springs from death, and
from the graves of patriot men and women spring living nations.
Men and women of Eire, who is with me?

VOICES.
Up Emmet!
We are with you! Up the Partisans!
Fuck a bal la! Emmet leads!

SPEAKER. But hark, a voice in thunder spake! I knew it. Slaves and
dastards, stand aside!

VOICES (*with great waving of arms*). Rathfarnham! Rathfarnham!
(*Singing.*)
> Yes, Ireland shall be free
> From the centre to the sea,
> Then hurrah for Liberty!
> Says the Shan Van Vocht.

(*Terrific enthusiasm. A queue forms.*)

OLDER MAN (*ringing a hand-bell*). Line up, line up, ladies and gents.

41

This way for Rathfarnham. All aboard for the Priory. Leaving An Lar every three minutes. Plenty of room on top. No waiting. This way ladies and gents. Seats for Rathfarnham.

TWO TOUTS (*distributing handbills*). Next bus leaves in ten minutes. All aboard for Tir-na-n'Og. Special reduced return fares at single and a third. The Radio Train for Hy Brasail. No waits. No stops. Courtesy, efficiency and punctuality. Joneses Road, Walsh Road, Philipsburg Avenue, Clontarf, Clonturk, Curran's Cross and the New Jerusalem.

OLDER MAN. Now then, quietly, quietly please. There is room for one and all. Step this way please. All those in favour will say 'Taw'.

> Put your troubles on the shelf.
> Country life restores the health.

(*Many gentlemen and ladies shake hands with the* SPEAKER *as they file past.*)

TWO TOUTS. Schoolchildren, under twelve half price. Senior Citizens free. Uniformed social workers will meet young girls travelling alone. Special Whit facilities when not on strike. Penalty for improper use, five pounds. Empyrean Express, Park in Paradise. Hearts' Desire Non-stop picks up and sets down passengers only at the white pole. Please do not spit in or on the conductor.

HANDSHAKERS.

> Proud to meet you, sir.
> Look us up any time you're in Sandymount.
> Jacobs Vobiscuits.
> The country is with you.
> My! how you've grown!
> Remember me to the boys.
> D'ye vanta vuya vatch?
> Magnificent, sir!
> Would you sign a snap?
> Have ye e'er a Green Stamp?

TWO TOUTS. Excursions for schools and colleges. Boy Scouts and Girl Guides in uniform admitted free. Tea and boiled eggs may be had from the conductor. Special comfort facilities on all vehicles, except when standing in the station.

(*The queue queues. Presently the* SPEAKER *finds himself shaking hands with the old* FLOWER WOMAN. *There is silence.*)

WOMAN. Wait, me love, an' I'll be with ye.

SPEAKER. You!

WOMAN. I thought I heard th' noise I used to hear when me friends
come to visit me.

Oh, she doesn't paint nor powdher,
An' her figger-is-all-her-owin.
Hoopsie-daisie! The walk of a Quee-in!

SPEAKER. Hurry on please.

WOMAN (*patting him roguishly on the shoulder*). Ah, conduct yerself. We're all friends here. Have ye nothing for me, lovely
gentleman?

SPEAKER. What do you want?

WOMAN. It's not food or drink that I want. It's not silver that I
want. Ochone.

SPEAKER. I have no time to waste talking to you.

WOMAN. What is it he called it? . . . the cheapest thing the good
God has made . . . eh? He-he-he. That's all. For your own old
lady.

SPEAKER. I've nothing for you.

WOMAN. Gimme me rights . . . me rights first!

SPEAKER. Go away!

WOMAN. Me rights! Me rights first . . . or I'll bloody well burst ye!

VOICES. Get on! Get on!

WOMAN (*turning on the crowd*). Aw ye have a brave haste about
ye. Ye have a grand wild spirit to be up an' somewheres, haven't
ye! Ye'll be off to a betther land will yez? Ye will . . . in me eye!

VOICES.

Ah, dry up!
What's she talking about?
Up Emmet!

WOMAN. An' a nice lot a bowsy scuts youse are, God knows!
Emmet! He-he-he! Up Emmet! Let me tell youse that fella's
not all he says he is!

VOICES. What's that? Not Emmet?

WOMAN. Look at him, ye gawms! Use yer eyes an' ask him for
yourselves.

A VOICE. But the costume?

WOMAN. Five bob a day from Ging.

(*She disappears into the crowd, whispering and pointing.*)

SPEAKER. My friends . . .

OLDER MAN. Is this true?

SPEAKER. My friends . . . we must go on . . . at once.

OLDER MAN. I asked you a question.

VOICES.
> Look at him.
> Well, what about it?
> Perhaps she's right.

SPEAKER. We can wait no longer.

VOICES. Can't you answer the gentleman's question?

OLDER MAN. Are these charges true?

SPEAKER. What are you talking about?

YOUNGER MAN (*in a beret*). What's all this?

OLDER MAN. This chap says he's Robert Emmet.

SPEAKER. I am.

OLDER MAN. Oh, you are, are you?

SPEAKER. I am.

OLDER MAN. Well answer me this then. *What's happened to your boots?*

VOICES.
> Ah-ha!
> Look!
> What about his boots?

SPEAKER. My boots!

OLDER MAN. He comes here an' says he's Robert Emmet, and where are his boots?

VOICES.
> That's right.
> Such an idea.
> He's an impostor.
> Throw him out!

SPEAKER. I don't know . . . I thought they were . . . I see your point . . . I . . .

VOICES. Well?

SPEAKER. Perhaps I had better explain . . . You see . . . someone took them from me when I was playing Robert Emmet and . . .

OLDER MAN (*with heavy sarcasm*). Oh so you were *playing* Robert Emmet? A play-actor are you? Some of this high-brow stuff I suppose?

SPEAKER. Oh no, not at all.

VOICES. High-brow! Ha!

OLDER MAN. I suppose you consider yourself a member of the so-called Intelligentsia? One of the Smart Set.

SPEAKER. Me?

VOICES. Smart Set! Ha! Ha!

OLDER MAN. A self-appointed judge of good taste, eh?

44

SPEAKER. I don't want to judge anything.

VOICES. Good taste. Ha! Ha! Ha!

OLDER MAN. You want to pose before the world as representative of the Irish people? Eh?

SPEAKER. I only want to ...

VOICES. Representative. Ha! Ha! Ha! Ha!

OLDER MAN. Tell me (*suddenly*) how much do you get for this?

SPEAKER. That's none of your business!

VOICES.

A job! A job!

He does it for a job!

He's related to someone!

And has a job!

OLDER MAN. Honest friends and anti-jobbers! This so-called leader, this self-appointed instructor of the Irish people, is owney linin' his pockets at the expense of the poor. His downy couch, debauched with luxury is watered with the sweat of the humble. A traitor's pillory in the hearts of his countrymen would be a proper reward for such an abattoir of licentiousness.

SPEAKER. (*assuming a Parnellesque attitude*). Who is the master of this party?

OLDER MAN. Who is the mistress of this party?

SPEAKER. Until the party deposes me I am leader.

A VOICE. You are not our leader. You are a dirty trickster.

A VOICE. Committee Room Fifteen!

SPEAKER. So you won't follow me any longer?

VOICES. No!

SPEAKER (*after a pause*). Very well. I shall just have to go on by myself.

OLDER MAN. Oh no you don't. You're not going out of this.

SPEAKER. Who's going to stop me?

OLDER MAN. We are. You're not going to be allowed to hold up this country to disgrace and ridicule in the eyes of the world. Throwing mud and dirt at the Irish people.

VOICE. Give him a taste of backwoodsman's law.

SPEAKER (*to* YOUNGER MAN). Tell him to get out of my way. You won't allow this.

YOUNGER MAN. It's nothing to do with me. The army has no interest in civilian affairs. All the same I don't like to see my country insulted by indecent plays.

OLDER MAN. That's right.

YOUNGER MAN. A high-spirited race resents being held up to scorn before the world, and it shows its resentment (*He takes out a revolver and hands it to the* OLDER MAN.) in various ways. But as I say it has nothing to do with me.

(*He walks away.*)

OLDER MAN (*with revolver*). Take off that uniform.

SPEAKER. Put up that revolver. I warn you, I am serious.

(*He stretches out his hand and gently takes it from him. The crowd slowly closes in upon him with sheeplike heedlessness.*)

SPEAKER. Stand back or I will have to shoot. I warn you I won't be interfered with, I am going on at all costs.

VOICES. Traitor. Spy. Cheat. Cur.

SPEAKER (*hidden in their midst*). Back! Back! Slaves and dastards, stand aside! Back! Back! or I'll...

(*The revolver emits a dull pop. The crowd melts away to the side and he is disclosed standing there alone with the smoking weapon still clenched in his fist. There is a deathlike silence.*)

A VOICE. Oh, my God!

OLDER MAN (*very quietly*). Now you've done it.

SPEAKER. Done what?

OLDER MAN. You've plugged somebody.

A VOICE. Oh, my God! My God!

SPEAKER. I've what?

A MAN (*looking out*). It's Joe.

SECOND MAN. Joe?

FIRST MAN. He's got it in the breast.

YOUNGER MAN (*reappearing*). Who fired that shot?

OLDER MAN. Joe's got it. Right through the left lung. He can't last long.

SECOND MAN. Christ!

FIRST MAN. It wasn't any of us, Tom. It was this chap.

SPEAKER. Stand back, stand back, I tell you. I'm fighting. This is war.

YOUNGER MAN (*quite unperturbed*). There's a man out there. You've put a bullet through his breast.

OLDER MAN. God rest his soul!

SPEAKER. I warned you – I warned you all.

YOUNGER MAN. He's going to die. You did it. That's what comes of having guns.

VOICES.

He's going to die.

You did it.

You did it.

SPEAKER. I had to. It wasn't my gun.

(*Two men appear bearing between them the body of another. The people take off their hats and stand mutely with bowed heads.*)

JOE. It's welling out over me shirt, boys . . . Can't anybody stop . . . it?

YOUNGER MAN. A good man . . . a true man . . . That is what you did.

OLDER MAN. That is what he did.

VOICES.
You did.
He did.
Robert Emmet did.
Who did it?
He did it.
He there.

SPEAKER. I had to . . . (*All hands point.*)

JOE. Give me . . . me beads . . . before the life . . . has ebbed out of me . . . I can't breathe . . . oh, lads, I'm going . . .

SPEAKER. What could I do? I ask you, what could I do? It was war. I didn't mean to hurt him.

OLDER MAN. Joe, old scout. We're sorry . . . we're . . . O God!

JOE. God bless you boys . . . sure I know . . . I know well . . . it wasn't any of . . . you . . .

SPEAKER (*flinging down the revolver*). Shoot back then! It is war. Shoot! I can die too!

YOUNGER MAN. Will that give him back the warm blood you have stolen from him?

OLDER MAN. Ah, leave him alone, Tom, leave him alone.

VOICES (*whispering*).
Leave him alone.
He shot Joe.
Through the breast.
Poor Joe.
Leave him alone.

JOE (*as he is carried off, followed by the crowd*). O my God . . . I am heartily . . . sorry . . . for having offended . . . Thee . . . and . . . I . . .

VOICES (*chanting*).

> *Lacrymosa dies illa*
> *Qua resurget ex favilla*
> *Judicandus homo reus.*

47

Huic ergo parce Deus;
Pie Jesu Domine
Dona eis requiem
Amen.

FLOWER WOMAN (*appearing in the shadows, but speaking with the voice of* SARAH CURRAN).
Do not make a great keening
When the graves have been dug tomorrow.
Do not call the white-scarfed riders
To the burying . . .
(*Hoarsely*). Ay misther – spare a copper for a cuppa tea – spare a copper for a poor old lady – a cuppa tea – (*Whisper.*) a copper for your own ole lady, lovely gentleman.
(*She fades away.*)
SPEAKER. Sally! Sally! – where are you? – where are you? Sally!

THE CURTAIN FALLS

PART TWO

Through the Curtain, amidst a hearty round of applause, comes the
MINISTER'S *talented daughter,* MAEVE. *She has on a nice white
dress with a white bow to match in her long, loose, black hair
which reaches quite to her waist. Around her neck on a simple
gold chain hangs a religious medal. She curtsies in charming embarrassment and commences to recite.*
MAEVE.

> Kingth Bweakfatht.
> The King athed de Queen
> And de Queen athed de Dar-med
> Could – I (*a little breathlessly*) – se – butter
> For-de-roy – – – thlaice – a – bwead?
> Queen athed de Dar-med
> De Dar-med thed Thertinley
> Ah goan tell – Cow now
> For he goeth tebed . . .

(*She continues this amusing piece to the very end, when the
Curtain parts amid general applause disclosing a fantastically
respectable drawing-room loud with the clatter of tea things.
A party is in progress under the aegis of the* MINISTER FOR
ARTS AND CRAFTS *and his nice little* WIFE. *The guests consist
of one of the* REDCOATS, *now a* GENERAL *in a green uniform,
the Statue of* GRATTAN, *rather a nice woman called* LADY
TRIMMER – *one of those people whose expression of pleased
expectancy never for a moment varies, the old* FLOWER
WOMAN *who is seated unobtrusively in the background eating
an orange, and a small but enthusiastic* CHORUS. *Side by side
upon the sofa reading from right to left are* O'COONEY *the
well-known dramatist,* O'MOONEY *the rising portrait painter,
and* O'ROONEY *the famous novelist.* O'COONEY *wears a cloth
cap, blue sweater and a tweed coat.* O'MOONEY *has a red shirt
and horn-rimmed spectacles, while* O'ROONEY *is dressed in*

49

full saffron kilt together with Russian boots. The MINISTER
himself bears a strange resemblance to the STAGE HAND. *It
is all very nice indeed.*)

CHORUS.

Oh very nice nice
Oh very nice nice nice
How old how nice how very nice don't you think so
Oh yes indeed yes very nice indeed I do think so indeed don't
    you indeed.
(*Teaspoons clink.*)

LADY TRIMMER. What was that one, my dear?

MAEVE. Kingth Bweakfatht pleathe.

LADY TRIMMER. Very nice indeed, Maeve. I must teach that one to
    my two chicks. Where do you learn, my dear?

MAEVE. The Banba Thcool of Acting, Lower Abbey Thweet.

CHORUS. The Banba School of Acting, Lower Abbey Street.

O'COONEY. Wasn't that bloody awful?

O'MOONEY. The question is, is she an aartist? A real aartist?

O'ROONEY. O'Mooney sounds better with his mouth shut.

WIFE. Of course, she hasn't been learning very long. But she has
    the language, and that's half the battle these days. Show them,
    Maeve.

MAEVE. *Caed mile failte.*

LADY TRIMMER. Oh very good indeed. But of course, she has her
    father's talent.

MINISTER. Ah, well, now . . .

WIFE (*pleased*). Oh, Lady Trimmer!

MINISTER. Well, now, all the same I don't know about that. But
    mind you I do say this, Talent is what the country wants.
    Politics may be all O.K. in their way, but what I say to *An
    Taoischach* is this, until we have Talent and Art in the country
    we have no National Dignity. We must have Talent and Art.
    Isn't that right?

CHORUS. We must have Art have Talent and Art.

LADY TRIMMER. Quite. And cultivated people of taste. You musn't
    forget them, Mr Minister. Art cannot live you know by taking
    in its own washing – if I may put it that way.

O'COONEY. Aw Holy God!

O'MOONEY (*ruminatively*). The reel aartist must be fundamental.
    Like Beethoven. Now, *I'm* fundamental.

O'ROONEY. Fundament, all right.

MINISTER. Now see here. I'm Minister for Arts and Crafts, you see.

Well, a young fellow comes along to me and he says, Now look, Liam, here's some Art I'm after doing . . . it might be a book you see, or a drawing, or even a poem . . . and can you do anything for me, he says? Well, with that, I do . . . if he deserves it, mind you, only if he deserves it, under Section 15 of the Deserving Artists' (Support) Act, No. 65 of 1926. And there's none of this favouritism at all.

CHORUS. The State supports the Artist.

GRATTAN. And the Artist supports the State.

CHORUS. Very satisfactory for everybody and no favouritism at all.

MINISTER (*confidentially*). And of course, then you see, it helps us to keep an eye on the sort of stuff that's turned out, you understand.

CHORUS. Clean and pure Art for clean and pure people.

LADY TRIMMER. What we need most is a small Salon.

GENERAL. That's right. A small Art Saloon.

WIFE. We often have people in on Sunday evenings for music and things. Won't you sing something now, General?

GENERAL. Aw, I have no voice at all.

O'COONEY. He's bloody well right there.

O'MOONEY. The question is . . . Is he fundamental?

LADY TRIMMER. Just somewhere where the nicest people . . . the people one wants to meet . . . like Mr O'Cooney and Mr O'Mooney . . .

O'ROONEY (*suspiciously*). And Mr O'Rooney.

LADY TRIMMER. *And* Mr O'Rooney, can get together quietly and discuss Art and common interests.

WIFE. Haven't you brought your music?

CHORUS. You must have brought your music.

GENERAL. Well now . . . if you insist. Maybe I might find something.

O'COONEY (*to* O'MOONEY). Ay, have *you* put my cap somewhere?

WIFE. Do, General.

GENERAL. I don't know for sure, mind you. I might . . . just happen to have something on me.

(*He produces a roll of music from inside his tunic.*)

CHORUS. The General's going to sing.

GENERAL. Ah, but . . . sure there's no one to play th' accompanyment.

WIFE. Maeve will play. Won't you, darling?

MAEVE. Yeth mammy.

(*Signs of distress from the sofa.*)

51

WIFE. Of course you will dear. Give her the music, General.

CHORUS. Ssssh!

(*The* GENERAL *gives her the music rather doubtfully and they are opening the performance, when there comes a loud, peremptory knock at the door. General surprise.*)

WIFE (*bravely but apprehensively*). What can that be?

LADY TRIMMER. Strange!

MINISTER. A knock at the door?

GENERAL. Ah now, isn't that too bad!

CARMEL (*entering*). There's a gentleman at the door, ma'am, looking for the Rathfarnham bus.

WIFE. What kind of a gentleman, Carmel?

CARMEL. A gentleman in a uniform, ma'am.

MINISTER. A uniform? Tell me, does he look like the start of a Daring Outrage?

CHORUS. Possibly the Garda Síothchána.

CARMEL. He has a sword, sir.

MINISTER. A sword?

CARMEL (*primly*). And a pair of slippers.

WIFE. Slippers?

GENERAL. I don't think I know that unyform.

CHORUS. Can't be the Garda Síothchána after all.

WIFE. Did he give any name, Carmel?

CARMEL. Yes, ma'am. A Mr Emmet.

LADY TRIMMER. Not *the* Mr Emmet?

CARMEL. I don't know I'm sure, ma'am.

MINISTER. Ah, yes I remember. That's him all right.

GENERAL. Aw, the hard Emmet.

MINISTER. The old Scout.

WIFE. The gentleman who is far from the land. Show him up at once, Carmel.

CARMEL. Yes, ma'am. (*She goes, muttering.*) Doesn't look like a sailor to me.

LADY TRIMMER. How nice of him to call.

WIFE. Yes, indeed, but you know we can't be too careful since the Trouble.

MINISTER. Emmet's all right. I know him well. Used to work with him in the old days.

GENERAL. Aw, the rare old Emmet.

LADY TRIMMER. You know I've wanted to meet him for such a long time. My husband always says that we of the old regime ought to get into touch with those sort of people as much as possible. We can assist each other in so many ways.

MINISTER. That's right. We must all get together for the good of the country.

WIFE. I wonder has he brought his music too?

GRATTAN. I expect he has.

(CARMEL *enters, cocking her head contemptuously towards the* SPEAKER, *who follows her with a strange, hunted look in his eye. He glances round apprehensively as though prepared for the worst and yet hoping against hope.*)

CHORUS. Oh how do you how do you how do you how do you how . . .

WIFE. How do you do? Bring another cup, Carmel.

CARMEL. Yes, ma'am. (*She goes, muttering.*) I'll have to wash one first.

SPEAKER. Excuse . . . me.

WIFE. Come and sit down and let me introduce you to everybody. It was so nice of you to call. Liam has just been speaking about your work.

SPEAKER. I only came in to ask . . .

CHORUS. Have you brought your music?

WIFE. This is Lady Trimmer, Mr Emmet.

CHORUS. Of the old regime.

LADY TRIMMER. Dee do.

SPEAKER (*after peering closely into her face*). No, ah, no.

LADY TRIMMER. You must come and visit us too, Mr Emmet. First Fridays. Now promise.

WIFE. And General O'Gowna of the *Oglaigh na h-Eireann.*

GENERAL (*affably*). And many of them.

SPEAKER. It was you who hit me.

WIFE. And of course you know my husband, the Minister for Arts and Crafts.

CHORUS. Vote *Fianna na Poblacht.*

MINISTER. *A chara.*

(*The* SPEAKER *tries to remonstrate but is hurried on.*)

WIFE. And Mr Grattan's statue from College Green.

GRATTAN. Welcome Don Quixote Alighieri. Did I speak the truth?

(*The* SPEAKER'S *head goes up.*)

WIFE. And this is Mr O'Cooney, the great dramatist.

SPEAKER. Cap?

WIFE. Oh, Mr O'Cooney always wears his cap in the drawing-room.

O'COONEY. And why the bloody hell shouldn't I wear my cap in the drawing-room?

53

(*General laughter.*)

SPEAKER. I see.

O'MOONEY. Now me.

WIFE. This is Mr O'Mooney, the artist, if you can remember everybody.

O'MOONEY. The reel Aartist.

O'COONEY. The owl cod.

WIFE. Oh, please, Mr O'Cooney!

CHORUS. I love the way he talks, don't you?

O'MOONEY. Oh, don't mind O'Cooney. He's a great friend of mine, really.

O'COONEY. He is not!

WIFE. And this is Mr O'Rooney, the well-known novelist. Now I think you know everybody.

SPEAKER (*indicating the costume*). You play the pipes?

(O'MOONEY *laughs shrilly.*)

O'ROONEY. I do not. I do not believe in political Nationalism. Do you not see my Russian boots?

WIFE. Mr O'Rooney believes in the workers.

O'ROONEY. I do not believe in the workers. Nor do I believe in the Upper Classes nor in the Bourgeoisie. It should be perfectly clear by now what I do not believe in, unless you wish me to go over it again?

LADY TRIMMER (*archly*). Mr O'Rooney, you dreadful man!

SPEAKER. I'm sorry.

WIFE. Sit down now and have a nice cup of tea.

(CARMEL *meanwhile has been back with a dirty cup.*)

CHORUS. I do like a nice cup of tea.

SPEAKER. So she is here, too!

WIFE. What's that?

SPEAKER. That damned old flower woman who turned them all against me!

WOMAN. Ay, mister, have ye e'er an old hempen rope for a neck-cloth?

WIFE. You're joking, Mr Emmet. There's no old flower woman.

SPEAKER. I mean . . . look there.

WIFE. Have some tea, Mr Emmet. You're a little tired, no doubt.

SEMICHORUS. Delightful drink.

SEMICHORUS. Pity it tans the stomach.

WIFE. You'll feel much the better of it. And we'll have a little music afterwards. We often have music in the evenings.

MINISTER. Are you interested in Art, Mr Emmet?

LADY TRIMMER. I suppose you're a member of the Nine Arts Club?

WIFE. And the Royal Automobile Academy?

CHORUS. Celebrity Concerts. The Literary Literaries.

SPEAKER. I don't feel very . . . Did you say that statue of Grattan was there?

WIFE. Oh yes, that's Mr Grattan's statue from College Green. We always have a few of the nicest statues in on Sunday evening. My husband is Minister for Arts and Crafts, you know.

LADY TRIMMER. Just to form a little group you know. A few people of taste.

WIFE. Of course we're only amateurs, but we're doing our best. (*Pause.*)

SPEAKER (*suddenly*). Let me be persuaded that my springing soul may meet the . . .
   (*Pause.*)

LADY TRIMMER. I beg your pardon?

SPEAKER. Let me be per— (*He shakes his head hopelessly.*) I am Robert Emmet.

GRATTAN. You are not.

SPEAKER. Who are you to question me?

GRATTAN. You are only a play-actor.

SPEAKER. Look well to your own soul, Major Sirr!

GRATTAN. Have you found your Holy Curran, Galahad?

WIFE. I always say to Liam, Liam you really *must* get a proper statue of Mr Emmet. It's positively disgraceful that we haven't got a good one, don't you think?

MINISTER. Ah, well, dear, you know, expense, expense.

LADY TRIMMER. What a nice uniform! Tell me, do you admire the plays of Chekhov?

WIFE. Perhaps he acts for the Civil Service Dramatics.

SPEAKER. Act? . . . No. No cake, thank you.

CHORUS. Benevente Strindberg Toller Euripides Pirandello Tolstoy Calderon O'Neill.

LADY TRIMMER. I'm sure you'd be good.

CHORUS. An annual subscription of one guinea admits a member to all productions and to all At Homes.

MINISTER (*confidentially*). Say the word and I'll get you into the Rathmines and Rathmines. I know the man below.

LADY TRIMMER. Now do tell us, Mr Emmet, about your wonderful experiences in the Trouble.

(*The* SPEAKER *spills his tea and looks around wild-eyed.*)

SPEAKER. What do you mean?

GRATTAN. Ah – ha!

WIFE. Never mind. It's quite all right. I'll pour you out another cup.

LADY TRIMMER (*hastily*). You must have had such interesting times all through the fighting.

SPEAKER. I shall never fight again!

(*He buries his face in his hands.*)

MINISTER. Oh come, Mr Emmet! What's the matter?

WIFE. Are you not felling well?

LADY TRIMMER (*aside*). Ssssh! Don't pay any attention. I understand. Do tell us about it, Mr Emmet. Talk. Talk someone.

SPEAKER. God have pity on me.

CHORUS. Oh the fighting everyone talk don't pay any attention wonderful experiences those were the attention fighting days how wonderful do tell us about the fighting days interesting and wonderful.

SPEAKER. It was I who shot him and you all know it! You all know! Isn't it enough for you? Haven't I suffered enough?

CHORUS (*louder*). Oh tuttut poor man don't talk do talk as hard as you can fighting wonderful pay no attention shellshock probably to have seen it all wonderful is he better yet poor man everybody pretend not to fighting notice.

SPEAKER. They trapped me! A good man . . . a true man . . . and I did it!

WIFE. Well what if you did shoot somebody? Everybody's shot somebody nowadays. That'll soon be over.

LADY TRIMMER. Yes, yes; of course we didn't approve of it at the time, but it's all so interesting now.

SPEAKER. Interesting!

CHORUS. Perhaps we had better how is he change the subject change the subject getting on what's the wonderful experiences matter with him matter with him at all?

WIFE. How about a little song?

CHORUS. How about a little little song song song?

WIFE. Do you sing, Mr Emmet?

SPEAKER. What do you all want with me?

LADY TRIMMER. Nothing, nothing at all, Mr Emmet. Perhaps you'd like to act us a little snippet from your play?

WIFE. We often have plays on Sunday evenings. Poor man. There, there. We are all friends here.

LADY TRIMMER. The General has just obliged us.

GENERAL. I have not. I was interrupted before I got going.

WIFE. You're better now, I'm sure. Of course you are. Aren't you?

56

MINISTER. Well, I believe in supporting Art and acting's Art. So you have *my* consent anyhow.

WIFE. You'll act something for us, Mr Emmet, won't you?

GRATTAN. Ah, leave him alone. Can't you see he's beaten.

SPEAKER. That voice! That voice!

GRATTAN. I said that you were beaten. You should have taken my advice from the first; but you would go on with your play-acting. Now, perhaps you know better. Rathfarnham! Ha! Sarah Curran! Ha-ha-ha!

SPEAKER (*slowly rising*). I am not beaten. I still believe. I will go on.

CHORUS. Oh good, he's going to do something for us.

WIFE. Oh do, Mr Emmet.

GENERAL. But look here . . .

GRATTAN. Don't be a fool. Do you imagine that they'll listen to you if you do?

MINISTER. Nothing political. That's barred of course.

O'COONEY. For God's sake make it short anyhow.

O'MOONEY. Nothing Iberian. There's no Iberian real Art.

O'ROONEY. See that it's not pompous. That would be an insult to the people of this country.

GENERAL. Hey, what about my song?

GRATTAN. Go on. Tell them all to go to hell.

SPEAKER. Please, please . . . if you want me to do it . . .

CHORUS. Oh yes yes, do Mr Emmet.

MINISTER. I suppose it will be all right. I wouldn't like anything by somebody with the slave mind, you know.

SPEAKER. Nobody can object to my play.

MINISTER. Or calculated to excite you-know-what.

CHORUS. Emmet's play is all right.

GENERAL. Well you needn't expect me to sit down quietly under this sort of behaviour. When you ask a man to sing . . .

SPEAKER (*advancing towards the audience*). It's very hard without Sally. It may seem a little strange here . . . but I'll do it.

GRATTAN. Very well. Have it your own way.

LADY TRIMMER. Did I hear him mention somebody called . . . er, Sally Somebody?

WIFE (*confidentially*). I think it must be his young lady.

LADY TRIMMER. How charming.

GENERAL (*determinedly*). One of Moore's Melodies entitled 'She is Far from the Land'.
(*He bows.*)

O'COONEY. Aw, this'll be bloody awful. (*Settles down.*) D'ye remem-

57

ber that night, Liam, when the two of us hid in the chimbley from the Tans?

MINISTER. Will I ever forget it? Ah, those were the days, Seamus.

SPEAKER. I had got to the part where I am arrested, hadn't I? No. I think I was . . .

WIFE. We always have music and things on Sunday evenings.

LADY TRIMMER. Just a nucleus. A few nice people.

GENERAL (*to* MAEVE). Have you got the place?

MAEVE. Mammy.

WIFE. Yes, dear?

MAEVE. Why ith that man wearing hith thlipperth in the dwawing woom?

WIFE. Hush, dear, you mustn't ask questions. You must be a good girl.

MAEVE (*plaintively*). You never let me –

GENERAL. Ah, go on when I tell you!

(MAEVE *commences the introduction to 'She is Far from the Land'*.)

SPEAKER.
The air is rich and soft – the air is mild and bland.
Her woods are tall and straight, grove rising over grove.
Trees flourish in her glens below and on her heights above,
Oh, the fair hills of Eire, oh.

O'ROONEY. Will you move up on the sofa and breathe into yourself.

O'MOONEY. We'd be better off if your hips were as soft as your head.

(*Simultaneously.*)

SPEAKER.	GENERAL (*singing*).
Down from the high cliffs the rivulet is teeming	She is far from the land where her young hero sleeps
To wind around the willow banks that lure me from above;	And lovers around her are sighing:
Ah, where the woodbines with sleepy arms have wound me.	But coldly she turns from their gaze and weeps For her heart in his grave is lying.

MINISTER (*solo*). And do you remember the day, Seamus, of the big round-up in Moore Street when the 'G' man tried to plug me getting out of the skylight?

SPEAKER, GENERAL, *and* O'COONEY (*simultaneously.*)

SPEAKER (*louder*).	GENERAL
But there is lightning in my blood; red lightning tighten-	She sings the wild songs of her dear native plains,

ing in my blood. Oh! if there
was a sword in every Irish
hand! If there was a flame in
every Irish heart to put an end
to slavery and shame! Oh, I
would end these things!

Every note which he loved
awaking.
Ah! little they think, who
delight in her strains,
How the heart of the ministrel
is breaking.

O'COONEY.

Aw, Jesus, and the evenings down in the
old I.R.B. in Talbot Street, picking out the
'Soldiers' Song' on the blackboard.

SPEAKER, MINISTER, *and* GENERAL (*simultaneously*).

I have written my name in
letters of fire across the page
of history. I have unfurled the
green flag in the streets and
cried aloud from the high
places to the people of the
Five Kingdoms: Men of Eire,
awake to be blest! to be blest!

He had lived for his love, for
his country he died,
They were all that to life had
entwined him;
Nor soon shall the tears of his
country be dried,
Nor long will his love stay
behind him.

MINISTER.

Sometimes I wish I was back again on the
run with the old flying column out by the
Glen of Aherlow.

(O'MOONEY *and* O'ROONEY *join in in low undertones*.)

O'ROONEY

My good woman, I said, I'll
tell you what's wrong with
you. Virginity, my good
woman, that's all. And believe
me, its nothing to be proud
of.

O'MOONEY

Saint Peetric d'ye see because
Saint Peter was the rock and
Saint Patrick was the seed.
That makes Saint Peetric, d'ye
see. For the rock is under-
neath and the seed lies above,
so Saint Peter and Saint
Patrick are Saint Peetric.

(*At the same time.*)

O'COONEY

And that night waiting up on the North
Circular for word of the executions. Ah,
not for all the wealth of the world would
I give up the maddenin' minglin' memories
of the past . . .

SPEAKER.   GENERAL

Rise, Arch of the Ocean and

Queen of the West! I have
dared all for Ireland, I will
dare all again for Sarah
Curran. Their graves are red.
O make her a maddening
mingling glorious morrow . . .

O! make her a grave where
the sunbeams rest
When they promise a glorious
morrow . . .

(The black curtain closes behind the SPEAKER, *blotting out the room, and the voices fade away. The* SPEAKER *himself has somehow chimed in upon the last few lines of the song, and is left singing it by himself.)*

SPEAKER.

They'll shine o'er her sleep like a smile from the west,
From her own loved island of sorrow . . .

(The BLIND MAN *comes tap-tapping with a fiddle under his arm and a tin mug in his hand. He bumps lightly into the* SPEAKER.)

BLIND MAN *(feeling with his stick)*. Peek-a-boo! Peek-a-boo!

SPEAKER. Damn your eyes!

BLIND MAN *(looking up)*. That's right.

SPEAKER. You're . . . blind?

BLIND MAN *(with a chuckle)*. That's what they say.

SPEAKER. I didn't know. I didn't mean to hurt you.

BLIND MAN. Ah, not at all. I'm not so easy hurted. *(Feeling him over.)* Oh, a grand man. A grand man. A grand man surely, from the feel of his coat.

SPEAKER. Do you know where I am?

BLIND MAN. Well, isn't that a rare notion now! Asking the way of an old dark fiddler, and him tip-tappin' over the cold sets day in and day out with never sight nor sign of the blessed sun above.

SPEAKER. I give it up.

BLIND MAN. And where might you be bound for, stranger?

SPEAKER. The Priory.

BLIND MAN *(with a start)*. Ah, so! So you're bound for them parts, are you, stranger dear?

SPEAKER. Yes.

BLIND MAN. Up the glen maybe as far as the edge of the white mist, and it hanging soft around the stones of Mount Venus, eh stranger? He-he-he!

SPEAKER. That's right.

BLIND MAN. Oh, I know you. I know you. Sure all the Queer Ones of the twelve counties do be trysting around them hills beyond the Priory.

SPEAKER. The blessed hills!

BLIND MAN. It's sad I am, stranger, for my light words of greeting and the two of us meeting for the first time. Take my arm now, and walk with me for a while and I'll put you on your way. Come – take my arm! Why should you not take my arm, stranger, for I'm telling you, my fathers are Kings in Thomond so they are.

SPEAKER (*taking his arm gingerly*). There.

BLIND MAN. That's better now. He-he-he. 'Tis proud I am to be walking arm in arm with the likes of you, stranger. Tell me now, or am I wrong? Would you by any chance be Mr Robert Emmet?

SPEAKER. You know me?

BLIND MAN. Uh! I thought I recognized them words I heard you singing.

SPEAKER. Yes. I am Robert Emmet. He said that I wasn't. But I am. It was the voice of Major Sirr.

BLIND MAN. Ah, poor Bob Emmet. He died for Ireland. God rest his soul.

SPEAKER. He died. I died?

BLIND MAN. You did indeed. You remember the old song we used to sing?

(*They sit down together.*)

SPEAKER. You mean 'The Struggle is Over'.

BLIND MAN. That's right. Ah, the rare old lilt of it. How does it go, now? (*He sings.*)

The struggle is over, our boys are defeated,
    And Erin surrounded with silence and gloom.
We were betrayed and shamefully treated
    And I, Robert Emmet, awaiting my doom.
Hanged, drawn and quartered, sure that was my sentence,
    But soon I will show them, no coward am I.
My crime was the love of the land I was born in.
    A hero I've lived and a hero I'll die.

BOTH.

Bold Robert Emmet, the darling of Erin,
Bold Robert Emmet will die with a smile.
Farewell companions, both loyal and daring,
I'll lay down my life for the Emerald Isle.

(*Pause. From somewhere comes faint dance music.*)

BLIND MAN. Ah, them are the songs. Them are the songs.

SPEAKER. He died for Ireland. I died. I?

BLIND MAN. High Kings in Thomond, my fathers are. Lords of the Gael. You'll know them, stranger.

SPEAKER. How can I have died for Ireland? What is that I hear?

BLIND MAN. Ah, never mind that. That's nothing. Nothing at all. (*A young man in evening dress and a pretty girl are walking out of the darkness into the edge of the light. It is the* TRINITY MEDICAL *and his friend, now a little older. They are smoking and laughing together.*)

SPEAKER. Go away.

BLIND MAN. Never heed them stranger. That's nobody at all.

SPEAKER. And I am dead this hundred years and more?

BLIND MAN. What would the likes of you have to do with the likes of them? He-he-he.

HE. I remember when I was a kid in Clyde Road how wonderful I thought a private dance was.

SHE. Now I suppose you've quite grown out of us all.

HE (*laughing*). Oh, well, I wouldn't say that. But of course when one's lived abroad things do seem a little different, when you come back.

SHE. I suppose so.

HE. Small in a way and rather provincial. But that's to be expected.

SPEAKER. I wonder is Sally dead too?

BLIND MAN. Dust to dust and ashes to ashes.

HE. Of course, there have been a lot of improvements. But over there . . . well, after all, it takes over an hour and a half to get into the country.

SHE. And you like that?

HE. Well, you know how it is. It makes one feel one's sort of *in* the world. Everything seems more serious, somehow.

SHE. While we and the old days never seemed serious at all.

HE. Oh well, I didn't quite mean it that way.

SPEAKER. O God help me!

BLIND MAN. Coming and going on the mailboat. And they thinking themselves the real ones – the strong ones! I do have to laugh sometimes and I hearing the wings of the Queer Ones beating under the arch of the sky.

HE. Of course I liked the old days. We had some jolly good times together, didn't we?

SHE. I liked them too.

HE. I was crazy about you.

SHE. My eye and Betty Martin.

HE. I was. I was, really. I often think about it all. It's a bit lonely sometimes over there, and often – Oh, I don't know. Do you ever think about me?

SHE. Sometimes.

HE. I hope you do. You know, Daphne, sometimes I wonder whether you and I oughtn't to have . . .

SHE. Have what?

HE. I think we ought to have . . . maybe we still could . . .
   (*The music stops. There is a pause.*)

HE. Hello. The music's stopped.

SHE. Yes. I suppose it has.

HE. Like to go in and have a drink?

SHE. I think we might as well.

HE (*briskly*). Funny, you know, how the old place can get you for a bit. But after all, one can't get away from the fact that it's all so damned depressing – (*They vanish.*)

SPEAKER. O God, make speed to save us! I cannot tell what things are real and what are not!

BLIND MAN. Oh, but it is not myself that is dark at all, but them – blind and drunk with the brave sight of their own eyes. For why would they care that the winds is cold and the beds is hard and the sewers do be stinking and steaming under the stone sets of the streets, when they can see a bit of a rag floating in the wild wind, and they dancing their bloody Ceilidhes over the lip of Hell! Oh, I have my own way of seeing surely. It takes a dark man to see the will-o'-the-wisps and the ghosts of the dead and the half dead and them that will never die while they can find lazy, idle hearts ready to keep their venom warm.

SPEAKER (*up*). Out of the depths I have cried to Thee, O Lord: Lord, hear my voice!

BLIND MAN. In every dusty corner lurks the living word of some dead poet, and it waiting for to trap and to snare them. This is no City of the Living: but of the Dark and the Dead!

SPEAKER. I am mad – mad – mad! Sally!
   (*During his speech the stage darkens until both figures are blotted out and the* SPEAKER *is left groping in the dark.*)

SARAH'S VOICE. Robert! Robert!

SPEAKER. What was that?

SARAH'S VOICE (*singing*).
   She stretched forth her arms,
   Her mantle she flung to the wind,
   And swam o'er Loch Leane
   Her outlawed lover to find . . .

63

SPEAKER. Sally! Sally! Where are you?

SARAH'S VOICE. Why don't you come to me, Robert? I have been waiting for you so long.

SPEAKER. I have been searching for you so long.

SARAH'S VOICE. I thought you had forgotten me.

SPEAKER. Forgotten you! Forgotten you, Sally! Is that your hand, dear? *A cuisle geal mo chroidhe* – 'Tis you shall have a silver throne – Her sunny mouth dimples with hope and joy: her dewy eyes are full of pity. It is you, Sally – Deirdre is mine: she is my Queen, and no man now can rob me!

(*The lights go up. He is in the dingy room of a tenement house. The plaster is peeling off the walls. On a bed in the corner a young man with the face of* JOE *is lying with an expression of serene contentment upon his pale, drawn features. Two men – the* OLDER *and the* YOUNGER MAN – *are playing cards at a table opposite, upon which stands a bottle with a candle perched rakishly in the neck. The* SPEAKER *himself is affectionately clasping the arm of the old* FLOWER WOMAN. *When he sees her he bursts into hysterical laughter.*)

WOMAN. Ah, me lovely gentleman, is it me yer calling?

SPEAKER. Well done! Well done! The joke is on me! Well done!

WOMAN. The Lord love ye, an' how's the poor head?

SPEAKER. Robert Emmet knows when the joke is on him! Kiss me, lovely Sarah Curran!

WOMAN (*archly*). Ah, go on owa that! D'jever hear the like!

OLDER MAN (*looking up from his game*). Drunk.

YOUNGER MAN. Aw, disgustin'.

WOMAN. Sit down now. Ah, go along with ye! Sit down now there, an' take no heed a them ignerant yucks . . . an' I'll get ye a small drop.

SPEAKER. My lovely Sarah Curran! Sweet Sally!

WOMAN (*aside to the* OLDER MAN). Ye bloody rip! I'll twist the tongue of ye, that's what I will.

SPEAKER. Her sunny mouth dimples with hope and joy.

YOUNGER MAN. Ho, yes, you'll do the hell of a lot, ma . . . in me eye!

WOMAN. Don't heed them. Don't heed them at all mister. He's no son of mine that has ne'er a soft word in his heart for th' old mudher that reared him in sickness and in sorra te be a heart-scaldin' affliction an' a theef a honest names.

OLDER MAN. Now ye can say what ye like, but there's a Man! There's a Man! Drunk, an' it's hours after closin'! Drunk, an' in th' old green coat! (*Singing.*) Oh, wrap the green flag round me, boys.

SPEAKER (*joins in.*) Ta-ra-ra-ra-ra-ra, Ra! Ra!

WOMAN. Sure, he's not drunk are ye, gentleman, an' if he was itself it's none a your concern. (*To* SPEAKER.) Isn't that right, son?

OLDER MAN. And why the hell shouldn't he be drunk? Tell me that. We're a Free State, aren't we? Keep open the pubs. That's my motto. What man says we're not a Free State?

YOUNGER MAN. I say it, ye drunken bastard!

OLDER MAN. Drunken bastard . . . hell! I declare to God I'm sober'n you are, me bold, water-drinkin' Diehard. God knows I'm cold an odd time, but sure a true Patriot is always drunk.

YOUNGER MAN. Have you no love for Ireland?

SPEAKER. God save Ireland!

OLDER MAN. Ho yes – 'The Republic still lives'. Aw – go te hell!

YOUNGER MAN. I've been to hell all right, never fear. I went down into hell shouting 'Up the living Republic', and I came up out of hell still shouting 'Up the living Republic' .Do you hear me? Up the Republic!

SPEAKER. Up the Priory!

OLDER MAN. Oh, I hear you well enough. But you'll not convince me for all your bridge blasting. Looka here, I stand for the status q-oh, and I'll not be intimidated by the gun.

WOMAN (*handing the* SPEAKER *a precious black bottle*). Here, have another sup and never heed that old chat of them!

SPEAKER. A health, Sarah Curran! A toast to the woman with brave sons!

WOMAN. Aw God . . . If I was young again!

YOUNGER MAN. And who needs to convince you?

OLDER MAN. Oh, you needn't think . . .

YOUNGER MAN. Every day and every night while you were lying on your back snoring, wasn't I out in the streets shouting 'Up the living Republic'?

OLDER MAN. Ah, don't we remember that too well.

SPEAKER. Up the living Departed!

YOUNGER MAN. Every morning and every night while you were sitting in the old snug, wasn't I out on the hills shouting 'Up the living Republic'?

SPEAKER. Up the pole!

OLDER MAN. Well?

YOUNGER MAN. Every hour of the day that you spent ⌐ ˙ 'our

belly and gassing about your status q-oh, wasn't I crying
'Republic, Republic, Republic'?

OLDER MAN. May God give ye a titther a sense some day.

SPEAKER. Up the blood-red Phlegethon! Up Cocytus, frozen lake
of Hell!

OLDER MAN (*turning for a moment*). Aw, wouldn't that languidge
disgust ye!

YOUNGER MAN. So one day, me laddo, you woke up and found that
the Republic did live after all. And would you like to know
why?

OLDER MAN. 'Tell me not in mournful numbers' ...

YOUNGER MAN. Just because I and my like had said so, and said so
again, while you were too drunk and too lazy and too thick in
the head to say anything at all. That's why. And then, with the
rest of your kidney you hunched your shoulders, spat on your
hands, and went back to your bed mumbling 'Up the Status
q-oh'. So why the hell should I try to convince you?

SPEAKER. A long speech. A strong speech. A toast to the son that
speaks. A toast to the son that swills!

OLDER MAN. Aw, that's all words. Nothing but bloody words. You
can't change the world by words.

YOUNGER MAN. That's where you fool yourself! What other way
can you change it? I tell you, we can make this country – this
world – whatever we want it to be by saying so, and saying so
again. I tell you it is the knowledge of this that is the genius and
glory of the Gael!

SPEAKER. Up the Primum Mobile! Up the graters of verdigreece.
Up the Apes Pater Noster.

JOE.
> Cupping the crystal jewel-drops
> Girdling the singing of the silver stream ...
> (*He tries to scribble on the wall.*)
> What was it? ... the singing of the silver stream.
> Damp acid-cups of meadowsweet ...

SPEAKER. Hello! There's the fellow I shot. Is he not gone yet? A
toast to the son that dies!

WOMAN. Ay ... are ye lookin' for a bit of sport tonight?

SPEAKER. I have had brave sport this night!

WOMAN. Aw, mister ... have a heart!

SPEAKER (*flaring up.*) A heart!
> (JOE *gives a short, contented laugh.*)

SPEAKER. Do not do that. That is not the way to laugh.

66

YOUNGER MAN. I tell you, what the likes of me are saying tonight, the likes of you will be saying tomorrow.

OLDER MAN. Is that a fact? And may I be so bold as to in-quire what awtority you have for makin' that observation?

YOUNGER MAN. Because we're the lads that make the world.

OLDER MAN. You don't say!

SPEAKER (*passionately*). Then why have you made it as it is? Then will you stand before the Throne and justify your handiwork? Then will you answer to me for what I am?

YOUNGER MAN. What are *you* talking about? You're only a bloody play-actor. If you were a man and not satisfied with the state of things, you'd alter them for yourself.

OLDER MAN (*holding out a bottle*). Aw, have a sup and dry up for God's sake!

(JOE *laughs again.*)

SPEAKER. That blasphemous laugh! Do you not know you're going to die?

JOE (*laughing again*).

>Soft radiance of the shy new moon
>Above the green gold cap of Kilmashogue
>Where . . .

SPEAKER. Kilmashogue!

JOE.

>Where of a summer's evening I have danced
>A saraband.

SPEAKER. What of Kilmashogue? Look around you. Here! Don't you know me? I shot you.

JOE. Well, please don't interrupt. (*He coughs.*)

WOMAN. It's the cough that shivers ye, isn't it, son? Me poor lamb, will ye tell the gentleman . . . (*She goes as if to touch him.*)

JOE (*through his teeth*). Strumpet! Strumpet!

WOMAN. Blast ye! ye'd use that word t'yer own mudher, would ye! God, I'll throttle ye with me own two hands for the dirty scut ye are!

SPEAKER. Go back!

YOUNGER MAN (*seizing her from behind and flinging her away*). Away to hell, ye old trollop!

OLDER MAN. Ah, leave her alone.

WOMAN. Awlright, awlright! Yer all agin me. But it won't be th' cough will have th' stiffenin' of him not if I lay me hands on his dirty puss before he's gone. When I get a holt a ye I'll leave me mark on ye never fear.

YOUNGER MAN. Aw, shut yer mouth, ma!

JOE. I'd like to do it all again . . . That's right . . . Again . . . It's good . . . to feel the wind . . . in your hair . . .

(*He laughs weakly.*)

SPEAKER. Don't! Don't do that I tell you!

JOE.

> Stench of the nut-brown clay
> Piled high around the headstones and the yews,
> My fingers clotted with the crusted clay,
> My heart is singing . . . in the skies . . .

(*He coughs again. The* BLIND FIDDLER *enters slowly through the door.*)

OLDER MAN. You know, some of that stuff is very hard to follow. I'd sooner have the old stuff any day.

> 'Oh I met with Napper Tandy
> An' he took me by the hand.'

SPEAKER. Sssssh!

YOUNGER MAN. What do you want here?

BLIND MAN. Wouldn't I have a right to pay my respects to one, and he passin' into the ranks of the Government? Isn't it a comely thing for me to be hopin' that he'll remember a poor old dark man an' he sittin' in the seats of the mighty in his kingdom out beyond?

JOE (*very soft*). Well . . . so long, lads. It was . . . a grand life . . . so long, lad . . . that plugged me . . So long . . . (*He dies.*)

WOMAN. Burn ye! Burn ye!

BLIND MAN. Be silent now, and a new shadow after being born! Do you not know, woman, that this land belongs not to them that are on it, but to them that are under it.

YOUNGER MAN. He's gone. Stiffening already, poor chap. Hats off, lads.

SPEAKER. Gone! And I am only a play-actor – unless I dare to contradict the dead! Must I do that?

BLIND MAN. Let them build their capitols on Leinster Lawn. Let them march their green battalions out by the Park Gate. Out by Glasnevin there's a rattle of bones and a bit of a laugh where the presidents and senators of Ireland are dancing hand in hand, with no one to see them but meself an' I with the stick an' the fiddle under me arm.

OLDER MAN. Well . . . a wake's a wake, anyhow. So pass over the bottle and give us a tune on the ole instrument.

BLIND MAN (*tuning up*). It's many's the year an' I fiddled at a wake.

WOMAN. One son with th' divil in hell, an' two more with th' divils on earth. (*She spits.*) God forgive me for weanin' a brood a sorry scuts!

> (*The* SPEAKER *is seated silently at the foot of the bed, staring at the body with his back to the audience. There is a knock at the door.*)

WOMAN. Wha's that?

> (*The* YONGER MAN *goes to the door, pauses, and flings it open. On the threshold stands* MAEVE.)

MAEVE. My mammy thez...

WOMAN. Ah love, is it yerself?

MAEVE. My mammy thez I'm to play the accompaniment of 'The Thruggle Ith Over'.

WOMAN. Come on in, duckie. God love ye an' welcome. The ole pianner's waiting for ye, love.

MAEVE. Yeth pleathe. My mammy...

> (*She comes in and, catching sight of the* SPEAKER, *she points, and bursts into tears.*)

WOMAN. There, there! What's the matter, lamb? Ah God help her! What ails ye at all?

MAEVE (*gulping*). Thlipperth...

WOMAN. There, there now...

OLDER MAN. Aw, will ye dry up?

WOMAN (*with an impatient flap of the hand*). There's the pianner, so do what yer mammy says before I slaughter ye.

BLIND MAN. Play on now, young one. And when you've played, 'tis meself will fiddle for the shadows and they dancing at the wake.

MAEVE (*sniffling*). My mammy thez...

> (MAEVE *sits at an old cracked piano, upon which presently she commences to thump out carefully 'The Struggle Is Over'.*)

WOMAN. There now. Ah God, hasn't she the gorgus touch on th' ole instrument!

> (*Another knock at the door. The* YOUNGER MAN *opens it. The* MINISTER FOR ARTS AND CRAFTS *is on the threshold in top hat, frock coat, and carrying one of those hemispherical glass cases full of white flowers.*)

MINISTER. Deep concern – Government grieved to learn – struck down in prime – Requiem Mass – life for Erin – send a gunboat – bitter loss – token of our regard. (*He presents the case.*)

69

WOMAN (*very unctuous*). Ah, aren't ye the kind-hearted Government, and isn't them th' gorgus flowers. God will reward ye, sir;
He will indeed at the next election, for th' blessed pity ye've
shown to a poor woman in her sorra.

(*Another knock at the door. The* YOUNGER MAN *opens it.*
LADY TRIMMER, *dressed in widow's weeds, enters.*)

LADY TRIMMER. So sad! So sad indeed! I can't simply say how sad
it is. Quite a poet, too, I hear. Can any of his books be purchased?

WOMAN. At Hodges an' Figgis ma'am. Be sure ye get the name right.
Come in, come in!

(*Before the* YOUNGER MAN *has the door properly closed there
comes another knock. He abandons it, leaving it open. The*
STATUE OF GRATTAN *is on the threshold.*)

GRATTAN. A word-spinner dying gracefully, with a cliché on his
lips. The symbol of Ireland's genius. Never mind. He passed on
magnificently. He knew how to do that.

WOMAN (*her head quite turned*). An' he was me favrit', too lady . . .
never a bitter word . . . never a hard glance. Sure, it's them we
love th' best is took th' first, God help us. Ullagone! Ullagone!
Ochone-a-ree!

(*Enter the* GENERAL *with crape upon his arm.*)

GENERAL . . . a grand song called 'Home to Our Mountains'. No. 17
bus passes the door or a bus to Ballyboden, whenever the road's
not up. But of course if you don't want me to sing, I won't force
myself on you. Won't I?

WOMAN.

> Low lie your heads this day
> My sons! My sons!
> The strong in their pride go by me
> Saying, 'Where are thy sons?'

(O'COONEY, O'MOONEY *and* O'ROONEY *enter, all in black
gloves and top hats.*)

ALL THREE. Who's a twister? I'm a twister? You're a twister? He's
taken a header into the Land of Youth. Anyhow, he was a
damn sight better man than some I could name, and there's no
blottin' it out.

LADY TRIMMER. So yellow-haired Donough is dead! Dear, dear!

(*A few more stray figures crush in, chattering and pressing
forward in file before the body.*)

WOMAN.

> Gall to our heart! Oh, gall to our heart!

70

Ullagone! Ochone-a-ree!
A lost dream to us now in our home!

MAEVE (*stopping her playing*). Will that do, Daddy?

BLIND MAN (*mounting upon a chair*). The shadows are gathering, gathering. They're coming to dance at a wake. An' I playin' for them on the gut box. Are yez ready all?

(*He tunes up. The lights in front have dimmed, leaving a great sheet of brightness flooding from the sides upon the back-cloth. The walls of the room seem to fade apart while the crowd draws aside and seats itself upon the floor and upon all sides of the stage. The SPEAKER has vanished.*)

THE VOICES OF THE CROWD. The Shadows are gathering, gathering: he says they must dance at a wake. Seats for the Shadows the gathering Shadows . . . The Shadows that dance at a wake.

(*The BLIND MAN commences to fiddle a jig in the whole-tone scale.*)

THE VOICES.
Overture started
Seats for the Shadows
Gathering, gathering
Dance at a wake
Loosen his collar
Basin of water
Dance Shadows
Oooooooh!

(*Upon the back-cloth two great SHADOWS appear gesturing and posturing in time with the music.*)

THE FIRST SHADOW (*stopping his dance and striking an attitude*).
Come clear of the nets of wrong and right;
Laugh, heart, again in the grey twilight,
Sigh, heart, again in the dew of the morn.
Your Mother Eire is always young . . .

(*Hand clapping. The SECOND SHADOW jostles the FIRST aside and points one long arm vaguely in the direction of the FLOWER WOMAN.*)

THE SECOND SHADOW. Stone traps of dead builders. Warrens of weasel rats! How serene does she now arise! Queen among the Pleiades, in the penultimate antelucan hour: shod in sandals of bright gold: coifed with a veil of gossamer.

(*Applause. Amidst shrieks of laughter the FLOWER WOMAN rises, curtsies and dances hilariously once round the fore-*

71

ground. Two more SHADOWS *have elbowed the first pair aside and are now dancing to the music.*)

THE VOICES.

Dance! Dance!

Speak, Shadows, speak!

THE THIRD SHADOW. It is difficult not to be unjust to what one loves. Is not He who made misery wiser than thou?

(*Applause, mingled with some booing. The* THIRD SHADOW *throws up its arms and flees.*)

THE FOURTH SHADOW. Every dream is a prophecy: every jest an earnest in the womb of time.

(*Shouts of laughter and applause. The* SHADOWS *change into a tumbling mass of blackness.*)

THE VOICES.

Dance! Dance!

Speak, Shadows, speak!

A VOICE. There are no Shadows left to speak.

BLIND MAN. Speak, great Shadow! Shadow of Ireland's Heart.

VOICES (*whispering*). We see him. He is here.

(*The shadow of the* SPEAKER *precedes him as he comes slowly in from the back.*)

BLIND MAN. Speak, shadow of Robert Emmet.

SPEAKER. I know whom you are calling. I am ready.

BLIND MAN. The eyes of the people are fixed on your face.

VOICES. Justify! Justify! Shadow of the Speaker, speak!

VOICES. Sssh!

SPEAKER. The souls in the seven circles of Purgatory cry out, Deliver us O Lord from the mouth of the Lion that Hell may not swallow us up. The Word Made Flesh shall break the chains that bind me. Three armies may be robbed of their leader – no wretch can be robbed of his will.

Yes, there is darkness now, but I can create light. I can separate the waters of the deep, and a new world will be born out of the void. A challenge, Norns! A gage flung down before you! Justify! Justify!

VOICES. Justify! Justify!

(*The* SPEAKER *continues to address the audience.*)

SPEAKER (*continues*). Race of men with dogs' heads! Panniers filled with tripes and guts! Thelemites! Cenobites! Flimflams of the law! Away! while Niobe still weeps over her dead children. I have heard the angels chanting the Beatitudes to the souls in Malebolge, and I have done with you.

72

I do not fear to approach the Omnipotent Judge to answer
for the conduct of my short life and am I to stand appalled here
before this mere remnant of mortality? I do not imagine that
Your Lordships will give credit to what I utter. I have no hopes
that I can anchor my character in the breast of this court. I only
wish Your Lordships may suffer it to float down your memories
until it has found some more hospitable harbour to shelter it.

(*Voices, shuffling, applause.*)

SPEAKER (*continues*). For now is the axe put to the root of the tree.
My fan is in my hand, and I will burn the chaff with unquench-
able fire.

VOICES.
Up Emmet!
Up Rathfarnham!
Up the Up that won't be Down!

(*He draws his sword and turns upon them all. During the
following commination the* VOICES *give the responses in unison
and the* FIGURES *in turn fling up their arms and take flight
before him. The light fades, gradually blotting out all vestiges of
the room.*)

SPEAKER. Cursed be he who values the life above the dream.
VOICES. Amen.
SPEAKER. Cursed be he who builds but does not destroy.
VOICES. Amen.
SPEAKER. Cursed be he who honours the wisdom of the wise.
VOICES. Amen.
SPEAKER. Cursed be the ear that heeds the prayer of the dead.
VOICES. Amen.
SPEAKER. Cursed be the eye that sees the heart of a foe.
VOICES. Amen.
SPEAKER. Cursed be prayers that plough not, praises that reap not,
joys that laugh not, sorrows that weep not.
VOICES (*dying away*). Amen. Amen. Ah – men.

(*The last of the* FIGURES *fling up their arms and vanish. As
the* SPEAKER *comes down stage they come creeping back
again, crouching in the darkness and watching him with many
eyes. It is dark.*)

SPEAKER. I will take this earth in both my hands and batter it into
the semblance of my heart's desire! See, there by the trees is
reared the gable of the house where sleeps my dear one. Under
my feet the grass is growing, soft and subtle, in the evening dew.
The cool, clean wind is blowing down from Killakee, kissing

my hair and dancing with the flowers that fill the garden all around me. And Sarah . . . Sarah Curran . . . you are there . . . waiting for Robert Emmet.

I know this garden well for I have called it into being with the Credo of the Invincibles: I believe in the might of Creation, the majesty of the Will, the resurrection of the Word, and Birth Everlasting.

(*He flings aside his sword and looks around him in triumph. It is very dark, so dark that for all we know perhaps it may be the garden of the first scene. Perhaps those may be the trees and the mountains beyond the Priory. For a moment we hear the tramp of feet and the distant sound of the Shan Van Vocht. His voice falters and he staggers wearily.*)

SPEAKER. My ministry is now ended. Shall we sit down together for a while? Here on the hillside . . . where we can look down over the city, and watch the lights twinkle and wink to each other . . . Our city . . . our wilful, wicked old city . . .

(*The gauze curtains close slowly behind him.*)

I think . . . I would like to sleep . . . What? . . . On your shoulder? . . . Ah, I was so right to go on!

(*His head sinks drowsily and his eyes stare out into the auditorium. He is lying just where the* DOCTOR *left him some time ago.*)

Strumpet city in the sunset
Suckling the bastard brats of Scots, of Englishry, of Huguenot.
Brave sons breaking from the womb, wild sons fleeing from their Mother.
Wilful city of savage dreamers,
So old, so sick with memories!
Old Mother
Some they say are damned,
But you, I know, will walk the streets of Paradise
Head high, and unashamed.

(*His eyes close. He speaks very softly.*)

There now. Let my epitaph be written.

(*There is silence for a moment and then the* DOCTOR *speaks off.*)

DOCTOR. . . . do, fine.

(*He appears bearing a large and gaudy rug. He looks towards the audience, places one finger to his lips, and makes a sign for the front curtains to be drawn. When last we see him he is*

74

covering the unconscious SPEAKER *with his rug. That is the
end of this play.*)

BLOOMSBURY, 1926 – DALKEY, 1976.

A NOTE ON WHAT HAPPENED

(The following note was originally written nearly fifty years ago in advance of the production of the play in the United States. It is published here for the first time.)

Walking back from Sorrento with Mr Yeats he gave me what was probably the most incisive criticism this play has received. 'I liked your play,' he said, 'but it has one or two faults. The first is, the scenes are too long.' He was silent for a time, while we both gazed with some signs of embarrassment at a cargo boat rounding Dalkey Island. 'Then', he added finally and after considerable thought, 'there are too many scenes'.

Needless to say I was grateful for this opinion.

To say that the scenes are too long and that there are too many of them goes right to the root of the matter. Why do it at all? And if it does mean anything, isn't it better left unsaid?

A distinguished member of the audience who sat through most of the performance with his eyes closed remarked very aptly as he took himself home, 'I suppose people must have nightmares, but why inflict them on us?' I am afraid I can supply very little in the way of an answer. Perhaps nightmares – or dreams, if you're that kind – don't really mean very much, and probably a good many of them would be better left unremembered. Ireland is spiritually in a poor condition at the moment and I don't know that homoeopathic treatment is the best for her complaint. A young lady having seen the play said of it that it made her blush. Not because of its vulgarity – ordinary vulgarity was a commonplace on the stage. But this was different. She had blushed for me – that such thoughts should ever have entered my head.

This play, if plays must be about something, is about what Dublin has made a good many of us feel. And if it is a very wrong and vulgar feeling that could only have been experienced by people with nasty minds, we aren't worth bothering about anyway. But it

76

is no good saying that it isn't true, because we happen to know that it is.

I was warned during rehearsals by various friends that the play would be denounced as anti-National, or as Republican propaganda, or as a personal reflection on so-and-so – opinions which were given with the best of good will but whose only common denominator was that the play would be denounced. In this they were right, but only in their conclusions. For as it turned out when the production was complete the assault came from a most unexpected quarter. It was well patronised by *l'ancien regime* and was stoutly defended in the press and elsewhere by more than one physical force Intransigentist. But exception was taken to the play on the ground that it was blasphemous.

It appeared that the language of the Holy Writ was used in obscene circumstances – ranted and raved by a mad actor to the accompaniment of a chorus of curses and swearwords – that the scene in which some of these lines were spoken was a brothel – and that the final Commination was a ribald parody of Jesus driving the money-changers from the Temple.

I need hardly say that I was not prepared for this, although I was ready to be philosophic about the charge that I was trying to write a silly lampoon of living persons. But now that I come to think of it, I have noticed before that the words of Holy Writ when used in circumstances in which they are liable to be taken seriously sometimes incur the suspicion of being either insanity or blasphemy.

I can quite appreciate the point of view which holds that the ethics of religion are solely a matter for the pulpit and have no place upon the stage.

But granted that we have persuaded all those members of the audience to leave the theatre if they are the kind who experience a shock on discovering that their own theological ideas have a human and a dramatic meaning as well as a symbolic one; how then, are we to express on the stage the idea of the triumph of the Word over environment – the dogma of the Resurrection? It seems to me that the most straightforward way – especially in a play where all other ideas are conveyed by the thematic method – is to call up the desired association of ideas by suggesting the words of the Liturgy.

Whether or not I have succeeded in doing this myself is another matter, but the fact that I appear to have suggested to the minds of some of my critics the picture of the expulsion of the money-changers from the Temple – an analogy which was not before my

77

own mind – would indicate that I have not entirely failed.

And lest it should be thought that criticisms of this kind are not of much consequence these days, I should add that nearly every night indignant women walked out during the last act, and strong representations were made to the authorities to have a blasphemy prosecution set on foot. Needless to say the authorities had no time to waste on such small fry as the little Gate Theatre or myself, but the threat had high ramifications and results that it would be amusing but totally wrong of me to disclose.

* * * *

I think that it must be a result of the long predominance of narrative drama to the exclusion of all else that people get so worried when one cannot tell them what a play is about. Yet the dithyrambic outbursts from which both western and eastern theatrical conventions have developed had nothing to do with a plot. It would be difficult to interpret the religious ecstacy of a mediaeval miracle play or the intricacies of a No Play of Japan for inclusion in French's 'Guide to Selecting Plays'.

It seems to me that the real play must be regarded as what goes on in the mind of the audience. What, therefore, a play is about depends entirely on who is listening to it.

Anybody who has done any acting will know that a performance to an audience is quite a different affair from the most complete Dress Rehearsal – as different as War is from Salisbury Plain. And furthermore, a good play – that is to say, a play which is succeeding in registering its effect whether we personally approve of it or not – is a different play from night to night according as the reflex of the House varies.

And these ideas and emotions can be stimulated without the assistance of a narrative plot at all, whether melodically as in music, by direct statement as in continental Expressionism, or by simple association of ideas. Strindberg in some of his later work provides one of the best modern examples of the fact that dramatic experience is not dependent on physical actuality and is in fact hampered by it. In the 'Spook Sonata' there is for example, the wretched wife who sits all day in a dark cupboard from which she cries like a parrot, 'Pretty Polly! Pretty Polly!' This genius with which he conveys an attitude of mind in terms of a fantastic physical reality has, on me at any rate, a most real and horrifying effect, but the intention of the author is completely defeated if the audience insists on regarding the picture as one of narrative fact.

The melodic method has been greatly developed since the War by the Russians, principally in the Constructivist Theatre of Meierhold and in the Moscow Jewish Art Theatre, where an attempt is made to stimulate the desired attitude of mind by means of acrobatics and dancing and the elimination of all unnecessary detail in the way of stage decor or scenery. The development of electric lighting has of course opened up limitless possibilities in all those directions.

Toller and Kaiser taking the dangerous course of direct statement have so simplified the stage by throwing out unnecessary lumber that nothing will convince a British audience, schooled to the loud technical camouflage of Mr St. John Irvine, that they are really saying anything at all. They have however discredited their school to some extent in the eyes of non-industrial audiences by a complete absence of humour and by the Frankenstein complex that seems to have dominated the stage of Central Europe ever since the War.

In English-speaking countries on the other hand, the tradition of Pinero, Barker and Shaw, culminating in the 'Problem Play', is still well entrenched in the path of any further development of the theatre. We have the Play that leaves you with a Thought. What would I do if I met an Escaped Convict? How would I like it if Father married a Prostitute? Is War Right? I need hardly say that as a natural consequence nobody can go to an ostensibly serious play without feeling that he must concentrate upon what it is all About.

But surely this is all wrong, just as it would be in the case of music! All that is needed to enjoy and appreciate a work such as E. E. Cummings' 'Him' is a simple faith, a little human experience, and a receptive state of mind attained by a process the reverse of concentration. This being the normal condition of my own mind I need hardly say that I find little difficulty in preferring Strindberg's 'Dream Play' to 'Emperor and Galillean'.

* * * *

'The Old Lady says "No"!' is not an expressionist play and ought never to have been mistaken for one. I have attempted to evolve a thematic method based on simple association of ideas, a process which has as many disadvantages as the opposite. For it presupposes at the start a set of recognisable figments in the minds of the audience – figments which from their very nature are bound to be somewhat local. In consequence of this, the play to be intelligible to a non-Irish audience requires to some extent to be translated.

The theme of the Romantic temperament seeking for an environment in which to express himself is a universal one, but everybody cannot be expected to know about Robert Emmet. When an old lady appears upon the stage and maunders about her four beautiful green fields, it is too much to expect of a London audience that it will recognise the traditional figure of romantic Nationalism for whom Mangan and Pearse sighed. It is only in the Free State that the O'Donovan Rossa speech and Committee Room 15 (where Parnell was betrayed) can be relied upon to call up any recollections without the aid of a footnote.

Yet the search for the Land of Heart's Desire is as old and as universal as the Holy Grail. The tale might also be the tale of such diverse figures as Juan Ponce de Leon, of the great Danton, of Abelard, of John Brown of Harper's Ferry and even of poor William Blake. Every land has had its store of Emmets, preaching their burning messages to the accompaniment of farmyard noises, and Ireland has more than her share.

It was Plato who first told us that if we don't like our environment it is up to us to alter it for ourselves, and the vigorous philosophy of Nietzsche's Man-Gott and the biology of Buffon and Lamarck are in somewhat the same line of business. If the Emmets in particular or if intransigent Irish Republicanism in general are to be taken as having made any contribution to the world of applied philosophy I feel that it is this characteristic attitude of mind. 'The Republic still lives' is not the expression of a pious hope, but is in itself a creative act, as England knows to her cost.

I understand that there is a correct psychological explanation of all this. Ned Stephens, for instance, tells me that the play represents the breaking down of something called a 'synthetic personality' by contact with reality and the creation of a new one in its stead. I am much too scared of Freud, Adler and McDougall ever to have attempted any such thing, but I feel that if a play is true to experience in its emotional aspect it may well have a sound psychological meaning thrown in as well. As a small boy I used to make pictures for myself with a box of blocks. When the work was completed I used to find that by turning the whole over you found another finished picture constructed on the other side.

But I should add that all this is not intended to be by way of explanation. All that I do wish to do is to answer the objection levelled at much of the post-war spirit both in art and in letters;

that it is insincere, intentionally obscure and that it lacks fundamentality. Lucidity seems to me to be the *sine qua non* of any effort of this kind. It has not been my desire to detract attention from my lack of craftsmanship by muddling people's minds. Neither have I any desire that the play should be unjustly enhanced by the 'false glitter of quotations', as one critic very threateningly put it. The method is thematic and a motif in the realm of thought is carried best by a name or a quotation.

Some years ago I used to have to play a game where some large, blindfold person, groping round with a cushion, would sit on my knee and tell me to 'Make a noise like a camel'. Well in this play when I want to make a noise like the Old Ireland, I do it in what seems to me to be the easiest way – by means of a potted anthology of the 'Erin a tear and a smile' school that preceded Geoffrey Phibbs. The play with which the first part opens, and which crops up again at intervals, is almost entirely composed of well-known lines from Mangan, Moore, Callinan, Blacker, Griffin, Ferguson, Kickham, Todhunter and a dozen more. The voices of the Shadows are the easily recognisable words of some of Dublin's greatest contributors to the World's knowledge of itself. The long speech with which the play concludes contains suggestions from Emmet's speech from the dock, the resurrection thesis of the Litany, and the magnificent, though sadly neglected, Commination Service of the Anglican Church.

I have already drawn attention to the Old Woman's lines. For the rest I have not consciously or wilfully bowdlerised anybody, except one line of Blake's which I freely admit I am not entitled to, but which is too apt to be surrendered. You may have it if you can find it!

But whatever may be said of the play, there can be no two opinions as to the merits of Hilton Edward's production. It was staged on a space roughly 16 feet by 12 feet – an incredible feat, when it is remembered that at several points there are mass movements of crowds that have to be carried out in a manner not dissimilar to a ballet, and that sets have to be changed while the action is proceeding.

The rhythmatic chanting of the Choruses was carried out to the throb of a drum, for which purpose a considerable portion of the dialogue had practically to be scored – the parts coming in one on top of the other as in instrumental music or a madrigal. It was an unusual and amusing sight at rehearsals to see the spoken lines being conducted from the front by the Producer. It would be invi-

81

dious to refer to the players. The elan of Michael MacLiammoir as the Speaker, the virtuosity of Meriel Moore in the difficult double role of Sarah Curran and the old woman, and the very trying work of the Chorus were the real cause of the play's success.

May I respectively thank them – not forgetting to include my friend Kate Curling for her help and for her contribution.

PERTISAU, 1929.

THE SCYTHE AND THE SUNSET

A Play in Three Acts

UP THE REBELS!

WHEN Sean O'Casey first came to live in London in the 'twenties, he was strap-hanging one late afternoon in a crowded Tube train. After contemplating for some time the unbroken vista of open newspapers, bowler hats, rolled umbrellas and shopping bags, he was finally heard to remark: 'Look at them – all burning with indignation over the Irish question.'

Since that time, a plethora of publishers have sponsored many volumes of Tan War memoirs written strictly from a Flying Column angle, and usually stopping short at the end of 1921, just when the story starts to get interesting. From this fact one might conclude that, outside our verdant island, there is still a widespread excitement over Ireland's military affairs. However, this is an assumption in which I do not readily concur, and I feel sure that some explanation is needed for pushing my way into so congested a district at an advanced stage of the western winter, by writing what has been described as 'another damned play about 1916'.

I was not myself a participant in any of the stirring underground activities that made the New Ireland, principally for a reason that may have contributed to some present sourness on the subject. At the age of sixteen I attempted to join the I.R.A., but did not rise even to the dignity of being blackballed – having failed ignominiously to obtain either a proposer or a seconder, which I was assured by my contacts was necessary. At the age of fifty-four I had much the same experience with the Royal Irish Academy; and these being the only two occasions in my life when I have rashly attempted to join anything without first being asked, I have subsequently affected an air of detachment about both the Academy and the Anglo-Irish War that is understandable, though not wholly sincere. This attitude, however, does not apply to the Easter Rising, in which for a few days I was allowed to play a very minor role as a juvenile civilian internee.

As far as I am aware, only one other play about 1916 was per-

85

formed prior to my own, in spite of all impressions to the contrary. It only seems as if there were more, thanks to the long line of motion pictures glamorizing the later struggle, that have been put out by the film studios. The other Easter Week play is, of course, Sean O'Casey's finest piece of writing, *The Plough and the Stars* – the play of which the title of mine is an obvious parody. Herein any intentional similarity ends, as it would be the act of an idiot for any dramatist to measure his play against such a yardstick as *The Plough*.

Neither in verbiage, plot nor sentiments does this play of mine presume to bear any relation to its magnificent predecessor. The only point in so titling it lies in the fact that *The Plough* is essentially a pacifist play, implying that if only man had 'a titther o' sense', these outbreaks of destruction and bloodshed would never occur. As a quiet man who, nevertheless, is not a pacifist, I cannot accept the fact that, theatrically, Easter Week should remain indefinitely with only an anti-war comment, however fine. So also, it may be noticed that the mouthpiece for most of O'Casey's pacifism is provided by his women; whereas in actual fact the women of Ireland, ever since the Maud Gonne era, have been the most vocal part of its militancy. If I can claim nothing else, I can at least point with some complacency to the fact that – when it comes to the point – both my women are killers.

The Scythe and the Sunset shows every sign of turning out to be one of those elusive phenomena – a play without a public. Apart from whatever intrinsic demerits it may have – and I must confess that I like it very much myself – an antimelodrama on what has now become a sacred subject is distasteful to the sea-divided Gael, and is concerned with a matter that the Sassenach has chosen to forget. As for the Anglo-Irishman, who might perhaps be expected to applaud a few of its less important sentiments, he has become an invisible man, hardly capable of joining in the singing of 'God Save the Queen' in the confines of St Patrick's Cathedral on Armistice Day – an act of defiance that, until recently, was the last kick of this very passé ascendancy.

I have described my play as an antimelodrama, which may require some explanation. Most plays about national uprisings are based upon an assumption that the embattled rebels are always romantic, and that the forces of oppression are totally in the wrong. A dramatist whose historical experience makes it difficult for him to accept these rather shopsoiled axioms as a matter of course, is usually regarded as being either satirical or deliberately confusing, unless he is prepared to waste a lot of time in disproving such conclusions.

I was a schoolboy at the time of the Rising, and for the greater part of three days my home was occupied and fortified by four male members of De Valera's battalion, while we of the family were held, supposedly as prisoners, but actually as hostages. (My father was a judge at the time.) It all sounds more dramatic than it was. Our captors were soft-spoken and apologetic young men who did the least damage they could, compatible with their orders to turn the house into a fort and to prevent us from leaving. On the third day, feeling I suppose that they had by then done enough for Ireland, they stripped off their accoutrements and disappeared through the front gate, shortly before the outbreak of the major pitched battle of the week which began at the other end of the road. I still possess a slouch hat and a bayonet that I saved from confiscation by riding off on my bicycle to a friend's house on the opposite side of the operations, with these incriminating objects concealed as far as possible in a school satchel.

Consequently my recollections of the week are personal and undramatic. Of the rebels, I principally remember their charm, their civility, their doubts, and their fantastic misinformation about everything that was going on. Of the men in khaki there remains an impression of many cups of tea, of conversations about everything except the business in hand, and of a military incompetence of surprising proportions, even to my schoolboy's eye. I could have told them that the best way to cross the Grand Canal was to go round the back by way of another route, rather than by means of a series of frontal bayonet charges against fortified houses, overlooking a narrow bridge. I could also have told them that cavalry in O'Connell Street would be unlikely to get into the General Post Office.

It is a pity that the 'Sinn Fein Rebellion' – as it was wrongly described at the time – has never been properly reported by an objective professional historian. Before long it will be too late to do this from first-hand information, and the accumulating legends, exhibitions of wisdom-after-the-event, and arguments as to who did what (which are so much less interesting than the truth) will have taken command of the record. Until recently little has been written about it from the point of view of Dublin Castle – that symbol of imperial government that was actually in the grasp of the rebels for about half an hour, and could have been completely captured for the first time since its construction by King John, if the intruders had gone on instead of withdrawing. This was the only uprising in the annals of our island of which the secret was perfectly kept beforehand. This triumph of concealment was due to the fact that the rebels had announced so publicly and so often what their belligerent intentions were, that nobody would believe a word they said, and all assumed, as usual, that they were talking through their kepis.

It is not generally known that for the first five hours of the upheaval there was nobody in command of His Majesty's forces in Dublin except a garrison adjutant. Late on Easter Monday afternoon, somebody higher than a major arrived at Kingsbridge from the Curragh, and took charge of the affairs of the Empire. Sir John Maxwell – a soldier who had previously distinguished himself by placing the defences of the Suez Canal on the western bank, I suppose under a mistaken idea that Turkey lay in that direction, and who is generally credited with having suppressed the rising – did not arrive from England until a little more than twenty-four hours before the cease-fire, and barely in time to preside over the least intelligent part of the proceedings – the executions.

Meanwhile, four days were spent in isolating the Post Office by a brigadier with most of the city facilities at his disposal. At which point, fire rather than firing drove the main body of the insurgents into Moore Lane, where they finally gave themselves up. Most of the other strongholds then followed suit – some of them without having been seriously attacked at all. We have also the feat of the gunboat *Helga*, which came up the river to shell Liberty Hall (empty since Monday), and which landed its first projectile in Phoenix Park, greatly endangering the Lord Lieutenant.

Little was done during the first two days to ascertain the dispositions of the Republicans. On the third day a brigade of infantry landed at Kingstown, and proceeded to march up to Dublin by two parallel roads, without either proper reconnaissance, or any other known source of information. A large military barracks stood within one block of their principal hazard. Nevertheless no warning appears to have been given to or asked for by these troops as to what lay ahead, as a result of which one battalion ran up against six or seven valiant Cuchulains, defending a bridge over the Grand Canal, and suffered there most of the casualties of the week, in an engagement that probably had the effect of prolonging the rising from Thursday till the following Sunday.

Indeed it is an eloquent sidelight on the handling of the whole affair by the forces of the Crown, that during the opening days of

the fight, the only real road-block in the way of the rebels was
provided by the amateurs of the Dublin University Officers' Training Corps, with the assistance of a few colonials on leave, who held
their college – and with it a key position in the city – until they
were finally reached by the shaken professionals from Kingstown
some time on Friday morning.

There are also a few aspects of the conflict from the Republican
angle that have been somewhat glossed over. With an exaggerated
respect for the prowess of their opponents, they refused to believe
that they had captured His Majesty's Under-secretary and the seat
of government in Ireland, when in fact they had. They left the
telephone system of the city in full working order under the impression that the exchange was heavily guarded – this on the day
of Fairyhouse Races! Few of the strongholds that they did occupy
had much tactical value, and in several cases had to be abandoned
at the first sign of an attack. But most serious of all from their own
point of view, they harassed and interfered with the work of the
Dublin Fire Brigade – if the word of the Fire Chief is to be believed
– thereby sealing their own ultimate fate. For fire turned out to be
their greatest – their inescapable, enemy.

But perhaps most interesting of all is a matter that has never yet
been commented on at all – the question of Republican leadership.
At the end of the week it was P. H. Pearse who surrendered as
Commander-in-Chief of the Republican Army and 'President of
the Provisional Government'. But how he ever got this lethal office
and who, exactly, appointed him (apart from himself) are matters
that have never been disclosed.

Before the rising, Commandant Pearse – although a leading light
in the military counsels of the secret Irish Republican Brotherhood
– was far from being the leader of the Irish Volunteers. He was
merely a staff officer in charge of organization, and did not even
command one of the city battalions. It would appear from the
order of the signatures on the Proclamation of the Republic (printed
as late as Easter Sunday) that Thomas J. Clarke, the old Fenian,
was originally intended to head the Provisional Government. The
person selected to lead in Dublin the combined forces of the Citizen
Army and the Irish Volunteers, was James Connolly of the first-
named body, while the ranking officer among those of the Irish
Volunteers who took the field was not Pearse but Thomas Mac-
Donagh, who commanded the Dublin Brigade. All that Pearse
mobilized under his own signature on that fateful morning was a
company, which received its directive from him in a handwritten

postscript at the bottom of MacDonagh's brigade order. Furthermore, when the main body marched into O'Connell Street to occupy the Post Office, the column was led by Connolly, with Pearse marching in company with others, further to the rear – surely a very odd position for the Commander-in-Chief, and even more so for the President of a forthcoming revolutionary government.

It is also of interest to note that when, at the end of the week, Pearse signed a document accepting unconditional surrender, De Valera refused to recognize it, when it was presented to him in his embattled Mount Street area. He would take orders, he said, only from his military superior, Thomas MacDonagh. Nor would MacDonagh, in Jacob's Biscuit Factory, accept this surrender either, until after 'consultation with Commandant Ceannt and other officers' he agreed to endorse it on his own behalf.

None of these clues gives us any information as to whether Pearse really held the position in which he has been enshrined ever since in the hearts of his countrymen, or, if he did, how and when he got it. Was the office of Commander-in-Chief an unpopular one, once the affair had started to run its fatal course? Was Pearse the only leader present at headquarters who, in the end, was prepared to assume these grave responsibilities, and to offer himself to General Maxwell as a blood sacrifice on behalf of the others? Or was his leadership largely an invention of his own? None of these questions has ever been publicly asked – much less answered.

My lack of personal knowledge of any of the leaders is my principal reason for not presuming to depict any of them by name, or even by implication, on the stage. Nevertheless there is a certain similarity between what one hears of the views and militant idealism of Pearse and some of those expressed by my character Tetley. The circumstances of the surrender, as depicted in my play through the conversations of Tetley and Palliser, are of course fanciful. Nor is there any reason to believe that some earlier efforts to negotiate were actually frustrated by the firing of a machine-gun. Apart from these dramatic inventions, the other details of my play are as factual as I can make them. I have listened to many accounts of those last days, as described to me by men who had to run the gauntlet of O'Connell Street under fire, and I remember very clearly the conversations of the rebels in my own home. But what I recollect most clearly of all is the aspect of Easter Week that is the most happily glossed over today – the intense hostility with which the whole affair was regarded by the Dublin public.

At this distance it is hard to realize the widespread contempt in which the 'Sinn Fein Volunteers' were generally held prior to the Rising. Ireland, as a whole, was enthusiastically in the War on the side of the Allies, and these non-combatant warriors were figures of fun in a world that was engaged on a very considerable struggle elsewhere. It is probable that this contempt was more instrumental in driving the Volunteers into action at that time than any political or economic motives. 'Face', not slogans, is one of the most power-ful motivating forces in the breasts of men, and these men had to prove that they were soldiers, or disband in the face of ridicule.

So it is not surprising that the prospect of picking up free sweets from the shattered window of a toffee shop should draw away the bulk of the crowd from the first reading of Ireland's Declaration of Independence. Standing at the corner of Stephen's Green, close to the Shelbourne Hotel, I listened with some youthful amusement to a small crowd of citizens shouting sarcasms at the insurgents behind the railings of the park. From time to time one of the latter would step out and wave a rifle in our direction, at which point the entire mob would scamper off up Merrion Row shouting abuse as it ran, only to return again a few minutes later to its old position, from which the comments were resumed. This sort of thing is not much spoken of today. Everybody is now convinced that he was in the Post Office with Pearse.

In spite of these objections to the official picture it is far from my intention in this play to debunk 1916 – a stupid accusation that I am glad to say is more generally made by those who have never fired a shot in anger, than by those who have. Whether or not we hold that the actual fighting was widespread or of first-rate quality, we must agree that the affair, on the whole, was a humane and well-intentioned piece of gallantry. And the more one sees of how these uprisings have since been conducted elsewhere, the more reason everybody has to be pleased with Easter Week. In those days nobody had much experience of warfare, or of what would be likely to occur if the British Army were challenged in open rebellion for the first time in three or four generations. Nowadays, there is hardly a corner of the globe that has not got plenty of data on this subject, but we must not forget that the Irish Volunteers were the first to try. For this reason alone, the Republicans must be credited with considerable courage in taking the field at all; and in at least two engagements in the course of the week they showed military aptitude of the highest quality, as did, also, the poor old British Tommy, when driven to perform impossible tasks that only tanks would be employed upon today.

Brave men are always exciting to write about, particularly when they are afflicted with doubts, and deficient in technical training; and in a wider sense *The Scythe and the Sunset* presents a picture that has been repeated so often in the course of the past forty years that one may legitimately doubt whether its local significance is of very much importance after all. The passing of an imperial civilization in which many of us were brought up is a process that has usually presented the same pattern – although not always so coherently – ever since the opening phase in Dublin. It is not an Irish but a world phenomenon, that the man who loses is often the man who wins, and that each side usually expends as much energy in playing the other fellow's game as it spends in furthering its own.

The conflict of the man with the idea against the man of action is as old as the battle of Pope and Emperor, and what each has to say for himself is as important now as it has been since the trial of Jesus. And whether in Cairo, Delhi, or in Jerusalem, or in Nicosia, I can still visualize some local Palliser rigging that machine-gun in a fury. And I would still be asked afterwards why he did so – this in a world where we not only rig machine-guns for our foes but supply them in bulk to the other side with unfailing regularity.

The fact is, that, outside the theatre, men do not act from logical motives as often as they act under the promptings of the urge that I mentioned before – this thing that the Orientals call 'face'. If it is not permissible to depict this well-known phenomenon on the stage without elaborating the reasons for it, that is the theatre's look-out. Not mine.

The Scythe and the Sunset

This play was first produced at the Poets' Theatre in Cambridge, Massachusetts, on March 14th, 1958, with the following cast:

Dr Myles MacCarthy	JOHN FRID
Roisin	CATHERINE AHERN
Emer nic Gabhann	SUSAN McCLINTOCK
Micheál Maginnis	RAY GIRARDIN, JUNIOR
Endymion	MICHAEL LINENTHAL
Sean Tetley	JUDGE SPRINGER
J. Williams	JACK ROGERS
Liam O'Callaghan	EDMUND ROCHE
Captain Anthony Palliser	JOHN LASELL
Captain Clattering	JOHN A. COE
A Volunteer	JOHN KING

The play produced by William Driver; the setting designed by Nyna Brael.

First European production was by the Abbey Theatre Company in Dublin, on May 19th, 1958.

The action of the play takes place in a small café in the centre of Dublin.

ACT ONE	Scene 1	Opens shortly before noon on Easter Monday, 1916.
	Scene 2	Continues about an hour and a half later.
ACT TWO		Tuesday afternoon.
ACT THREE		Friday evening.

ACT ONE

Scene 1

An unpretentious restaurant, known as the Pillar Café, one floor up in a building facing on to a wide street. It is the kind of place where, whatever the hour of day, the meals maintain the same quality, centering around bread and butter, bacon and eggs, and strong stewed tea which comes from an urn on the counter. On this counter are also a number of glass-covered stands containing packets of biscuits, chunks of plum cake, currant buns, and jam pots. There is also a dingy showcase exhibiting a mixed collection of chocolate bars, tins of toffee, raffle tickets, and condiments. On the wall behind the counter is stored the crockery, and there is also a hatch, leading through to the kitchen. The room is furnished with a number of small tables covered with stained cloths and surrounded by rickety chairs. On the opposite side to the counter is a low platform on which stands an upright piano with a pile of sheet music on top. A wide window to the rear looks out across the street to an Ionic colonnade, the interior of which is plastered with recruiting posters. Towards the rear, a narrow pillar holds up a portion of the ceiling, and there are two doors: one behind the counter, leading to the kitchen, and the other a swing door on the opposite side, leading to a landing from which presumably a flight of stairs goes down to the street. The whole impression is unappetizing, and should convey the ever-present smell of cabbage-water. Yet there is an air of sordid Latin gaiety mixed with this solid Dublin background, that shows itself in the décor. The flags of what used laughably to be called 'the Allies' decorate the pillar, and on the walls are pinned coloured reproductions of scenes from the Bay of Naples, pictures of Bonzo dogs, Bairnsfather cartoons, religious emblems, and a portrait of Victor Emmanuel.

When the Curtain rises it is a bright, sunlit morning, and two customers occupy adjoining tables. One is a handsome, earnest-

95

looking woman in her late twenties, plainly dressed in the lower-middle-class mode of the period. She is wearing dark glasses and is reading a religious magazine as she finishes her lunch. The other is a saturnine gentleman in the middle forties whose clothes, although stamping him as a member of the professional classes, have a rumpled appearance that suggests that he has not been to bed for a night or two. From his lapel dangles the admission check to the enclosure of a race-course. He is studying a menu card with some distaste. Beside him, waiting for his order, stands a pretty young shop-girl who is in her street clothes and hat but wears an apron. Offstage, in an adjoining flat, somebody is playing a piano. It is actually heard before the Curtain rises, and continues into the scene. Bartok's 'Evening in the Country' is suggested, but any music of a similar type that would be considered modern in 1916 will do if the mood is right.

MACCARTHY (*with a shudder*). Haven't you got anything more suitable for breakfast?

ROISIN. Breakfass? And it ten of twelve?

MACCARTHY. Yes, I know that it's a little late. Would I be patronizing this fly-parlour if breakfast was still to be had in any of the more sanitary hotels?

ROISIN. You wouldn't be here at all if it was closed the way it should be a Easter Monda.

MACCARTHY. How true. Today we celebrate the opening of a tomb in Palestine by closing all the local tombs. Wilde thyme is blowing now in all the banks, and the officials are at large, airing their tots on Kingstown Pier. (*He turns to the other customer.*) What is this lady having? No, don't tell me. I can see for myself.
    (*The woman – EMER – gives him a cold glance around her magazine.*)

MACCARTHY (*politely*). Good morning. (*Then, to* ROISIN.) Do you suppose that was a snub?

ROISIN. Would that surprise ya?

MACCARTHY (*with a happy thought*). Maybe she takes me for a masher. Is this music your own selection, madam? Because it affects my metabolism.
    (EMER *stares at him again without replying.*)

ROISIN. That's coming from the nex door. In Miss Garrity's.

MACCARTHY. Miss Garrity's Palm Court Restaurant?

ROISIN. No. It's owney a Servants' Registry. But she does be practising on the pianna when there's no one in. D'ye know.

MACCARTHY. I'm not surprised there's no one in. (*He rises.*) Let us indicate our disapproval to Miss Garrity.

(*He crosses and knocks on the wall. The music stops.*)

MACCARTHY. Results, by God! I wish I was as successful in my practice. (*He returns to his table.*) And now to business before you go off to wherever you're going. Send out the chef.

ROISIN. The which?

MACCARTHY. No. I realize that would be a misnomer. The proprietor.

ROISIN. Oh, the boss. He's off at Fairyhouse.

MACCARTHY. At the races! Dear me. What time did you say it was?

ROISIN. The Angelus will be anny minnit now.

MACCARTHY. There's no need to bring religion into it. Bring me the usual – a cup of stewed, lukewarm tea, a piece of damp toast, smeared with what is alleged to be butter, and half a portion of potato jam.

(ROISIN *tosses her head and goes off to the counter.*)

ROISIN. Ennuf ole guff to float a battleship.

MACCARTHY. I see you have a telephone. (*He rises and goes to where it hangs on the wall near the window.*) Maybe it works. I have a sure tip for the second race, and must engage an outside car.

(*He lifts the receiver as a young man enters rather sheepishly from the street. He is in the uniform of a minor tramway official, and has shiny black hair, long lashes, and a friendly, intelligent expression. In his lapel is a Pioneer shield, bearing the symbol of the Sacred Heart.*)

MAGINNIS. Hello.

ROISIN. So it's you, Mickser Maginnis!

MAGINNIS. *Dias Muire dhuit.* I tought I'd maybe find ya.

MACCARTHY (*at the phone*). Is there anybody there?

ROISIN. I tought you said you was goin route-marchin?

MAGINNIS. They called it off.

(EMER *smiles significantly.*)

ROISIN (*indignantly*). Called it off! Is this the time to be tellin me that?

MAGINNIS (*a little shrilly*). It's not my fault, Roisin. It's not my fault.

ROISIN. I mighta known.

MAGINNIS. It's early yet. Can ya not come now?

ROISIN. Come now is it? An' no one in the place excep meself! (*She slams a plate and a knife on* MACCARTHY'S *table.*)

Let's go to Bray, sez he, a Monda,

97

Or maybe join the lads at Blackrock Baths.
We might, sez I, for there's a day due te me.
But then, it's No. They've called minoovers for the Volunteers.
Ah, never fret, sez I, I'll work a Monda so
An' save me hollyer for a better day.
So off goes the Boss te the races,
Glad enuff te have me stop behind.
An' out comes the sun,
Te warm the jarvies on the jaunt te Fairyhouse.
An' buckets an' prams on Merrion Strand.
An' chizlers feedin' ducks in Stephen's Green,
Or peddlin' their way up te the Pine Forest.
But once he has me spancelled te the sink
Where are yer man's minoovers now?
Like tealeaves – up the spout.

MAGINNIS. It's not my fault. It's orders from the chief a staff.

ROISIN. That's what I am meself . . . the chief an' all the staff.
There's no playin' at wars for this Judy. It's hard labour for me.

(MAGINNIS *turns petulantly to the window, and looks out.*)

EMER (*who has been collecting her things*). Can I have my bill,
please.

MACCARTHY. This lady speaks, after all. Which is more than can be
said for the exchange.

(*He rattles the phone, and then gives it up.* ROISIN *works out
the bill.*)

MACCARTHY. What's all this pother about a route march? This is
not a military uniform, is it?

ROISIN. The Flyboy Fusiliers.

MAGINNIS. Ah, dry up for God's sake.

ROISIN (*pursing her lips*). Ninepence the spaghetti . . . threepence
the bread an' butter . . . and three ha'pence the cuppa tea.
One . . . an' a penny ha'penny.

MACCARTHY (*to* EMER). Clearly the course of true love is not running
smoothly. May I sit down here for a moment?

EMER. No.

(*She pays the money which* ROISIN *takes to the cash register.*)

MACCARTHY (*sitting down*). Thank you. You are a stranger in this
country, I expect. So you will hardly understand the difficulties
we Irish are up against in our sex relationships.

EMER (*enigmatically*). What makes you think that I'm a stranger?

MACCARTHY. There is an air of mystery behind those enigmatic
glasses. Something tells me that you are a beautiful spy. Nobody

but a stranger to our city would look for a feast on a Feast
Day.

EMER. Then why are *you*?

MACCARTHY. My circumstances are very special.

ROISIN. Been on the tiles, I'll be bound.

MACCARTHY. On the tiles!

ROISIN. How well I know the signs. He's afeared to go home.

MACCARTHY. A neo-Thom-cat descending from the chimney-pots
after a night of what is laughably called sin. Please don't scold
me while I have this taste of linoleum in my mouth.

EMER. What you need is a good purgative.

MACCARTHY. My dear lady, medical advice is quite useless to me.
I am a doctor myself, and I know how unreliable it is. You're
not a member of the D'Oyly Carte Opera Company, by any
chance, required to rehearse this glorious afternoon?

EMER. No, I'm not.

MACCARTHY. 'Full to the brim with girlish glee.' No? Well then
perhaps you will share a car with me to Fairyhouse?

EMER (*going through her bag*). No.

MACCARTHY. Too bad. My wife can't stand me, either.

EMER. I'm really not interested.

MACCARTHY. I suspect it's much the same with Marie Bashkirtseff
behind the samovar. She also finds her lover unsatisfactory.

ROISIN. Now don't be puttin' me into one o' me tantararums.

MAGINNIS. What's that you said?

MACCARTHY. Notice? You might suppose they were objecting to
the word 'unsatisfactory'. But it's not that at all. It's because I
referred to them as lovers.

MAGINNIS. You'll be finding yerself in trouble one a these days.

MACCARTHY. You see. They love each other, but it only embarrasses
them. I often wonder how this race of ours has managed to
propagate itself at all, with the age of consent at thirty-five.
Good God, man, there's nothing derogatory in being her lover!
The birds and the bees do it too.

MAGINNIS. I'm not askin' about any birds or bees.

MACCARTHY. Because you disapprove of any rumours you have
heard on the subject.

MAGINNIS. Would you like a puck on the gob?

MACCARTHY. Don't be deceived by our charm, madam. None of us
are any damn good as lovers. No regard was taken of our native
peculiarities when the formula of passion was being worked out.
Dr Yeats, our national poet, expressed it clearly. (*He intones.*)

'What's the use of kissing your girl
Only once a night?
Only once a night.
You know it isn't right.'

EMER (*sarcastically*). Dr Yeats, indeed!

MACCARTHY. Printed, I assure you, by the Cuala Press, with hand-coloured illustrations by a hairy fairy. I'll send you a copy if you leave me your address.

ROISIN. That one has a great nose for other people's business.

MACCARTHY. This sort of bullying is every Irishman's business. Because he doesn't sweep you off your feet, he's blamed for everything else – even when his friends fail to turn up for a route march. Er . . . what is this organization, by the way?

MAGINNIS. The Volunteers.

MACCARTHY. Which of the many varieties?

ROISIN. A Mickey Dazzler – that's what he is, drillin' for Ireland in the Banba Hall.

MAGINNIS. And what's wrong with that?

ROISIN. Oh, nuttin at all. You'll be a gineral with that lot before yer brother's a serjeant in the Munsters.

MACCARTHY (*to* EMER). My confusion is due to the fact that we have so many armies in this country – north and south – in addition to His Majesty's. Five, I believe, is the actual number at present.

MAGINNIS. It's not Ireland's war.

MACCARTHY. The only thing that they all have in common is the fact that they do not take part in any fighting. The Boy Scouts are the only independent belligerents in the present war. You follow this, I hope, Miss . . . er . . . what did you say your name was?

EMER (*looking at her watch*). Smith.

MACCARTHY. Smith. Oh well, keep it a secret if you insist. One incognito is as good as another.

EMER (*with a grim smile*). As a matter of fact, it *is* Smith.

MACCARTHY. I understand your caution, however much I feel personally hurt about it. Mary Smith, I suppose.

EMER (*with some distaste*). They once christened me Pearl, believe it or not.

MACCARTHY (*delighted*). The snowy-breasted Peril! How sensible you English are! Micheál here has got to live up to the moniker of an archangel, but you are content to nestle in the modest oyster. It's a pity our two races can never communicate. Yours is the world of 'Keep the Home Fires Burning' – of cupie dolls

100

and *Nash's Magazine*. You have Billy Bunter to rag and slackers to give white feathers to. You have your Empire and your House of Lords to provide you with endless amusement. You don't give a damn whether you are an Angle, a Saxon or a Jute, and you are fortunate enough to be fighting for your bloody lives. Here we have only a land of saints and cemeteries that laughs at nothing but itself, and where even the route marches to glory never come off.

EMER. Before long you're in for a big surprise.

(MACCARTHY *goes back to the telephone carrying a milk jug.*)

MACCARTHY. You must have a word with my wife. You won't like her, but she's English too, and it may divert her attention from me. A penny? Ah yes.

(*He feels in a pocket, holding jug and receiver in one hand.*)

ROISIN. Lippin' full, at this hour!

MACCARTHY (*into the telephone*). Hello.

MAGINNIS. As well oiled as Kelly for Bykes if ye ask me.

ROISIN. All you was asked was if ye'd be free for Easter Monda.

(MAGINNIS *turns away rather shamefacedly to the window.*)

MACCARTHY. 2663 please. Sorry to disturb you at your devotions.

(ENDYMION *pushes open the street door causing MacCarthy to spill the milk over the side of his face. He is a fantastic figure wearing an old-fashioned small bowler hat with a string attached to it, a long-skirted sports coat, and a very high hard collar. His trousers are tucked into leggings. He wears an eyeglass and carries a bundle of sticks, umbrellas, and a sword in a scabbard, all of which are tied together with red tape and with a seat card reading 'Engaged'.*)

ENDYMION. Did you want to speak to me?

MACCARTHY. Ow!

ROISIN. Jeesus Mary Joseph!

ENDYMION. Endymion. At Home today. R.S.V.P.

MACCARTHY. Never startle a man when he's in a certain condition.

ENDYMION.
> I just dropped in to see
> That all is ready for the party.

MACCARTHY. Then drip out again. Nobody wants you here. (*Into the phone.*) Oh hello, my love. Sorry I can't speak to you now. My ear is full of milk.

(*He hangs up.*)

ROISIN. It's owney Endymion. He put the heart across me.

EMER. Is he one of your patients?

MACCARTHY. Not any longer, so don't encourage him. He'll have no parties at my place.

EMER. What is this place of yours?

MACCARTHY. The Little Flower Refuge for Nervous Complaints. Drop in any time.

ENDYMION. St Vitus's Ballroom.

EMER. Does this mean you're mental?

MACCARTHY. Not personally, of course. But some of my patients are.

ENDYMION.

> At twelve noon.
> Uniforms and desecrations will be worn
> And half the Civil Service will be there.

MACCARTHY. That's a damnable lie about the Civil Service. At least half of them were never at my place.

ENDYMION.

> Carriages in six days' time.
> And for the few who will not leave,
> Beds are provided by the Lord Lieutenant.
> I hope to see you all.

(He bows and stalks out.)

MACCARTHY. It's always a pleasure to see the last of him.

ROISIN. Why do they let the poor *omadhaun* wander in the streets at all?

MACCARTHY. He's quite harmless . . . a personal friend of the Chief Secretary and a very gallant fellow in his day. As a matter of fact, we do sometimes have very pleasant little parties out at my place.

EMER. I suppose nobody can distinguish the guests from the patients?

MACCARTHY. Bless you, we don't mix socially with the patients. They only serve the drinks. I wish you'd come to one.

EMER. Can you do ordinary doctoring? Regular work, I mean?

MACCARTHY. My dear young lady, I am one of the best-known doctors in Dublin, and as for my regularity, it is . . . very good indeed.

(She rises, looks at her watch, and puts another bag on the table.)

EMER. Well, maybe you can be of some use.

MACCARTHY. I can indeed. To begin with, I can show you the sights of the city. Guinness's Brewery – the corpses in St Michan's – Lady Gregory . . .

EMER *(opening her bag)*. You don't have to show me around Dublin.

MACCARTHY (*going to the window*). Now here we have the finest
street in Europe, not forgetting the Nevsky Prospect . . . immortalized in folk-lore and ballad as 'The Meeting of the
Waters'. You know the song, no doubt?

EMER. I know the song, and it has nothing to do with O'Connell
Street.

MACCARTHY. Yes, O'Connell begins it in person. To the left – our
Liberator, standing on his pedestal, surrounded by his large
illegitimate family, looking out over the water. Next we come
to the effigy of a nonentity who is said to have brought the
water-supply to Dublin . . . a memorial to an unknown plumber.
And here, to the right, between us and the public urinal, pre-
siding over the entire vista – Lord Nelson . . .

(*The tramp of feet is heard behind his voice.*)

ROISIN. What's that I hear?

(*As the Angelus starts to ring,* EMER *blesses herself.*)

MAGINNIS. It's the Angelus. (*He blesses himself.*)

ROISIN. No, listen.

MACCARTHY. . . . Lord Nelson who made his name on the water . . .

ROISIN (*pushing him aside as she goes to the window*). Eggscuse me,
It's marchin' I hear.

MACCARTHY. . . . a one-eyed English sailorman with an eye for only
one thing . . .

ROISIN. No minoovers how are ya! What's that I see comin' down
the street? The Christian Brothers, I suppose, on their way to
a sodality?

MAGINNIS (*looking out too*). What's on ya at all?

MACCARTHY. . . . a sailorman with a bacchante by Romney, pregnant
in every port. Don't push me.

MAGINNIS. The Volunteers! But they tole me . . .

ROISIN. They tole me this. They tole me that. The war's put off
till half pass five. Don't shoot till ye see the green in the white
of me eye.

MAGINNIS. Roisin, they tole me it was off. I don't understand it at
all.

ROISIN. The warrior's late for the battle. The bombadier has missed
the boat. Oh, wait till I tell the brother an' he home on leave.
He'll burst his britches with the laughter. An' you callin' him a
renegade not two years ago for joinin' up with the fightin'
men.

MAGINNIS. Roisin, will ye listen to me . . .

ROISIN (*bitterly*). Ah, youse ones give me the sick. I'd be ashamed

103

te be seen walkin' out wid ya an' the men in kharki dyin' in Flanders Field.

MAGINNIS (*hysterically*). I'll leave the Volunteers that's what I'll do. I'll not be made a mock of any longer. I'm no flyboy fusileer.

(*There is a crash of glass outside in the street, following a shouted command. A confused babble of voices is next heard. In the room there is a sinister pause. From the room next door, the piano is heard once again. Albeniz's 'Cordoba' is suggested.*)

EMER (*finally*). Has it started?

MACCARTHY (*looking out of the window*). Most extraordinary.

ROISIN (*who is back at the bar*). Well? What's the latest from the front?

MACCARTHY. Most extraordinary thing I ever saw.

(EMER *is taking off her glasses and hat.*)

MAGINNIS. Begob, they're in action.

MACCARTHY. Swarming into the Post Office . . . breaking the windows, and turning the people out into the street.

ROISIN. Janey Mac, let's have a luk at this. Turning the people out?

(EMER *starts to pull some of the tables over towards the window.*)

MAGINNIS. Posted in Orders so it was. All minoovers is cancelled by the chief a staff.

MACCARTHY. If those are Minoovers, give me a night at the Tivoli.

MAGINNIS. If they're goin' inta action why wouldn't they let me know?

MACCARTHY (*covering his eyes and coming away*). Maybe they just want to buy some stamps.

EMER. Move over please.

ROISIN. Ay, what are ya doin' with them tables?

EMER. We want this place. They'll be in here shortly.

MAGINNIS. There's two of them coming over now.

MACCARTHY (*sitting down and closing his eyes*). Pardon me . . . the feet . . . painful . . .

ROISIN. Whatja mean – want this place? Who are you anyways?

MACCARTHY. Don't ask her. Let's forget it and start looking for a cuke buke.

EMER. I'm sorry we'll have to disturb you. But this is war.

ROISIN. War?

MACCARTHY. About a hundred men with a cab. Yes, I saw a cab too. And a couple of drays filled with pikes and guns. No. I saw nothing.

MAGINNIS. Why wouldn't they tell me? Do they take me for an informer or a scab?

EMER. I told you to expect a surprise.

(*The piano stops, and two men enter from the street, dressed in green uniforms, with felt hats fastened up at one side. The first is the younger of the two* – TETLEY – *a quiet, clean-shaven man in the thirties with a square, resolute jaw and far-away eyes. He wears a greatcoat over his Sam Browne belt. The other* – WILLIAMS – *is a stouter man in his forties, with a bushy moustache, and a revolver on his belt. He has no overcoat.* EMER *turns to them expectantly.*)

TETLEY. Is this the place?

EMER (*her eyes shining*). Yes, Commandant.

WILLIAMS. Is there any way through to the rear?

EMER. You'll have to knock a hole through the wall of the kitchen. In there. (*She points*).

WILLIAMS. That's simple.

TETLEY. I'll send up a couple of men with a crowbar. (*He bows politely to those present*). Excuse us, please. (*He goes out*).

WILLIAMS. And you'd better collect your equipment from the dray.

EMER. I know what I have to do.

(*She takes off her overcoat, disclosing a green tunic and skirt. Putting the overcoat on a chair, she takes a hat from her bag and leaves the room.* WILLIAMS *goes to inspect the kitchen.*)

ROISIN. Knock a hole with a crowbar? In the name of God what's goin' on?

MAGINNIS (*grimly*). Well, if that's the way it is, it's nuttin te do wit me.

MACCARTHY (*his eyes closed*). Corporation officials – that's all they are.

ROISIN. Carryin' guns?

MACCARTHY. Perhaps they intend to raise the rates.

(*A shot is heard outside. Everybody jumps.*)

MACCARTHY. There! They've raised the rates.

MAGINNIS (*sarcastically*). A Risin' – that's what it is. But owney for them that's let in on it.

MACCARTHY (*opening his eyes*). Once it was too many strangers in the house. Now it's a damn sight too many friends.

(TETLEY *enters followed by two* VOLUNTEERS *carrying tools and a crowbar.*)

MACCARTHY (*wincing and closing his eyes again*). Suppose we discuss

105

drink. In Singapore, I hear, the climate makes them sweat, so rendering whiskey auto-somatic.

TETLEY (*with grave politeness*). I'm sorry to have to disturb you people, but we're taking over this entire block. There's no cause for alarm.

MAGINNIS (*hostile*). Who's alarmed?

MACCARTHY. I am. Definitely.

(WILLIAMS *enters. He speaks much more brusquely.*)

WILLIAMS. Across here in the kitchen. Be sure a passage goes through to the rear. And all the window glass will have to be broken.

ROISN (*getting in their way*). You will not! Not in my kitchen.

TETLEY. Any damage will be repaid in full by the Irish Republic.

ROISIN. Irish Republic how are ya! No yuck in fancy dress is taking a crowbar inta my kitchen excep the plumber.

WILLIAMS. Keep out of the way, girl.

ROISIN. I will not.

MACCARTHY (*hastily rising*). Now listen, my dear, let's not forget these men are dying for their country.

ROISIN. Let them die somewhere else so, an' give their country a chance.

WILLIAMS. Look, I'm warning you . . .

MACCARTHY. Please, please, let's have no acrimony, please. Why not begin by telling us in simple language just what this Irish Republic is?

TETLEY. It will be proclaimed in a few minutes' time.

MACCARTHY. Proclaimed? Who by?

TETLEY (*after a brief pause*). As a matter of fact . . . I've got to arrange about that. Thanks for reminding me.

(*With a swift, charming smile he hurries off.*)

WILLIAMS (*motioning impatiently to the* VOLUNTEERS). Out of the way now, miss. Go on in, men. (*As they hesitate.*) Ach, will I have to shift her myself?

(*He grabs* ROISIN *and pushes her aside. She struggles and tries to slap his face. As the two* VOLUNTEERS *slip by into the kitchen* MAGINNIS *interferes, and* WILLIAMS *turns on him, his hand on his gun.*)

ROISIN. Leave go of me ye scut or ye'll find there's more scrappin' in me than in the whole of yer windy militia.

MAGINNIS. Leave that girl alone.

WILLIAMS. Keep off me – you!

ROISIN. Easy, Mickser. Can't ya see he has a gun?

106

(*As they freeze for a moment into inaction,* MACCARTHY *hastens to the piano.*)

MACCARTHY. Let's have some gay music. I hate hearing my teeth chatter.

(*He raps on the wall without any result. From the kitchen comes the sound of hammering and smashing, which continues at intervals till the end of the scene.*)

WILLIAMS. Who are you?

MAGINNIS. A volunteer.

WILLIAMS. Then why aren't you outside with the men?

MAGINNIS. Because I take me orders from the chief a staff. Whose orders am I supposed to take?

WILLIAMS (*with a contemptuous laugh*). I don't know anything about your chief of staff. If it wasn't for us in the Labour movement the Volunteers would still be forming fours. But you're in it now, all right. We're all in it together.

(EMER *enters staggering under a folded stretcher and several boxes of medical supplies. She drops the stretcher on the floor, and carries the boxes to the counter, where she takes out a Red Cross apron and starts to unpack.*)

EMER. We've taken the Castle and three barracks. Two brigades of Germans have landed in Kerry. The whole country has risen.

MAGINNIS. My God, is this true?

WILLIAMS (*nodding his head*). There'll be no going back on this. (*He turns his head as scattered cheers come from outside.*) Oh, are they reading the Proclamation? I suppose I'd better go down.

(*He goes out without any great show of enthusiasm.* EMER *flies to the window, as a voice outside is heard reading the Proclamation.*)

EMER. To think that I've lived to see this day! A new flag flying over the Post Office!

MACCARTHY. I suppose it's too much to hope that there's a policeman somewhere?

EMER (*jubilant*). No more police! We're free of those bosthoons for ever.

MACCARTHY. Woman, you have been deceiving me. You *are* a beautiful spy after all. My God, what did I say to her that I shouldn't? Guinness's – the corpses – Lady Gregory . . .

EMER. This place is picked as a dressing station, and . . .

MACCARTHY. And I am to be your Christian slave. I see it all now.

EMER. If you're really a doctor there'll be plenty of work before long.

MACCARTHY. I love work. I can sit looking at it for hours.

ROISIN. Two peep-o'-day boys making poor little Belgium outa my kitchen! Can nobody stop them?

EMER (*at the window*). Be quiet girl, and let me hear the words of the Proclamation.

ROISIN. If that fella could suck as well as he can blow they'd give him a job at the waterworks.

(*She stares indignantly into the kitchen, as* MAGINNIS *sits down gloomily.*)

EMER (*banging on the window*). Oh, cheer, everybody! What's the matter with them all? Why can't they cheer? Don't they know they're free?

(*There is a crash of glass, followed by some scattered cheering.*)

ROISIN (*turning*). What's that?

MACCARTHY (*pointing sardonically out of the window*). The Birth of a Nation.

EMER (*sinking down in despair*). Oh, no!

MAGINNIS. Well anyway, the crowd is cheerin' him at last.

MACCARTHY. I'm afraid not. They're only breaking into Noblett's toffee shop.

(*The hammering continues from the kitchen, as the cheering grows from outside.*)

CURTAIN

Scene 2

It is about an hour later. The glass in the window has apparently been knocked out, and some of the tables and chairs have been piled in front of the aperture to make an ineffective barricade. EMER – *now wearing a Red Cross apron – is unpacking bandages and bottles of disinfectant on the counter, and clearing away the cups and cake stands to make room for them.* MAGINNIS *is still sitting gloomily in a chair with his hands in his pockets, while* ROISIN *and* MACCARTHY *are gossiping near the window.*

108

ROISIN. Will I ever forget the night this body-builder outa Maguire and Gatchell's used te be oxin' his way up an down Henry Street with the string a hurley medals he fecked from Moran's on the Quays doin' His Lordship with a strap with straw hair how are ya up from Tullamore oh beef te the heels ye'd tink soap an wather cost a fortune. (*She raises her head and listens.*) Lissen! It's my belief som'in's comin'.

(EMER *is now putting a Red Cross flag on a pole.*)

EMER. What is it?

MACCARTHY. Whatever it is, it'll still be pleasanter than home. Heigh ho. There's no place like home . . . for which we can be heartily thankful.

ROISIN. The people are clearin' off the street.

(*Horses' hooves approach.*)

MACCARTHY. Hark, I hear hooves!

ROISIN (*gleefully*). It's horses . . . an' men on them. Fightin' men for wonct.

MAGINNIS (*hurrying to the window*). Let's see.

ROISIN. Them's the lads . . . the real McCoy at last.

MACCARTHY. My God, you don't mean proper soldiers?

ROISIN (*as the hoof-beats grow louder*). It's the Lancers.

MACCARTHY. Lancers! Woman, give me that flag.

ROISIN. A whole troop a them.

(MACCARTHY *struggles to take the flag from* EMER.)

MACCARTHY. Have you no morals, woman? Don't you realize the importance of hanging out this rag? Don't crowd me.

(*He obtains possession of it, and sticks it out of the window.*)

ROISIN. Will ye look at them . . . gallopin' straight at the Post Office . . . flags flyin' on their lances . . . cobbles sparkin' under the hooves! Them are the boys'll banjax the lot of them!

MACCARTHY. There now.

ROISIN (*shouting*). Up the Lancers! Up the Royal Irish!

MACCARTHY. Thank God, we're safe now.

(*There is a volley of shots, followed by some confused shouting and the hooves then gallop off.* MACCARTHY *appears to swoon.*)

MACCARTHY. Is anybody still alive?

(*Distant cheering.*)

ROISIN. Oh God! They opened fire from the Post Office.

EMER. Can't you act like a man?

MACCARTHY. I have no intention of acting like a man.

EMER. Well at least pull yourself together.

MACCARTHY. I am perfectly pulled together. In fact I'm in a knot. Don't tell me that ammunition was real?

EMER. What did you expect? Confetti?

ROISIN (*incredulously*). They fired on them! . . . fired on the men and the horses!

MAGINNIS. One o' them is down. Will ya look.

ROISIN. The poor horse! Lyin' there in the middle a the road. Oh, the murderin' blagards.

MAGINNIS. Here come the Volunteers. They're pickin' him up. They're carryin' him over here.

MACCARTHY. What? The horse?

MAGINNIS. No, ye eediot! The Lancer.

MACCARTHY. You're quite sure? I have no experience as a vet.

EMER. Get that door open.

MACCARTHY (*peering carefully out the window.*) What's happening now? Aren't the soldiers still there?

ROISIN. They've ridden off up the street. I can't see them now.

(*A third rebel – O'CALLAGHAN – and one of the* VOLUNTEERS *carry in a British officer –* PALLISER *– whom they place on the stretcher. This rebel is more exotic and striking than either of the others whom we have seen. He has the high colour and burning eyes of an invalid. Around his neck is wound a white scarf, and he coughs frequently. From one side of his belt dangles an enormous pistol in a hanging holster. On the other side he carries a sword. His uniform is neat and complete, and on one of his wrists is a slave bangle. He is highly strung, and over-dramatic in his gestures.* PALLISER *– who appears to be unconscious – is a man of about twenty-five, with a clipped military moustache.*)

O'CALLAGHAN. Can't anybody lend a hand?

(MAGINNIS *runs to their assistance, and the other* VOLUNTEER, *when relieved of his burden, hurries off again.*)

MAGINNIS. Here. Let me.

ROISIN. Oh, the poor fella.

MACCARTHY (*suddenly becoming businesslike*). Don't carry him like that, unless you want to break his neck. Get him down on the stretcher.

ROISIN. Is he killed?

O'CALLAGHAN (*fanatically*). We got him with the first volley! Then all the rest turned tail and galloped off like rats. Lord, it was magnificent.

MACCARTHY (*rapidly examining the body*). Galloping rats indeed!
Get me hot water – quick.

(MAGINNIS *runs for it to the counter.*)

ROISIN. You've killed him, ya scut!

O'CALLAGHAN (*exalted*). The insolence of them – riding up the street
like that . . . expecting that we'd all come out with our hands up,
I suppose. But we showed them something. We showed them.

ROISIN. Have ya no shame on ya for what ya did?

O'CALLAGHAN. This is war, girl. War!

MACCARTHY. Never mind what it is. Just hand me one of those
napkins.

EMER. You don't need them. I've got dressings.

MACCARTHY (*taking them*). Clean, I hope.

O'CALLAGHAN. Who is this man?

EMER. He says he's a doctor.

O'CALLAGHAN. We'll need doctors. Let him carry on if he's
willing.

ROISIN. Murderers – that's what youse are . . . you an' yer dirty . . .

PALLISER (*opening his eyes*). Goddam and blast. Damn. Damn.
Damn.

MACCARTHY. Quite a coherent corpse.

ROISIN. Is he not dead at all?

MACCARTHY. He's dislocated a knee. Must have been knocked out,
falling off his horse.

PALLISER. Hell and damnation blast it.

O'CALLAGHAN. Don't swear like that. There are women present.

MACCARTHY. Let him swear if he likes. He probably thinks he's at
home .Cut the rest of that puttee off. And gently!

ROISIN (*going out to the street*). What about the poor horse? Some-
thin' must be done about it.

PALLISER. Horse be damned. How did it throw me?

MACCARTHY. It didn't throw you, old boy. It just passed out with a
bullet in the bum. There now. Hold him steady, you people,
and I'll set it right away.

(*As* MAGINNIS *and* O'CALLAGHAN *hold his arms, and* EMER
holds his head, MACCARTHY *sets the leg with a deft jerk.*)

PALLISER. Ow! What the hell . . . ?

MACCARTHY (*with a friendly pat and a smile*). There. All over now.
Old Macan used to say, 'Always get the worst over before the
patient knows what happening.' Now, a tight bandage and a
couple of splints and you'll be all fixed up.

(*He snaps his fiingers at* EMER, *who fetches splints and ban-*

111

dages. Meanwhile MacCarthy *feels him over with expert fingers.*)

PALLISER. Call yourself a doctor?

MACCARTHY. Quite some time now since I've had the chance to do a bit of surgery. I always liked it. Keep that leg steady till I . . . No, you don't seem to have anything else.

O'CALLAGHAN. Will he be all right?

MACCARTHY (*putting on the splints with* EMER'S *help*). He'll not be able to get around for a bit, but he'll be all right.

O'CALLAGHAN. In that case, don't forget, everyone, that he's our first – no, our second – English prisoner.

PALLISER. Who are you calling English?

O'CALLAGHAN. Well, whatever you are there's no need to worry. You'll be treated strictly in accordance with the Hague Convention.

PALLISER. You mean the Geneva Convention.

O'CALLAGHAN (*stiffly*). I said the Hague Convention.

MACCARTHY. Just settle for the Firemen's Convention, and hand me a pair of scissors.

PALLISER. What happened to the rest of my troop?

O'CALLAGHAN. They turned tail and fled.

PALLISER. Oh, they did, did they.

MAGINNIS. They're still down there somewheres . . . hidin' behind the Parnell Monument.

O'CALLAGHAN. Wondering, no doubt, what hit them.

PALLISER. I shall stop somebody's leave for this.

O'CALLAGHAN. We mustn't be too hard on them. They little knew what they were up against. (*He offers his cigarette case.*) Cigarette?

PALLISER (*looking him over quizzically*). Well . . . that's very handsome of you. Thanks. (*He accepts one. Then, to* MACCARTHY.) Quite a fellow.

MACCARTHY (*fixing the splints*). Give him a light.

O'CALLAGHAN. You'll give your parole, of course?

PALLISER. What does that consist of?

O'CALLAGHAN. You know. Your honourable undertaking not to try to escape if we don't lock you up.

PALLISER. From all accounts, I'm not likely to get very far with this leg.

O'CALLAGHAN. Then you agree?

PALLISER. Certainly . . . if the alternative is to be locked up.

(*The telephone rings.* MACCARTHY *goes to it irritably.*)

MACCARTHY. Yes, yes, I'm coming. Who is it? As if I care a damn. No, it's not the Pro-cathedral. This is the Hell Fire Club.

(*He hangs up.*)

O'CALLAGHAN. Has that telephone not been cut? Can nobody carry out the simplest instructions?

(*He wrenches out the wires.*)

MACCARTHY. Now that was a tiresome thing to do. I still have several calls to make.

O'CALLAGHAN. Well, you can't make them from here.

(MACCARTHY *remains behind for a little while examining the severed wires, before returning to his patient.* TETLEY *appears in the door, carrying a machine-gun.*)

TETLEY. See what I've got.

MAGINNIS. A machine-gun!

O'CALLAGHAN. Splendid. How did you capture it?

TETLEY. Someone found it in the Post Office.

O'CALLAGHAN (*excited*). You mean to say they had that when we stormed the place?

TETLEY. Well – yes. It was somewhere upstairs.

O'CALLAGHAN. But this is tremendous. (*To the others.*) Look – we've captured a machine-gun.

TETLEY (*with a ghost of a wicked smile*). Well – yes. There was no ammunition. That's probably why nobody fired it.

O'CALLAGHAN (*disappointed*). Oh.

TETLEY. But we have some ourselves. That's why I brought it over. To see if somebody could tell us how to work it.

(*He gives a sly look at* PALLISER.)

MACCARTHY. Look here, you can't fire that thing from here. Don't you see the Red Cross flag?

TETLEY. We can't fire it at all unless somebody can put it together. Can you, Seamus?

O'CALLAGHAN. My battalion never had one. Don't you know anything about it?

TETLEY. How should I? I got my military training in the Board of Works. (*He looks at* PALLISER.) Pity.

PALLISER (*after a pause*). There's no good looking at me. I'm a prisoner.

TETLEY. Oh, of course. We could hardly expect an Englishman . . .

PALLISER. Listen. I was born and brought up in Greystones.

TETLEY. Oh, I beg your pardon. Then you certainly won't want to help us. I have an idea that it goes in this way.

MAGINNIS (*interested*). No, no. It goes the other way round.

O'CALLAGHAN. It does not! The belt obviously has to be on the other side.

MACCARTHY. Look – please will you leave that thing alone. Just to oblige me.

O'CALLAGHAN. Don't interfere. I happen to know that it must be this way up.

PALLISER. As a matter of fact, you're all wrong.

TETLEY. Oh?

PALLISER. For a bunch of alleged soldiers, I've never seen such ignorance.

TETLEY. There you are. I told you it goes the other way. He knows.

PALLISER. That nut on the left has to engage the . . . Here, pull it over here somebody. (*They do so*). It has to engage with this thing here.

MACCARTHY. Look here, this is all most improper. Who's rigging this machine-gun for what?

PALLISER (*stopping his work*). He's right. Why the hell should I be showing you how to fix it?

TETLEY (*with an amused shrug of his shoulders*). Why indeed?

PALLISER. I'm a prisoner. He told me so himself.

O'CALLAGHAN (*to* MACCARTHY). Why do you have to stick your nose into this?

MACCARTHY. Because I have some respect for the sanctity of my profession. That's why.

TETLEY. Never mind. We'll leave it here, and get Williams to fix it for us, when we can find him.

O'CALLAGHAN. I'll send for him. I think he's trying to get into Trinity. (*He goes.*)

MACCARTHY. My difficulty was to get out of Trinity. It took me seven years.

MAGINNIS. There's a man in my battalion was in the Boer War.

TETLEY. I suppose they had machine-guns then. Who are you, by the way? A Volunteer?

MAGINNIS. I was. But I'm going to leave.

TETLEY. That's too bad. Why?

MAGINNIS. Why yourself? Why wasn't I mobilized?

EMER. He's a renegade if he's leaving now.

MAGINNIS. It's well for you you're not a man – callin' me that.

TETLEY. I'm sure he's not that, Miss Nic Gabhann. He probably got the countermanding order.

MAGINNIS. I got me orders from the chief a staff. If I was wanted why wasn't I mobilized?

EMER. The chief of staff is to be ignored. He's not fit to lead a thing like this.

MAGINNIS. Ignored? What sort of an army is it where yer tole te ignore the chief a staff?

TETLEY. Not a very orthodox one, I'm afraid. We're all acting according to our lights. Nobody will blame you afterwards if you obey the chief of staff.

EMER. Nobody except all true Irishmen.

TETLEY. You mustn't be so bitter, Miss Nic Gabhann. I'm sure the chief of staff is doing what he feels is best for the country. It's we who are being insubordinate.

EMER (*passionately*). There you go again . . . trying to save the face of everybody but yourself! When you're the last man left in that Post Office, you'll die trying to find excuses for the others that have walked out on you.

MAGINNIS. I'm not walkin' out on anyone. All I want to know is whose orders I'm supposed to take.

TETLEY. You'll have to work that out for yourself. All I can say is that some of us have decided that now is the time to strike. If we wait any longer there'll be no Volunteers left, and this generation will go down in history as being as craven as the last. Personally I'm not going to accept that.

MAGINNIS. But have we any . . . any . . .

TETLEY. Do you mean, have we any chance?

EMER. Of course we have a chance. It's now or never. France is out of the war for want of men. The old enemy is on the run at last.

TETLEY. Well, we hope so, at any rate. As for France – we only have rumours to go on. But some people tell us that if we can manage to hold out for a certain number of days we'll have the right to be recognized as belligerents at the peace conference.

MAGINNIS. Is that the truth?

TETLEY (*with a shrug of his shoulders*). I hope so. But all I can say is this: that the greatest war in history is being fought – a war in which millions of men are laying down their lives for their countries. And as I'm a soldier too, I'd feel pretty mean if I didn't seize the opportunity of fighting for mine. That's all.

EMER. In years to come, every decent man in Ireland will be wishing he could say 'I was in the Post Office in 1916.' You have your chance now, Maginnis. Are you going to take it, or are you what that girl called you – a Mickey Dazzler?

(ROISIN *enters in some excitement.*)

ROISIN. The chizlers is all over the street eating sweets from Nob-

115

lett's. The women are dancing jigs in Talbot Street. I've never seen the like in all me born days.

MAGINNIS. Where can I get a gun?

TETLEY. Over in the Post Office. What's your unit?

MAGINNIS. C Company – Third Battalion.

TETLEY (*putting a hand on his shoulder*). Then they'll be wanting you out at Ballsbridge. I hope you're not going to regret this.

MAGINNIS. I don't give a damn if I do.

TETLEY (*laughing*). A lad after my own heart. Come on. I'll see to your orders myself.

ROISIN. Mickser – where are you going?

MAGINNIS. Where no one will call me a Mickey Dazzler.

(MAGINNIS *and* TETLEY *go out, followed by* EMER. ROISIN *runs to the window to look after them. Next door, the piano starts to play again. This time it is Satie's 'Gymnopédie, No. 3'.*)

ROISIN. Mickser!

MACCARTHY (*rising from his final bandaging*). There. That should repair itself if you give it a chance. Now how about another cup of your abominable tea, my dear?

PALLISER. Suits me too. Who's the pianist?

ROISIN. The oul wan next door. They ought te get her out.

(*She goes thoughtfully to the urn and pours out three cups.*)

MACCARTHY. And some of those nice Digestive Biscuits. We won't have them if they're not digestive. (*He lifts the receiver.*) Oh, hello! Are you there already? 2663 please. Of course it's an official call. This is the Chief Secretary speaking.

PALLISER. I thought he pulled out the wires of that thing.

MACCARTHY. Yes, but I stuck them back again. I suppose it's too much to hope that my home has been burnt to the ground. No – somebody answers. A penny? Oh! I would have thought that official calls were free. However . . . (*He puts a coin in the box.*) let's not be captious in such times. Ah – is that my love? This is your Tristram. I just wanted to tell you that I can't get home because of this er . . . this revolution . . . Yes, I said revolution . . . haven't you heard? Blood is flowing in the streets, my darling. And I . . . what? Now don't be vulgar, Margery. As a matter of fact I did have milk in my ear. Listen, darling, the most frightful things are happening in Sackville Street . . . dead horses everywhere. Well I'm damned. She doesn't believe me! (*He hangs up.*) It just shows the importance of never telling the truth.

116

ROISIN. (*bringing the cups*). Do youse take sugar?

PALLISER. No thanks.

(*Another crash of glass is heard, followed by cheering.*)

MACCARTHY (*feeling in his pockets*). Do you suppose that could be a tobacconist's? I'll come back for my tea after taking a peep. (*He goes.*)

PALLISER. Wouldn't you like to go too? I'll be quite all right, you know.

ROISIN. Are you sure, now? I've half a mind to go and see what's happening to Mickser.

PALLISER. Off you go, and take your time. I can look after myself now that I've got my tea.

(*She goes.* PALLISER *puts down his cup and pulls himself across to the window, where he takes down the phone, and looks out.*)

PALLISER. Hello. Hello. Put me through to the Royal Hospital . . . Certainly it's a military call. Hello. (*He puts in a penny.*) Yes. Get me Colonel Kennard quickly. Captain Palliser speaking. No . . . Kennard. K – E – N – the garrison commander . . . There must be somebody in charge of the British Empire, even if it is a bank holiday . . . Hello . . . Oh, it's you, Bunny. I thought I recognized the adenoids. (*He settles down cosily.*) I know this is going to be a surprise to you all in Intelligence, but there's some sort of a rebellion going on. (*A voice yaps indignantly in reply.*) All right, you know already. But you may not know that this is your old friend, Tony Palliser – yes, 6th Reserve Cavalry, and I'm here in an O.P. right opposite the G.P.O., from which point I am going to direct you in cleaning the whole thing up, before any red tabs come back from the races. Now listen, Bunny, you can settle it with a company if you come through the right way . . . No, not over the bridge. They're barricading Elvery's. Try Beresford Place and in by the back of Clery's. I'll keep you posted . . . And Bunny, send me down a packet of Players, there's a good chap . . . No you can't ring me here, but I'll ring you whenever I can . . . Now Bunny, listen while I explain . . .

THE CURTAIN HAS SLOWLY FALLEN

ACT TWO

It is a dull, showery afternoon, a day later. The place is in a mess, and someone has removed the flags of the Allies, and drawn a full beard on Victor Emmanuel. The unmounted machine-gun still stands on the floor near the window. PALLISER is reclining on a bed improvised from a few chairs, and is smoking a cigarette as he reads Emer's religious magazine. He has a crutch beside him. MacCARTHY and ROISIN are sipping cups of tea at one of the tables. From the street comes an occasional crash and sometimes some distant shouting. Next door, the piano is playing Granados's 'The Maiden and the Nightingale'.

MACCARTHY. Actually, I once did have a patient who thought he was Napoleon. Very rare, you know, that Napoleon business, although it's what loonies are usually supposed to do. Usually they go in for more up-to-date selections.

ROISIN. Like Charlie Chaplin?

MACCARTHY. Yes – or somebody really amusing, like Lloyd George. This Napoleon was very popular with the students until one day Endymion got hold of him and taught him to say, 'I'm Johnny Doyle of Drimnagh'. Imagine my embarrassment before a whole classful of tittering medicals. 'Now tell us who you are,' I said. And the bloody fellow answered, 'I'm Johnny Doyle of Drimnagh.' And the annoying thing is that he wasn't Johnny Doyle either.

ROISIN. So it was after that, you put out poor Endymion?

MACCARTHY. Of course. Couldn't have that sort of sabotage on the premises.

(ROISIN *starts to examine the tealeaves in her cup.*)

PALLISER. That woman next door is still there. I thought they took her out yesterday.

MACCARTHY. So they did. She must have come back.

ROISIN. D'yever read the cups?

118

MACCARTHY. I can't say that I do. I'm usually apprehensive enough about the future.

ROISIN. There's some queer things in this one.

MACCARTHY. I once had my horoscope cast by a Parsee Graduate in Surgeons. He warned me against taking part in an official ceremony where a platform would collapse under me. I never liked to make any further inquiries.

PALLISER. Obviously a hanging.

MACCARTHY. An interpretation that had also occurred to me. But I don't think it's very nice of you to mention it. Why don't you concentrate on your magazine?

PALLISER (*putting it down*). I've already read it twice through including the advertisements for altar wine.

MACCARTHY. It ought to be very good for you. However, we'll send across to Eason's and loot you a lot of old newspapers. Then you can brood over happy bygone days that you spent in the trenches.

PALLISER. You might get me a few books.

MACCARTHY. Make your choice. You'll never have a chance like this again. Anything from Bertha Ruck to William Blake.

PALLISER. I think I'd prefer the last.

MACCARTHY (*surprised*). Blake? Really? Mightn't it seem a little affected to sit there reading Blake during a rebellion?

PALLISER. No better time to understand him.

ROISIN. Hey-ho. I wish I understood meself.

MACCARTHY (*indulgently*). So do we all, my dear. And those who succeed don't usually enjoy the discovery.

ROISIN. I'd like to ask you a question, all the same.

MACCARTHY. Why pick on me, my dark Rosaleen?

ROISIN. I dunno. Mebbe it's because what you say is sort of . . . original. D'ye know.

MACCARTHY. Original? My dear, I pride myself on never having made an original remark in my life.

ROISIN. That's a queer thing to be proud of.

MACCARTHY. The only people who make original remarks are my patients. They're all completely original.

ROISIN. All the same I'd like to ask you something I've offen wunnered. Mebbe you'd tell me, an' you married all these years, an' . . .

MACCARTHY. And had the nerve taken out. Go on.

ROISIN. Is there . . . is there such a ting as true love at all, Doctor Mac? D'ye know what I mean?

119

MACCARTHY. I know just what you mean . . . unfortunately.

ROISIN. Is there such a ting at all? Or is it something the bukes
and the pictures has cuked up to cod us? You know, Doctor
Mac, like . . . like Christmas.

MACCARTHY (*sadly*). So Christmas is only a cod.

PALLISER. She's right, you know. There is no Santa Claus.

ROISIN. Ah, it is an' it isn't . . . that's no matter now. But I wish
you'd tell me about the other, Doctor, for I wudden want to be
disappointed in that. D'ye know.

MACCARTHY. I find such a question disturbing, after my Easter
celebration.

ROISIN. Ah, ye know I'm not talkin' about anyting nasty.

MACCARTHY. Really! The arrogance of these women over the problems they arouse themselves! Did you hear how she described
my Easter?

PALLISER. I did, and I dare say she's right. You would say that the
lust of the goat is the bounty of God.

MACCARTHY. You mean Blake would say it. I only wish I still had
some of the goat's problems. Of course I had them all in T.C.D.
and enjoyed them enormously. But now, alas, I have only a few
simple complexes left, and they haven't even got the glamour
of looking ridiculous.

PALLISER. Too simple by half, I'll be bound.

MACCARTHY. Well, all great art is simple. That's why second-rate
people sneer at it.

ROISIN. What does he mean, Captain? Who's trying to sneer at
what?

PALLISER. You wouldn't understand, Roisin. You're a woman, and
have a soul above the gymnastics the Doctor is talking about.

MACCARTHY. Exactly. She's a woman. All she wents from life is just
the sky and the moon.

ROISIN. An you mean I'll . . . never find them?

PALLISER. Here's hoping you will, my dear.

MACCARTHY (*determinedly*). She'll never find anything until she
accepts the fact that no primula can live that isn't planted in a
reasonable amount of dirt. But no woman ever will.

ROISIN. Will what?

PALLISER. He means that life itself is a dirty business, and we've got
to put up with it.

MACCARTHY. I mean nothing of the sort. What I'm trying to convey
is the fact that love is a vegetable that must be planted in a bed
pan, and watered with a nice supply of disappointments.

120

ROISIN (*primly*). There's nuttin' nasty about true love.

MACCARTHY. Then for God's sake don't say so. Nature has wisely provided that most of the important things we have to do seem wicked. There is great wisdom in that. So don't disabuse us of the idea, or we may lose interest in Nature, and stop doing them.

ROISIN. I mighta known I'd never get an answer. It's Mickser and me I wanted to know about . . . not either a yous.

PALLISER. We should have remembered. But all we do is talk about ourselves.

MACCARTHY. I suppose the next question is: 'Can Galahad be Galahad if he's only a boy employed by the tram company?'

ROISIN. It's not his job I mind. Sure what better am I meself? But . . .

MACCARTHY. But you know in your soul that you are a heroine. Where, on the other hand, are the heroes?

ROISIN. Well, I wouldn't put it that way.

MACCARTHY. No. But you mean it.

PALLISER. One of the things about my profession is that it sometimes enables us to find out who the heroes are.

MACCARTHY. My dear fellow, even in your profession it needs influence to be a hero. How often have you been allowed to try?

PALLISER. Not very often. But perhaps that's just as well. People shouldn't be encouraged to pursue these second-rate ambitions.

MACCARTHY (*dumbfounded*). Heroism? A second-rate ambition?

PALLISER (*crisply*). Certainly. Just another form of self-advertisement.

MACCARTHY (*after a pause*). I think the trouble is that most of us are in the wrong occupations. Palliser, here, would probably have made an ideal tramways official if his family had allowed him to take it up, while Mickser is the real military genius.

PALLISER. Thanks. Thanks a lot.

MACCARTHY. After all, who but a tramways official would have thought of leading a cavalry charge against the General Post Office? Mickser would never have tried that.

ROISIN. Cavalry charges, moryah! That's all I hear about, an' me wonderin' whether it's love I feel.

MACCARTHY. If you want to know whether you're capable of that emotion, take him across to Holyhead on the mailboat. If you can contemplate each other being seasick without losing interest, then you are both ripe for parenthood. Not before.

ROISIN. Ah, I knew I'd never hear any sense.

(*She takes the cups over to the counter. The music concludes.*)

PALLISER (*who has been slightly offended*). Isn't it about time you went home? If you don't go soon, all your patients will be getting better.

MACCARTHY. I am quite aware of that possibility. (*He rises and goes to the telephone.*) Hello.

(ROISIN *screams as* ENDYMION *enters from the kitchen. He has donned a pair of celluloid cuffs on his ankles.*)

ENDYMION. You *do* want to speak to me.

MACCARTHY. Never again. (*Then, into the phone.*) This is the head of the Fire Brigade. Get me 2663 at once.

ROISIN. Where did you come from?

ENDYMION. Through the official funk-holes.

PALLISER. You should blow a horn or something.

ENDYMION.

Some day I shall be heralded by horns.
Enter Endymion – Chorus to these large events,
Coming to limn the progress of the offstage scene.

PALLISER. Well, what's happening?

ENDYMION.

High preparations.
Colonels and brigadiers, coralled from the Curragh
And from the better types of house of ill repute,
Will soon be planning operations in the Castle yard
To burn the city to the ground.

PALLISER. Don't be absurd. Why should they?

ENDYMION.

Because they have artillery.
Would you expect them not to use it –
Affirming the royal peace with great explosions?

PALLISER. Nonsense. None of that is necessary. I've told them myself how to . . . I mean, I . . . (*He hesitates in some confusion.*)

ENDYMION. I know. You've spoken to them on the telephone.

MACCARTHY. The telephone! Why you sly old fox! You know you're not allowed to use the telephone. Hello. (*He drops a coin in.*) Got you that time, my dear. Yes darling. It's me again.

ENDYMION.

And they have called you in return to say
That not an item of the news has changed.
Verdun holds out.
No Prussian sole has bruised the soil of Kerry.

122

PALLISER. I know. It's only a matter of time.

ENDYMION.
> Till what?
> Haha! Till what?

PALLISER. Till it's all over.

ENDYMION.
> Till generals and ministers arrive
> Bringing a bloody sunset from the east.

MACCARTHY. I thought I'd better warn you, my love, that the end of the world has begun, so you'd better start packing. On second thought, don't bother to pack, for the same reason.

ROISIN. Tell us what's happening to the rebels.

ENDYMION.
> They, too, are doing their best to earn unpopularity.
> Out near Ballsbridge, a few old men
> With wooden guns that will not fire
> Have been shot down.

ROISIN. I don't believe it.

ENDYMION.
> The issue's knit,
> And every fellow plays the other fellow's game.
> The Green makes murder and the Crown makes martyrs,
> And the great and unwashed Liberated loot.
> Victory's the crown, my friends, for him
> With the least power to engineer his own defeat.
> In short, the situation's normal.

PALLISER.
> Marry, here's grace and a codpiece;
> That's a wise man and a fool.

ENDYMION (*staring at him coldly*).
> No, I will be the pattern of all patience;
> I will say nothing.
> I am Endymion – beloved of the Moon.
> I wear my cuffs upon my ankles.
> So, in a world that's upside down,
> I walk upon my hands.
> Good afternoon.

> (*He stalks off towards the street.*)

MACCARTHY. Margery, that's no way to talk to a man who's doing his bit ... B – I – T ... No, I wasn't referring to you. Dammit, she's rung off.

PALLISER (*pointing after* ENDYMION). There's your hero for you.

The most gallant gentleman in Ireland. And what has it profited him?

MACCARTHY. Some day the worm will turn. But nobody will notice. Who knows one side of a worm from another? You were saying?

PALLISER. I said he was a hero. A man who met with fate in Guinness's.

MACCARTHY. So they say. But that was twenty years ago.

PALLISER. Leapt into a vat to save a drowning man, and struck his head. So now – a hero and a lunatic!

(*He bursts into a sardonic laugh, as* WILLIAMS *enters from the kitchen.* MACCARTHY *hastily replaces the receiver, which he has still been holding.*)

WILLIAMS. Who came through this passage?

PALLISER. Only Field-Marshal Endymion.

WILLIAMS (*suspiciously*). I thought I saw someone else. (*He goes to the telephone.*) Has anyone been using this telephone?

MACCARTHY. I'm afraid I did, my dear fellow. I have to keep the wife posted.

WILLIAMS. Why weren't these wires pulled out?

MACCARTHY. They were, old boy. But I pushed them back again.

(WILLIAMS *wrenches them out and takes the receiver under his arm.*)

WILLIAMS. You'd better not do that again. You must be looking for trouble.

MACCARTHY. Looking for it! You obviously don't know my wife. She's beginning to show her age. (*To* PALLISER.) She's already got some grey hairs in her moustache.

ROISIN. Is it the trut you plugged some old G.R.s out at Ballsbridge?

WILLIAMS. Who told you that?

ROISIN. Never mind. Is it the trut?

WILLIAMS (*looking at* PALLISER). Has anybody else been using this phone?

MACCARTHY. Rather a silly question! Who else would want to talk to my wife?

WILLIAMS (*to* PALLISER). If you've been playing the spy – Oh, never mind. I'm going to call a meeting over here.

PALLISER. Why over here?

WILLIAMS. Because it may concern you.

PALLISER. That's very cryptic. Isn't the war going too well?

WILLIAMS. It's going fine. What makes you think it isn't?

PALLISER. Oh, nothing. Those Huns . . . soon be here?

WILLIAMS. You'll see. (*Then to the others, as cheering breaks out quite close.*) We've taken three more barracks, and there's a German submarine out in the bay. Men from the country are pouring in every hour.

ROISIN (*sceptically*). Game ball. You'd think he had seven toes.

MACCARTHY. Actually he has. (*Then with a deprecating laugh.*) Though not all, of course, on the same foot.

(EMER *comes in from the street in some excitement.*)

EMER. Something will have to be done about that crowd. Now they've broken into the shop downstairs.

WILLIAMS. No one can stop the workers from taking a few of their needs.

EMER. Who's talking about their needs? If it was food or blankets I could understand. But toffee shops and fancy dancing shoes, hats and children's toys . . .

WILLIAMS. What do you expect us to do? Fire on them? (*Then, with a slight laugh.*) If a few chizlers get a bag of sweets or a teddy bear, it'll be the first time they've ever had something for nothing.

EMER. Next thing it will be drink.

MACCARTHY. Drink? Where? Tell me, woman.

EMER. In Meagher's round the corner. Somebody broke in during the night and set it on fire.

MACCARTHY (*agitated*). On fire! My God, this must be put out at once. (*He prepares to go.*)

ROISIN. It's all right. The Brigade has put it out.

MACCARTHY. But is the place still open?

ROISIN. How should I know?

MACCARTHY (*making for the door*). Will you excuse me, folks. I think I'll . . .

EMER. Where are you off to?

MACCARTHY. Just to get a few medical supplies. We need them, you know.

PALLISER. Bring me back a quart while you're at it.

EMER. Is it liquor you're after?

MACCARTHY (*pausing in the doorway*). What an abominable suggestion! When I'm only going to call on a little chemist round the corner. A teeny-tiny chemist.

EMER. I'm going along to see what you're up to.

MACCARTHY (*in mock horror*). Ah, the peasant mind! Always full of suspicion.

125

WILLIAMS. The bourgeois mind. Not one of you understands the poor.

PALLISER. I do. I'm absolutely broke. Make it Scotch.

MACCARTHY. I have no idea what any of you mean. Goodbye.

(*He hurries off followed by* EMER. *The piano is heard next door, playing from Griffes's 'White Peacock'.*)

EMER (*To* WILLIAMS *as she goes*). How can we have a government of our own if we don't have law and order?

WILLIAMS (*suddenly losing his air of confidence*). Ah, what does it matter what they take? It'll all be up in flames by morning.

PALLSER (*alarmed*). In flames? Why?

WILLIAMS (*viciously*). Because your people are bringing artillery on to the Quays. That's why.

PALLISER. Artillery! So that's the game.

WILLIAMS. It may be a game to you but it's no game to the people.

ROISIN (*mockingly*).
> 'So-wil-jers are we
> Whose lives are pledged to Eye-er-land.

WILLIAMS (*turning on her*). Ah, will you dry up!

ROISIN. Who's banjaxed now? Slattery's Mountain Fut.

WILLIAMS. Get out of here, woman. Go and join your friends if that's the dirty fighting you admire.

ROISIN. Me friends is me own concern. I'll go an' warn me friend Miss Garrity to mind the fire.

WILLIAMS (*rather pompously*). Yes. Get her out of there. Get all civilians out of the area.

(ROISIN *tosses her head and walks out by the street door.*)

PALLISER. Funny how indignant you civilians always get whenever you find that there are two sides to every war.

WILLIAMS. Are you calling me a civilian?

PALLISER. Well, aren't you acting like one? If you want to have a fight you must expect to get hit.

WILLIAMS. With big guns! Against a few lads with shotguns and scapulars!

PALLISER. Ttt-ttt. I know. And all of them so difficult to keep clean. Of course, it's always unfair to be beaten.

WILLIAMS (*passionately*). Yes it is when it's done by holding women and children to ransom.

PALLISER. You're not only a civilian. You're a journalist.

WILLIAMS. I'm not exaggerating. Your people are getting ready to blast the whole city to hell in order to get at us.

PALLISER. That was one of the hazards of starting it in the city.

WILLIAMS. I'm not going to argue with you. I want to see your commanding officer. Do you know him?

PALLISER. I know the present one. But he won't be here for long.

WILLIAMS. I'm going to get some of our leaders. So don't attempt to escape. We may want you. (*Indicating the telephone receiver.*) And this I'll take with me.

(*He goes out by the street door. As* PALLISER *stands up on his stiff leg, a British Captain –* CLATTERING – *also rises, from behind the counter. The piano stops.*)

PALLISER (*startled*). God!

CLATTERING. About time that bloody fellow went.

PALLISER. Bunny! Where the hell have you come from?

CLATTERING. Through those dashed little holes. Why the devil haven't you been keeping in touch? The Colonel is furious.

PALLISER. I can't keep in touch while they're here, and they're here all the time. Now he's taken away the telephone.

CLATTERING (*going to the window with a notebook*). Good thing I came to see for myself. Had quite a ride on a fire engine.

PALLISER. Why didn't you send those men yesterday?

CLATTERING. My dear chap, we could hardly start off before everyone was back from the races. Then we got a better idea. I say, they've made quite a mess of the old Post Office, haven't they?

PALLISER. Who got a better idea? Who's in command now?

CLATTERING. Oh, some brigadier from the Curragh. Not a bad sort. Of course all the usual jobbery and backbiting is in full swing – you're lucky to be out of it, old boy. But I think we've got him to see the light.

PALLISER. Bunny, is it true you've got some guns on the Quays?

CLATTERING. Yes, old boy. That's the new idea. In fact, that's why I'm here. To take a look-see before we open fire.

PALLISER. But Bunny, that's crazy. If you open fire with artillery you'll burn half the town.

CLATTERING (*still busy taking notes at the window*). Got to do something fast, old boy. Two brigades from home are due at Kingstown some time tonight. By tomorrow that ass Hempenstall will have them all marching up the Rock Road with drums beating and colours flying. If we don't do something ourselves before that crowd turns up, we'll find ourselves in Q jobs in Liverpool – you as well as me.

PALLISER. But Bunny, this mustn't be treated as a military operation.

CLATTERING. I know they're only a bunch of Sin Feeners, but . . .

PALLISER. I tell you, they're just about ripe to be plucked. I've talked to them. If we can only bluff them into coming out with their hands up, it's all over.

CLATTERING. Who cares where their hands are? About time we did a bit of shooting ourselves.

PALLISER. But Bunny, you don't undertsand. A lot of fireworks will only make them look important.

CLATTERING. I don't follow.

PALLISER. Let's march them through the streets without their pants, and ship them off in a cattle boat to their friends – the Huns. That'll put 'paid' to the whole business.

CLATTERING. Sounds to me as if you want to make everything look damn silly. What's the idea?

PALLISER. I want to make *them* look damn silly.

CLATTERING. A bit fanciful. What?

PALLISER. It's the answer. I know this country.

CLATTERING (*becoming rather arch*). Ah, yes. Scratch a Paddy and you're all the same, no matter what uniform you're wearing.

PALLISER. What the devil do you mean by that?

CLATTERING. I mean, old boy, frankly – you don't mind my being frank, do you?

PALLISER. No, I don't mind you being frank.

CLATTERING. Well what I'm getting at is this. You're a horseman and I'm a gunner. And basically – one can't shut one's eyes to the facts – basically you fellows always hate to see a gunner firing his guns. Isn't that so?

PALLISER. It is not so. You can fire your blasted guns to your heart's content. But not just now. Don't you understand?

CLATTERING. Pity you can't be frank, like me. But you Paddies! (*Archly.*) Always love a spot of intrigue, don't you? Do you know what that fellow Braithwaite tried to do?

PALLISER. God, give me patience.

CLATTERING. Tried to get me taken off the circulation list. Me, of all people! I don't know who these old dug-outs think they are. Haven't heard a shot fired since Ladysmith, and now they're hand in glove with the Territorials, trying to run the show as if they owned it. Of course your crowd in Marlboro Barracks doesn't come under that heading, but we all know what camp you're in.

PALLISER. I'm not in any camp. I just want to get this thing licked.

CLATTERING. Oh come now. You're not going to ask me to believe that you're not up to the neck in that Bisley business?

128

PALLISER. What has Bisley got to do with it?

CLATTERING. We all know who you fellows have been backing for captain of that shooting team.

(PALLISER *pulls himself together, and drums with his fingers for a short time, while* CLATTERING *returns to the window, having triumphantly made his point.*)

CLATTERING. What do you suppose has happened to the populace? Gone to ground in the pubs, I suppose, now that a little bit of shooting has begun. How's morale? Fairly low, you say. And their O.P.s . . . where did you say they are?

PALLISER. None of them even know what an O.P. is. Listen Bunny. I can tell from your remarks that you're a pretty astute fellow.

CLATTERING. Uh-uh! Flattery. What's coming now?

PALLISER. Nothing about the guns, Bunny. But I've been thinking over what you said about the Bisley team.

CLATTERING (*interested*). Oh?

PALLISER. You don't mind me speaking frankly, do you?

CLATTERING (*really interested*). No, no. Be as frank as you like. Only don't try to pull the wool over my eyes. I know.

PALLISER. Well, I'm ready to admit that we've been backing the wrong horse.

CLATTERING (*gratified*). Ah!

PALLISER. But I'm not going to admit it in public without a *quid pro quo*. That's frank, isn't it, Bunny?

CLATTERING. Yes. We know where we are now. Nothing like being frank.

PALLISER. So I'll do a deal with you.

CLATTERING. Well, what's the proposition? Do come on.

PALLISER. I'll back you up over the Bisley team, if you hold up on those guns till tomorrow. My God, there's somebody coming! Hide!

CLATTERING (*reluctantly going back behind the bar*). I never could understand how anyone could imagine that a fool like Wilbraham-Northwood could – Oh, excuse me.

(*He sinks from sight, as* O'CALLAGHAN *enters from the street.*)

O'CALLAGHAN. Who was talking?

PALLISER. Nobody. I was just talking to myself.

O'CALLAGHAN. I thought I saw somebody else at the window.

PALLISER. You must have been mistaken.

O'CALLAGHAN (*looking around*). About this parole of yours . . . you realize what it means, of course?

PALLISER. That I'm not to leave here without your permission.

O'CALLAGHAN. That you're not to take any further part in this business in any way. You've undertaken that, on your honour as a soldier.

PALLISER. Have I?

O'CALLAGHAN. You don't seem certain. Do you realize what may happen if you break your parole?

PALLISER. The whole subject is rather a dull one.

O'CALLAGHAN. You forfeit your rights as a prisoner of war, and are liable to be shot.

PALLISER. Why keep on about it?

O'CALLAGHAN. Because Williams thinks, and I agree, that both you and the enemy know a damn sight too much about what's going on, ever since this thing started.

PALLISER. Maybe it's just natural intelligence.

O'CALLAGHAN. Maybe it's intelligence that goes by the name of spying. Is this your hat?

(*He picks up* CLATTERING'S.)

PALLISER. Yes.

O'CALLAGHAN. I thought you were in the Lancers.

PALLISER. O what the hell! Maybe it's somebody else's I borrowed.

O'CALLAGHAN. I don't remember you having a hat when we carried you in.

PALLISER. Miss Garrity found it in the street, and very kindly brought it up.

O'CALLAGHAN. I see.

(H*e looks around the room, and even over the counter, but apparently sees nothing.*)

O'CALLAGHAN. Well, maybe I'll leave you now. Goodbye.

(*He goes out by the street door.*)

PALLISER. Goodbye. (*Then, after a pause.*) Are you still there?

CLATTERING (*reappearing*). I've been thinking that over about the Bisley team. What exactly is it that you want?

PALLISER (*in a low voice*). I want you to have that brigadier standing by to treat with these fellows. It may come quite soon – perhaps even this afternoon.

CLATTERING. You know he can't give them terms without first talking to the frocks.

PALLISER. Yes he can if he likes. To hell with the frocks.

CLATTERING. Oh, I agree with you there. All the same –

PALLISER. Get them in the bag on any terms you like while the spirit's low. Then we can talk about the next step. But no shell-fire till we see how they're going to jump. Keep those guns quiet, no matter what the Castle says. Have the wrong ammunition. Tell everybody all the lies you like, but let's get them in the bag first.

CLATTERING (*after a pause*). About the team . . . of course I don't care much who's adjutant.

PALLISER (*impatiently*). All right – Bertie's adjutant. Is it a deal?

CLATTERING. Not that I want to be unreasonable. But it does seem obvious that if somebody isn't in command who has a lot of pull in Whitehall, everybody's going to get the wrong end of the stick, the most ghastly quarters to begin with and . . .

(O'CALLAGHAN *is standing in the doorway with revolver drawn*.)

CLATTERING. Oh. This fellow's back again.

O'CALLAGHAN. Put up your hands.

CLATTERING. Put up what?

O'CALLAGHAN. Your hands.

CLATTERING. I shall do nothing of the sort.

O'CALLAGHAN. I'll shoot you if you don't.

CLATTERING. Stop behaving like a cowboy, my man. As I haven't got any weapons the idea of putting up my hands is absolute nonsense.

O'CALLAGHAN. I warn you. You'll be plugged. I mean it.

CLATTERING. Don't be ridiculous. You can't shoot an unarmed man. (*Very deliberately, he turns his back. After a dreadful pause,* O'CALLAGHAN *dashes to the window and shouts*.)

O'CALLAGHAN. Hey, below there! Send up some men. Hurry – I've caught a spy.

PALLISER (*to* CLATTERING). Quick. Now's your chance.

(CLATTERING *leaps out by the kitchen.* O'CALLAGHAN *is about to run after him, but collapses across the counter in a violent fit of coughing*.)

PALLISER. You should take something for that.

O'CALLAGHAN (*almost in tears*). Damn you! Damn you!

PALLISER. Why didn't you shoot? No ammunition, I suppose.

O'CALLAGHAN. None of . . . your damn . . . business.

(MAGINNIS *runs in from the street carrying a rifle*.)

MAGINNIS. What is it?

O'CALLAGHAN. Enemy spy – through there – catch him . . .

(*As* MAGINNIS *runs to the kitchen door he collides with* MAC-CARTHY *coming in, and grabs him.* MACCARTHY *has a number of bottles which he struggles to get behind the counter.* PALLISER *shouts with laughter*.)

131

MACCARTHY. Don't touch me, you guerrilla.

O'CALLAGHAN (*still between his coughs*). Not him – officer – in uniform . . .

MACCARTHY. Not with the child in my arms.

(MAGINNIS *runs off after* CLATTERING, *and* WILLIAMS *hurries in from the street.*)

WILLIAMS. What's happening?

MACCARTHY (*concealing the bottles*). Everybody's dashing about – wearing different uniforms. I can't keep track of what side I'm on.

O'CALLAGHAN. Enemy spy.

PALLISER. A spy in full uniform! Don't be absurd.

WILLIAMS (*drawing his revolver*). Where is he?

(O'CALLAGHAN *tries to point.*)

O'CALLAGHAN. Someone's gone . . . after him.

MACCARTHY. If it's the gentleman who hurried past me, he seemed to be going to the cloakroom. (*He throws a book to* PALLISER.) There's what you asked for.

PALLISER (*delighted*). 'The Marriage of Heaven and Hell.'

MACCARTHY. You'll never guess where I found it.

O'CALLAGHAN. He was talking to . . . (*He points at* PALLISER.)

WILLIAMS (*grimly*). Ah, I see. Passing information.

MACCARTHY (*to* O'CALLAGHAN). That's a terrible cough. Let me see.

WILLIAMS. And over the telephone as well. I see it all now.

MACCARTHY (*looking at* O'CALLAGHAN'S *throat*). Have you ever had T.B.?

WILLIAMS. Why hasn't he been kept under proper guard?

O'CALLAGHAN. Can't get away . . . Gave me . . . his . . . parole.

MACCARTHY. Stop trying to talk.

WILLIAMS. Well, he's under guard from now on till we decide what to do with him.

(*He draws a pair of handcuffs from his pocket and, putting away his gun, he pinions* PALLISER'S *hands around the pillar.*)

PALLISER. If you're all so damned incompetent as to leave a telephone in a place like this, what do you expect?

WILLIAMS. Shut up.

O'CALLAGHAN. I cut . . . it. Somebody . . . fixed it . . . again.

MACCARTHY (*authoritatively*). Sit down at once and let me have a proper look at your throat.

(O'CALLAGHAN *obeys, as* TETLEY *comes in, following* EMER. *He has lost much of his vigour and seems to be deeply depressed.*)

132

EMER (*pointing at* MACCARTHY). There he is! How well you gave me the slip.

MACCARTHY (*snapping his fingers*). About time you appeared, nurse. Give me a swab, and then hold my torch.

> (*After a moment's surprised hesitation she hurries obediently to his assistance, and presently* O'CALLAGHAN'S *coughing subsides, as swabs are taken and examined.*)

TETLEY (*looking at* PALLISER). What's happening to this officer?

WILLIAMS. Whatever's supposed to happen to spies and informers. Everybody knows their fate.

PALLISER. And the fate of civilians who try to play at soldiers.

WILLIAMS. He's been in touch with the enemy ever since yesterday.

PALLISER. Talk about me charging the Post Office! They don't even know enough to occupy the telephone exchange.

TETLEY (*incredulously*). But surely this isn't possible? This officer gave his parole.

WILLIAMS. You must be even simpler than I thought. But there's other things more urgent at the moment. You know they're bringing artillery on to the Quays?

TETLEY (*tonelessly*). Yes, I know.

WILLIAMS. Once they open fire with that it's goodbye to both the city and the population.

TETLEY. It's happening to a good many cities besides this one. Does it matter very much?

WILLIAMS (*loudly*). Does it matter?

TETLEY. If we hadn't considered that possibility, why did we ever start?

WILLIAMS. We started it to make a public protest – not to force the workers to commit suicide along with us. Now we've made that protest.

MACCARTHY. These instruments are a disgrace. Take them and . . . No, not you. Where's that Roisin girl?

EMER. I don't know.

PALLISER. Next door talking to a piano player.

> (MACCARTHY *strides to the wall and bangs on it.* MAGINNIS *re-enters, out of breath.*)

MAGINNIS. He got away. There's an enemy barricade across Marlboro Street.

WILLIAMS. Damn it, are they on that side now? Well, this just confirms what I think.

MACCARTHY (*shouting*). Roisin Whateveryouare, I want you.

> (*He returns to* EMER *and* O'CALLAGHAN.)

TETLEY (*to* MAGINNIS). I thought you'd gone to the Third Battalion?

MAGINNIS (*rather sulkily*). The men on the canal don't understand their orders. They sent me back to ask is this a war or is it not?

TETLEY. What's this all about?

WILLIAMS. I told them off for opening fire on a detachment of Veterans.

MAGINNIS (*indignantly*). They were marchin' into Beggarsbush with guns on their shoulders.

WILLIAMS. Those aren't the people we're fighting. It's had a very bad effect.

MAGINNIS (*shrilly*). A bad effect!

WILLIAMS. They ought to have had more sense. But it all adds up to the same thing. Artillery . . . this trouble at Beggarsbush . . . and now this fellow being allowed to get away.

MAGINNIS. That wasn't my fault.

TETLEY. What's in your mind?

WILLIAMS. I was going to suggest that this man (*indicating* PALLISER) should be sent across to find out what terms we can get.

EMER. Terms?

WILLIAMS. Now it will obviously have to be somebody else.

TETLEY. I thought it was going to be something of this sort.

O'CALLAGHAN (*weakly*). The Provisional Government will never agree to ask for terms.

WILLIAMS. The Provisional Government needn't know about it, until I can tell them what the terms are.

MAGINNIS. Terms? Does he mean surrender? And we not in action for two days yet?

WILLIAMS (*confidently*). In those two days we've accomplished a great deal. We've captured five barracks and nearly taken the Castle. The country's up . . . alive and kicking. There's nothing dishonourable in discussing terms after that.

PALLISER. You've taken no barracks.

WILLIAMS. Keep out of this please.

PALLISER. You've taken no barracks. Not a county has risen, except for a skirmish in Wexford. Two brigades of infantry are landing at Kingstown, and will be marching on the city within twelve hours. These are the facts. But don't let them bother you. You'll be given terms – good ones – if you're quick about it.

TETLEY. Captain Palliser, is it in your role as a parole-breaker that you have all this information?

PALLISER. Never mind how I know. Is it true or is it not? That's the question.

WILLIAMS. Pay no attention to him.

TETLEY. I don't know anything about reinforcements arriving at Kingstown. As for the rest – according to my information, it's perfectly true.

EMER (*astonished*). True?

WILLIAMS. Don't be a fool, Tetley.

TETLEY. It's perfectly true. Let's be realistic about this for once, now that we're talking about the future. We've driven off a very determined attack on the Mendicity Institute, and we've scattered a small party of idiot Lancers . . . if our prisoner will forgive the expression. As for any offensive operations against armed men, we have not – so far – taken and held as much as a sentry box.

WILLIAMS. We took the Magazine Fort.

TETLEY. Are we there still?

EMER. We took Dublin Castle.

MACCARTHY. Are you assisting me, nurse, or are you talking politics?

TETLEY. We took the Castle – yes – and we came out again as soon as somebody fired a pistol out of one of the windows.

WILLIAMS. What kind of a way is this to talk?

TETLEY. It's a very good way. I'm not blaming the men. They have all shown great courage in being with us at all, and what we've failed to do is simply a matter of ignorance. Dammit, we're only taking on the British Empire in open warfare for the first time in three generations. It takes us a little time to learn. But we'll never learn by pretending that we've done things that we haven't.

MAGINNIS. What about the Germans? Haven't they landed in Kerry?

TETLEY. At least we've been spared that indignity. Nobody else is going to come and save us.

MAGINNIS. Jaze!

WILLIAMS. Tetley, we've got to keep up morale.

MAGINNIS. D'ye mean by that we've got to be tole a lot of lies?

WLLIAMS. Everybody does it, Maginnis. Look at the 'Official War News'. Men won't fight unless they think they're winning.

TETLEY. Men won't fight until they believe that all is lost. Why must we imitate the enemy even in his illusions?

MAGINNIS. I don't give a damn whether we're winnin' or not. I just don't like bein' tole a lot of lies.

135

WILLIAMS. It was never a question of winning. It was a matter of making a protest, and that we've done.

ROISIN (*entering from the street*). Well, I got ole Miss G. to go home at last.

MACCARTHY. There you are, you tiresome girl. Put on some boiling water and sterilize these disgusting implements. I'm going out to get some proper equipment.

(*He rises and starts to jot down a list.*)

ROISIN (*to* MAGINNIS). Aw, wait till ye see Napoleon! What brings you back from the Gran' Canal?

MAGINNIS (*sulky again*). There was nuttin' doin' out there.

ROISIN. Nuttin' excep for te plug a few ole gorgeous wrecks. Murderin' blaggards!

MAGINNIS. God forgivus is there no pleasin' that one at all? If I stop out of it I'm a flyboy. When I go into it I'm a murderin' blaggard. They call us soljers and' send us into action, and when we loose off at the red, white an' kharki they say it has a 'very bad effect'.

WILLIAMS. I said that, in this case, your target was unfortunate, that's all.

MAGINNIS. Unfortunate is right. It's unfortunate we ever got inta it. But I'll tell ya this, when I go back an' tell the men at the bridge that they're to inquire the name, address and occupation of every man in kharki before they open fire, I know what they'll do. They'll go home to their tea that's what they'll do an' small blame to them. An' for God's sake will ye give me a cup now.

(*He goes indignantly into the kitchen after* ROISIN, *passing* MACCARTHY *on his way out towards the street.*)

WILLIAMS. Where are you off to?

MACCARTHY. To Jervis Street Hospital.

WILLIAMS. Don't you know they're shooting down that way?

MACCARTHY. That melancholy fact has not escaped me. However, if I can't get to Jervis Street, I shall borrow what I need from His Majesty.

WILLIAMS. His Majesty! Look here, whose game are you playing?

MACCARTHY. Don't adopt that tone with me. Whose game is everybody playing? It's painfully obvious from all the nonsense I've heard that nobody knows whose game is what. My patient Endymion was perfectly right when he said that this campaign will be won by whoever manages to do the least for the other side.

136

WILLIAMS. Listen to me. If you're game enough to go as far as the British barricades, would you go further – and come back?

EMER. Don't be an eedyet. The man would never go near a barricade. Sure he's scared to death already.

MACCARTHY. Madam, do I look like the kind of man who is scared at the call of duty?

EMER. Yes.

WILLIAMS. Well, are you?

MACCARTHY. Certainly I am, you miserable shop steward. (*With a change of tone.*) What do you want me to do?

WILLIAMS. I want you to get through to the British commander and ask him to meet me by the O'Connell Monument in about half an hour.

EMER (*passionately*). No! Not that!

MACCARTHY. Supposing he's having cocktails in the Shelbourne?

EMER. Don't let him go, Sean.

TETLEY (*with a calming gesture*). Easy.

WILLIAMS. In that case have one with him, and bring me back word of his alternative.

EMER. You fool – once he gets over there, he'll never come back.

WILLIAMS. Is it clearly understood that whatever the answer is, you'll come back with it?

EMER. He'll just give away more information.

MACCARTHY. There is no information of the slightest interest to anybody, if it's what I've been hearing. However, I shall be your dove, on the strict understanding that it's kept quiet afterwards. I don't mind a bullet, but I'm not going to run the risk of knighthood over this.

WILLIAMS. Then off you go.

(MAC CARTHY *leaves by the street door.*)

EMER. Fools! Fools! That's the last you'll ever see of him.

MACCARTHY (*looking in again*). I'm going now. But I shall come back, my dear Peril, if only to show you how to put on a roller bandage without wrecking the circulation of the blood. Well, *au revoir*, everybody.

EMER (*to* TETLEY *and* O'CALLAGHAN). Haven't you two got anything to say about this?

O'CALLAGHAN (*rising*). I think . . .

MACCARTHY (*reappearing*). I'm going now. About half an hour. At the O'Connell Monument? Is that right?

WILLIAMS (*roaring*). Yes. And hurry up.

MACCARTHY. Bye-bye. (*He goes.*)

137

O'CALLAGHAN. I was about to say that this is not something any of us can decide. It's a matter for . . .

MACCARTHY (*reappearing*). It was proved by statistics that under the age of forty-five we live longer than over it. Isn't that encouraging?

WILLIAMS (*throwing the magazine at him*). Will you get out of here!

MACCARTHY. I'm going now. Let me be the first at your post mortem. (*He goes.*)

TETLEY. Yes, Seamus? What were you saying?

O'CALLAGHAN. I was trying to say that . . . (*He pauses and looks at the door, but nobody reappears.*) Trying to say that I'm going across to the Post Office to call a meeting.

EMER. Yes – call a meeting. The Council will soon vote this down.

WILLIAMS. We'll see. I'll go with you. What about you, Sean?

TETLEY. No. I'm going to stay here.

O'CALLAGHAN. Why?

TETLEY. Because I feel that way.

EMER. Aren't you going to vote?

TETLEY. No.

WILLIAMS. Oh very well. Stop here and sulk if you must. But when we get before the Peace Conference ask yourself what was it that got us there? My realism, or your sulks.

O'CALLAGHAN (*at the door*). The firing's got bad in the street. We'll have to run.

WILLIAMS. All right. Off you go.

PALLISER. Hi. What about me?

WILLIAMS. We'll deal with you later, when we have time.

PALLISER. Supposing I want to leave the room for a certain purpose?

WILLIAMS (*throwing the key to the handcuffs to* TETLEY). Here. You look after him. Take the damn key.

O'CALLAGHAN. You go first. I'll be the slowest.

WILLIAMS. All the more reason for you to get a good start.

O'CALLAGHAN. I don't see that at all. Surely if . . .

PALLISER. Ah, let me give you a tip. The one that starts first will be half way across before they start shooting. It's the one behind that gets it.

WILLIAMS (*stiffly*). That was not what was in my mind.

O'CALLAGHAN (*laughing*). Oh come on. I'll race you neck and neck.

PALLISER (*shaking his head*). Amateurs!

(*They both disappear.* MAGINNIS *watches from the window, his cup of tea in his hand.*)

138

EMER. Why wouldn't you go too?

TETLEY. Because I never take part in votes if I'm not sure that I'm going to accept the decision.

EMER. Your vote might have made all the difference.

TETLEY. I don't think so. Williams can be very convincing – under certain circumstances.

MAGINNIS. They're running. An' not a shot bein' fired.

ROISIN (*from the bar*). Who'd waste bullets on men bound for Mountjoy?

EMER. Then you think . . .

TETLEY. I don't know what to think. I'd fight to the last building and the last man if I was sure of only one thing – that I was fighting for my country and for my people, and not just for my own satisfaction.

EMER. Do you doubt that?

TETLEY. I'm afraid I do. Look at that girl over there. You know how she feels about us. Are we fighting for her?

ROISIN. Ye are not.

EMER. Who would mind her? She's only a West Briton – a shoneen.

ROISIN. Call me that again an I'll gut ye for garters. I'm for John Redmond an there's no yella streak in our flag.

TETLEY. You see. She's the people. It's their hostility that's really shaken me – not any question of whether we're going to win or lose. I was watching their faces during the reading of the pro- clamation, and there was nothing but derision in those eyes – derision, and that murderous Irish laughter. It was as if we were putting on a rather poor entertainment for them, and they wanted their money back.

EMER. They'll change. We'll show them.

TETLEY. Show them what? That they're downtrodden? You can't show people that if they don't feel it. There we were – in our hands, the first declaration of our independence for the past seven hundred years. But there was no sign of understanding in those eyes. And then . . . at the words 'Ireland through us sum- mons her children to the flag and strikes for her freedom' . . . that crash of glass, and that terrible shout of 'Noblett's toffee shop'.

(*He sinks into a chair and covers his face with his hands.*)

TETLEY. Oh, these moments of doubt and self-examination! I can stand anything but them. Do I have to pretend to myself that I'm another Jesus Christ – that everyone's wrong except me? Endymion thinks like that. But I'm a sane man – amn't I?

(EMER *comes to him and is about to touch his head with her hand. We realize for a brief moment that she adores this man. But then something holds her back, and for a while she stands there in silence.*)

ROISIN. What we all need is a good square meal.

MAGINNIS. Game ball.

ROISIN (*going off*). Come an' lend a hand while I whip up what I can. Mr Vitali can charge it to the Irish Republic.

MAGINNIS (*getting out cups*). I never cared for that Citizen Army. I suppose we'll all be hanged now.

TETLEY (*pulling himself together*). No, Mickser. I don't think you'll be hanged. Maybe just a little . . . penal servitude. (*He smiles and* MAGINNIS *smiles back.*)

MAGINNIS. Penal servitude. I've offen wunnered what that's like.

(EMER *moves slowly away and sits silently beside the machine-gun near the window.*)

PALLISER. Pity you never attended an expensive public school. Then it would hold no surprises for you.

TETLEY. Tell me, Captain, was it at your expensive public school that you learnt to break your word?

PALLISER. That seems to be weighing on your mind.

TETLEY. It is, because it puzzles me. I always imagined that whatever we might say against the British Army, it had a certain code – a canon of good form, if you like to put it that way – that included a respect for the laws of war.

PALLISER. Indeed.

TETLEY. You don't wish to enlighten me? Am I wrong, or are you just an exception?

PALLISER. You have me at a disadvantage, Tetley. Make the most of it while you can.

TETLEY. Oh? I beg your pardon. Allow me to unlock this thing. (*He does so.*)

PALLISER. Thank you. I hope this doesn't get you into trouble. I understand that I'm to be court-martialled, or something.

TETLEY. Oh, I don't think that any of them will bother about you at the moment. In fact, if you'd like to go, I'm sure Maginnis will help you to a place of safety.

PALLISER (*puzzled*). Go?

TETLEY. Better now than later. The going may not be good, but it's still tolerable.

PALLISER (*suspiciously*). Are you inviting me to escape? What's the idea?

TETLEY. I suppose it's because I'm just a damned amateur. If I had your professional attitude, I'd let them shoot you as you probably deserve. But what's the point, now?

PALLISER. I don't see much point in being shot at any time. All the same I don't think I'll go just yet. Perhaps I'll stay and join you in that bite of food.

TETLEY. Stay if you like. But if you've no better explanation to give, I don't think *I'll* join *you*, Captain.

PALLISER (*taken aback*). You what? Is this a snub?

TETLEY. Maybe they'll be back later to shoot you, if you insist . . . and they haven't forgotten.

PALLISER. You sound rather patronizing. I believe it *is* a snub.

TETLEY. Interpret it any way you like. One thing I would be grateful to know. Is there really a column of reinforcements landing at Kingstown?

PALLISER. Yes. You haven't a hope, I'm afraid.

TETLEY. That's not why I asked the question.

PALLISER. Maybe you want me to pull a few strings for you?

TETLEY (*stiffening*). What do you mean by that?

PALLISER. I mean, about your own future – after you've surrendered I dare say I could get you off, if we concocted a good story now, and both stuck to it.

TETLEY (*offended*). I don't need to have any lying done for me, thank you.

PALLISER. It's tit for tat. After all, isn't that why you're letting me go?

TETLEY (*with a flash of temper*). I always suspected that you weren't a gentleman, but I'd no idea that you'd presume to think the same of me.

PALLISER (*furious*). What the devil do you mean? Whatever I am, I'm a gentleman.

TETLEY. Would a gentleman disregard his parole?

PALLISER. I disregard no promises that I give myself. I do disregard promises that are thrust on me by other people for their own convenience.

TETLEY. An officer and a gentleman is not supposed to break the laws of war. There's no getting away from that.

PALLISER. If you were a real soldier and not a sham one you'd know that all soldiers break the laws of war continually. They couldn't fight a war if they didn't. The whole art of war is to know when to break the rules intelligently. And it has nothing whatever to do with being either an officer or a gentleman. The fact that you don't know this, classifies you – both socially and professionally.

EMER (*rising in a fury*). How dare you talk to him like . . .

PALLISER. How dare he adopt that superior tone to me?

TETLEY (*calmly*). Now, don't let's get annoyed, please. We all know that Captain Palliser and his friends have a monopoly of a certain tone towards people like us.

PALLISER. I'm damned if I'll be patronized.

TETLEY (*to* EMER). So naturally he's annoyed at my offering him his life, and then not allowing him the satisfaction of saving mine.

(EMER *sits down again, silently.*)

PALLISER (*with a sneer*). So you think your life's in danger, do you?

TETLEY. Well, I would imagine so – after this. Of course there's no knowing what the Castle will do. But I imagine that some of us will have to be hanged or shot.

PALLISER. And you hope it's yourself. That would be so much easier than fighting to the last ditch.

TETLEY. On the contrary. Fighting to the last ditch seems to be extremely easy. Your profession is quite terrifying, Captain – it's so simple. It requires no special qualities, except an indifference to one's personal fate that I find rather pleasant.

PALLISER (*sarcastically*). Indeed?

TETLEY. In fact. I've found since yesterday that soldiering gives one a great feeling of release – especially when you're bound to be beaten. I suppose that's why so many stupid people make a success of the Army. It doesn't require much courage to be shot at.

PALLISER. So far, you've had damn little data on that.

TETLEY (*ignoring him*). But to be hanged is quite a different proposition. I'm very much afraid of that, because I don't know how I would react. It's easy to be brave up here in the mind. But what will the body do? Will it let you down? Will the stomach turn to water, no matter how often it's told that it mustn't? Who knows, whether hanging's a difficult thing to take, or if it's not?

PALLISER. All these doubts would be swallowed up in the enormous pleasure of being a martyr.

TETLEY. Now there you show your ignorance, Captain. I know that's what you think I'm after, but I don't want to be a martyr at all, and I'm sure I'd make a rotten one. But what can I do? If we were to 'concoct' some story – as you say – to get me off, it would have to take the line that I had had nothing to do with this rising, and disapproved of it.

PALLISER. Well, why not? It's a flop, isn't it?

TETLEY. Whether it's a failure or not, it has at least expressed the purpose of my life. You could hardly expect me to repudiate that.

PALLISER. Do you seriously mean to say that you know the purpose of your life?

TETLEY. Of course. Don't you?

PALLISER. Good lord no. What's more, I'd hate to, almost as much as I'd hate to know the date of my death. Is the purpose of your life to show that about seven hundred years of history have all been a mistake?

TETLEY. If you like to put it that way.

PALLISER. That's a bit pompous, isn't it? May I ask where you got these ideas from?

TETLEY. Oh, I don't know, really. Mainly from my father, I suppose.

PALLISER. I see. (*Pause.*) Your father, I suppose, was an old Fenian . . . a charming old failure, crippled from long years of imprisonment?

TETLEY. No. As a matter of fact, he was an English Nonconformist.

PALLISER. A what?

TETLEY (*with a smile of recollection*). And he was far from being a failure. He made quite a good living out of manufacturing rosary beads. That's how he came to this country and met my mother.

PALLISER. Well to hell with the English! I always said they were at the back of Ireland's troubles.

TETLEY (*cryptically*). That's why you're in the English Army, I suppose?

PALLISER. I'm in the army that we Irishmen have officered in all its most important victories.

TETLEY. I know. That puzzles me too. Why do you people enjoy fighting everybody's battles except your country's?

PALLISER. Look here, my friend, it's not the professionals who enjoy fighting battles. As a soldier, I believe in peace on earth – goodwill towards men. Can you say as much?

TETLEY. That's a well-known Protestant mistranslation. What the Vulgate says is 'Peace on earth to men of goodwill'. Quite a different thing.

PALLISER. Well, are you a man of goodwill?

TETLEY. I don't know. I suppose – since I've always hated evil and wanted to fight it – that I can't be a man of goodwill. Maybe that's why I have never been wholly devoted to peace on earth.

PALLISER. It's odd, then, that you're not going to fight it out.

TETLEY. How can I, if the others decide . . .

PALLISER. Blake says that if the fool would only persist in his folly. he would become a wise man. (*He rises and limps over to the piano.*) You should read Blake. He belonged to the Middle Nation . . like you.

TETLEY. I'll probably not have an opportunity for much more reading.

PALLISER. If I had my way, you'd have more opportunity than you expect. Now I'm beginning to wonder if that might not be a pity.

TETLEY. Are you hinting that I ought to persist in what you call my folly? May I ask why?

PALLISER. A fight that doesn't get fought out has a way of stinking afterwards. Besides, I'd rather like to see how much of a soldier you really are. There's more to it than this, you know. (*He gestures towards the window.*)

TETLEY. Much more, I'm sure. *I'd* also like the chance of finding out.

PALLISER. Even if you're licked?

TETLEY. Whether we lose or win is a matter that only God can decide. How we behave is something that depends upon ourselves.

ROISIN (*entering*). There's baked beans now, on the stove.

TETLEY. Thanks. I'll come in and get some.

(*He goes into the kitchen. From the next room the piano is heard again. This time, Respighi's 'Notturno' is suggested.*)

ROISIN. Will ya have some too?

PALLISER (*listening to the piano*). Yes.

ROISIN. Well lissen te that now! The ole one's back again. I tought I had her out for good an' all.

PALLISER. What's she like – this Miss Garrity? Another Maeve of Connaught, harping her warriors against Muirthemne?

ROISIN. Ah, not at all. She's an ole Loyalist in black bombazine, with a picture of King Teddy on the whatnot. (*She goes back into the kitchen.*)

PALLISER. Good for her! A diehard! As a neighbour, I salute Miss Garrity.

(*He strikes a few chords in harmony with the playing next door.* EMER *rises from her seat and approaches him.*)

EMER. Captain Palliser, will they really hang him if there's a surrender now?

PALLISER. I don't know. That depends on who's in charge.

EMER. You've been planning something else for him? Haven't you?

PALLISER (*with a laugh*). A fate worse than death.

EMER. But why? What is it that you've got against him?

PALLISER. Nothing – except that he's my enemy . . . that he wants to destroy most of the things that my country means to me. Isn't that enough?

EMER. Are you afraid of him?

PALLISER. Not as a soldier, certainly. As a corpse – well, that might be a different matter.

EMER (*thoughtfully*). Yes, you hate him. Is it because he said you weren't a gentleman, and wouldn't have tea with you?

PALLISER. Don't be ridiculous.

EMER. I think it must be that. Or else you hate him because he's got a purpose in life, and you haven't.

PALLISER. Life is much too complicated to define a purpose.

EMER. Except to the saints.

PALLISER. I don't know that I like saints.

EMER. That's what I said. You hate him.

PALLISER. I don't remember when I invited you to discuss my feelings with me, Miss Smith. You say that I hate him. What would you say if I were to suggest that you love him?

EMER (*getting upset*). I'd say you were a very impertinent man.

PALLISER (*interested*). By God, I believe you do! You're blushing (*She turns away her head.*) Don't worry, I won't tell.

EMER. It wouldn't matter if you did. It isn't with any woman that he's in love.

PALLISER. More fool he.

EMER. He's not a fool. Even if he did offer to let you go.

PALLISER. Yes, he offered to let me go. But I didn't go, Emer. At least not yet. So you needn't start asking me to save him in return.

EMER. It's *you* that's the fool if you think I'm asking you to save him!

PALLISER (*surprised*). You mean, you want to make sure that he's hanged?

EMER (*emotionally*). That's a cruel way of putting it.

PALLISER. It's a cruel thing to want.

EMER (*passionately*). I don't want him to be hanged, but I want his life to have its meaning – the meaning that he puts on it him-

145

self. I don't want him to have . . . whatever it is that you've been planning for him.

PALLISER. What's it got to do with me . . . what you want? We're not friends, are we?

EMER. No. Maybe that's the best reason for you to help him – just because you aren't friends. Isn't that what your Blake would say?

PALLISER. Help him? How?

EMER (*earnestly*). Don't let them make him surrender now. Don't let them. You can do something, can't you?

PALLISER. So that's what you call helping him! By making sure that he dies. You want a holocaust, do you, so that your lover can win the only crown he's fit for?

EMER. You *are* afraid of him – afraid most of all to see him die.

PALLISER. Why should I be afraid to see him die?

EMER. Because you know, for all your talk, that you couldn't face it the way he could.

PALLISER. So you think not?

EMER. What's death to him or me, so long as it's a good one? But, oh, what's the use of talking? Nobody can ever understand that, who hasn't got the Faith!

PALLISER. What invincible ignorance. Do you suppose that only a Catholic can die? You're like a child I once knew who couldn't understand why I didn't kill and rob when I hadn't got the Church to keep me good.

EMER. How could you ever understand death the way we do?

PALLISER (*furious*). My God, what do you suppose I am?

(*He takes a step towards her, colliding with the machine-gun on the floor.*)

PALLISER. Damn that thing. I nearly broke my . . . (*A pause, while he looks at the machine-gun, and then out of the window, where something else attracts his attention.*) Listen, my good girl. I've had about enough play-acting from you and your friend from the Board of Works. You want to know what war is, do you?

EMER (*doggedly*). We're ready to learn.

PALLISER. It's about time you did – calling yourselves soldiers. If I was to show you how to start a fight that may teach you more than you've bargained for, would you thank me for it?

EMER (*dully*). Yes.

PALLISER. I wonder. (*Pause.*) Well, let's see who's best fitted to look Azrael in the face – the saint or the unbeliever. Come over here to the window. Do you see our friend MacCarthy down there

146

beside the O'Connell Monument? That's my C.O. along with
him. They must have come to discuss terms with Williams.

EMER. I suppose so.

PALLISER. Well, here's your chance to turn wind into wonderment.
(*He lifts the machine-gun into the window, and makes a few
rapid, businesslike adjustments.*)

PALLISER. A lot of damned incompetence. Simplest thing in the
world to rig a machine-gun. Now my dear, if you really want to
open the Book of Revelation, all that you have to do is to (*He
limps away.*) . . . press the trigger.

EMER (*her eyes full of tears*). Thank you.

PALLISER. No thanks are expected. (*He turns and looks at her with
a slight smile.*) Better wipe the eyes first.
(*He hands her his handkerchief, which she takes and applies
to her eyes.* PALLISER *limps to the bar with a nonchalant
shrug of his shoulders.*)

PALLISER. I say, everybody. The doctor's down the street.

ROISIN (*entering with a plate of beans*). Then let him stop there.
I've no beans for that wan.

PALLISER (*taking the plate*). All prepared for high negotiations.
Thank you, my dear. And do be careful of that thing, Miss
Smith.

EMER (*blessing herself*). *Quam oblationem tu, Deus, in ominibus
quaesumus, benedictam, adscriptam, ratam, rationabilem,
acceptabliemque facere digneris.*

PALLISER (*eating*). Nothing like a nice plate of . . .
(*The machine-gun blazes out of the window. Amid general
shouting,* TETLEY *and* MAGINNIS *rush in. The piano has
stopped.*)

TETLEY. What the deuce . . .

MAGINNIS. What's up?

PALLISER. My God! She fired it!

TETLEY (*shouting*). Turn that damn thing off!

PALLISER (*shouting back*). She doesn't know how.

TETLEY. Then you do something.

PALLISER. Then get out of my way.

TETLEY (*to* MAGINNIS). Take in that flag, Maginnis.
(*The gun stops firing, as* MAGINNIS *struggles with the Red
Cross flag.*)

PALLISER. You really are a very careless girl.
(*He touches the gun again, and it bursts into action once
more. Both he and* EMER *appear to struggle with it.*)

147

TETLEY. You fool! Can't you see we have a Red Cross flag hanging out?

PALLISER. Sorry. My mistake.

(*The firing stops, but outside in the street is a confused noise of shouting and considerable rifle fire.*)

ROISIN. Will ye look at the doctor runnin' like a hare?

MAGINNIS (*rolling up the flag*). That'll be the last we'll see a him.

ROISIN. Bedad, you'll see him shortly. He's runnin' this way.

MICKSER (*dropping the flag and joining her at the window*). This way!

TETLEY. What possessed you to touch that thing? Not only is this a hospital, but they had a flag of truce.

PALLISER. Yes, the Brigadier will be furious. Two more laws of war gone down the plug hole.

TETLEY. How did it get fixed?

PALLISER. You'd be surprised, old boy. But not so surprised as me.

(MAC CARTHY *enters breathlessly amidst a roar of shooting.*)

PALLISER (*to* EMER). Now see what you've started.

MACCARTHY. What idiot fired that damn blunderbuss? Has nobody any respect for my cloth?

PALLISER. Nothing personal old man.

MACCARTHY. It was you, you miserable Horse Marine. Give me a drink, somebody.

MAGINNIS (*getting out a bottle*). He said he'd come back and bedad he did.

MACCARTHY (*pouring out*). If I hadn't known it was the shortest route to alcohol I would never have chosen it. Do you know, I had just said to the Brigadier – a somewhat ill-informed individual – that . . . (*Some artillery opens up.*) Cripes!

ROISIN (*flinging herself into* MICKSER'S *arms*). Jaze! What's that?

PALLISER. Artillery. (*Then, to* EMER). Yes, you do seem to have started something. Congratulations, and apologies.

TETLEY (*quietly*). I suppose we're for it now.

MACCARTHY. Let this be a lesson to everybody. Though I'm damned if I know what it is.

TETLEY (*crisply*). Maginnis, can you get through with a message to the men on the Canal?

MAGINNIS. I can try, sir.

ROISIN. Don't leave me, Mickser.

MAGINNIS (*disengaging himself tenderly*). It's all right, Roisin. I'll be back.

TETLEY. Tell the Commandant there's a column on the road from

Kingstown. Tell him to open fire and to keep firing while the buildings last. Tell him to fire at everything in an enemy uniform – armed or unarmed. Tell him that if he does that I'll see that nobody blames him afterwards.

MAGINNIS (*delighted with himself*). I'll tell him.

TETLEY. And Mickser. Tell him it's a hopeless cause. But to put up a bloody good fight.

MAGINNIS (*dashing off by the kitchen*). That's the kind of an order the lads will unnerstan'.

ROISIN (*in distress*). Mind yerself, Mickser.

TETLEY. As for me, I'm going across to the Post Office.

(*He strides off towards the street.* EMER *watches him go from the window.* PALLISER *limps slowly to the piano, and* ROISIN, *open-eyed, goes back behind the bar, covering her mouth from time to time as a heavy gun continues to fire.*)

MACCARTHY (*refreshed*). Ah, I feel a new man. Now how about another half for the new man?

CURTAIN

ACT THREE

*The piano is heard playing 'There's a long, long trail awinding'.
The Curtain rises upon the same scene, on an evening three days
later. The street outside is lit by the red glow of fires that grow
more intense as the Act proceeds.
EMER is bandaging the shoulder of a wounded VOLUNTEER who lies
on the stretcher while PALLISER is strumming the tune on the piano.
ROISIN stares out of the window. There is the occasional rattle of
rifle-fire from outside.*

ROISIN. When do you tink will Mickser come?

PALLISER. What makes you think he'll come at all?

ROISIN. He'll come.

EMER (*to the* VOLUNTEER). There now. Is that easier?

ROISIN. The fire is the worst this side a the street. It'll be up here
before long.

PALLISER. Then you'd better be going. We need no virgins on this
burning deck.

ROISIN. I wouldn't go without a word a Mickser.

PALLISER (*ending his playing*).
     Weep not for Ferdia, trusting bride.
     He lies embattled by the ford,
     Drunk with the bloodied waters of the Grand Canal.

ROISIN (*to the* VOLUNTEER). Did ye hear any news a the men at the
bridge?

EMER. Don't be bothering him with questions. You'll hear soon
enough.

ROISIN. If owney I knew what's keepin' him.

PALLISER. Here's someone coming now.

ROISIN (*excited*). Where?

     (MACCARTHY *appears from the kitchen with more bottles,
     which he places proudly on the counter, in full view.*)

ROISIN (*disappointed*). Ah, it's owney him.

150

MACCARTHY. Only me! What more did you expect, woman? King William the Third on a camel? You should shout 'Hooray! ' The MacCarthy Mor is still on his feet. (*He counts the bottles.*) A few more beakers full of the warm south.

(EMER *is noticeably less hostile towards* MACCARTHY, *and even gives him the flicker of a frosty smile.*)

EMER. So you've been looting again?

MACCARTHY. 'Salvaging in Wynn's Hotel' would be a nicer expression. Everything seems to be on fire. Let me see what you've been doing to that man.

(*He goes swiftly to the stretcher and begins a businesslike examination.*)

EMER. I suppose you can't help it. You're made that way.

MACCARTHY. Mm. Not bad, my love. Give me another dressing. How did he get this?

EMER. Fighting his way back from Mount Street. They've been fighting there for over two days.

MACCARTHY. As if anybody could be unaware of Mount Street. Mm. You seem to have done this quite well. Yes, very well. (*Rising.*) It has come to my attention, sister, that you can be a ministering angel in spite of a forbidding bedside manner.

EMER. You're not so bad yourself – in spite of some other things I won't mention. (*She smiles.*)

MACCARTHY. My God! A smile from Granuaile. Fellow, we're both going to pull through! The sun has come out on this blood-red evening. What about a little refreshment all round?

PALLISER (*promptly*). Yes, please.

EMER. Why do you have to spoil it all with drink? Nobody's supposed to touch that.

MACCARTHY (*opening bottles*). That is one of the seamier sides of this uprising. Do you know, some idiot locked up the bar of the Coliseum Theatre, as a result of which the entire contents have gone up in smoke! Bismarck was right. He said that the Irish and the Dutch ought to swop countries. In a few years – he said – the Dutch would make a garden out of Ireland, and the Irish would begin to neglect the dykes.

(*He hands round glasses.* ROISIN *and* EMER *refuse.*)

EMER. No thanks. You know my views.

MACCARTHY. After all I've been through to bring a hiccough to those rose-red lips! (*To the* VOLUNTEER, *who is hesitating about accepting.*) Doctor's orders. (*Then, taking a glass himself.*) Still . . . a Pearl of great price. However desperate the situation, she always manages to look as if she's just had a nice cup of tea. Why can't you be a little craven from time to time, if only to keep me company?

EMER. As a coward you're as big a fraud as ever.

MACCARTHY. But I *am* a coward! I am. Fear is such a healthy emotion. If only we could manage to be afraid together, we would both be in each other's arms for all time.

EMER. A nice ambition.

MACCARTHY. We must have met before – maybe in some past existence, half a hundred guilts ago. And now we have so little time left.

Swift speedy Time, feathered with flying hours
Dissolves the beauty of the fairest flowers.

EMER. You must be a terrible trial to your poor wife.

MACCARTHY. Is this a moment to bring her up? Under your left breast you keep a heart. Does it never beat a fraction faster when I appear? Or don't you like me at all?

EMER. I don't dislike you.

MACCARTHY. Come on. Be specific. Mention just one of the things you like about me.

EMER. I don't see why I should.

MACCARTHY. Because it would be good for my morale. Just one little thing. Do you like my nice white teeth, for instance.

EMER. They're all right.

MACCARTHY. They damn well ought to be. They cost me thirty-five pounds. Do you like my hair?

EMER. Ah, will you stop this nonsense.

MACCARTHY. That, at least, is genuine. Would you like me to give you a lock of it?

(*He picks up a pair of scissors*).

EMER (*indignantly*). I would not!

MACCARTHY (*disappointed*). You don't want a lock of my hair?

PALLISER. If she won't have it, I will.

MACCARTHY. No, sir. To have one of these you have to be not only civil but sober.

PALLISER. You flatter yourself that I could ever get drunk on what you provide.

MACCARTHY. If you don't like what we have in stock, you can take your custom somewhere else. You don't find me sitting around here, like an accident waiting for somewhere to happen.

PALLISER. Dammit, I've got a crack in my knee.

MACCARTHY. And ants in your pants. Well, anything you've got, you

152

must have brought in with you. These premises are inspected annually by the Corporation.

(MAGINNIS *enters from the street, covered with dirt and glory.*)

ROISIN (*running to him*). Mickser, yer back!

MACCARTHY. Is this a moment for clichés?

ROISIN. What happened to ya?

MAGINNIS (*exalted*). We fought them at the bridge since Wensda afternoon. Seven of us.

EMER. Against hundreds.

MAGINNIS. I dunno how many. We weren't countin'.

EMER (*with grim satisfaction*). But there's fewer now.

(*She turns to the wounded man and works on one of his dressings.*)

MAGINNIS (*transported*).

Like the sea on the beach at Bray,
Wave after wave lappin' the bridge
Then rollin' back an' comin' on agin.
Water that knows no better.
Brown breakers turnin' red,
An' bayonets flashin' in the sun.
They flung Mills bombs inta the garden of the house,
Roarin' bloody murder.
We fought from twelve till dusk
Dodgin' from winda te winda
With the Tommies' bullets playin' chunes in the pianna,
Till the fire druve us up over the roofs
And behind the chimney pots.
The gun was red-hot in me hands
An' I cooled it off with oil from a tin a sardines.
The smoke'd catch me by the troat
And tear the eyeballs from me face.
But it was them went back – not us . . .
Back, an then on agin,
Till all the terrace was a hell a flames
And the lead was rain runnin' from the gutters.

ROISIN. Glory be to God, how could flash an' blood stand the like a that?

MAGINNIS (*matter of fact*). I declare te God, I dunno. I wudden' reckernize meself.

ROISIN. It woulda put the heart across me. Were ye not scared te death?

MAGINNIS. At first I was scared, Roisin . . . scared that I was goin' to be afeared. D'ye know. But when it all got goin', I forgot. An' then when I remembered, I sez to meself, 'Begob, I forgot to be scared.' An' at that, God forgive me, I started to laugh, an' the most unholy joy come over me, for I knew then I was a soljer, an' nuttin' could ever take that from me. (*Pause.*) Has no one got a Woodbine?

EMER. Here. Take the package.

(*He lights up, as* MACCARTHY *pours out a bottle of stout.*)

MACCARTHY. You shall have more than a Woodbine, Mickser. You shall drink a flask of your own family beverage – Gwine's Twenty.

MAGINNIS. What the hell is that?

MACCARTHY. You probably only know it by the Milesian pronunciation. Maginnis is the more ancient and honourable form of the name.

(*He holds out the glass, which* MICKSER *takes.*)

MAGINNIS. I'll have it, begob, Pioneer or not.

MACCARTHY. Let nobody stop you. And after we have drunk, we will dally with the women.

ROISIN. You'll what?

MACCARTHY. Girl, do you not know that nature devised you to be the recreation of the warrior?

ROISIN. A nice warrior you are!

MACCARTHY. If I am not in Mickser's class, I am the next best thing – a bard.

(*The piano is heard off, playing Debussy's Piano Duet, 'Minuet'.*)

PALLISER. There she is again!

(*He joins with her in the duet.*)

MACCARTHY. Dance with your doxey, Mickser, while I describe her bosom in a *villanelle*.

ROISIN. Me what?

MACCARTHY. Your . . .

ROISIN. Never mind, if it's what I tought I heard.

MACCARTHY. Here, there are no such things as bosoms. The female frontispiece is only a plaque for medals, holy and Celidhe. (*To* EMER.) Well, shall I ignore anatomy and write about Cuchulain's much neglected bride?

EMER (*ignoring him, to the* VOLUNTEER). Are you comfortable now?

MACCARTHY. I can do it through the medium, if you insist, *acushla geal mochree*, my admirable *Feis Ceoil*, my darling little *Cruis-*

154

keen Lawn. You see, I am a native speaker. (ENDYMION *appears
from the street.*) Oh, go to hell, Endymion!

ENDYMION.

      Is this the last dance?
      Then may I have the pleasure?

EMER (*to* MACCARTHY). These are no times for foolery.

MACCARTHY. These times are fortunate – honoured above all other
times in being ours. Be brave. My wife will never know our
secret.

PALLISER. Your wife can find your secret written up in privies.

MACCARTHY. Pay no attention to the licentious soldiery. (*As he
turns away.*) Oh very well. Nobody cares.

    (*He claps his hand to his brow, and moves off in the throes of
composition. Meanwhile* ENDYMION *has commenced a grave
and dignified minuet with an invisible partner.*)

ENDYMION.

      Goodbye, my love.
      Familiar things must now be put away.
      Hard-riding squires
      Drink the last stirrup-cup of power.
      Another lordship's here to stay.

PALLISER (*as he plays*). Ladies to the centre.

ENDYMION.

      Spring's a raw season,
      Boisterous with words we do not know.
      We must pack up forbidden memories
      With the court suits of dead solicitors,
      And send the bundles to the prop rooms.

PALLISER. Swing your partners. Bow and retire.

ENDYMION.

The April wind blows cold on royalty,
Swift, Grattan, Sheridan, Wellington and Wilde,
Levees on Cork Hill,
The tramp of crimson sentries in the colonnade.
No more of Suvla Bay or Spion Kop.
The bunting under which we spilled our colours on the globe
Shall hang in gaunt cathedrals
Where no one goes.

    (PALLISER *suddenly crashes his hands on the piano in a loud
discord.*)

PALLISER. Be off, old zany. Who wants to hear your prophecies?

    (*He breaks into a jig-tune, drowning out the playing from the*

next room. ENDYMION *stops dancing and surveys* PALLISER
before speaking.)

ENDYMION.

You changed the tune –
Tired of the other, I suppose.

(PALLISER *stops playing, and* MISS GARRITY *is heard again.*)

PALLISER. About time too. I've had enough of you and old Miss
Garrity.

ENDYMION.

And tired, beyond all thinking, of ourselves,
A paradox that nobody
Will ever understand.
So, let us make our bows together –
Baron Hardup, the Prince and Cinderella.

PALLISER, I'll make my bow when I choose.

ENDYMION (*placing a hand on* PALLISER.)

This is my beloved son
Who sees more ways from Sackville Street than one.
So take the road, my lad,
With my permission and my Gaes –
That when you go, you never let them see you run.

(*There is an outburst of rifle-fire from outside. All freeze for
a moment.* ROISIN *with her head on* MICKSER'S *shoulder.
The piano next door has stopped.*)

PALLISER (*noticing the silence*). She's stopped.

ENDYMION. Carriages at midnight.

(*He bows and stalks from the room by the kitchen.* TETLEY
carries in O'CALLAGHAN *from the street. The latter's tunic is
splashed with blood, and his eyes are closed.* MACCARTHY *and*
EMER *spring to his assistance, and the wounded man is laid
on the floor.*

MACCARTHY. Here, let me take him.

MAGINNIS. What happened to him?

TETLEY (*serious, but not too emotionally*). We were running across
the street – more than half way over before they opened fire. He
was just in front of me when I noticed the little hole in the back
of his tunic. Suddenly there. Just a little hole. But he kept on
running – ten – fifteen – twenty steps, before he seemed to
realize what had happened. Then I caught him just as he was
falling, and carried him the rest of the way over. Is he gone?

MACCARTHY. No. But it won't be long. Water – quick!

(ROISIN *brings a glass of water and holds it to* O'CALLAGHAN'S

156

lips. PALLISER *strikes a chord on the piano, and listens for the answer. There is none.*)

PALLISER. I think . . . Miss Garrity's . . . in trouble too.

MACCARTHY (*to* EMER). Do you know an Act of Contrition? (*He rises and crosses to the bar, his hand over his eyes.*) I wouldn't trust myself . . . to remember it.

(PALLISER *strikes another chord, and listens.* EMER *whispers into* O'CALLAGHAN'S *ear. He opens his eyes and smiles.*)

ROISIN (*to* PALLISER). Sssh! Is this a time to be playin'?

O'CALLAGHAN. Don't stop him. Why are you all so . . . glum.

ROISIN. Don't try to talk. Let you listen to the Act of Contrition.

O'CALLAGHAN. I've said it myself . . . every day . . . for the past year. I'm ready.

MACCARTHY. Then you knew?

O'CALLAGHAN. I knew. If it wasn't this . . . it'd be . . . something else. Ah, cheer up, for God's sake. Look at Sean there. He knows who's . . . well off.

TETLEY. You think so?

O'CALLAGHAN (*gathering strength for a little*). It was a . . . good fight. Why don't you play something, Don Quixote? Are you in mourning for your horse?

PALLISER. Are you addressing me?

O'CALLAGHAN. Yes. I'm surprised to find you haven't run away.

PALLISER. You never told me I could go.

O'CALLAGHAN. As a soldier, you never used to have much difficulty . . . about breaking your word.

PALLISER. As a soldier who never carried any ammunition, you needn't be so smug.

ROISIN (*angrily*). That's no way to talk to . . . to a . . .

PALLISER. To a dying man. Why not?

ROISIN (*astounded*). You oughta have some respect. Is this a time for spite?

O'CALLAGHAN (*with a grin*). No, don't be spiteful, Captain. Just one thing . . . I'd like to let you know.

PALLISER. Well?

O'CALLAGHAN. I had ammunition . . . plenty of it.

PALLISER (*surprised*). Then why didn't you shoot?

O'CALLAGHAN. I'm glad . . . I didn't. I'd be thinking of him . . . now . . . if I'd killed him. Now I can . . .

PALLISER. Leave thinking to others? If you mean me, don't speak too soon. I haven't run yet.

157

O'CALLAGHAN (*sinking fast*). Bet you . . . I'll be here . . . after . . . you . . .

> (*He closes his eyes.* MACCARTHY *returns swiftly for a brief examination.*)

EMER. Is he gone? (MACCARTHY *nods. The Catholics cross themselves.*) May God grant peace to his great soul.

> (*They all rise except* PALLISER. MACCARTHY *goes behind the bar to have another drink.* EMER *goes to the window, and looks out.*)

ROISIN (*looking down at* O'CALLAGHAN). What's he smilin' at?

PALLISER (*savagely*). Why wouldn't he smile? He was going to die, and he knew it. We're all going to die, only we don't know it.

ROISIN (*softly*). Is it always like that?

TETLEY. I'd like to think so.

ROISIN (*turning on* EMER). It's all your doin'. But for you it mighta been over a Tuesda.

EMER. Keep out of this.

ROISIN (*shrilly*). I'll not keep out of it. Wasn't it you that fired that gun?

EMER. You know nothing about it.

ROISIN. But for you there's many a man would be still alive.

EMER (*contemptuously*). Alive for what?

PALLISER. Ah, leave her alone.

ROISIN. She fired the gun an' she supposed te be a nurse. What kind of a woman is that? Drivin' men te slaughter an' the flames. She fired it.

TETLEY. Maybe she did. But how did it get fixed in the first place? (*Pause while all eyes but* EMER'S *turn on* PALLISER.) Can you help us, Captain?

PALLISER (*to* ROISIN). Why are you glaring at me? I'm not the one you used to glare at.

ROISIN. It was you that fixed it. Why?

PALLISER. Why? Because . . . because Montaigne tells us that a glass of water night and morning is the best cure for constipation.

MACCARTHY (*gloomily*). That is not at all certain. (*He returns to his drink.*)

ROISIN. You did it because you didn't want the trouble to be ended. You wanted to see them all slaughtered.

EMER. You're a fool, girl. Why can't you keep your mouth shut?

ROISIN. Because I'm sick a killin', that's why.

PALLISER (*looking at* O'CALLAGHAN). Even the killing of killers?

ROISIN. Who did he ever kill? He was a better man than any a youse.

PALLISER. We always are, once we're in his condition. Strange . . . this importance of the dead.

ROISIN. Will ya stop sneerin'! I've just seen a man die for his country – his country an' mine.

PALLISER. And so you're going to change your views about the whole business?

ROISIN. What de ye expec'? Oh, I dunno what to tink.

(*She turns away to* MICKSER, *covering her face with her hands.*)

PALLISER. A pity that it wasn't me. I like my country too.

TETLEY. Captain Palliser, I hope we all like our country, however differently we may express it. I suppose you've heard you have a new commanding officer?

PALLISER. No. Who's that?

TETLEY. He landed this morning in the small hours. I don't know his name, but they say he's a soldier of the old school.

MACCARTHY. I know all about him. He was out in Egypt defending the Suez Canal. Only nobody told him who his opponents were, so he arranged matters to have the Canal defend him.

TETLEY. Yes, I think that's the man.

MACCARTHY. It's a damn scandal, that's what it is. We're entitled to a sledgehammer and they send us an oats-crusher. Another injustice to Ireland.

TETLEY. We hear, however, that he's very stern. The situation requires measures of the utmost severity.

PALLISER. Oh, God.

MACCARTHY. There *are* some acute Saxons, but these obtuse Angles are all we ever get over here. (*Pause.*) Personally, I thought that rather a good remark. I suppose you'll laugh at it next year.

PALLISER (*despairingly*). No, we laughed at it last year.

TETLEY. Dr MacCarthy, I really think we've had enough of you. Do you suppose you could get that wounded man out of here, to a place of safety?

MACCARTHY. Over to the Post Office . . . from the fire into the frying pan?

TETLEY. No. To Jervis Street Hospital. We've evacuated the Post Office, and broken our way through to the small shops in Moore Street. That's what we came over to warn you about. The Post Office has become quite untenable.

PALLISER. It was untenable from the start. I could have told you that.

TETLEY. It served us well enough against cavalry charges. But you see how we're all learning from experience. Maginnis will help you with the stretcher, and somebody else had better take that Red Cross flag.

MAGINNIS (*finishing his stout*). You'll need me in Moore Street.

TETLEY. Yes, you'll be needed Maginnis, but not in Moore Street. These are your instructions. You're to dump your equipment, and after you've got your man to the hospital, you will retire from these operations altogether, and keep out of internment if you can. (*With a smile.*) In particular, avoid being identified by Captain Palliser. It's absolutely essential that as many men as possible should remain at large. Is that understood?

MAGINNIS. You mean, this isn't the end?

TETLEY. I mean that it's up to you to see that it's only the beginning. Report to a Staff Captain Collins.

MAGINNIS (*delighted*). Come on youse.

ROISIN. I'll carry the flag.

(*He salutes, and* TETLEY *returns his salute.* ROISIN *takes* TETLEY'S *hand, and kisses it fervently, much to his embarrassment.* MACCARTHY *and* MAGINNIS *pick up the stretcher, and carry it out, following* ROISIN, *who carries the flag.* EMER *goes to the window to watch.*)

MACCARTHY (*as they go*). Now don't push me. You know I'm a very nervous man. It's all due to a governess who gave me complexes by insisting that I wear button boots when I was three. Ever since then whenever I see a button . . .

(*There is no firing as they go.*)

PALLISER. So there's going to be more fighting?

TETLEY. Yes, Captain. But of a different kind. We live – some of us – and learn.

PALLISER. From behind hedges, I suppose. You'll never get to the Peace Conference with that kind of fighting.

TETLEY. Oh who cares about the Peace Conference. That's just another illusion we're well rid of. The boys who come through this will have to do their own fighting. Only next time it will not be strictly in accordance with the rules.

PALLISER. I thought you loved the rules.

TETLEY. Somebody told me once, that the sign of a good soldier is his readiness to disregard the rules in an intelligent way. The

160

boys will be better at that than we of the older generation. By the way, I hope they got across!

EMER (*turning from the window*). They got across. Are you not going yourself?

TETLEY. Yes. But only on my way to another destination.

EMER. Where's that?

TETLEY. The Post Office has served its purpose. I had intended to stop in it till the end, but I've since thought that maybe we can win this war after all.

EMER. What do you mean?

TETLEY. Now that Captain Palliser has a new commanding officer, there's a better use I can make of the last few days of my life than by being burnt to death like a rat. So we're going to surrender.

EMER (*horrified*). Surrender! But if you do that they'll only hang you!

TETLEY (*with grave simplicity*). Yes. I hope I can face up to it. I think I can.

PALLISER (*disturbed*). That's not a soldier's end.

TETLEY. Then maybe you were right, Captain. Maybe I'm not much of a soldier after all. (*Then with a slight smile.*) Perhaps I'm something more significant.

PALLISER. You needn't think you'll get off, after this week's work.

TETLEY. If I thought there was any danger of that, I'd take the pleasanter course and fight it out. But this new man of yours seems to be quite a hangman. He'll hang the entire Provisional Government. He'll hang innocents for being related to us. He'll probably take the wounded from hospital and hang them too. There'll be court martial after court martial, and you, Captain Palliser, will be subpoenaed, I'm afraid, as a star witness for the Crown.

PALLISER (*grimly*). Indeed! So that's the role you've picked for me.

TETLEY. It's not my casting, Captain. It's Heaven that provides us with our roles in this fantastic pantomime.

PALLISER. Well Heaven can't ballyrag me. I pick my own parts.

TETLEY. I'm afraid you can hardly get out of it. And I'm sorry; because you did us a great service once.

PALLISER. *I* did?

TETLEY. Of course. I know who fixed that machine-gun. I believe you did it because you didn't want to see your countrymen climb down without putting up a good fight.

161

PALLISER (*vehemently*). I did it for no such melodramatic reason. (*He glares at* EMER *before turning back to* TETLEY.) And if you're proposing to thank me for anything, I shall take it as a damned impertinence.

TETLEY. Then why did you do it?

PALLISER. For no reason that I intend to discuss with you.

TETLEY. Why? Are you ashamed of what you've done?

PALLISER. Who wants to be thanked for letting himself be talked into playing the other fellow's game? But we always do. (*Gloomily.*) We deserve whatever's coming to us.

TETLEY (*shaking his head*). Look at him. I believe he's suffering from some absurd sense of guilt over having acted like an Irishman.

PALLISER. You go to hell.

EMER. Be careful Sean. He'll be crowing over you if you surrender now.

PALLISER (*lying viciously*). Yes, I'll crow! Cock-a-doodle-do!

TETLEY. I don't think so, Emer. You saw how that shopgirl behaved over poor O'Callaghan. What will she feel – what will the nation feel – when fifteen or twenty of us have been treated to what will be called our 'just deserts'?

EMER. But he mustn't be let feel that he's won.

PALLISER. No! Don't let me feel that!

TETLEY. I am not concerned with what the enemy feels . . . any more than with the Peace Conference . . . now. What matters to me is that this week can be turned from a disgrace into a triumph – that all our mistakes and incompetence can be made of no importance whatever by giving ourselves up to some fool of a general.

EMER. But how do you know it will end that way? This has got to be your triumph, not his. (*She points at* PALLISER.) You mustn't weaken now.

TETLEY (*with a wry smile*). I wish to God it was weakening, but it's not. If you will do something for me now, you'll soon see how it will work out.

EMER (*aghast at what she knows is coming*). *I'm* to?

TETLEY. Yes. I want you to go out with a white flag, and offer your commanding officer to that general.

EMER (*passionately*). No! It's unnatural! Let the others climb down if they have to, but let you and me stop in the Post Office.

TETLEY (*firmly*). No, Emer. We can do better than that. If he offers you any terms, we may have to fight on. But if he insists on

162

unconditional surrender, bring me back the good news at once to Moore Street. I shall be over there, trying to convince the others.

EMER (*bursting into silent tears*). No! I'll carry no white flag.

TETLEY. My dear, I know what I'm doing. (*Surprised.*) And crying does not become you.

EMER. Your dear! Don't call me that. You'd never ask me to do such a thing if you didn't know that it's never been true.

TETLEY (*puzzled*). What has never been true? (*She turns away her head.*) I don't understand. (*Pause.*) Do you want me to ask one of the other ladies to oblige? (*Pause.*) Well at any rate will you wish me good luck and goodbye?

(*He holds out his hand, but she turns away abruptly, pausing for a moment to glare at* PALLISER, *before going out by the kitchen. The smell of smoke begins to become noticeable.*)

EMER. No. But I'm ready to wish *him* goodbye.

PALLISER. Me?

EMER. I think *we've* managed to look Azrael in the face. What about you?

TETLEY. What are you two talking about?

PALLISER (*meeting her eye, gravely*). Quite a killer. Mm.

EMER. Now's *your* chance to turn wind into wonderment.

PALLISER. Fair enough. (*Pause. Then suddenly.*) Goodbye.

EMER. We'll see if it's goodbye.

(*She goes.* PALLISER *stares after her. Then he gives a little mirthless laugh.*)

TETLEY. Some women can never understand politics.

PALLISER. Some men can never understand women. I wonder which is the more ignorant.

TETLEY. This is hardly the time for enigmas, Captain. Let me help you to a place of safety before I go.

PALLISER. No, thanks.

TETLEY. I smell smoke. Come along. I can carry you if necessary.

PALLISER (*louder*). No, thanks.

TETLEY. But the fire will be here in five or ten minutes.

PALLISER. Will you kindly mind your own business and allow me to mind mine?

TETLEY. What's the idea? Are you proposing to commit suicide?

PALLISER. I have no such second-rate ambitions. I leave those to your sort.

TETLEY (*offended*). A prisoner of war who is judicially murdered does not commit suicide.

163

PALLISER. You don't have to be murdered. In fact, I'll give you a fair offer. If you'll undertake to let me save your life, I'll give you the satisfaction of saving mine.

TETLEY. You mean, I'm to join in some lies, that you will tell at the court martial?

PALLISER. Yes.

TETLEY (*indignantly*). I shall do nothing of the sort.

PALLISER. O.K. Off you go, then.

TETLEY (*distressed*). I've *got* to go through with this. Can't you see? But you've got nothing to die for by stopping here.

PALLISER. And nothing to live for except the honour of playing Judas to your Jesus. What do you take me for?

TETLEY. A professional in the service of the big battalions. Your own choice.

PALLISER. If you think I'm going to be a witness at your apotheosis you can think again. I've made you a fair offer, and if you won't take it, you can be the fellow who runs. Not me.

TETLEY. What earthly good will that do you?

PALLISER. It will show you and that bitch who's killing you for not marrying her that there are other people who understand as much about death as you do. And there's no pie in the sky to make it any easier for us.

TETLEY. So that's at the back of it! Palliser, you're a fool. It's not me she's killing, but you. If this is just a matter of showing off, I'm at least doing something the world will know about. But if you stop here until the building collapses, nobody will know about it except me.

PALLISER. Thank you. I shall know about it myself.

TETLEY (*after considering him for a moment*). And this is the fellow who had the nerve to call me pompous for knowing my own mind. I would never have believed in such vanity. But don't think that you can bully me out of my destiny. I warn you that if you insist, I shall leave you this bonfire for whatever satisfaction you can get from it.

PALLISER. Goodbye.

(TETLEY *goes to the door, and turns.*)

TETLEY. Listen, Palliser, I know that you people have a pride in your past. But isn't it our turn now?

PALLISER (*softening*). Of course it is. I know what's coming, and there's no hard feelings so long as I don't have to be part of the audience. When we built an Empire, Tetley, we didn't have much in the way of big battalions. But we had life and an

164

interest in ourselves. Now we're tired of being what we are, and we play the other fellow's game because we're sick of winning. I see it all as if it had happened already. Ireland's only the start. We're going to go on winning every war, but piece by piece we're going to give it all away – not because we're licked, but because we're bloody well bored. So don't be too proud of yourselves. It won't be the first time that people like you have loosened the foundations of a civilization – and at Easter too, by gad. You'll have it in chains again, as you had it before. But not me.

TETLEY. In chains? We, who are fighting for liberty?

PALLISER (*with a smile*). You don't give a damn about liberty. All you care about is a cause. And causes always let you down. Your admirers will find that out before they've finished.

TETLEY (*after a pause*). Perhaps it's just as well you won't be around. I think I shall defeat your general, but I must admit that in some ways you defeat me. Well, I must go now.

PALLISER. You'll walk across, I suppose. Just to show off.

TETLEY. No. I shall run like hell, as any soldier should. I've got a better use for my life than that.

PALLISER. You ought to walk. It'll come to the same thing in the end.

TETLEY. It may be the same end, but it will not be the same thing.

PALLISER. They're rotten shots. I know. I taught them.

TETLEY (smiling). I don't think I'll risk it all the same. Goodbye, Julian Imperator.

(*He salutes.* PALLISER *turns away abruptly and stares out of the window. With a little shrug of the shoulders,* TETLEY *leaves. When he has gone,* PALLISER *turns round and salutes.*)

PALLISER. See you shortly, Commandant General.

TETLEY (*off*). Thanks. I heard you.

PALLISER. Eavesdropper! Listener at doors! (*He returns to the window.*) Don't run, cowardy custard. Blast it, don't run. Shoot you fools, shoot! Not a bloody shot! (*Shots.*) Ah! Oh damn, damn, damn! He's got across. I always knew those musketry courses were no damn good.

(*From next door, the piano is heard once again, leading up to the crashing finale of Ravel's 'Le Jardin Feerique'.*)

PALLISER. Well I'll be . . . ! (*He turns to the body of* O'CALLAGHAN.) You hear, my friend? We're neither of us the last to go. (*He shakes his head.*) Winter gives back the roses to the frost-filled earth.

(*He goes to the piano, and joins in his part of the duet. For a time they play, as the glow of the fire grows deeper. Then there is a crash and the other piano stops.* PALLISER *continues alone. Presently the central pillar falls with a shower of plaster.* PALLISER *is still continuing to play as the Curtain slowly falls. That is the end of this play.*)

SOUTH HADLEY, 1957

STORM SONG

A Play in Three Acts

The original version of *Storm Song* was first produced at the Dublin Gate Theatre on January 30th, 1934, with the following cast:

Gordon King	NIALL MACGINNIS
Bob Bristow	EDWARD LEXY
Bride	RIA MOONEY
Jennifer Joyce	CORALIE CARMICHAEL
Deirdre Dobbs	SHELAH RICHARDS
The Earl of Clanbrassil	JACK DWAN
Martin Burke	JOHN IRWIN
The Captain	LANDON SORRELL
Alf Quilt	CYRIL CUSACK
Raymond Chenevix	RAYMOND PERCY
Szilard	HILTON EDWARDS
Paudeen	SEAMUS HEALY
Innkeeper	ART O'MURNAGHAN
Micheal	ROBERT HENNESSY
Commissionaire	LIONEL DYMOKE
Telegraph Boy	LESLIE COLLING-MUDGE
Maysie Bristow	BETTY CHANCELLOR

Men of the Islands, People of the City, and Mr Solberg: Messrs O'Connor, Monson, Byrne, Cotter, Kelly, O'Toole, Cassidy, Fassbender, Devoy and Collins, and Misses Hayes, Delany, McConnell, Clancy, Cox, Monson, Hill, Molloy, Lynch and N. Delany.

Production directed by Hilton Edwards.
Settings by Micheál MacLiammóir.

168

CHARACTERS

BOB BRISTOW

GORDON KING

RAYMOND CHENEVIX

SZILARD

DEIRDRE DOBBS

THE EARL OF CLANBRASSIL

MARTIN BURKE

JAL JOYCE

ALF QUILT

THE CAPTAIN of the Steamer

MICHEAL MÓR ⎫
SIBBY   ⎬ *Islanders*
MAGGIE'S BARTLEY ⎮
PAUDEEN   ⎭

MR COLLINS (*Tony's butler*)

THE COMMISSIONAIRE

THE TELEGRAPH BOY

MAYSIE BRISTOW

SOLBERG

Men and Women of the Islands and People of the City

The action of the play takes place on the seaboard of the North Atlantic, and also in London.

ACT I   Scene 1   The pier at Inishgarve, one of the Crioch Islands. Shortly after noon on a day in late September.

ACT II   Scene 1   The living-room at Szilard's house, Tigh na Beith. Late afternoon on the same day.

          Scene 2   Tony's house on the Mainland of Tyrcluain. Late afternoon, two days later.

ACT III   Scene 1   Szilard's living-room. Before dawn, on the following morning.

          Scene 2   The Foyer of the Majestic Cinema, London. After midnight, about two months later.

ACT I

The play opens outside Szilard's cottage, Tigh na Beith. The scenery is wild and rocky with the sea in the background, across which, about eight miles away, we can see the mainland, faintly studded with white cottages, behind which rises a group of mountain peaks. To the left is the whitewashed front of Szilard's house. It has a long, low window, a half-door and a thatched roof, while, somewhat incongruously, it is wired for electricity. The wires cross the stage to a squat, grey limestone building upon the other side, originally intended as a fisherman's store, but which is now fitted up as a laboratory. In the centre there is a rocky foreshore leading to a small pier, from which a flight of steps leads down out of sight to the water. On the pier there is a stone bollard, a pile of turf and some lobster pots and fishermen's nets. Outside the laboratory are a couple of stone jars for chemicals, while on the flat roof, to which a ladder leads, stands a cinematograph camera on a tripod. A portable gramophone which stands upon a rock at one side of the stage is playing a jig, while from the far side of the rocks we can hear the sound of shuffling feet, chatter and laughter. Inside the cottage somebody is apparently practising a phrase of some folk melody upon a violin. BOB BRISTOW comes out of the laboratory with a receptacle in his hands. It is the magazine of a movie-camera. He climbs the ladder to the roof and proceeds to load the camera, singing 'O sole mio' as he works. As, however, these are the only three words of the song that he knows, he keeps lustily repeating them. From the window of the cottage GORDON KING'S voice is heard.

GORDON. Musical this morning! Enough of that. Hey, enough of that!

BOB. What say, Gordon?

    (*GORDON KING comes out of the cottage. He is wearing dirty grey flannel trousers and a short-sleeved shirt open at the*

171

neck. Strips of cinematograph film are hanging around his neck.)

GORDON. How the hell do you expect anybody to work with this filthy racket going on? Shut up, Bulgy!

BOB. It's only a few of the locals having a dance. Must say I enjoy watching them.

GORDON. It's your own contribution that gets me down.

BOB. Well, it's another lovely morning and the post arrives today. Gosh, I feel good! (*He bursts into song once more.*)

GORDON. As for Romping Raymond practising his fiddle in there! Any sign of the boat yet?

BOB. I saw her leaving Inishmeadhon when I was up at the cistern. She should almost be in by now. Yes, there's her smoke.

GORDON. No more trippers, please God. I suppose it's getting a bit late in the year for them.

BOB. You'd never think it was the end of September. You can see the white cottages across there in Tyrcluain and the surf breaking all round Belgata. Gosh, what a summer it has been!

GORDON. Too damn good for Szilard's liking.

(BOB *sings again. The violin has stopped and* RAYMOND CHENEVIX *comes out of the cottage carrying the instrument and some manuscript music in his hand.*)

CHENEVIX. I wonder would you mind making a little less noise!

BOB. What say?

CHENEVIX. I'm trying to take down the notation of a folk tune from old Trady and its exceedingly difficult in the circumstances to hear him hum.

BOB. Him what?

CHENEVIX. Hum!

GORDON. Ha. Too bad, old man.

CHENEVIX. Thank you. I just thought I'd mention it.

BOB. Righty-ho! Come and see us again sometime.

(CHENEVIX *turns and goes back into the cottage upon which* GORDON *and* BOB *both break out into* 'O sole mio'. CHENEVIX *returns, opens his mouth as if to speak, thinks better of it and goes off once more, after petulantly throwing down some of his music on the ground. His playing is heard no longer.*)

GORDON. Naughty, naughty!

(*An islander appears, and stops the gramophone. He is a fine, upstanding, bearded man in the forties.*)

BOB. Had enough, Micheal?

MICHEAL MÓR. We'd have a right to be going now, Mr Bristow, for

172

to get the curraghs on the water. The steamer is in sight around the point. Thank you kindly, sir, for the loan of this instrument.

BOB. Always glad to play for you (*to* GORDON) You wouldn't like to hear a record or two yourself?

GORDON. There's nothing I'd like less.

BOB. Oh well, another time, perhaps. Put it in the cottage, Micheal. Good morning all!

(MICHEAL *carries the gramophone into the cottage as a number of islanders of both sexes enter and pass across the stage, exchanging kindly greetings and thanks with* BOB *and* GORDON.)

GORDON. Isn't there some fellow coming out today from the London office?

BOB. Yes. They sent a telegram on Monday about him. Solberg is sending him out to square up the books.

GORDON. That sounds sinister.

BOB. Yes. They're getting a bit uneasy, if you ask me. Think we've been out here long enough.

GORDON (*going back into the cottage and speaking out through the window*). God, don't I know it! I've been out here nine solid months myself. Nine months, with the mail only twice a week – weather permitting! I've almost forgotten what a policeman looks like. And as for a woman!

(BOB *comes down the ladder and meets* GORDON, *who emerges from the cottage with a reel of film in his hand, which he gives to* BOB. *He has discarded the film from around his neck.*)

BOB. Don't mention women, old man. That's why I'm here.

GORDON. This is ready for splicing. And look – I want a chemical mix wherever I've made a mark like this.

BOB (*looking at a strip of film*). I see.

GORDON. I wish to God Szilard would occasionally think of the matching up when he shoots. What the devil can you do with a sequence like that?

BOB. Oh, that will be all right. I can grade it in the next printing. But, I say, do you know you've put in some of these close-ups back to front?

GORDON. Of course I do. He shot them with the faces looking in the wrong direction, so I just turned them over to save a re-take. It's all right, isn't?

BOB. I'm not so sure. The emulsion will be on the wrong side. It may need an optical printer.

(He goes into the laboratory with the reel).

GORDON. Anyone who can work with Szilard and keep out of the lunatic asylum has my respect. Oh God, I'm just about exhausted! I hate this life. I'm going to chuck pictures altogether one of these days. Oh, by the way, did I tell you that I am applying for a job at the Institute?

BOB *(off)*. What Institute?

GORDON. The State Institute of Cinema in Moscow.

BOB *(emerging)*. Moscow! I say, you wouldn't go there, old man?

GORDON. Remind me to send the letter back by the boat.

BOB. All those Bolshies. Terrible. Free love and all that sort of thing. And no bath plugs either, they say.

GORDON. Oh well, who cares about bath plugs?

BOB. I knew a chap who went there once. Peculiar fellow of course. Very keen on all that sort of thing he was. But he soon had to come home. Couldn't stand the wild life in the blankets. Ordinary remedies no use at all, he told me. They have to use a specially strong stuff that goes off with a fizz.

GORDON. And above all I am sick and tired of these documentaries. God, what wouldn't I give for some roaring continental capital! Not a woman in sight since Christmas except Sibby and Bride and a language crank or two! That's not good for a boy like me.

BOB. Don't know about you, but it's good for me. I've mucked up that divorce of mine often enough.

GORDON. Canoe races this afternoon, aren't there? Suppose some ravishing thing from Shaftesbury Avenue were to drop in by that boat!

BOB. What for?

GORDON. Oh, to see me – and the races.

BOB. Bit of an optimist, aren't you?

GORDON. I don't believe I'd know what to say.

(Voices are heard off.)

BOB. Hullo, there's Szilard now.

GORDON. Have you everything ready? This light is perfect, and he sounds like business.

BOB. Oh damn, I suppose this will mean no lunch today. *(He looks at the sky.)* Please God, send a spot of rain before half-past two so that Bob can have his lunch.

SZILARD *(off)*. Don't stand around like a lot of blasted sheep. Get down to the shore and be quick about it! What good are you? You're brainless – hopeless! No damn use to me or to anybody

174

else. I hate the sight of you and you don't wash. Get down to
the rocks and spread the seaweed.

(*A few islanders run in and take up their positions on the
shore. They chatter to each other in Gaelic.*)

GORDON. Stormy weather!

(*He hurries into the cottage as* SZILARD *come down the path-
way in a whirl of energy.*)

SZILARD. Come along! Get ready, please. We can't idle around all
day. Where's the exposure metre? Is the camera loaded?

BOB (*handing* SZILARD *the metre as he climbs the ladder*). I've put
in about ninety feet. It's all we've got.

SZILARD. Another damn anti-cyclone! What's the weather coming
to out here? Nothing but semi-tropical days. Still, this light is
too good to lose, so let's re-take the drying of the kelp. Give me
the megaphone! The filters! Where the devil are you, Gordon?

(BOB *throws a megaphone up to* SZILARD *as* GORDON *runs out
of the cottage carrying a box of filters and lenses which he
carries up the ladder.* SZILARD *makes some rapid light tests,
followed by a few deft adjustments of the camera.*)

SZILARD. Now, you know what to do, everybody. You carry up the
seaweed and spread it out in the sun in your own way. You've
done it all before.

GORDON (*softly*). Only seventeen times.

(*There are murmurs of assent from the islanders.*)

BOB. Do you want any reflectors?

SZILARD. Get some light on the left side of the bollard if you can.

(BOB *runs to the cottage and emerges with a large reflector,
which he holds in the sunlight.*)

SZILARD (*to* GORDON, *who is handing him a lens*). Take it away. I
don't want a telephoto lens. Can't you see where the sun is?

GORDON. Shall I turn or will you do it yourself?

SZILARD. You turn this time.

(*There is a hoot from a steamship off.*)

GORDON. There's the steamer in the bay. If you don't watch out
we'll get some of those curraghs into the field.

SZILARD. The captain will be coming ashore today for the races.
Better offer him some lunch.

BOB (*mournfully, to himself*). Lunch! Once I used to have lunch!

GORDON (*hailing one of the curraghs through the megaphone*).
Micheal Mór! Tell the captain to come ashore for lunch!

(*There is a distant answer. One of the islanders turns.*)

ISLANDER. He can't hear you, Mr King, sir. He is too far out.

175

GORDON (*shouting*). Ahoy, Micheal!

SZILARD. Try Gaelic. One of you others tell him.

> (*The islander runs to the bollard and calls out.* SIBBY *comes out of the cottage.*)

ISLANDER (*shouting*). Abair leis an geaiptin theacht i dtir go bhfuigh' se a chuid dinneir!

SIBBY. Your dinner is on the table, Mr Szilard, sir. Will you kindly come down out of that and start to eat your food, there's a good man.

SZILARD. Now, get ready everybody! We're going to shoot right away. All set?

ISLANDERS. We are indeed, Mr Szilard, sir.

SZILARD. Then let's go. Camera!

> (*Some of the islanders commence to gather and to carry up baskets of seaweed from the lower rocks. The others receive it and spread it out to dry in the sun.* GORDON *cranks the camera.*)

SIBBY. Do you hear me now, Mr Szilard? And if you hear me, why do you not heed me?

SZILARD. That's all right, Sibby, the first thing first.

SIBBY. Your dinner is the first thing.

GORDON. Watch that curragh coming away from the ship. It will be into the field in a minute.

SZILARD. Cut! Hold it everybody!

> (GORDON *stops cranking. The islanders resume their original positions.*)

SZILARD. Who the devil are those people in that curragh? Get out of the field, blast you! Don't you see we are working? (*He seizes the megaphone and shouts.*) Get out of the eyeline, you goddam imbeciles! That's better. Now you men, let's do it again. And if those blasted trippers come near the steps while we're at it, pitch that turf at them with my compliments. Are you ready? I'll turn this time myself. Shoot!

> (*He starts to crank the camera himself as the islanders repeat their movements.*)

SIBBY. Will you come down when I tell you, Mr Szilard, and take your dinner. It's stone cold already and 'twill be time enough for you to go on with your play-acting in the afternoon. You think you can defy me because you know I can't climb a ladder, so you do.

> (SZILARD *stops cranking.*)

SZILARD. Cut! This camera is empty. Quickly, Bob, reload.

BOB (*putting down the reflector*). We've got no more.

SZILARD. No more what?

GORDON (*to the* ISLANDERS). Easy, boys.

BOB. No more stock. I told you I had only another ninety feet.

SZILARD. Do you mean to tell me that we have no more unexposed film?

BOB. Not an inch.

GORDON. They have been sending us nothing but short ends for the last three months.

SZILARD. Then why the devil haven't you written for more?

BOB. But I did – over three weeks ago. I asked for 7,000 feet, but they haven't replied yet.

SZILARD. Good God! What inefficiency! I give it up! I can rely on nobody. The light is going. And how the devil am I expected to finish a picture without film? When is it? Almost October. Do you realize it is almost October? We have been lucky with the light as it is. And now you stand there and tell me they haven't sent us any more stock!

GORDON. We've had nearly 100,000 feet already.

SZILARD. And what does that observation signify, may I ask?

GORDON. Oh, nothing.

BOB. Maybe this fellow from London office is bringing it out. He's due to arrive by this boat.

SZILARD. Ah, yes. I forgot. Hey, what the devil's going on down there?

(*At the pierhead one of the islanders is solemnly throwing sods of turf out to sea. At each throw shouts of indignation can be heard from an invisible boat approaching the steps.*)

SZILARD. What the devil do you think you are doing, Maggie's Bartley?

GORDON (*laughing*). Oh, good shot! Give the boy a coco-nut!

(*The young man at the pierhead turns and expostulates mildly in Gaelic.*)

BOB (*laughing*). He says you told him to throw turf if they came near the pier.

SZILARD. Stop that at once, Bartley. A nice way to treat visitors!

(*He climbs hastily down the ladder. There is a murmur of laughter and greeting from the pier.*)

BOB (*to* GORDON). Who are they?

GORDON. God knows. Trippers, I suppose. They seem a bit shaken.

(*He climbs down the ladder still laughing.*)

SZILARD. Oh, tut, tut! Too bad! Help the lady and the gentleman up the steps, Bartley. Come, come, we can't have any more of this tomfoolery!

SIBBY. How many of them are there? They'll all be wanting dinner, I'm thinking. Ah well, the creatures! Don't they deserve a bite after that kind of behaviour.

(DEIRDRE DOBBS *comes up the steps followed by* MARTIN BURKE *and the* EARL OF CLANBRASSIL. *She is distinctly shaken, and responds to the heartiness of* SZILARD'S *greeting with visible signs of nervousness. The Earl has apparently got something in his mouth.*)

DEIRDRE. Oh, dear! How very peculiar!

SZILARD. How do you do? I don't know who you are, but we're all delighted to see you. The turf was a pure mistake.

DEIRDRE. Thank you so much. We didn't quite understand. It's all right, Tony dear. We don't mind if you spit a little.

TONY. Thanks.

SZILARD. Pat him on the back, somebody.

(*They do, much to* TONY'S *discomfort.*)

DEIRDRE. It's so lucky he was dozing, don't you think? Otherwise he might have got a little bit in his eye, and that can be so painful.

SIBBY. 'Twould be better for him to keep his mouth closed.

SZILARD. Of course. Lay a lot more places, Sibby.

DEIRDRE. Oh, we couldn't dream of bothering you!

SIBBY (*going off to the cottage*). Didn't I say that would be the way of it? And the dinner destroyed entirely this half hour. Ah, well!

SZILARD. And which of you gentlemen is from London office?

DEIRDRE. I have a letter of introduction from Mr Solberg, the owner of your company. I met him at Fontainebleau, at the races. Let me see now, where is it?

(*She searches in her handbag.*)

SZILARD. From Mr Solberg! Well, well!

(SIBBY *returns with a bowl of soup, with which she stands behind* SZILARD).

GORDON (*to* BOB). Fontainebleau – at the races!

BOB (*to* GORDON). What price Shaftesbury Avenue now!

DEIRDRE. Such a charming man! He said we simply must call on the Unit out here the next time we were in the west. I think 'Unit' is the expression, or am I wrong? Ah, here it is!

(*She produces a letter from her bag and hands it to* SZILARD *who glances at it and puts it in his pocket unopened.*)

178

SZILARD. From Mr Solberg. Well, that makes you all doubly welcome. Which of you gentlemen is the Accountant?

DEIRDRE. Now, I really ought to introduce everybody, though it's
such a bore, isn't it? This is Mr Martin Burke of Calamore.
I'm sure you've heard of him. (*Confidentially.*) County family,
you know. He's terribly clever.

(SIBBY *shakes hands as well as* SZILARD.)

SZILARD. Indeed. That's Bristow and King over there.

MARTIN. Spare my blushes. We've come out to see the canoe races.
They are on today, aren't they?

DEIRDRE (*to* BOB *and* GORDON). How do you do? (*to* SZILARD.)
And this is Lord Clanbrassil.

SZILARD. Quite so. Glad to meet you all.

DEIRDRE. I'm sure you know his place – just across the Sound. Of
course it's usually shut up, but at this time of year he often
gives such jolly parties, don't you, Tony? Such a change, too,
from the Continent!

SZILARD (*to* GORDON). Well, send me Solberg's man immediately
he comes ashore. Thank you, Sibby.

(GORDON *and* BOB *vanish into the laboratory.* SZILARD *takes
the soup and walks off into the cottage, followed by* SIBBY. *All
the islanders except* BARTLEY *have by this time wandered away
from the pier.* LORD CLANBRASSIL *sits down and suns himself.*)

DEIRDRE. Oh dear, they've all gone. I do hope I didn't say anything
to offend him?

MARTIN. He probably saw that you were about to mention that
cousin of yours who frequently walks on at Elstree when the
hunting is over.

DEIRDRE. Well, as a matter of fact, I was. Everybody is interested
in the pictures nowadays, and after all, it is Mr Szilard's subject,
isn't it? You can't expect him not to be interested.

MARTIN. I dare say, my dear. But you shouldn't mention those
relations of yours except in prayer.

DEIRDRE. Oh Martin, you are awful! It's no wonder that Jal gets
into a fury with you.

MARTIN. I wish you didn't encourage all this girlishness in Jal. I
did no harm to that incredible Cockney. I was only pulling his
leg, and anyhow it all passed completely over his head.

DEIRDRE. Oh dear, I can't believe that we are really here. The great
Szilard's unit! Now I must remember everything. Tony, dear,
do you realize where you are?

TONY. What's that?

MARTIN. She thinks you don't know where you are.

TONY. Where I am? Of course I know where I am! Don't be ridiculous, Dreary dear!

(CHENEVIX *emerges from the cottage and collects the sheets of music that he has flung down. He is received in silence by the others and responds to their glances with a cold, pre-occupied stare.*)

CHENEVIX. Oh, pooh!

(*He disappears back into the cottage.*)

MARTIN. Did you see, Tony? A crook!

DEIRDRE. My dear, what an interesting-looking man! I wonder who he is?

MARTIN. Just a wandering sunbeam. A nice collection, I must say. The man Szilard is obviously suffering from some form of auto-intoxication. I can't believe that it's poteen at this hour of day. As for the others, Saint Vitus's Dance seems to be the most charitable explanation.

(GORDON *emerges from the laboratory and climbs the ladder.*)

DEIRDRE. Oh hush, dear!

MARTIN. Am I overheard?

(SIBBY *looks out of the cottage.*)

SIBBY. Would there be any more of ye coming, or is that all for dinner?

DEIRDRE. Only Miss Joyce, Mr Burke's – well she *was* his fiancée, at least we all thought – still, never mind – only Miss Joyce.

SIBBY. Is that so, now?

(*She goes back into the cottage. A girl's voice is heard off, cheerfully hailing the pier, and the remaining islander goes down the steps to help to unload the curragh.*)

THE VOICE. Don't shoot! Women and children only!

DEIRDRE. Oh, here she is in the next boat. It's all right, darling! It's only us!

THE VOICE. Don't tell me nobody was hit?

DEIRDRE. Only poor Tony. But it's all right – he seems to have got most of it out by now.

MARTIN. Had a nice crossing, dear?

THE VOICE. Mind you don't put your foot through the bottom when you're stepping out, Mr Quilt.

A MAN'S VOICE. Coo! I don't think much of this, I must say!

(JAL JOYCE *comes up the steps followed eventually by* ALF QUILT *and* MICHEAL MÓR, *who carries a sack of flour which he hands to* BARTLEY. *During the following dialogue the two*

180

*islanders unload a number of parcels, crates and sacks of
flour from the curragh which they pile on to a wheelbarrow.
GORDON, on the roof-top, shows a marked change of
demeanour as he watches JAL. BOB comes out of the laboratory and joins them.)*

JAL (*appearing*). Hello, everybody! (*to* TONY) Dr Livingstone, I
presume? Where are the enemy?

DEIRDRE. It was all a mistake, darling. They've been terribly sorry
about it. This is a Mr Bristow. Don't you like him?

JAL. Very much indeed.

(*She shakes hands with* BOB.)

BOB. Lovely day.

DEIRDRE. And that's a Mr King up there on the roof. He's very
busy. We don't quite know what has happened to Mr Szilard,
but my dear, there's a terribly interesting man with a beard who
appears from time to time. I do wish I knew something about
him!

BOB. That must be Romping Raymond. He's an expert on folk
music. Name of Chenevix.

DEIRDRE. Folk music. Mm. Isn't there a book about that in your
library, Tony?

(GORDON, *after exchanging a glance with* JAL, *has swarmed
down the ladder.*)

GORDON. How do you do? Why have you never come out before?

JAL. But I do. Frequently.

GORDON. Not since I've been here.

MARTIN. Ah, but you see, she didn't know.

JAL. Don't mind Mr Burke. It's Wednesday, so his clean com-
binations are itching him.

ALF (*whom nobody has noticed*). Name of Quilt.

BOB (*not very much interested*). Oh!

ALF. Come out to settle up those books of yours. 'Ope I don't
intrude.

BOB (*interested at last*). Oh, yes. We were expecting you. Look
here, have you brought us out any more stock?

ALF. Yes. I've got that, O.K. It's coming ashore with the mails in
the next boat.

BOB. Thank God for that. We haven't a foot left unexposed.

ALF. Nice little place you've got 'ere, I must say.

GORDON. Better send him in at once.

SZILARD (*from inside*). Is that the man?

BOB. Yes. Here he is now.

SZILARD. Has he got the stuff?

ALF. Yes, sir. Yes, sir.

GORDON. Three bags full.

SZILARD. Then what's keeping him? Send him in.

BOB. Come on, I'll show you to your room.

ALF. Very kind, I'm sure.

(BOB *takes* ALF *and his suitcase into the cottage.*)

JAL. Poor Mr Quilt! He looks so apprehensive. I do hope no harm is going to come to him.

MARTIN. I'll never forget his face when he first saw how he was going to be taken ashore.

JAL. He bore up very well. I won't have a word said against my Alf.

GORDON (*to* JAL). Have you come out to see the boat races?

JAL. Of course. We always do. What luck with the weather too!

GORDON. Yes, for everybody except us.

JAL. But surely it must be grand for cinema work.

GORDON. We've been waiting for the equinoctials for almost a month to get our storm sequence through, but they simply won't come. So you must excuse the somewhat tense atmosphere. We're all on edge for fear the summer should end before we have the picture finished.

MARTIN. Yes. It has been unusually fine. But you'll get all the weather you want in a month or two.

GORDON. I dare say. When it's too late in the year. That's the worst of exteriors in this part of the world.

(*The* ISLANDER *pushes the wheelbarrow off.* MICHEAL MÓR *goes back down the steps.*)

JAL. Oh, do look at Tony! He's asleep again. Dreary darling, isn't there any way of keeping his mouth closed? After all, repose can at least be dignified.

DEIRDRE. You know I can do absolutely nothing with him, darling. He's never been quite the same since he was knocked down by that Ambulance. So degrading to be knocked down by an Ambulance, don't you think?

(SIBBY *comes out of the cottage.*)

SIBBY. Can ye all eat rabbits?

DEIRDRE. Oh, really, please don't bother. We wouldn't dream of staying to lunch.

(TONY *opens his eyes.*)

TONY. Eh, what!

JAL. Hello, Tony's amongst us again!

MARTIN. That word always brings him to. Lord Clanbrassil can eat rabbits. They're the staple diet at Castle Corkscrew in the season, aren't they, Tony?

TONY. Well, as a matter of fact . . .

MARTIN. Hush – a statement.

JAL, Oh, do let's all listen to this. Go on, Tony!

TONY. Well, I do feel rather like a nice rabbit.

JAL. He feels like a nice rabbit.

MARTIN. Well I must say the illusion is perfect.

DEIRDRE. Don't mind them, Tony dear. They're awful.

(TONY *apparently doesn't, as he closes his eyes again.*)

SIBBY. And we have some nice rhubarb tart. That'll be good for your stomachs.

DEIRDRE. Really, it's so kind of you! We never dreamt of being offered lunch.

MARTIN. However, you don't have to believe that if you happen to have noticed the hour of our arrival.

(PAUDEEN, *the postman, arrives. He is a pleasant, fair-haired, fresh-faced youth, wearing a cap. The only thing that distinguishes him from the rest of the islanders is the brassard on his arm, which denotes his office.*)

PAUDEEN. Bail o dhia annseo isteach, a dhaoine uaisle.

SIBBY. Dia's Muire dhuit is Phadraic. You took your time this morning, Paudeen Og Donahue, and you the postman!

PAUDEEN. Ah, sure the bags aren't ashore yet, are they? (*to* MARTIN) We were watching ye coming off the boat from up at the post office. And where would ye all be from, because we'd be glad to know?

SIBBY. That's a Mr Burke and a Miss Joyce from Calamore. She's promised to Mr Burke, I'm thinking.

JAL. Indeed? And who said so, may I ask?

SIBBY. And that is a Miss Dobbs from outlandish parts.

(PAUDEEN *shakes hands all round.*)

PAUDEEN. I hope ye are well. I'm glad to hear that you're getting married.

JAL (*embarrassed*). Really! Hasn't this gone far enough?

PAUDEEN. So ye are from Calamore! It must be a strange thing for ye, now, to come out here and to find people living on an island.

MARTIN. Well, you know, when you come to think of it I live on an island myself.

SIBBY. And that's a Lord by the name of Clanbrassil, over there. Only mind you don't disturb him while he's resting.

PAUDEEN. And would ye have visited these parts before? I'm glad ye are able to stay to dinner, tho' mind ye there's a fine hotel down beyond in the village. The best hotel in Inishgaroo where they come from all parts to learn the Irish.

DEIRDRE (*politely*). Indeed? I didn't know there were any hotels on the island.

PAUDEEN. Oh, it's a very good hotel. It has a flushing water closet.

(JAL *and* GORDON *laugh heartily.*)

DEIRDRE (*hastily*). Well, I hope we'll see you some time across in Calamore.

PAUDEEN. Over in Calamore, is it? Oh, I wouldn't go there. They do say that's a terrible wild place.

MARTIN. There seems to be a widespread belief that people who don't live on islands never have any morals. I have noticed it before.

(SZILARD *comes out of the cottage, followed by* ALF *and* BOB. *He is now expansive and genial.* SIBBY *goes back into the cottage.*)

SZILARD. Yes indeed, Mr Quilt. I calculate that we will be finished now in a month or two. You can cable them to that effect when you get back to London. Well, well, and how is everybody? Are you quite all right, Miss – er . . .

DEIRDRE. Dobbs. Oh, quite, thank you, Mr Szilard.

GORDON (*to* JAL). Would you like to come along now?

SZILARD (*to* JAL). I don't think I have met you. Welcome to Tigh na Beith.

GORDON. She's a Miss Joyce. I'm going to take her to the canoe races.

SZILARD. Ah so. Miss Joyce. And Gordon is taking care of you? That will be pleasant, no doubt.

MARTIN (*taking* JAL *quietly by the arm*). As a matter of fact, I don't think Miss Joyce really needs to be taken care of.

SZILARD (*taking in the situation*). Good. That will make it all the more interesting.

(*He looks at* MARTIN *and then at* GORDON *and the girl.*)

GORDON. You will come, won't you? I can get you a curragh for yourself if you could manage one.

JAL (*disengaging herself from both*). There seems to be rather a lot of congestion about here. Excuse me.

SZILARD. Quite right, my dear young lady. Don't let them crowd you.

ALF. What cheer, all! Nice little place, I must say. Pretty views,

184

nice weather, and you don't have to be fussy about your clothes. Just what the Doctor ordered. Bit of a Bohemian I am at 'eart, you know.

SZILARD. Is the stuff ashore yet?

BOB. Here's the Captain coming over with it now.

DEIRDRE. I hope you don't mind our dropping in. But Mr Solberg – such a charming man – said we simply must. Don't you adore Mr Solberg?

SZILARD (*politely, but without much sincerity*). Oh yes. A very nice man.

DEIRDRE. And so bound up in his work.

SZILARD. Yes. Mr Solberg is our patron saint. But for him we wouldn't be here at all, I suppose.

DEIRDRE. Of course, I have simply no patience with Hollywood. But the better type of picture that Mr Solberg goes in for – don't you think . . . ?

GORDON. 'Happy Days', for example. And 'Rough in Bed'.

DEIRDRE (*a little confused*). Yes, of course. I mean there are so few people who realize as yet that the films are really an Art. So few really artistic pictures like yours, Mr Szilard.

(GORDON *grins as* SZILARD *winces.*)

SZILARD. Yes. I suppose Mr Solberg is interested in Art.

GORDON. Have you met his wife?

DEIRDRE. No. I don't think he had her with him at Fontainebleau. Oh dear, perhaps I shouldn't have mentioned that!

GORDON. He says her hands are so beautiful that he's going to have a bust made of them.

(JAL *and* GORDON *laugh again.*)

SZILARD. Now, Gordon, enough of that. I'm afraid that poor Mr Solberg is made the centre of every malicious witticism in the movie world.

DEIRDRE. I was telling Mr Solberg about Martin – that's Mr Burke here. He's a terribly clever critic and Mr Solberg said that I simply must introduce him to you. He was sure that he could be helpful in any number of small ways.

SZILARD. That's very kind of you. And what does Mr Burke criticize?

DEIRDRE. Oh, everything. Don't you, Martin?

MARTIN. Please, please.

JAL. Don't be a fool, Dreary. Please pay no attention to her, Mr Szilard.

185

DEIRDRE. Do tell me, Mr Szilard, what are all those corks and buoys floating out there?

SZILAR-. Mackerel nets – the fisherman's most precious possession after his boat. You shouldn't waste your time on the curraghs, Miss Dobbs. You should see the hookers putting out in a gale of wind to save the nets. There is real drama for you! It is magnificent. No art there, Miss Dobbs. But there is life and struggle and real meaning.

DEIRDRE. Oh, I should love to. When is the next?

SZILARD. Ah, if only I knew that! I have been waiting all summer for that climax to my picture. A sunlit storm. A big equinoctial gale. And the fishermen bringing in their nets. But this sea – look at it – it is not the Atlantic – it is playing the fool with me. Ah, here you are, Captain. I was complaining to these people about the weather.

(*The* CAPTAIN *comes up the steps smoking his pipe. He is an elderly, taciturn Scot.*)

CAPTAIN. Why, what's wrong with it? You may have more weather than you fancy some of these days.

SZILARD. Please God you may be right. I have almost given up hope. Well, we must have our lunch, I suppose, so let us all go in and get it over. Inside, everybody, if you please.

ALF. Well, I must say I do feel a bit peckish myself.

MARTIN. Wake up, Tony. Lunch.

TONY (*opening his eyes*). It's all right. I've sent for the troops.

GORDON. What was that?

JAL. Only Tony coming to.

SZILARD. Hurry up with that stuff, Micheal.

MICHEAL (*below*). That's so, Mr Szilard, sir.

SZILARD. Wait a moment, Bob – Mr Quilt. Help me to carry this. Which parcel is it?

(GORDON , JAL, DEIRDRE, MARTIN *and* TONY *go into the cottage in which somebody soon starts the gramophone.*)

ALF (*speaking down to* PAUDEEN). In the bag in the bow.

SZILARD. Who are all those people, Captain? Hand it up, Paudeen.

CAPTAIN. Och, they live in and around Calamore. They're well spoken of in the district, but some of them belong to a wild, drinking lot, I'm thinking, like many in these parts.

PAUDEEN. There you are, Mr Szilard, sir.

(*He hands him up two cans of film.*)

SZILARD. Hurry up. Where's the rest?

PAUDEEN (*out of sight*). That's the lot.

SZILARD. Nonsense.

PAUDEEN. There's nothing more down here except the mail bag.
(*He comes up the steps with the mail bag.*)

SZILARD. There must be more than this. Why, there's not more
than a thousand feet here.

ALF. That's O.K.

SZILARD. What do you mean?

ALF. Read the letters, old boy. You'll find out all about it.

SZILARD. Give us our letters, Paudeen. Never mind about taking
them up to the post office.

PAUDEEN (*rummaging in the bag*). I'll see if I can find them, Mr
Szilard. Wait now till I see. That would be the bundle, I'm
thinking. Five letters for Mr Szilard and a parcel and a postcard
for Mr Bristow. (*He looks at the postcard.*) From a young lady,
I'm thinking. Am I right?

(SZILARD *and* BOB *eagerly take their correspondence.*)

GORDON (*from the window*). Nothing for me, Paudeen?

PAUDEEN. Not a letter, as far as I can see, Mr King, though it's
sorry I am to have to tell you.

GORDON. Another good mail gone wrong.

(*He disappears*).

PAUDEEN. Ah, maybe now Mr Bristow will let you have a share of
his postcard.

(*He goes off with his bag*).

BOB. I say, this is a bit thick. It's from the wife. She really shouldn't
be so affectionate on a postcard. At least, not at the moment, I
mean – look!

(*He shows it to* ALF.)

ALF. Why, wot's the trouble, old boy?

BOB. That won't do our divorce much good, will it? I wonder does
the King's Proctor read postcards?

SZILARD (*reading a letter*). So Paramount want me to go to the
Congo! Well, I'm not going to the Congo for Paramount.
Where is Solberg's letter?

BOB. And a new gramophone record! That was decent of her. But
oh my God, look at the title!

SZILARD (*reading another letter*). Good God!

BOB. What say?

SZILARD. Do you know what Solberg is going to call the picture?
'Storm Song'!

BOB. Sounds like Sybil Thorndyke marooned in a lighthouse.

ALF. Good snappy title, if you ask me. And only nine letters. Save
a lot in lights, that will.

SZILARD. Well, maybe we should be thankful for small mercies.
But what's the meaning of this? Only another thousand feet of
short ends, and then I'm to finish up. But Mr Bristow says he
told the office that we wanted at least seven thousand. (*to* ALF)
Do you know anything about this?

ALF. No, old boy. It's nothing to do with me, you know. But if you
ask me, maybe I might tip you the wink, so to speak.

SZILARD. What the devil do you mean by that? How am I expected
to make a picture without stock?

ALF. Well, I mean to say, nobody wants to be unreasonable, but
you 'ave 'ad a lot, now 'aven't you, old boy? Fair do.

SZILARD. Well, what about it? Did you never hear of retakes?

ALF. And you 'ave 'ad nearly a year. I mean to say.

SZILARD. Nearly a year! Good God, what do you expect? Do you
realize what we have had to do! We've built a house, stocked
a laboratory, collected a cast from the corners of three islands,
trained them, laid on power and a water supply – why, man, we
hadn't any soup for three months, and we've had to shut down
every time the sun went in.

ALF. Oh, I daresay they don't realize all you've been up against,
but . . .

SZILARD. Nearly a year! And what, may I ask, do you expect? A
Studio Time Schedule in Inishgarve? Why I spent over two
years in Bali for M.G.M.!

ALF. It's nothing to do with me, you know, old boy. I'm only 'ere
to close the books.

SZILARD. To close the books! What the devil do you mean by that?

ALF. Well, you see there'll be no more accounts, will there? Another
thousand feet and you'll be finished.

SZILARD. Finished? I will not be finished. I have still got to take
the storm sequence.

ALF. Sorry, old boy. Afraid it can't be done. Money's a bit tight,
you know, these days.

SZILARD. Do I understand you to say that Solberg is having the
impertinence to tell me to shoot another thousand feet and
then come home? Who the devil does he think he's dealing
with?

ALF. Well, after all, old boy, 'asn't 'e been fair enough? I mean to
say . . .

SZILARD. But I tell you I haven't finished. I'm waiting for the weather. And don't call me old boy.

ALF. I'm sorry, Mr Szilard. But after all, you can fake up what you've got, back in the Studios, can't you?

SZILARD. Fake it! Fake it! (*He gives a roar, and then suddenly he is icily polite.*) Mr Bristow, will you kindly show this gentleman where the books are. I believe that they are what concern him here.

(BOB *touches the terrified* ALF *on the arm and indicates the laboratory. The pair of them file out, but before* BOB *has gone he is called back.* SZILARD *smokes fiercely, lighting one cigarette from the previous butt.*)

SZILARD. Bob! Bob, what the devil do you make of this?

BOB. I don't know. Suppose the weather does blow up, couldn't you finish with another thousand feet?

SZILARD. Maybe. If the light holds and the rollers come in and the rain keeps off before the money gives out. Am I expected to make all these arrangements?

BOB. God knows.

(*He smokes philosophically.*)

SZILARD. I expected something of the kind from that bastard, Solberg. They warned me before I started. What the devil does he care! Just another damn Quota Picture. He's got his 'Happy Days', and all his other blasted boob-catching musicals. If he has to spend a few thousands over here I suppose he thinks he may as well put himself right with the highbrows. That's all he wants with me. That's all his interest in the Criochs. Blast him!

BOB. Oh, I don't know. Solberg is a good business man. I really think he believes in you.

SZILARD. A damn good business man to order me home with the climax of my picture unfinished. Oh, a hell of a good business man! He knows what's good enough for his half-grown public and that's good enough for Solberg.

(SIBBY *comes out from the cottage carrying a plate of food.*)

SZILARD. But he'll not treat me like that. I'm finished with him. We shut down. I wash my hands of the whole thing. The whole picture is off. Oh, what is the matter now, Sibby?

SIBBY. There now, if you won't eat it inside you can eat it outside. But inside or outside, you must eat your dinner.

SZILARD. Good heavens, I was forgetting all about lunch!

BOB (*feelingly*). Yes, you do sometimes!

SZILARD. And all those people! Really, Bob, you mustn't allow me

189

to neglect my guests like this. It's too bad. (*He hurries to the cottage door followed by* BOB *and* SIBBY) Ah, good morning everybody. Are you quite all right?

(*There are murmurs of polite greeting from inside as the three of them disappear into the cottage. Presently the laboratory door opens and* ALF *peers out. He crosses cautiously and looks wistfully into the cottage window. From inside comes a burst of laughter and music and the merry clatter of plates. He taps cautiously on the window. Suddenly there is a heavy silence inside.*)

ALF (*timidly*). Could I have a small plate of – a – (*The silence continues*) Just a small piece of bread and butter. I mean to say . . .

(*The silence continues. Then there is a burst of loud laughter from inside as the*

CURTAIN FALLS)

ACT II

Scene I

It is about five o'clock in the afternoon of the same day. We now see the interior of the Living Room. Looking at the stage from the front there is a door at the left end of the rear wall leading out to the site of Act I. Beside it is a long window which runs along the back wall and through which we can see the foreshore. Below the window is a cushioned window-seat upon which lie a number of books and magazines. The right-hand corner up-stage (from the point of view of the audience) is cut off by a light portable screen which masks a reclining chair and a washstand and basin occupying the corner. In the right-hand wall is a door leading to the Projection Room upon which somebody has laconically chalked the words: 'Go away'. Down stage, below this door, is the Cutting Bench upon which stand piles of film cans, a portable typewriter, a couple of winders, several spools, a splicing outfit, a tray of wire paper clips, a notebook and scissors, knives and so on. On the wall above it is a shelf carrying piles of film cans and a number of boxes, bottles, lanterns, and other apparatus and a small wooden horse from which strips of film hang suspended. The roof over the bench is pierced by a skylight. In the left-hand wall there are two doors, the upper one leading to the kitchen, and the lower one leading to the visitor's bedroom, occupied by MR CHENEVIX, *but now also intended for* ALF QUILT. *On the floor, along the left-hand wall, stand a number of transit cases and metal reflectors, a camera case and a tripod. In the centre of the stage is a table. Its top lifts off and turns over, becoming when required a miniature billiard table. The room is wired for electric light. The invisible fourth wall contains the fireplace. The only occupant of the room is* GORDON KING *who is working away at the Cutting Bench. Strips of film lie about everywhere and even hang around his neck. He searches through these holding them in turn above his head in such*

191

*a way as to get the skylight behind them, and having found a
desired strip he roughly measures so many feet between his outstretched hands, tears off the required footage and roughly splicing
the ends by means of a paper-fastener to a reel already in composition on one of the winders, he then rolls it on, makes an entry in
his notebook, and then proceeds to search for the next piece, with
which he repeats the process. He appears to be in high spirits and
hums as he works. Presently* CHENEVIX *enters from his bedroom.*

CHENEVIX. By the way . . .

GORDON (*turning for a moment*). Hello, Folk Music.

CHENEVIX. Do I understand that this man Quilt is being put in to
share my bedroom?

GORDON. I shouldn't be surprised. You'll be able to have some long
talks.

CHENEVIX. Quite. We've had one already.

(ALF *enters from the bedroom.* CHENEVIX *winces.*)

ALF. Ah, there you are, old boy. Well, as I was saying to Mr Szilard,
look 'ere old boy, I said, you don't mind us 'aving a strite talk,
do you?

CHENEVIX. I'm afraid I must get my things ready.

ALF. I say, you're not going away, are you?

CHENEVIX. I must go back by the boat. I have some thing to look
up at the National Library.

ALF. Well, well, isn't that too bad! 'Ere were we all looking forward to a good old chin wag this evening! Isn't that right, Mr
King?

GORDON. That's right, Mr Quilt. Couldn't you persuade him to stay?

ALF. Come now, old boy . . .

CHENEVIX. No, no. Really I can't. I'm sorry. Where is my violin?

ALF. Your violin? (*He sees it*) Oh, 'ere you are. Mustn't forget that.
You'll be wanting a bit of music on the train, I daresay.

CHENEVIX. I don't play on trains. My interest is folk music.

GORDON. No use at all for trains.

CHENEVIX (*glaring at him*). What are you talking about?

ALF. Well, as I was telling you just now, I said to Mr Szilard down
at the engine 'ouse, I don't like to mention it, old boy, but you
know, I said, you're wearing out your big end. You'll be sorry
some day, I said. Oh cheerio, Mr Bristow.

(BOB *comes in from the open air with a spool of film which
he hands to* GORDON.)

BOB. There's the first print of yesterday's rushes.

192

CHENEVIX. Excuse me. I really must dash off.

(*He goes into the bedroom.*)

ALF. Good work! You'd like me to step along and lend a 'and, I know.

(*Still talking, he follows* CHENEVIX *off.* BOB *and* GORDON *are intent upon the film.*)

GORDON. That looks good. Are there any more spots? Romping Raymond has been dislodged at last.

BOB. What spots? Why so suddenly?

GORDON. You know – those spots that were on the last lot of positive. Yes – there's one. They're putting Quilt in to share his bedroom.

BOB (*blankly*). Oh. I don't suppose that's anything. (*cheerfully*) Good for Alf.

GORDON. Wait a minute till I give you the rest of this sequence. It's ready to be spliced.

(*He attaches a final shot to the reel upon which he has been working, spins it round and gives it to* BOB, *after which he proceeds to tidy up the strips of unused film.*)

BOB. What's this about? (*He looks at the reel which he has been given.*) Cliffs?

GORDON. I'd like to project it for Szilard this afternoon. Might as well get the row over at once.

BOB. You think he won't like the way you've treated it?

GORDON. Well, I've cross cut it with some cheat shots and close ups. You can't get any impression of the real height of those cliffs from straight photography. It has to be treated or it is meaningless.

BOB. You know, old man, sometimes I think you go a bit far. After all, you're not the Director.

GORDON. Pah, what the hell is the Director, anyway! Camera angles and amateur dramatics! Cutting is the only thing that counts in this job.

BOB. I say, you'd better not let the old man hear you talking like that.

GORDON. He's heard me often enough. I'm not afraid of Szilard.

BOB. Then you're the bravest man I know.

GORDON. Anybody can shoot 100,000 feet if they've got the stock. But to make a picture out of it is a different matter. Now that Solberg has cut off the supplies who is it that is stumped – Szilard or I?

BOB. Well, have it your own way. Anyhow you've heard him say

193

that the whole damn thing is off. He's going to throw it all up again.

GORDON. If we stopped work every time Szilard resigns a hell of a lot would be done, wouldn't it! He'll be roaring round this afternoon just as if nothing had happened. Don't you know that nothing will stop Szilard taking pictures so long as there's a foot of stock left in the cameras?

BOB. I suppose you're right. I'd better take this over to Bride at once if you want it back this afternoon. She oughtn't to take long.

GORDON. Have you seen that girl, by the way?

BOB. Oh, a frightful woman, isn't she! They're all down at the beach watching the races, thank God.

GORDON. I don't mean the enthusiast from Fontainebleau.

BOB. It now appears that she has an aunt in Madrid who knows somebody or other.

GORDON. I mean the other one. She's attractive. I think I'll just take a stroll down to the beach myself.

BOB (*at the door*). Here's one of them coming up. Hello, Miss Joyce, we were just talking about you.

(GORDON *hastily goes to the window as* JAL *comes in. She appears to be agitated and annoyed.*)

JAL. May I come in?

BOB. Of course. Everybody welcome. I must be toddling, but Gordon will entertain you, unless he still wants to go down to the beach. Bye, bye.

(*He goes.*)

JAL. Am I disturbing you?

GORDON. Very much indeed. Do come in and sit down. You must be tired, watching all those activities down there.

JAL. It's our own activities that tire me. How did you know that sods of turf were the proper welcome for us?

GORDON. We were wrong. You are the most welcome visitor we have had in six months.

JAL. God help you. Things must be rotten in the State of Denmark.

GORDON. Don't you like your friends?

JAL. Oh, they're all right. Dreary is a good sort even if she has no sense, and Tony has had a most expensive education. He has ties for all the schools he has been asked to leave.

GORDON (*laughing*). What a devastating description! Your friend, Burke, couldn't do better.

JAL. Let's not talk about him, please.

194

GORDON. With pleasure. I could easily suggest something more interesting.

JAL. Oh dear, if only friendship could survive indigestion! But I suppose you're much too busy to be conscious of things like that?

GORDON (*with some bravado*). Oh, I don't know. I'm glad you came up to talk to me. You'll find that I'm really much the most interesting person here.

JAL. Are you? I didn't know.

GORDON. Of course we're all raving mad. You realize that? Szilard is completely bats and even I am in the first three.

JAL. I shouldn't have thought so. You're not old enough, are you?

GORDON. What's that got to do with it? You don't know what it means – living here and making pictures.

JAL. I think I should like it.

GORDON. No, you wouldn't. You couldn't stand it. You'd go off your head after a week. I've decided to chuck it all up.

JAL. I like what I've seen of Szilard.

GORDON. Who? Oh, Szilard. (*His voice changes.*) Yes, he's a grand man. He's worth working with. (*After a pause he resumes his old manner.*) Of course we're always disagreeing. I'm the only one who stands up to him. You see, his job isn't so important as mine, and he knows it. Though of course he wouldn't admit that.

JAL. Why, what do you do?

GORDON. The editing. I've got to put together about seven thousand feet of what he takes into a picture that will mean something. That's where the brains and intelligence come in.

JAL. I see.

GORDON. In fact, I'm a great man too.

    (*Pause.*)

JAL. I love it out here.

GORDON. You heard what I said?

JAL. When?

GORDON. Just now.

JAL. Which thing?

GORDON. About my being a great man.

JAL. Yes, I heard that.

GORDON. Well?

JAL (*smiling*). You look as though you think I ought to be shocked? If you're not very careful, perhaps it will turn out that you really are a great man, and then who will get the shock?

GORDON. I suppose you object to my talking like this?

JAL. Like what?

GORDON. Oh, that way. You don't believe me. You think I'm only boasting. But you're going to hear about me before long. I'm going to go all over the world, before I'm finished.

JAL. Yes. How old are you?

GORDON. Why do you keep on at that?

JAL. Twenty-three?

GORDON. Twenty-four. But I've knocked around a lot.

JAL. You've been working hard. And you haven't any sisters, have you?

GORDON. I wish you wouldn't be so damned irrelevant.

JAL. But you haven't. I know that from the way you think you ought to talk to women.

GORDON. You must be crazy. If you think that I don't know how to talk to women . . . Well, I like that! (*He laughs mirthlessly.*)

JAL. You have a funny, pugnacious face, and your ears stick out. I'm afraid your parents must have neglected them at a critical age.

GORDON. Never mind about my ears! The extraordinary thing about you is your entire lack of sex appeal.

JAL. Oh, who cares! You're nice. Especially when you start boasting like a little boy. It's so straightforward and young. While we're all so damned sophisticated in Calamore. That's what tires me so much.

GORDON. Sophisticated in Calamore! You *are* crazy!

JAL. And I liked the look you put on when I praised Szilard. I wasn't meant to see it, I know, but I did, and I appreciated it. You can say anything you like after that.

GORDON (*awkwardly*). Well, he's my Boss.

JAL. Of course.

(*There is a pause.*)

GORDON. That was a damn silly thing for me to have said about you just now.

JAL. Which thing?

GORDON. Oh hell, don't you remember anything I say? I mean – about your sex appeal.

JAL. Oh, there was great provocation, I'm afraid. Forgive me too.

GORDON. You're quite right about me, really. I know nothing. But I'm going to, some day.

JAL. Tell me about yourself.

GORDON. I want to go to the Soviet. That's the place. Nobody knows anything about the Cinema anywhere else. Probably not there either. But they are trying. It's all still in the beginning. We know nothing at all.

JAL. You will some day, I'm sure.

(*There is a pause.*)

GORDON. I say, you're not going back on that boat?

JAL. Yes.

GORDON. Amn't I going to see you again?

JAL. I hope so.

GORDON. You live somewhere over there? We won't be here much longer now. Couldn't you come across again?

JAL. I might. I sail a little boat. That's how I usually come over.

GORDON. Do come. Will you?

JAL. Why not?

GORDON. You must.

JAL. Here are the others.

GORDON. Oh hell! Don't bring them the next time. Do you mind?

(DEIRDRE *enters, followed by* TONY *and* MARTIN.)

DEIRDRE. My dear, we've been having such an exciting time watching the boat races. It's fascinating. You shouldn't have left us.

JAL. I was tired.

MARTIN. Well, let's hope you are having a nice rest. No doubt Mr Bing – by the way, that is the name?

JAL. Shut up, Martin.

MARTIN (*to* GORDON). We've been having a lot of trouble with our Miss Dobbs. I'm afraid she has been making advances to your bearded expert. We scarcely knew which way to look.

DEIRDRE. Oh, Martin, you are awful.

MARTIN. We'll really have to do something about her or she'll be making some good man unhappy one of these days.

DEIRDRE. I tell you, we were only discussing tonal values.

JAL. It's all right. His mother will probably have warned him about women.

TONY (*his voice breaking out into a surprising bellow.*) Has anybody seen my hat? (*to* GORDON, *confidentially.*) I had to get a new one, you know, because someone was sick on the last.

(*He wanders about disconsolately and eventually sits down and soon falls asleep.*)

DEIRDRE. I assure you, Martin, when I went up the sandhills with Mr Chenevix, all that took place was . . .

JAL. Don't confess your sins to Martin, dear, because he's very broadminded and will only wave them aside, and then you'll be raging.

DEIRDRE. Don't be ridiculous, Jal. I never – Oh, there you are, Mr Chenevix.

(CHENEVIX *enters.*)

DEIRDRE. We were afraid we had lost you, Mr Chenevix. (*To Jal.*) Do you know, darling, we had such a terrible argument. Hadn't we, Mr Chenevix?

CHENEVIX. I'm afraid that I was a little ruthless with poor Miss Dobbs.

DEIRDRE. Ah, Mr Chenevix, I knew that you were ruthless the very first moment I saw you. Martin, didn't I say to you 'That man is an artist – a ruthless artist'?

MARTIN. Positively shaking like an aspirin, my dear. Has anybody got a blunt instrument?

(ALF *enters.*)

ALF. Well, well, the more we are together – eh, what!

CHENEVIX. You must excuse my apparent rudeness when we first met. Sometimes my work so dominates me that I am inclined to overlook my social obligations. I must apologize.

DEIRDRE. I quite understand. So many artists are like that. Folk music. I am simply fascinated by anything folk.

CHENEVIX (*rapidly thawing*). Really? Perhaps you'd care to hear the little air I have been working on?

DEIRDRE. Oh, I should love to. Do you sing?

CHENEVIX. I play the violin.

(*He goes and gets his instrument.*)

GORDON (*to* JAL). You don't have to listen to this. We've had it once or twice before.

CHENEVIX. I picked it up from a very old fiddler on the middle island. Just a gaunt, stark little thing, but quite fundamental. I want Szilard to use it for the sound synchronization of the film.

DEIRDRE. We never hear of these things on the Continent. Are you listening, Tony?

(ALF *has discovered the billiard table as* CHENEVIX *begins to play. Nobody listens to the latter, except* DEIRDRE, *who makes a few distracted efforts to do so.*)

ALF. What O! Billiards! 'Ow about a nice little game of billiards, all?

MARTIN. That's a good idea. Let's turn it over.

(*They turn the table top over.*)

ALF (*to* CHENEVIX). Don't mind us, old boy. We like it.

198

MARTIN. Play, Dreary?

DEIRDRE. I should love to. I'm afraid I have never played before, unless, of course, you count bagatelle. (*She helps with the table and then recollects herself*.) Oh excuse me. I do feel we really ought to listen to this.

ALF (*to* TONY). Nice game of billiards, yer lordship?

TONY (*waking up*). Eh, what?

ALF. Billiards.

TONY. No thanks. Too much running round.

(BOB *re-enters with the spool of film and turns on the electric light*.)

BOB (*to* GORDON). There's some more back.

GORDON (*to* JAL). I'd like to show you this sometime. He's managed to get some marvellous shots. Can you see that?

(*He holds it up to the light for her*.)

MARTIN. Going to play with us?

GORDON. No thanks. I shall have to show this sequence to Szilard, but Bulgy will join you, I'm sure.

BOB. Certainly, if no one else wants to.

ALF (*to* MARTIN *and* BOB). I mean to say, I'm free and easy as you are. But if you only 'eard what 'e said to me, when I told him about the customs' requirements!

BOB. Who? Szilard?

ALF. Yes, 'im. I'm broadminded as you are, and I know a bit o' wot's wot. But there's some things that turn me up. Oh, my Gawd, 'ere 'e is!

(SZILARD'S *voice is heard off and presently he enters, followed by the* CAPTAIN *and* PAUDEEN. CHENEVIX'S *playing withers up with his arrival*.)

JAL. Hide me, somebody!

SZILARD. Of course they'll be able to do it. It's perfectly simple. Ah, good evening, everybody. Are you all quite all right? Don't smoke near that cutting bench, if you please.

DEIRDRE. Oh that was lovely, Mr Chenevix. I did enjoy that.

(*She applauds alone*.)

PAUDEEN. Would any of ye have anything for the post going back?

GORDON. God! I nearly forgot (*He produces his letter*.) Here you are, Paudeen, and the money. It's very important.

PAUDEEN. I'll put the stamp on myself. Oh, that's going a long way, surely. Russia, is it? (*He puts it in his bag and goes off*.) Well, goodbye all. I hope ye will have a pleasant crossing.

(*The billiards continues*.)

199

DEIRDRE. It has been so interesting to see the place where you work, Mr Szilard. You will let me see your scenario, won't you? I try to write them myself, you know, but I'll promise not to steal a thing.

SZILARD. Scenario? I've got no scenario.

DEIRDRE. No scenario?

GORDON (*to* JAL). Now she's put her foot in it! That's heresy out here.

DEIRDRE. Oh dear, I don't understand.

SZILARD. Don't mind him. If you stay here a little longer, you'll soon understand Gordon, Miss – er.

DEIRDRE. Dobbs.

SZILARD. He's our theorist. His idea is that moving pictures should be made with a scenario and a pair of scissors. I however prefer to use a camera. I know what I want and I take it. What use is a scenario for a documentary film? Nobody ever looks at it anyhow.

DEIRDRE. Fascinating!

GORDON. But a gross slander on me.

JAL. Oh, Mr Szilard, I know you're going to be asked this sooner or later. How about your Montage?

GORDON. Ha!

SZILARD. I'm afraid you'll have to explain.

DEIRDRE. Oh, now you really are making fun of us, Mr Szilard. You can't convince me that you've got no Montage.

SZILARD. I've heard the word. I've seen it in one or two articles that I'm afraid I failed to understand. Perhaps you could be so good as to assist me?

DEIRDRE. Indeed I was hoping that you would tell me. Everybody says you get such fascinating Overtonal Montage into all your work. I have one of the latest Film Reviews here, with a long article about you. Now you're not going to tell me you haven't even read it.

SZILARD. Let me see. (*She does so.*) Never heard of it. Is this about me?

DEIRDRE. Why yes. You simply must keep it. No, not at all. It's a pleasure. You'll find it most helpful.

ALF. 'Ere, wot about this game?

DEIRDRE. Oh, I'm sorry. Is it my turn to play. Am I holding this thing right, Mr Quilt?

ALF. Well, I won't deny I 'ave seen it 'eld differently.

CHENEVIX. What time do you sail, Captain?

CAPTAIN. At half-past five sharp. We have to catch the high tide at Calamore, or we won't get over the bar. How many of you are coming back with me?

MARTIN. Four.

BOB. Don't forget Chenevix.

CHENEVIX (*ironically*). Would you be so kind as not to bother about my arrangements.

SZILARD. You're not going, Chenevix?

CHENEVIX. Yes. I have to make some annotations from the Petrie Collection.

SZILARD. Indeed. Ah well, we'll soon be after you, thanks to Mr Quilt here and his superiors.

CAPTAIN (*to* ALF). And how are you getting across?

ALF. Oh, I'll take a day or two to finish up. When will you be back?

CAPTAIN. Not till the end of the week.

ALF. You don't say! Coo, that's Irish, isn't it!

JAL. We'll be down at Tony's place on the far side, the day after tomorrow. If I came across for you in a pookawn we could take you up to Calamore in the evening by car.

GORDON. That's a good idea.

ALF. Very kind, I'm sure. But what's a pookawn?

GORDON. Nice little boat. You'd love it.

MARTIN. Oh yes, delightful. That's why we all came today on the steamer.

GORDON. Of course. Then you'll come out the day after tomorrow?

ALF. Really, it's very kind, I am sure, but I shouldn't bother.

GORDON. Indeed she will.

SZILARD (*who has been examining the film at the cutting desk*.) I see there are some more of these spots on the positive. I have been down to the laboratory and I have found them on the negative as well. Most peculiar brown stains. What do you suppose that is?

BOB. No idea, I am sure. Unless . . .

(*His voice dies away and a spasm passes over his face.* SZILARD *turns and speaks with slow deliberation*.)

SZILARD. So we will be seeing you again, Miss Joyce? You are very kind to Mr Quilt.

ALF. Oh, but really, I shouldn't bother. I'd just as soon wait for the boat.

JAL (*to* SZILARD). I like to do what I can for others.

SZILARD. I hope you are a good sailor, Miss Joyce. There are sometimes storms that should daunt a lone woman in a pookawn.

JAL. Thank you, Mr Szilard. I think I know my way about.

SZILARD. I hope so, my dear young lady, I hope so. It's more than most of us can say.

DEIRDRE. I love a good storm. Don't you? I always think it makes the west even more picturesque.

SZILARD. Picturesque! My dear madam, do you realize that the people of these islands carry up the sand and the seaweed from the shore to lay on the bare rock to make the earth of their fields? Do you realize what the wind means to these people – the wind that may sweep away not merely the crops, but the precious earth itself? Do you consider that 'picturesque' is an adequate way of describing such conditions?

DEIRDRE (*shaken*). No. Perhaps it was the wrong word.

SZILARD. You are right. It was the wrong word.

TONY (*opening an eye*). Do you know any of these film stars?

SZILARD. Excuse me, ladies and gentlemen, while we see this sequence. Come along, Gordon – if Miss Joyce can spare you.

TONY. There's a nice one called Jessica Jobson.

SZILARD. Yes, we all know her. The soul of a rat!

(*He goes into the projection room as* TONY *wakes up with a start.*)

CAPTAIN. Well, I must be away to the ship. Remember now, you must all be aboard before she hoots or it will not be my fault if you are left behind.

BOB. We'll see to that, Cap.

TONY. Could I have a wash?

BOB. Certainly. There's a basin in there behind the screen.
(TONY *goes in.*)

CAPTAIN. Well, I hope I'll be seeing you all aboard in a wee while.
(*He goes.*)

SZILARD (*off*). What the devil is keeping you, Gordon?

GORDON. Coming. (*to* JAL.) Don't go. We won't be long.
(*He disappears into the projection room and closes the door.*)

DEIRDRE. Oh! Are they showing some of the picture? I'd adore to see a little. Just the tiniest bit!

BOB. Afraid you can't go in there now. Things get a little heated sometimes and they don't like other people about. By the way, would anybody like to hear a tune?

CHENEVIX. Come on, Bristow, it's your turn to play.

DEIRDRE. How disappointing! Is this your ball, Mr Quilt?

ALF. Don't move them! Oh, come, come, that's too bad!

DEIRDRE. Oh, I'm so sorry! Did I do wrong?

MARTIN (*to* JAL). So glad you've got into the Girl Guides at last, my dear.

JAL (*in a hoarse whisper*). How would you like me to offer him a shakedown in your dressing-room, eh?

> (MARTIN *winces. The lights dim slightly and a distant humming comes from the next room, above which can be heard the shouting of voices.*)

DEIRDRE. Good gracious! What's that?

CHENEVIX. They've turned on the projector. It always affects the current.

BOB (*at the gramophone*). Which one would you like? Do you know one that goes: 'Tum Tum Ti Tum'?

MARTIN. Well, the words seem familiar.

ALF. Have you got the Lard Song? That's a good 'un.

BOB. No, what's that?

ALF. You know: (*sings.*)

> Let's all sing the Lard Song
> Lardi da di da
> Lardi da di da
> Let's all sing the Lard Song
> And drive all your cares away –

MARTIN. Here, try a cigarette. Take a whole one.

> (*The lights brighten as the humming stops. The voices can be distinctly heard now in violent altercation.* BOB *abandons his gramophone.*)

DEIRDRE (*listening at the door*). Dear me! Are they putting in the sound?

BOB. Oh, no. The final cut version will be dubbed in the Studio. Post synchronized, I mean. We take it all silent out here.

DEIRDRE. Then what are they shouting about?

BOB. Oh, that's all right. They always fight a bit over a new sequence.

> (*The lights dim once more, and the humming starts again.* BOB *comes back to the game.*)

DEIRDRE. They're off again!

ALF (*to the men at the table*). Do you know what 'e said to me? Going a bit far, I call it. All I told 'im was that if 'e wanted to get the stock back into England, duty free, the Regulations provide that there must be a flash of the Director's face every hundred feet – just a flash, you know, for identification purposes.

BOB. We never heard that before.

ALF (*sotto voce*). Well, 'e said 'e'd give 'em a flash of 'imself all right, but it wouldn't be of his face. Well, I mean to say, I'm broad-minded as you are, but I don't like these double-entenders.

DEIRDRE. They're shouting something about the height of the cliffs. Oh, do you think I ought to be listening?

CHENEVIX. We'll hear it all when they come out.

ALF. If you ask me, Solberg's right to call 'im 'ome. Knows 'e's balmy, that's what Solberg does. After all, you've got to draw the line somewhere.

(*The door of the Projection Room opens and* SZILARD *looks out, places a hand on* DEIRDRE *and pulls her in.*)

SZILARD. Come in here, somebody.

JAL. Well, that's the end of our Dreary.

(*In a few moments, there is an even louder shout from inside, and* DEIRDRE *shoots out again, and the door closes behind her.*)

DEIRDRE. Oh, dear.

MARTIN. Congratulations, dear. So you've seen it after all.

DEIRDRE. Oh, dear, I do hope I didn't say the wrong thing.

JAL. What happened?

DEIRDRE. They were showing a picture of the sea breaking below some cliffs and they asked me how high would I say they were. I do hope I didn't say the wrong thing.

JAL. Why, what did you say?

DEIRDRE. Well, I said that I liked it awfully, but I simply had no head for heights. It seemed the safest thing to say, but it didn't appear to satisfy either of them.

CHENEVIX. Ah! I've just had an idea for an article. Excuse me while I make a few notes.

DEIRDRE. Oh, you must show me some of your writings, Mr Chenevix, won't you?

CHENEVIX. I'm afraid I haven't written anything for some time. I can only write when I feel that way. I can't imagine how some people manage to do creative work all the time. Take Szilard, for instance. It can't be genuine. Though of course he's a Hungarian and that may account for it.

DEIRDRE. It must be marvellous to have inspirations. Do tell me more!

MARTIN. My dear, one more skirt off and home you go.

(*The lights come up again, and stamping is heard off.*)

DEIRDRE. Oh, dear, here they are!

(SZILARD *stamps into the room followed by* GORDON.)

SZILARD. I'll stand no more of it! There I spend two days on the end of a rope shooting those cliffs from the lower ledges, and you have the impertinence to treat it like that!

GORDON. Well, it's your picture, I know, but that seems to me to be the only way to treat it.

SZILARD. You and your wipes and your fades and your lap dissolves! Had Chaplin any of these? Do you suppose Griffith ever wanted them? But that's all you've got nowadays. Stunts, stunts, stunts! (*Suddenly polite.*) Ah, good evening, Miss Dobbs. Are you quite all right?

DEIRDRE. Oh, yes, thank you, Mr Szilard. Are you?

SZILARD. Me? Good God, no!

(*He lights one cigarette from the butt of another. From the anchorage, the ship hoots.*)

CHENEVIX. Good Lord, there's the boat! We must run. (*He grabs his violin case.*) Auf wiedersehen; everybody!

DEIRDRE. Oh, thanks so much, Mr Szilard. We've had a lovely time. You've got my film magazine, I hope?

SZILARD. Yes, thank you, Miss Dobbs. Come again. But be quick now.

GORDON. Goodbye. You'll be back, won't you? The day after tomorrow. Don't forget.

JAL. Goodbye!

(CHENEVIX, MARTIN, DEIRDRE, *and* JAL *run madly out of sight, while* GORDON *and* SZILARD *watch from the doorway.*)

SZILARD. Be quick, be quick! For God's sake run! (*He flings himself into a chair.*) I hope that wasn't rude of me.

ALF (*to* GORDON). Look 'ere, old boy. It's very decent of 'er, I dare say, but I don't want to go across in that wot's-its-name. I don't like the sea, and the steamer's bad enough for me. No, old boy, I think we'll send 'er a telegram not to bother.

GORDON. Listen to me, Dogsbody. You're going across in that pookawn the day after tomorrow, and you're going to like it.

ALF. Well, I mean to say . . . !

SZILARD (*reading* DEIRDRE'S *paper*) 'Having no control over the secondary visual characteristics of the material he collected, he was forced to make the interaction of the content of the film events more powerful than their appearance. This was done by impressing a more or less temporal metric on the film, to emphasize, echo or run contrapuntal to the intellectual relations.' For God's sake will someone tell me what that means?

205

GORDON. That's all about you and your doings, I suppose.

BOB. Anyone mind if I put on this record the wife sent me?
(*He does so.*)

SZILARD (*flinging the paper into the grate*). God deliver me from all Artists! – a lot of tom cats chasing their own hindquarters. The Greeks had no Art Critics! Christ! What a paper, what a day, and only another thousand feet of stock! (*He strides to the door and looks out*) Pah – call this the Atlantic! Bath-water – that's all it is. Where are the breakers? Where is the part of Hamlet? God dammit – a gale. Send me a gale of wind to whip some life into our last days!

BOB. Michael O'Flaherty says he thinks there's wind in the west.

GORDON. If Michael O'Flaherty had a couple of bottles of stout on board he probably had wind in his stomach.

SZILARD. Well, let's be thankful for small mercies. That crowd has gone. And not another boat till Saturday.

BOB. Listen.
(*There is a snore from behind the screen. They all look round.* BOB *stops the gramophone.*)

BOB. Did anyone else hear what I heard?
(*He and* GORDON *creep up to the screen.*)

GORDON. I declare this exhibition open!
(*They pull the screen aside. On the reclining chair* TONY *lies fast asleep.* BOB *shouts with laughter.* SZILARD, *with a cry of anguish, takes up a bottle and flings it on the floor, where it shivers into fragments.*)

SWIFT CURTAIN

Scene II

About 5.45 p.m. two days later we find ourselves in Lord Clanbrassil's house at Belgata, on the mainland across the Sound. The over-riding characteristic of the scene is that it must be possible to set it quickly within the previous set or, alternatively, to adapt it therefrom, as it is of importance that the interval should be of the briefest duration. The room can scarcely be described as a drawingroom and scarcely as a hall, being the principal apartment in the house, offensively known as Castle Corkscrew, and having been rebuilt during the middle period of the nineteenth century at a time when there was a good deal of money available and when peculiar ideas of good style in feudal or baronial residences were current. The place is a glaring caricature of the medieval carried out in three-ply wood, most of which has been subsequently painted over by a discouraged successor-in-title. On the wall there are a few bad portraits, a couple of illuminated addresses dating from early political days, and numerous stuffed fish, antlers and other sporting relics added by the present holder of the title. There is a big window at the rear through which the foreshore and the sea are visible, while in the distance, about every thirty seconds, through the deepening twilight, can be seen the flash of a light-house on the island across the Sound about eight miles away. There is a wireless set to one side and a barometer hanging on the wall. Around the table, centre, on which are the remains of a meal, sit DEIRDRE, ALF, *and* TONY. MARTIN *is at the window. He is restless and ill at ease but carries it off with sardonic humour, fortified by alcohol. He comes across and helps himself freely from time to time from a decanter of whisky and a syphon of soda on the table.* TONY *dozes over a plate of pie, while* ALF, *after a safe crossing, is glowing with relief and has become even more familiar and friendly than ever over a bottle of Guinness. As the curtain rises the wireless is playing some modern orchestral music.*

ALF. Now, just take Solberg. You may say what you like, but 'e's a gent, that's what I say. You treat me like a 'uman, and you can twist me round your little finger (*gesture*) like that. I am soft in some ways I dare say, like a lamb with little children or dumb animals, as you are too. But what I mean to say is, some of those chaps in London office, they just turn me up.

DEIRDRE. Really? What an extraordinary thing to do.

MARTIN. Did King give any reason for coming over in the boat with you? Damn that thing!

(*He turns off the wireless.*)

ALF. No. 'E just wanted the sail, I suppose. Takes all sorts to make a world, don't it?

TONY. Did somebody turn off the wireless?

ALF. I'll just give you an illustration. Take Carter – that's the 'ead Scenarist – 'e thinks 'e's Gawd just because 'e was at Giggles-wick. 'Im and 'is Old Boy's tie. Well, I mean to say, if you're a Man, like 'is Lordship 'ere, I'll shake you by the 'and and who

cares about Giggleswick? But Carter! 'I'm going out to look
at the barometer in the break,' says I, quite quiet like. 'What?'
'e says, 'at break of dawn? Well I 'ope you don't break it.' But
nobody laughed. Not a smile, I'm glad to say. Oh, but it turns
me up, as it does you.

DEIRDRE. Quite.

TONY (*eating*). Nothing like a nice piece of apple tart.

MARTIN (*examining it*). You're right. Not the slightest like one.

TONY. Have some more, Quilt, eh?

ALF. No thanks, your Lordship, not for me.

MARTIN. You needn't think there's anything better coming, because
there's not. How do you suppose he intends to get back?

ALF. No. Solberg's not like that. 'E may 'ave 'is faults. 'Oo 'asn't?
But 'e knows a man when 'e sees one. Knows old Szilard, all
right. As for yours truly – well, I 'aven't much in the way of
style, I dare say, but I'm a good clean man as you are. That's
one of the things about being married. It keeps you straight,
old boy. You know what I mean. Or maybe you're not inclined
that way?

TONY. What way?

ALF. Oh, you know, your Lordship. Or maybe I oughtn't to 'ave
mentioned it.

MARTIN. Of course you shouldn't. Haven't you heard? When his
Lordship is expected anywhere on a visit, the women of the
house go round beforehand oiling the locks in all the bedroom
doors.

ALF. You don't say? Not for safety!

MARTIN. No. For silence.

DEIRDRE. Oh, Martin!

TONY. I don't know what you're talking about.

MARTIN. That's all right. It's a bit above your head.

DEIRDRE. Don't you think we'd better go out and help Jal and Mr
King?

MARTIN. I'm sure we'd better not. Didn't they say they were going
to stow the sails? Supposing we found that they were.

ALF. Now me and the wife 'as an understanding. Worktime, no
drink. 'Oliday time, drink what I like and no questions asked.
She's a good sort is Annie, and we're all 'uman I say. We
weren't engaged when the war was on, thank goodness. A man
needs to 'ave no care those times. If you 'ave any care it kills
your patriotism (*gesture*) like that. You know what I mean. I
do my best as you do yours, and if a man wants a fight I don't

lose my goat. I just say, 'Oh, do calm yourself, old boy. 'Ave a cigarette.'

TONY. Very creditable, I'm sure.

ALF. Now that's what I like about you folks – all free-and-easy and go-as-you-please. Not stand-offish. I'm a bit of a Bohemian myself, I dare say. You like me and I like you, and so you come all the way across just to get me up to Calamore. Now that's friendly, I do say. Though mind you, I don't mind saying I was a bit nervous coming across in that there what's-its-name. Didn't like it at all, did we, your Lordship? Still, I couldn't let you folks down after all your kindness, and we're over now any'ow, thank God. So 'ere's 'ealth!

(MARTIN *looks out of the window.*)

TONY (*rising and doing a few peculiar stretching exercises*). Had a terrible two days. No decent mattresses, and the natives all insist on shaking hands with you when they wake you up in the morning . . .

MARTIN (*indicating* TONY). He has to have lead in his shoes to prevent him falling over.

(TONY *turns on the wireless and sits down again.*)

ALF. I'll just leave you my address, and when you come up to town the wife and I'll be glad to show you the sights. She'll be glad to meet your Lordship. Ever been to Madame Tussaud's? Nice little air, that. What's it called?

MARTIN. 'Oh, I don't know the size of his collar, but my fingers just meet round his throat.'

ALF. Oh, damned good! Where'd you hear that one? Now there's another thing. You folks are always on for a good laugh, I must say. I'm like you in that respect. Always ready for a bit of fun so long as it's clean, old boy.

> 'Smile a little every day
> As you pass along life's way,
> Just a merry bit of chaff,
> Just a tiny, gladsome laugh
> Brings more 'appiness than gold
> Far more joy than wealth untold.'

(*The* FAMILY SERVANT *comes in carrying a lighted lamp which he places on the table. He is a courtly, decayed old man. The wireless concludes.*)

SERVANT. Mrs Collins and I are very relieved that you are all across safely. They have the north cone hoisted at the pierhead and the men say that there's likely to be a gale.

THE WIRELESS. This is the National Programme from London. Here is the weather forecast for tonight and tomorrow. General inference. Anti-cyclones are situated over Russia and near the Azores. A large depression centred near north-west Iceland is filling up, while a disturbance in the Central Atlantic is likely to move north-east. Weather will be unsettled and stormy and somewhat cooler. All districts – wind north-west, backing to west – strong, with gale locally – cloudy – sea rough. Here is the first news, copyright reserved.

(JAL *and* GORDON *enter. He is wearing oilskins and she a belted raincoat.*)

MARTIN. Ah, so here you are!

JAL. Hello everybody. It's a perfect evening.

THE WIRELESS (*softly*)

Speaking at Geneva today, the Prime Minister said that the cause of world peace must not be jeopardized by new armaments. He hoped for a better and fuller understanding amongst the peoples of the world. A Bill authorizing the issuing of ten thousand million francs of Treasury Loan was authorized today by the French Chamber. The Premier declared . . .

GORDON. Ah-ha. The voice of London. And does that make me homesick? Well, well, so the same old things are still going on!

MARTIN. We can't hear what you're saying, but we're sure it's appropriate.

JAL. What's the news?

(MARTIN *turns off the wireless.*)

MARTIN. Only the hee of one Government followed by the haw of the next.

SERVANT (*to* GORDON). You're not thinking of going back to Inishgarve this evening, are you, sir?

GORDON. Well, I don't know.

SERVANT. It's going to be a bad night.

JAL (*at the barometer*). Hello, that's good! This thing has suddenly gone up to Much Rain. Never saw it up there before.

SERVANT. Don't tap it, Miss, or it will fall off. A rising glass is as likely to mean more wind as less. There's a full gale somewhere out there in the Atlantic. You can tell by those rollers. And if the wind backs a little to the west, we're going to get it here.

GORDON. That's good news for Szilard. I ought to get back at once.

JAL. Mmm. Don't much like the green colour of that sky or those oily looking clouds. I think you'd better come up to Calamore

210

with us in the car and go back by the steamer tomorrow.

GORDON. Very well. If you think so. They'll all be hopping with excitement out there if there are any signs of a storm.

SERVANT. Mrs Collins and I will be very relieved if you don't go tonight.

GORDON. I really shouldn't have come across. I'm the only sane man in the unit.

(*The* SERVANT *goes off, leaving the lamp.*)

MARTIN. Too bad, if you're not going to get another little sail.

GORDON. Oh, I'll bear up.

TONY. Why did you turn off the wireless? I wanted to hear all the political news.

MARTIN. Isn't it a solemn thought that no General Election can shake this hereditary ruler out of his seat in the Lords!

TONY. I've never taken my seat yet.

JAL. Dear Tony. He has spent years looking for the address of the Liberal Party.

TONY. My old father was a Liberal. He used to say . . .

MARTIN. That's all right. We'll discuss your old father when we're both sober.

DEIRDRE. Martin, how could you! Tony's perfectly sober.

MARTIN. As far as I can see, I'm the only sober one here.

JAL. I'm afraid that's only as far as you can see.

MARTIN. Really, my dear, you're damn funny. Now let's all laugh. (*Mirthlessly*) Ho, ho, ho.

(TONY *closes his eyes.*)

JAL. Don't be so offensive, Martin. If you're expecting to drive us up to Calamore this evening, hadn't we better be starting?

MARTIN. Really! Back to Calamore! Just one excitement after another. Be sure you keep me in touch with any further project, my dear.

JAL. Oh, don't let's have a row, Martin. I'm tired. You know you've had quite enough to drink, if you expect to drive the car.

ALF. That's right, old boy. Got to think of the car, you know.

MARTIN. Ah, Mr Quilt, so there you are.

ALF. No offence, old boy. I just thought I'd mention it.

MARTIN. Offence? Why, not at all, Mr Quilt. There's nobody to whom I would go sooner for advice when in doubt.

ALF. The same with me, old boy. It's the slackers and snobs that turn me up. Now take that Carter I was telling you of.

MARTIN. A little louder, Mr Quilt. For his Lordship's sake.

ALF. He just used to look at me whenever he'd pass and never

211

would say a word, until one day I met him on the stairs and I
said to 'im, 'Look 'ere, old boy, let's 'ave a straight talk', I said.
'You know the type of man the War made – the man who'd do
it again for the country – that's me, old boy,' I said, 'and yet you
snub me and snub me and snub me'. Of, if you felt as I felt! It
was like trying the devil. I offered him fair fight, but I didn't
strike a blow, I'm glad to say. (*To* GORDON.) Who's he, anyway?
Is he a war-made Britisher such as you and I profess to be?

GORDON. I'm afraid I can't profess to be that.

MARTIN. I daresay.

ALF. Well, what about it, old boy? If you were too young to fight
who's fault was that? Wasn't it for the coming generation that
we all made the great sacrifice?

MARTIN. And what a generation! All magnitude but no position.
A race of professional hypocrites. They knew everything and
can do nothing. Except like Pantagruel, they can cover armies
with their tongues.

JAL. Martin, you're drunk.

MARTIN. And how do you suppose, my dear, I learnt to drink?

ALF. That's right. Drink was the only thing that got you through the
War. Whenever I meet a man with a medal I say to him, 'Tell
me, old boy', I say, 'in what condition were you when you
performed your act of chivalry?'

MARTIN. Yes, Mr Quilt, that's what we went through for the coming
generation. And what does their freedom mean to them? Only
so much opportunity for expressing their prurient puberty!

GORDON. I'm not sure whom all this is directed at, but I certainly
didn't ask you to go through anything for me.

MARTIN. A lost generation. God forgive us for ruining our lives for
such a brood.

GORDON. Why, what's wrong with your life?

MARTIN. My dear boy, don't bother your little head about something you'll never understand. How the hell could you? I tell
you, the generation that hasn't been through the War knows
nothing. Absolutely nothing. There's a great gulf . . .

GORDON. Ah, come down to ninety-eight point four! Hasn't that
War been made an excuse for enough by now?

MARTIN. Are these your natural manners or are you by any chance
trying to be rude?

GORDON. No more than you are. I just made an observation.

MARTIN. And how much have you observed, may I ask? How could
you know what it feels like to have all your ideals shattered.

Nobody has any ideals nowadays. There's nothing but cynicism. A lot of bloody Bolsheviks. God, what a world! Only two species that can breed in any part of it – man and the swine. I wouldn't bring a child into this world for anything under the sun. I'd strangle it first.

GORDON. Well, it seems to me that the Bolsheviks, as you call them, are the only people who aren't cynical nowadays.

MARTIN. Are you talking about anything, or just talking? Have you ever been to Russia?

GORDON. No, unfortunately.

MARTIN. Exactly. Now let's talk about something else we know nothing about. Any suggestions?

GORDON. All I suggested was that if you like ideals you should like the Russians because they still have them, while you apparently haven't.

MARTIN. Who says I haven't got ideals?

GORDON. Didn't you say you lost them all in the war?

JAL. Oh, do come on. Let's stop this and go home. I'm so tired.

MARTIN. Tired? Maybe you went too far with Mr King. (*To* GORDON) What was it you said about me?

JAL. Please don't argue with him, Gordon.

MARTIN. Excuse me. Who says I've got no ideals?

JAL. Martin, you're giving me a headache. Give me the key of the car, and I'll drive.

MARTIN. And why should you drive?

DEIRDRE. That's all right, Martin dear. We only thought you might be tired.

ALF. I can drive a car, you know, old boy.

MARTIN. Leave me alone. I want to have a few words with this young man.

DEIRDRE. Oh, I do hope we're not going to have any unpleasantness.

MARTIN (*stridently, to* GORDON). I'm an individualist. I've got ideals and a soul, thank God! Do you hear me? A soul! You never heard of that, I suppose. Who are you to say I've got no ideals?

GORDON. All right. You've got ideals, then, and a soul too, if you like. I thought I was only repeating what you had said yourself.

MARTIN. There's no good in deliberately trying to misrepresent me. Or in being insulting. It doesn't add an inch to your stature.

GORDON. Look here, I don't know what the hell . . .

JAL. Gordon, please!

GORDON. I'm sorry.

213

MARTIN. 'Gordon, please.' So we're on Christian name terms now, are we?

JAL. Martin, I won't stand this. If you won't either give me the key of the car or drive it yourself, I suppose we'd better stay the night, if Tony will have us.

DEIRDRE. That's a good idea.

ALF. Top 'ole! Let's all stay the night. Must say I'd rather do that myself, all things considered.

MARTIN (*laughing raucously*). So that's the latest, is it? Stay and have another little walk in the moonlight, I suppose! Stay and hear your fiancé insulted a few more times by knowledgeable members of the post-war generation, eh?

JAL. You're not my fiancé.

DEIRDRE. Have some more tart, Tony dear?

TONY. What's all this going on?

JAL. What right have you to talk like this? Those people are doing work here we don't even know the beginnings of. You might at least have the decency to keep sober until nobody can hear you but your friends.

MARTIN. Doing work! The Pictures! The God Almighty, omnipresent, holy and undivided pictures! This colossal globe of achievement poised above forty million cosmopolitan foreheads respectfully inclined!

JAL. They're real people. They're doing something in the world. And, my God, how I envy them for it!

MARTIN. Ladies and Gentlemen, Mr Szilard's false premises will now be reopened under an entirely new management.

JAL. Yes, I mean it. With all our malice, with all our intelligence, what are we? What will any of us ever leave behind?

MARTIN. A few personal pronouns. But who cares. The world will be none the poorer.

JAL. We're a lot of sorry specimens. I want to get out of it.

DEIRDRE. Oh, really, Jal. Is that necessary?

MARTIN. My darling. Nobody had a better right to put a name on us than you. But whatever we are, let's thank God we're not a lot of stallions neighing after our neighbours' womenkind!

(GORDON *rises to his feet.*)

DEIRDRE. Martin!

ALF. Are you interested in psychology, your Lordship?

MARTIN. Do you think I don't know why you want to stay the night? What do you take me for?

ALF. Very important these days. I'm like you in that respect. Any job in reason.

TONY. What?

MARTIN. Five senses are too much for a sorry specimen. We must be blind as well as dumb, I suppose.

(GORDON *takes a step towards him.*)

JAL (*to* GORDON). Stop – please.

DEIRDRE. Oh dear.

MARTIN. All right, all right. Let him hit out if he has to. It's quite in character and will get us no further.

TONY. Stuff and nonsense. Had on H.M.'s armour myself, but I don't make a fuss about it.

JAL (*to* MARTIN). You can do what you like. I'm going.

MARTIN. When I'm ready.

JAL. You can take your car and go to hell. I don't need your assistance or permission. You'll let me have the pookawn, Tony?

TONY. Absolutely.

JAL (*to* GORDON). Do you want to go back to Inishgarve now?

GORDON. Yes – but didn't you say it would be better to wait for the steamer?

JAL. Very well. Wait for it, then. I'm sailing up to Calamore by myself. Good night, everybody.

DEIRDRE. Oh, Jal, dear, don't be absurd!

(JAL *takes her coat and puts it on. Everybody rises.*)

GORDON.
DEIRDRE. } Oh, look 'ere, you can't do that. It's going to be a
ALF. filthy night. Jal, this is absurd!

(JAL *goes out.*)

DEIRDRE. Oh, dear! Can't anybody stop her? She oughtn't to go by herself.

(GORDON *seizes his oilskins and hurries out, calling after* JAL.)

GORDON. Make it the Island then! I'll go back now. I ought to. (*To* MARTIN *as he goes.*) Blast you, anyhow!

(*The hall door slams.*)

DEIRDRE (*at the window*). Oh, dear! She really is going. And there's the wind starting!

(*The first stirring of the wind is heard.*)

MARTIN (*hysterically*). Go then! What do you expect me to do? Go anywhere you like! Oh, God, I'm a sick man!

DEIRDRE. He's asking her to come back. She won't come. Now he's going with her. Oh, dear, isn't this all very, very unwise?

215

ACT II

TONY. Excuse me, Dreary dear. Just keep looking out of the window for a moment. There's a dear. (*He hits* MARTIN *a resounding whack on the jaw.*) There! (*He walks vigorously away.*) That's for Ole Lang Sang.

SWIFT CURTAIN

ACT III

Scene I

It is shortly after 3 a.m. on the morning of the following day. We are back in the living-room at Tigh na Beith, except that on this occasion we view the room from another angle. Opposite to us is the wall containing the kitchen and bedroom doors. The latter stands almost centre of the stage. To the right, from the observer's point of view, is the window and front door. To the left is a wall, hitherto unseen, containing a big open fireplace in which a turf fire is burning. Along this wall, in the upper left-hand corner, stand several theatrical flood lamps, a cinematograph camera and tripod, a camp bed and a few suitcases and boxes. We can no longer see Bob Bristow's screens, the door of the projection room or the cutting bench. The centre table has been moved away and in its place SZILARD *is working away with another camera in the centre of a flood of artificial light and a half circle of reflectors. He is busily photographing the reflection in a large mirror of Bob's gramophone which is resting on a stool.* BOB *himself, looking very weary, is holding the mirror, which he turns and swings around in accordance with* SZILARD'S *directions. Outside, a wild wind is raging and from time to time we can hear the thunder of the surf.*

SZILARD. Now up a bit. Now back. Now sideways. Now track the whole thing back. More to the left. Stop. That's splendid. It gets a sort of zooming effect.

BOB. It's the reflection of the gramophone you want, isn't it? Tell me if I'm not holding this thing right. (*He yawns.*) Wouldn't like me to put on a record, would you? Might remind me of supper with Maysie at the Café Anglais. (*He sighs.*)

SZILARD. This has never been properly exploited yet. You can get an infinite variety of angles and distance by moving the glass without having to alter the position of either the camera or the object. Now let us try again.

217

BOB (*as he continues to move the glass*). I was up with Maggie's Bartley on Dun Emer watching the big rollers coming up the bay from the Atlantic. (*He yawns.*) Nearly a quarter of a mile between each crest. The spray is coming right over the island from the far side.

SZILARD (*impetuously stopping his work*). Du lieber Gott, is it not morning yet! When will it be light? Three months waiting for this moment and now it must come in the dark!

BOB. Is that why you stopped the hookers from going out after supper?

SZILARD. Waiting, waiting! If those nets are lost before the light comes, our last chance of finishing will be gone. But if not – my God, what a sequence it will make! Tremendous! Why doesn't the dawn come?

BOB. To tell you the truth, it will surprise me if they're able to get out at all by morning. I believe it's getting worse.

SZILARD. Don't talk nonsense. It's no worse than it was. They must go out, Bristow. Don't you realize, we've got to shoot this time? It is our last chance, damn him!

BOB. Damn who?

(*Half a dozen* ISLANDERS *troop in headed by* MICHEAL MÓR. *They are all highly excited but show a respectful restraint.*)

SZILARD. Hello! I thought you were all in your beds.

MICHEAL. It's a rough night, Mr Szilard, sir.

SZILARD (*airily*). Oh, yes. So-so.

MICHEAL. About the nets, Mr Szilard.

SZILARD. Yes? Well, what about them?

MICHEAL. The men are thinking that if this sea lasts the way it is, the nets will be lost surely.

(*The men murmur assent amongst themselves.*)

MICHEAL. It's the way we feel, if we have to wait any longer 'twill be too wild for the hookers to put out at all.

SZILARD (*addressing them in low, earnest tones*). Listen to me, men. You understand the position. Of course we must save the nets. But not until the light comes. I cannot work until then. We must wait just a little longer.

MICHEAL. We understand you, Mr Szilard, sir. But 'tis a terrible wind that is rising, and 'tis likely to be blowing for a day itself or maybe two or more.

SZILARD. Micheal Mór, Seán Power, Colm Ruadh – we know each other. Haven't we worked together for nearly a year now? God knows you've had little enough in return for it, but it has been

218

good work – real work – work that we're not going to be sorry
for. Amn't I right?

ISLANDERS (*murmur*). You are indeed, sir. We've liked it well
enough.

SZILARD. You know that your nets mean as much to me as to any
man on this island – that if they're lost through any of my
doing I shall get you new ones, if I have to rob or murder to
do so.

MICHEAL. We're not looking for that at all, sir.

SZILARD. I know you're not, Micheal. But I mean it. You realize
what we have been making here. This is no six-reel melodrama
that you could see any Saturday night over in Calamore. We
are making a memorial to your fathers and to your fathers'
fathers, and to the age-long struggle for life that has gone on
in these islands – the struggle that is yourselves, and your very
existence here. And now we are finished, all but this one scene
– this storm – the sea – the nets. Something that could be shot
in an hour – that we will be able to start on maybe half an hour
from now, when once the darkness lifts. Are you going out now,
when it is useless for me to come with you? Or can you have
the patience to wait just a little longer for the sake of all that
has gone before?

(*The men speak in whispers one to another.*)

AN ISLANDER (*gloomily*). There's bad luck and all in them photo-
machines. How will we live itself and our good nets gone?

BARTLEY. Ah, damn the nets, anyway! I say we'd have a right to
wait for Mr Szilard, sea or no sea.

(*There are murmurs of assent.*)

AN ISLANDER. Have you no regard at all for all that Mr Szilard has
done for the people?

ALL. It's little enough to do for a man the like of Mr Szilard! We
will wait so!

MICHEAL. Just as you say, sir. We will wait for you till you say we
are to go. And if by the grace of God the nets are still there,
we will take you out in the hookers and do the best we can.

SZILARD. Good man! I knew you would. Is all my gear loaded on
to the boats?

MICHEAL. It is indeed, sir. They are loaded and tossing at the pier
these two hours.

SZILARD. Then set a watch on Dun Emer for the first sign of dawn,
and the rest of you go back to your homes and sleep till you

hear the bell. If the floats are still to be seen, we go out at dawn.

(*The* ISLANDERS *go out, leaving* MICHEAL *behind for a moment.*)

MICHEAL. Would you not be thinking of taking a bit of a rest yourself, Mr Szilard?

SZILARD. Time enough for me, Micheal Mór. I shall have rest and to spare before long.

(MICHEAL *follows the others out.* SZILARD, *with a sigh of weary relief, relaxes and returns to his camera.*)

SZILARD. Come on, Bob! Let us get on with something. Hello, this camera has run out! Damn these short ends they send us. I shall have to go down and reload.

BOB. None of my business, I know, but you won't have much of that thousand feet left if you go on like this all night.

SZILARD. Dammit, you're right. I must do something while we are waiting, but I suppose we must save the little stock we have. Intolerable! And what right had Gordon King to go off at such a moment! The sort of thing that always happens when a woman turns up. I knew it from the first. I can rely on nobody.

BOB. He'll be back. And I'll do the best I can. (*He yawns again.*)

SZILARD. Not in this weather. (*surprised*) You're not sleepy?

BOB. Well – a bit. Doesn't matter.

SZILARD. Go and lie down, but don't undress.

BOB. Well, let me go across to the lab and reload this for you first.

SZILARD. Very well.

(BOB *takes the camera and goes out by the front door.* SZILARD *clears the centre of the floor by switching off the flood lights and piling the gear back against the left-hand wall. Presently horses' hoofs sound faintly.*)

SZILARD. Hello, who's this?

(*There are voices off, and then* GORDON *and* JAL *enter. They are very wet and bedraggled.*)

SZILARD. Well, I'm damned. So you've turned up at last!

GORDON. All those people aren't on the look out for us, are they?

SZILARD. No. We didn't expect to see you for a very long time.

GORDON. Come over to the fire, Jal, and warm yourself.

JAL. Thanks. I think I will.

(*He takes her to a seat by the fire.*)

GORDON. You remember Miss Joyce?

SZILARD (*with a sardonic glance*). Of course – welcome back, Miss Joyce. This is a fresh evening for a sail in a pookawn.

JAL. Oh, we weren't out when it was as bad as this.

GORDON. Please God, no! She was amazing. I was scared stiff. Thought we'd never get out of it.

SZILARD. More to the point, why did you ever get into it?

JAL. Oh, it was safe enough when we started. The sea didn't get really bad till about midnight. Then we made the far end of the island and got ashore while we could.

GORDON. What really kept us out till now was that I couldn't find a car for ages. Nearly all the men seem to be over here.

SZILARD. Yes. We're making a night of it. However, I suppose that is of no interest to you.

GORDON. I'm sorry. I had no idea that you'd be working. But anyway, here I am if there's anything to be done.

SZILARD (*putting on his oilskins and boots*). Oh, tut, tut. Never mind us. You attend to your social obligations.

JAL. I'm sorry for turning up like this, Mr Szilard. I hope that my craving shelter for a night won't inconvenience you.

SZILARD. My dear young lady, you are welcome to occupy, or even share, any apartment in Tigh na Beith that you may fancy – though for my own part, I would prefer it not to be mine. And now excuse me. I must go down to the hookers. The first thing first.

(*He goes out*).

JAL. Well, there's a raspberry for someone.

GORDON. Please don't mind him. He's a nasty old man, when he's working.

JAL. What does he mean by 'the first thing first'?

GORDON. Only that he intends to go on doing whatever happens to suit him. Oh, God, I'm glad to be across.

JAL. I'm afraid he doesn't like me.

GORDON. Nonsense. He's in a fuss. That's all.

JAL. Listen to that. The old sea moaning like a monster pained. Don't you love the Atlantic? It's the only sea in the world. (*He kisses her suddenly on the lips. She appears not to notice.*) People who live in towns never really understand that there is such a thing as weather, do they?

GORDON. God dammit!

(*He kisses her again.*)

JAL. What's the matter? Aren't you well?

GORDON. I wish I knew what's going on in your head. What do you think of me?

JAL. Listen to that. I love the sea because it's my enemy. Do you

221

ever feel like that? (*He shakes her violently.*) Oh! What do I think of you? Well, I like you too. Probably for much the same reason.

GORDON. Do you know what I'm thinking?

JAL.

> 'He sipped the honey from her lips
> As 'neath the moon they sat,
> And wondered if ever a man before
> Had drunk from a mug like that.'

GORDON. Oh, curse our damnable language. It makes us so incoherent. I want to say something terribly important. I want to – oh, what the hell do I want?

JAL. I'm afraid it's only too evident.

GORDON. Well! What if I do? Why not? Do you know what you mean to me?

JAL. Why should I mean anything to you?

GORDON. We might have been drowned tonight, but we weren't. I was scared stiff. We've been through something together.

JAL. And who got you into it? Me.

GORDON And who got me through it? You're a grand person. I love you.

JAL. I wonder.

GORDON. Let me show you.

JAL. How?

GORDON. Tonight.

JAL. Tonight?

GORDON. Yes. I love you.

JAL. You love me. Those are words. Better be careful. Words mean things.

GORDON. They certainly do. Those ones mean a lot to me – happiness. . . .

JAL. Happiness? What bait can tempt the stars swimming in the fountain? Somebody said that.

GORDON. Ah, do stop quoting at me. Tonight?

JAL. You've got work to do. Szilard wants you. I'm only a social obligation.

GORDON. Oh, damn work! What do you suppose he matters! I've had about enough of it. I'm going to chuck it altogether before long. You're the only thing of importance to me. Don't you realize that?

JAL. Let me think for a moment.

GORDON. No. Don't think.

JAL. I wish I could think tonight. It must be the storm. I hope I'm not going to do something we'll both be sorry for.

GORDON. Well, what the hell! We might have been dead. We will be dead some day. But now we can love each other. Oh, God, I could shout the wind down! I want to break something. How many times in our lives do you suppose we will feel like this? Is this a moment to let slip just because of something we may have been told by so many scared old wrecks who understand nothing except their own terror of life?

JAL. Oh, my dear, do you think that I mind the old wrecks! It's ourselves I'm thinking of.

GORDON. That's right. Nothing matters except ourselves. Can't you see that? I shall come ...

JAL. Hush, dear. Here's somebody coming.

(SIBBY *enters. She comes across and shakes hands.*)

SIBBY. Is that yourself, poor lamb. May God and His glorious Mother bless you. That is a terrible wild night for the likes of you to be out. Sure you must be drowned dead.

JAL. Thank you, Sibby. I'm quite all right.

SIBBY. It's straight to bed you'll go now and not a word out of you, for I will not take no. I'll have the best room in the house ready for you inside of five minutes. Wait till you see what I'll do now. Ah, sure, God help the poor creature!

(*She goes in through the centre door as* BOB *enters from outside.*)

BOB. Well, well, and where have you sprung from?

GORDON. Hello, Bulgy. We're back from Belgata.

BOB. You don't say? Not in a pookawn? How are you, Miss Joyce?

JAL. Hello.

BOB. Couple of telegrams arrived late this evening. One from Chenevix at Calamore to say that there'll probably be no boat for him tomorrow as there's a storm on.

JAL. Observant creature!

BOB (*folding up the telegram*). Well, that's one good bit of news. Do you know, perhaps I oughtn't to say it, but I don't much like that chap.

GORDON. Wouldn't you like to hear all the small talk from the museums?

BOB (*lighting his pipe*). Think I can hold out a bit. The other is from Maysie.

GORDON. Who's she? Oh, your wife?

223

BOB (*sadly*). *Was* my wife. She wires to say our decree *nisi* is through.

(*He sighs deeply and shakes his head.*)

GORDON. Well, I suppose that's good news also.

BOB. Maysie says now is the testing time – We've got to stay six months apart or the King's Proctor will be after us, like the last time. Damned good thing I am out here.

JAL. But was there a last time?

BOB. Twice. Damned hard to get a divorce, you know, and damned expensive, too. Got to go off somewhere with some frightful woman, and mind you, it's not enough just to say you have gone. They make you really do it nowadays. Damned particular about that sort of thing, although it seems most improper to me. But I'd do anything for Maysie, poor little woman. It's hard to stay away from her for six months, you know.

JAL. But why do you want a divorce?

BOB. Oh, I don't want it, you know. It's Maysie. She likes to be free. And now and then we have such dreadful rows if she's not.

JAL. Poor Bulgy. Well, let's hope you are successful this time.

BOB. Hope so. Do you know, I wouldn't be surprised if that fellow, Chenevix, was a King's Proctor's spy. I don't like the way he snoops around. And that beard of his looks a bit phoney to me.

(SZILARD *enters in a whirl of excitement and wind. He tears off his oilskin.*)

SZILARD. About those Leica shots. Do you remember the spots on the negative?

BOB. Er – yes. I . . .

SZILARD. Smears on the positive and mysterious brown spots on the negative. Well, I've been across to the lab and what do you suppose I have found?

BOB. What?

(SZILARD *produces a couple of bars of chocolate from his pocket and flings them on the floor.* BOB *winces.*)

SZILARD. There's your brown spots on the negative! Fry's Creamy Twopenny Bar. (*Pointing an accusing finger at* BOB.) The man's a secret eater. Chews chocolate over the soup!

BOB. Well, you see, when I can't smoke . . .

SZILARD. Get out and watch for the light.

(BOB *hurries into the oilskins.*)

BOB. Only a bar or two, you know.

SZILARD. Get out, get out! Your perambulator is outside. Get out and watch for those nets.

(BOB *hurries off while* GORDON *and* JAL *shake with laughter.*
SZILARD *turns to them with a twinkle in his eye.*)

SZILARD. Spots on the negative! My God!

(SIBBY *enters from the next room.*)

SIBBY. There you are now, ma'am. I have your bed all hot and
warm for you. Let you be getting into it at once.

JAL. Thank you, Sibby. You're very good to me.

(*She looks at* GORDON.)

SZILARD (*to* GORDON). We were talking about stereoscopy earlier
this evening. I don't believe that it can be done without either
some form of eyeglasses or else a dividing partition. You see
there must be two separate images – one for each eye. And
they mustn't blend until after they pass through the iris.

(*He sits down and draws a sketch on a piece of paper.*)

GORDON. Good night. (*He presses her hand.*) I shall be here. (*She
smiles.*) All night, if necessary.

SIBBY. Ah, now, Mr Gordon, let you not be delaying the creature.

SZILARD. Stereoscopy is a process that can only take place inside
the brain. Suppose we take two images of the one object from
the distance apart of the space between the eyes. Then to get
the effect of three dimensions – Ah, good night, Miss Joyce, I
hope you're quite all right.

JAL. Good night, Mr Szilard.

SIBBY. Good night to you, ma'am. And I'll bring you a nice cup of
hot tea in the morning. Sound sleep to you now, and sure
never mind if the wind is rising itself. Please God tomorrow
the sun will be high in the sky. (*She closes the door firmly and
turns to Szilard.*) My cousin's son Paudeen and my brother
Seán and my sister's son Colm Ruadh, and my daughter's husband Micheal O'Flaherty are down at the pier. What now would
you be wantin' with them down there, Mr Szilard, on a wild
night the like o' this?

SZILARD. We're waiting until it's light, Sibby.

SIBBY. You wouldn't be thinkin' of goin' out in the hookers in a
storm the like of that?

SZILARD. Oh, it's not too bad yet, Sibby, I hope.

SIBBY. To bring in the mackerel nets?

SZILARD. If they can be found.

SIBBY. That's a bad thing to be hearing, surely. I'll be telling my
sister and my daughter Sarah. I think we'd better be going down
to the chapel.

225

(*She shakes her head and goes off, drawing her shawl over her grey hair.*)

GORDON. You're not going out in this weather?

SZILARD. Well, the nets won't come in by whistling for them.

GORDON. But I never heard anything more unbelievable! Do you realize there's a full gale blowing?

SZILARD. Ah, I see you've been reading Mr Chenevix's telegram.

GORDON. But you can't be serious about this!

SZILARD. Serious! Here am I with less than a thousand feet of stock left. Do you expect me to let slip the last chance of finishing my picture? What the devil do you think we are here for? A bicycling tour?

GORDON. But no islander in his senses will go out with you.

SZILARD. Oh, yes, they will. Nobody who doesn't want to do so need come. But they'll do it all right. They are that kind.

GORDON. Yes, I know they'll go with you. They'll do anything you tell them. That's why it's the next thing to murder to ask them.

SZILARD. Don't be so hysterical. Amn't I going too? It's the same for all of us. If you must blame anybody, blame Mr Solberg. It's he who is sending us out.

GORDON. But I tell you the picture can be finished with what you've got. You've taken nearly 100,000 feet and with proper cutting . . .

SZILARD. Cutting, cutting, cutting! That's all you can think of. Moving Pictures are made with a camera, not with a pair of scissors. A box with a film inside and a handle that you turn. Have you ever seen one?

GORDON. But I keep telling you that you've already taken nearly 100,000 feet. Let me have a chance now.

SZILARD. And I keep telling you that I haven't taken the storm shots or the hookers saving the nets.

GORDON. That doesn't matter.

SZILARD. I know, I know. We'll fake it in the studios. We'll use the wind from six aeroplane propellers and a baby's boat in a bath tub. We'll have magnesium lightning and glycerine tears pouring down over Sibby's bodice. And if that isn't good enough we'll stick in a lot of old stock shots taken in 1910 by Adam, the first cameraman, and in the end there won't be a dry-eyed servant girl from Bloomsbury to Baghdad.

GORDON. No, we won't. We'll cut and cross-cut it with the test shots.

SZILARD. And call the result 'Overtonal Montage'.

GORDON. No. We'll call it a bloody great storm. And people will cheer it. I tell you straight, Szilard, you've got great stuff here – probably the best stuff you've ever shot. But it's not enough. It's still only a cameraman's picture.

SZILARD. Well, I'll be damned!

GORDON. I've never dared to say it before, but I'm going to say it now. It's going to be a great picture with one thing wrong with it. Nobody will believe it.

SZILARD. What!

GORDON. Yes. I mean it. You've photographed real cliffs, and real waves, and real fish, and now you're going to photograph real men being drowned. But what's the good? They'll only say, 'faked', and that's the pity of it, not even well faked. They'll all have seen King Kong.

SZILARD. What! (*smoking furiously*) Listen to me, young man. I was in pictures when they were a dime peep-show on the Board Walk of Atlantic City. I remember Hale's Tours. I worked under Griffith when he first thought of the close-up. I remember the first tracking camera and the days when sound was first tried and discarded. And believe me, I've forgotten more about pictures than you'll ever learn out of your text books on cutting.

GORDON. I know that. It's absolutely true. That's why I can't see . . .

SZILARD. Of course you can't see. Nobody can see anything till they're old men, and then it's usually too late. Listen to me. All my life, I've been making fake pictures for fake firms for morons to gape at. But not any more. Now I've got my chance, and I'm going to make something that means something. When first I came out to these islands and met these people – saw the lives that they lead – the strength, the character, the primitive dignity of everything they do, I knew that I had found something I had been looking for all my life. I made up my mind to make a record of it. A full, true, authentic record, with nothing shirked or nothing left unsaid. And then Solberg sent across asking for his High Art Quota Picture and gave me my chance.

GORDON. But all that Solberg wants . . .

SZILARD. Don't talk to me about what Solberg wants, or what the public wants. Do you think I give a curse for either of them! I've worked for the public long enough and now it's my turn. This time they're going to get what I want. It's these islands that matter to me and these islanders. This picture is going to

227

be none of your big popular successes. But it's going to be a picture the like of which nobody has ever seen before. And if Mr Solberg thinks that he is exploiting me, he's going to find out that the boot is on the other foot.

GORDON. Perhaps he has found that out already.

SZILARD. Then he's found it out too late. I'm to take another thousand feet and then come home, am I? Very well. I shall come home. But if those nets are to be found anywhere this side of hell when this night is over, I shall come home with my picture finished, and Mr Solberg has found me out too late. Ha! Just too late!

GORDON. I used to think that I hadn't a conscience, but really . . .

SZILARD. I love these people. They are folk after my own heart. And before I have gone – which won't be long now – I shall have done one thing of which I am proud.

GORDON. You mean you will have drowned half a dozen Islanders.

SZILARD. Should I expect any less from them than I am prepared to give them?

GORDON. But don't people mean anything to you as individuals? It's against human nature, this!

SZILARD. Ah, don't run down human nature. It's the grandest thing that God has made. Do you suppose that human nature can't stand a wetting when it has managed to survive the Christian religion!

GORDON. I tell you I won't be a party to any such butchery! My God, a grand way to show your love for them!

SZILARD. Nobody expects you to come if you don't feel like it. Besides, you have other ties now.

GORDON. That has got nothing to do with it.

SZILARD. Das Ewig Weibliche, as we used to call it in my youth. Love has come.

GORDON. Mr Szilard, I beg to resign.

SZILARD. By all means. There is not much opportunity in my unit for a man with as many interests as you seem to be acquiring.

GORDON. What exactly do you mean by that?

SZILARD. I mean that in all probability your attention in the future will be concentrated less on the cutting-room, and more on the bedroom.

GORDON (*shouting*). You can go to hell. I resign. I'm done with pictures altogether. Finished! Do you hear me?

SZILARD. Yes. I hear you. Finished – God help you.

228

GORDON. God nothing! Your only idea of God is yourself on stilts.

SZILARD. Yes, Love is a most engrossing thing. Think of it! All over the world innumerable activities are going on. Dirty old landladies are peering through keyholes and policemen are flashing torches into odd corners, saying 'Hello, what's going on here?' All thanks to Love!

GORDON. This is a filthy racket! I wish to God I had never got into it. But I'm done with it now. You're a raving lunatic and I'd have been one myself in another six months if this hadn't happened.

SZILARD. Pah, don't be a fool, Gordon. Go off with your woman if you must, but remember when she lets you down that work never lets you down, if you stick to it. I'm an old man now and I know.

(*Outside a bell begins to peal.*)

SZILARD. Was that the bell?

(BOB *rushes in followed by four or five* ISLANDMEN.)

SZILARD. Yes?

BOB. Light! Clouds breaking up to the north-west. Maggie's Bartley up on Dun Emer – seen the nets. Dragging their sinkers, but still holding, in the swell about a mile out.

(*The* ISLANDMEN *chatter excitedly in Gaelic.*)

SZILARD. Is every foot of stock down in the hookers?

BOB. Yes. It's all there.

SZILARD (*seizing his camera and tripod*). Then back to the lab and start charging the batteries!

BOB. Don't you want me with you?

SZILARD. No! You're in charge here on shore. If anything happens to me, wire Solberg and see that the exposed negative is got safely away. (*He turns to the* ISLANDERS.) Any man who would rather not come can stay behind and nobody will hold it against him. The rest of you, down to the hookers. (*They all dash off after* BOB.) There's human nature for you! (*He dashes after them.*) Stand to! Stand to below, there!

(*His voice dies away into the distant shouting. As* GORDON *watches from the window,* JAL'S *door swings slowly open. He turns and crosses to it. Then he turns back towards the shouting. Suddenly his eyes blaze with excitement and he hauls on an oilskin coat and seizes the second camera and tripod. The tripod leg is entangled with the flex of one of the flood lamps. With a curse, he wrenches it free, and as*

229

it comes away, it fuses all the lights in the room, leaving as the only illumination the light that streams through the open door of JAL'S *room, centre. He dashes out by the front door carrying the camera and tripod.*)

GORDON (*his voice dying away*). Hey! Wait for me. You'll need a second camera – I'm coming too.

(*The shouting grows more distant. Then* JAL'S *voice comes softly from the next room, the door of which swings gently in the wind.*)

JAL. Gordon . . .

(*The light from the swinging door glows intensely, but the only answer to her voice is a wild shriek from the wind.*)

SLOW CURTAIN

Scene II

A corridor in the Majestic Cinema, London. It manages to resemble at one and the same time a Turkish Bath, one of the larger railway stations, and a sumptuous setting for trick cyclists in an old-fashioned music-hall. At the side there are doors and to the rear there are big archways, now curtained over, leading into the foyer. Nine large spangled letters hang from the ceiling and read

STORM SONG

On an easel is resting a large board bearing the announcement: 'Solberg's "Storm Song" – the last Gesture of a Giant.' It is 1 a.m. on an evening two months later. From the auditorium can be heard the music of the concluding sequence of the film. It is a highly orchestrated version of Chenevix's folk melody, crashing and wild. A number of waiters pass across the stage carrying champagne on ice and plates of food. With them are one or two members of a dance band carrying their instruments. They all pass through into the foyer. A uniformed COMMISSIONAIRE *is on duty.*

COMMISSIONAIRE. This way, please. Pass right into the foyer. 'Urry up now! They'll all be coming out in a few minutes.

(*A* Telegraph Boy *enters and accosts the* Commissionaire.)

COMM. Well, what do you want, my lad?

BOY. Cable for a Mr King.

COMM. Well, you can't find 'im now. 'E's inside. Give it 'ere to me and I'll see that 'e gets it.

BOY. Say, what's going on 'ere, Mister? Ain't the pictures over yet?

COMM. Private Show on tonight. This big Cryoch Islands picture they've just released.

BOY. Coo, I've 'eard about that un. It's in all the papers! The Last Gesture of a Giant they calls it.

COMM. That's right, my lad. That there Mr Szilard. 'E was drowned at sea making it. It's going to be a big 'it, if you ask me. I seen a bit myself and I know what they like.

BOY. Let me in, mister, just for a minute. Go on. Be a sport.

COMM. None of that, my lad. Nobody's let into a Private Show except the nobs. What do you suppose would 'appen to my job if Mr Solberg was to catch you?

BOY. Coo, is Mr Solberg 'ere too?

COMM. Yes. 'E's come all the way over to see it 'imself.

BOY. I'd like to see 'im, I would. What's 'e like?

COMM. That's all right my lad, you 'op it before 'e comes along and you find out.

BOY. Oh, go on, mister. Nobody'd mind me. I want to see Mr Solberg and them big storms.

COMM. You'll see them soon enough, when they comes out 'Ighgate way.

(*Loud applause blends with the music off.*)

COMM. 'Ere now, 'op it! They're coming out. You can't keep 'anging around 'ere. I've got to see to my doors.

(*He hustles the boy off as* GORDON *and* JAL *come through the curtains from the foyer. They are in evening dress.* JAL *looks tired and seems rather spiritless in these surroundings.*)

GORDON. God! Isn't it loathsome?

COMM. Mr King, sir?

GORDON. Yes, what is it?

COMM. Cablegram for you, sir – just arrived.

GORDON. What? A cable? Oh, thanks.

(*The* COMMISSIONAIRE *goes off.* GORDON *crams the envelope into his pocket unopened.*)

GORDON. It's intolerable. I can't stand it any longer.

231

JAL. It's a success. Just listen to the applause. I believe they actually like it.

GORDON. Of course they like it. The Last Gesture of a Giant – the picture that drowned Szilard. They love it ! My God, it's ghoulish!

JAL. Poor Szilard! If he could only have seen that poster! Still he's lucky to have had you.

GORDON. Why? What did I do?

JAL. Didn't you shoot most of the climax? Didn't you cut it and edit it and synchronize the sound?

GORDON. Nonsense! It's no more my picture than it's Solberg's. I only worked according to Szilard's plan.

(*The applause swells.*)

JAL. They are still clapping. Won't Solberg be pleased!

GORDON. If only I could have taken him that night, lashing his camera to the mast as the hookers put to sea – his oilskins streaming out behind him in the wind and an unholy exultation in his eyes – that would have been greater than any shot in the picture. But what's it all been for? Why did we do it? For thousands of ladies and gentlemen in fancy dress. The satisfied public! Solberg's Storm Song! God, it makes me vomit! He was a great Director. I used to fight with him, I know, but I've no right to have my name even on his credit titles.

JAL. I think he would have been satisfied. Deep down he suspected that in some ways you were rather like him.

(*The music stops. Bursts of applause follow, presumably as various people make their bows in the invisible auditorium.*)

GORDON. I'll never be like him. His sort of work only seems to come from an extraordinary combination of inspiration and guts. If you're all inspiration but no guts you play the Artist like Alastair Chenevix, while if you've got the guts without the inspiration you become what he always said I was – a Theorist. Men like Szilard don't work to theory. It is the Theorists who try to explain them afterwards.

JAL. Inspiration or guts. What of all the people who have neither?

GORDON. Like most of the inhabitants of Calamore, they become Critics.

JAL. Poor Martin!

GORDON. But Szilard had them both, and he was like nothing on earth, except himself. He wanted this to be a real picture, and by God he got what he wanted. There was no fake about that storm.

232

JAL. It's going to be his biggest popular success.

GORDON. Of course. That's the irony of it. The one time they were to have had what he wanted! There's the greatest cameraman in the world gone to make a trailor slogan for Solberg.

JAL. Well you must admit Solberg is marvellous. Such personality! He patted me on the head and gave me a visiting card with 'Mr Solberg wants to see you' on it. I loved him at once, especially in that waistcoat.

GORDON. Solberg! The friend and patron of the new Art of the Cinema! Oh, I've done with pictures. I had to finish this one, but it's definitely the last.

JAL. You know, I think it was a grand end for Szilard. He was the kind of man who wouldn't have wished for anything else.

GORDON. Yes, you are right there. That's why I finished his picture as he would have finished it himself. But it doesn't alter the fact that it wouldn't have really meant anything to that filthy crowd out there if he hadn't been drowned – if it hadn't been for that slogan.

(*The clapping thins out as the music recommences to play the audience out.*)

JAL. They're stopping now. By the way, don't you want to see what your cable is about?

(*He takes it out and reads it.*)

GORDON. It's from Moscow!

JAL. Oh! What do they say?

GORDON. They're offering me a job at the Institute. Good God! A job at the Institute! To start at once.

JAL. Gordon!

GORDON. Yes. (*He looks at her.*) It would come now – when . . .

(*The curtains to the foyer are drawn back by the attendants exposing the full stage, as the crowd begins to troop in from the auditorium chattering and laughing. Many of them shake hands with* GORDON, *in the course of which he is separated from* JAL. *Everybody is in evening dress.*)

VOICES. A great Artistic success! Such montage! Terrific. Very fine, indeed! Most entertaining! Another triumph for Solberg. Such a pity he was drowned! How do you do, King? We were just saying how much we like Szilard's picture. You had something to do with it yourself, hadn't you? Marvellous metric! I told you Solberg would pull it off again. He knows what's what. A most interesting new theory of overtones, did you notice?

(*Among the crowd* CHENEVIX *and* QUILT *appear.* CHENEVIX

233

*has shaved off his beard and has now noticeably developed
several of* SZILARD'S *mannerisms.*)

CHENEVIX. Art? Pooh! Dynamic undoubtedly but not artistic. Of
course the hardship out there was terrific, but after all what is
hardship? The first thing first.

SOMEBODY. Then you do believe in the importance of this picture,
Mr Chenevix?

CHENEVIX. Well, it's a little embarrassing to praise something that
one has contributed to in some small way oneself. Besides, what
use is criticism? The Greeks had no Art Critics. But since you
ask me, my considered opinion is that it *is* an important picture.
Quite on a par with the Silly Symphonies or even the earlier
work of Chaplin – though I know that that is a daring thing to
say.

SOMEBODY. Oh, Mr Chenevix, it must have been such a privilege
to have worked with Szilard.

CHENEVIX. I agree. Take the folk medley for instance, that we
orchestrated for the final sequence, I found that on the Middle
Island in a . . . (*His voice is drowned.*)

ALF (*to* GORDON). What cheer, old boy! Glad to see you again. Very
nice little bit of work, I must say. And by the way, the boss
wants to speak to you.

GORDON. Who?

ALF. The boss. Mr Solberg. 'E told me to send you along. And
believe me, he's pleased, old boy. Wouldn't be surprised if he
was going to hand you out a little bit of all right.

GORDON. Oh? Thanks.

(GORDON *wanders off through a haze of polite appreciation.*)

CHENEVIX. Yes, that was the most surprising thing about Szilard.
He had none of the recognized badges of an artist whatsoever.
In fact if you hadn't known him you would probably have put
him down as an energetic auctioneer. Yet he turned out work
like this. You see what I mean.

ALF. Well indeed, if it isn't good old Mr Chenevix!

CHENEVIX (*wilting*). Ah, good evening, Mr Quilt. Are you quite all
right?

ALF. I declare I wouldn't 'ave recognized you, old boy, without the
face 'air if it 'adn't been for your voice. And Miss Joyce, too!
Well, well, like old times, I must say.

JAL. What cheer, Alf! How are you, Mr Chenevix?

CHENEVIX. Are you quite all right?

ALF. Of course she is. And looking as charming as ever, and I

234

don't care 'oo knows it. Sorry I couldn't bring along Annie, the wife. She doesn't much like dressing up for these affairs. You must look in on our little love nest before you go back. Will you be in town for long, Mr Chenevix?

CHENEVIX. Well, as a matter of fact, I'm just on my way to the Balkans.

ALF. You don't say! Passing through Paris, I'll bet!

CHENEVIX. Yes, I believe I shall.

ALF. Paris, oh-ho! I'll say you're going to 'ave a nice little bit of just what the doctor ordered, eh?

CHENEVIX. I'm afraid I don't quite understand.

ALF. Oh, come off it! No offence, Miss Joyce, where none's intended. I'll give you a tip about Paris, old boy. Don't give in to those programme girls.

CHENEVIX. Really . . .

ALF. 'Pourboir,' one of them said to me. 'Pourboir?' said I. 'Pourquoi un pourboir? Je vous demande. Je peut promenader a mon chaise sans vous, ma bonne femme.' And believe me, old boy, she just crumpled up (*gesture*) like that!

CHENEVIX. I know my way about Paris all right, thank you.

ALF. I'll bet you do, vieux garçon. I'll bet you do!

JAL. Did I hear you telling Gordon that Solberg wanted him?

ALF. That's right. And believe me 'e's in good form tonight. 'E's just bought the film rights of something called the 'Song of Solomon'. Says 'e 'ears it's good sexy stuff.

CHENEVIX. Good God, he's not going to make a picture out of that!

ALF. That's right. Music and all.

(DEIRDRE *and* TONY *come in.* CHENEVIX *rapidly conceals himself and moves off.*)

DEIRDRE. Oh, Jal darling, there you are! I heard you were here. We've been trying to find you all evening.

JAL. Hallo, Dreary. Doesn't it seem years. Oh, Tony, what a nice suit. Is it paid for?

(TONY *mumbles something.*)

DEIRDRE. He says he's suffering from fleas.

JAL. Dear Tony! I suppose he slept through it all.

DEIRDRE. Oh, no. It was much too good for that. He kept awake and even made one or two comments.

JAL. Tony! Is this true? Look me in the eye.

TONY. Which eye?

JAL. This one. Did you really keep awake?

TONY. Damned good little show. All hand done too. Saw them at it myself.

DEIRDRE. My dear, Mr Solberg will simply be world famous. We are all sure he'd get a knighthood if only he'd get naturalized. Ahem – was that Gordon King I saw him talking to just now?

JAL. Probably. He sent for him.

DEIRDRE. Of course, it's really Szilard's picture, but I suppose even the cutter gets some reflected glory. I even feel entitled to a little myself.

JAL. Good for you, darling.

ALF (to TONY). Come along, your Lordship. Beer and skittles next door.

TONY. Thanks. I think I will.

ALF. 'Ow about a nice glass of bubbly for the ladies? Just 'alf a glass will do you no 'arm, I'm sure.

DEIRDRE. Thank you so much, Mr Quilt. We'll follow you directly.

ALF. Cheerie-bye then! Come along, old boy. We'll all be merry and bright!

(TONY and ALF leave for the foyer.)

DEIRDRE. Darling, how are you?

JAL. All right, thanks.

DEIRDRE. We've heard absolutely nothing from you since that dreadful night at Belgata.

JAL. No, I suppose not.

DEIRDRE. Don't talk about it, darling, if it's too painful.

JAL. Why should it be painful?

DEIRDRE. That's splendid, my dear. Always keep a stiff upper lip, or whatever it is. Of course we heard – er –

JAL. That I was living with Gordon King. Quite true.

DEIRDRE. Yes darling. I'm so glad. Love is terribly important, don't you think?

JAL. Some seem to think so. Others not so much.

DEIRDRE. Just what I was saying to Tony. I do hope you're happy, darling.

JAL. Oh, we've got along so far.

DEIRDRE. Goodness! Only that?

JAL. I daresay we're both a bit difficult at times.

DEIRDRE. Well, of course, darling, I must frankly admit he did seem rather a terrible young man to me. But then I'm really no judge of character, and he may not have liked me. Has he – I mean – is he . . . ?

JAL. No, he hasn't anything. He had quite a good job while he was finishing this picture. But now that's over.

DEIRDRE. I see. So wise of you both not to have got married. And of course everybody's so much more broadminded nowadays, don't you think? But what are you going to do now, darling?

JAL. God knows! I think I could get a job in the Studios from Solberg. He is very approachable these days. As for Gordon, I suppose he ought to go to Russia.

DEIRDRE. You don't mean to say you're going to part, darling?

JAL. I don't know.

DEIRDRE. But don't you want him any more?

JAL. I suppose I do. I'm not exactly in the habit of doing this sort of thing you know. But what's the good of attempting the impossible? All he really cares for is his work. I've known him long enough now to know that. So you see it all rather depends on how much he wants me.

DEIRDRE. Oh dear! Really, aren't men awful?

JAL. Nonsense! It'll all come right in the end. How's everybody? Is Martin well?

DEIRDRE. Well, as a matter of fact dear, nobody knows. He's married!

JAL. Martin?

DEIRDRE. Yes, dear, isn't it overpowering? He has married that enormous Slater woman from Spiddal and has hardly been seen since.

JAL. Well, indeed! Poor Martin! I hope he hasn't been overlain!

DEIRDRE. We were sure you'd take it in that spirit, dear. Yes, he did it soon after you left. Of course she always did have her eye on him, but nobody ever thought it would come to anything while you were there. Still, you never can tell with people nowadays, can you? And that reminds me, I wonder where Tony is?

JAL. Martin married! That was very precipitate of him. But a fine gesture all the same.

DEIRDRE. Yes, darling, but excuse me just a moment. I really must go and rescue poor Tony from that awful Mr Quilt! (*brightly*) I see that nice Mr Chenevix is here. But such a pity about his beard, don't you think?

(*She goes. Another batch of guests passes through. Amongst them is* BOB BRISTOW. *On his arm is a pretty, fluffy young woman with a baby voice. Dance music comes from the foyer.*)

237

BOB. Hello Jal! Hope you enjoyed the show.

JAL. Hello Bulgy!

BOB. How do you think I'm looking?

JAL. Splendid. I believe you're plumper than ever.

BOB. Not lost but gone before, eh?

HIS LADY FRIEND. Aren't you going to introduce me, Bob?

BOB (*embarrassed*). Oh, er. This is Miss Joyce who was out on the islands with us. Miss Joyce – er – well, as a matter of fact . . .

JAL. Bob! You don't mean to say . . .

BOB. Well – to tell the truth . . .

JAL. Bob, it's not Maysie?

MAYSIE. Oh, how did you guess, Miss Joyce? You're much, much too clever! You see, nobody's supposed to know. But you won't tell a soul, will you?

JAL. Oh, Bob, you've ruined it all again!

BOB (*shamefacedly*). I know. It's awful, but we couldn't help it. Could we, dear?

MAYSIE. No, darling. We simply *couldn't*. But Miss Joyce won't give us away, I'm sure.

JAL. And in a public place like this, too. Oh, Bob! The King's Proctor is probably on his way down already.

BOB. I know. I know. It can't be helped. I daresay we'll have to start all over again. But it's worth it! Isn't it, dear?

MAYSIE. Of course it's worth it, my big strong handsome! Do you love Maysie?

BOB. I should just say so!

MAYSIE. Oh naughty! Suppose the nasty King's Proctor were listening! Do excuse us, Miss Joyce, but he *is* rather a dear, isn't he?

JAL. Of course he is!

MAYSIE. Sometimes Maysie almost doesn't want to be free. Aren't I awful!

BOB. We're both awful, I'm afraid. I can see I shall have to get a job in Australia the next time.

MAYSIE. Now, take Maysie to the nice drinks. Good night, Miss Joyce! I'm sure our little secret is safe with you.

JAL. Not a word! Goodbye!

(*They wander off in a dream into the foyer.* GORDON *returns, and the crowd thins out, leaving him eventually alone with* JAL.)

GORDON (*gloomily*). Aren't you coming in, Jal?

JAL. In a moment. What did Solberg want with you?

238

GORDON (*without much enthusiasm*). He wants to give me a contract. Editing dozens more musicals and eventually directing.
(*With a wry smile.*) It's a good contract, really, particularly the
salary.

JAL. So that's it, is it? I thought that he would sense what this
picture owes to you. Trust Solberg!

GORDON. I suppose it's a compliment to my new market value.

JAL. He wants to use your name and your connection with Szilard
as an advertisement for every leg-show he turns out for the
next ten years.

GORDON. Oh, it's not as bad as that. If Solberg thinks that good
pictures can catch the public, I daresay he'll make them as
cheerfully as bad ones.

JAL. What's the matter with you? You seem very broadminded all
of a sudden. You're not thinking of accepting his offer?

GORDON. Well – after all – it will mean money.

JAL. But Gordon! The Institute! What about that?

GORDON. Oh, that's out of the question.

JAL. But you've been longing to go there for years. You're not going
to give it up now?

GORDON. It's out of the question. It means three years of damned
hard work and sweat, with little more in the way of wages than
my keep. I might as well be in the trenches.

JAL. But wouldn't you love that?

GORDON. Oh, I don't know. I might have once. But now – oh, well.
Let's forget it.

JAL. You mean you can't bring me?

GORDON. Of course not.

JAL. I see. (*Pause.*) Well, I think you ought to go.

GORDON. Thanks. But as I won't, let's change the subject.

JAL. What's the use of pretending? We've had two months together.
It's been fun, I know, but we've lived apart before this and we
can do it again.

GORDON. I don't want to stop loving you.

JAL. And how long do you suppose you'll love me if I keep you
from this? Oh, my dear, do you think I don't know you well
enough to be able to foresee that? You love me, I daresay, but
I'm not your life. If you accepted this offer and we went out to
Solberg, every time we had a row for the rest of our lives, I
would see resentment in your face – I would see words on your
lips that I could never bear.

GORDON. Nonsense!

239

JAL. After all, what's love anyhow? Do you think I don't know that there's only one thing that really matters to you? Do you remember how scared you were that night crossing to Inishgarve with me in the pookawn? That was all just an adventure and you didn't want to pass out that way. But you never even thought of what you were doing when you went out with Szilard a few hours later in far worse weather.

GORDON. That was different. I had to.

JAL. Of course it was different. It was something real to you. Not just a woman.

GORDON. I see. You're trying to give me up so that I can go to the Institute. Don't be so damned self-sacrificing and superior. What sort of a fool do you take me for? I'm not going and there's the end of it.

JAL. It seems to me that it is you who are being self-sacrificing and superior.

GORDON. In what way?

JAL. And why should you be so sure that leaving you must be self-sacrifice on my part?

GORDON. I don't understand.

JAL (*after a pause*). Well, I've been talking to Deirdre and Tony.

GORDON. Yes, I thought I saw them.

JAL. It was like old times seeing them again. You know, dear, you're not all my life any more than I am all yours.

GORDON (*after a pause*). You mean, you're thinking of Martin Burke?

JAL. Why not?

GORDON. I see.

JAL. He has got lots to give me.

GORDON. That futile swine!

JAL. You needn't be so emphatic. His only trouble is that he can't stop laughing. And I suppose I can give him something too.

GORDON (*rather hysterically*). What do you mean, give him something? Why should you be kinder to him than to me?

JAL. How could anybody be kind to you? Kindness is about the last thing that you inspire.

(*The* COMMISSIONAIRE *looks in.*)

COMMISSIONAIRE. Mr Solberg wants you, sir.

(*He disappears again.*)

GORDON. Szilard was right. He said you'd let me down.

JAL. Did he?

GORDON. Yes, that's what he said.

JAL. How well he knew. (*Holding out her hand.*) Well, goodbye.

GORDON (*after a pause, taking it*). All right. I'll start in the morning.

JAL. Tomorrow?

GORDON. Why not? What's to keep me?

JAL. Nothing at all. Then you'd better go home at once and start collecting your things. I'll do the honours for you here.

GORDON. Thanks. I'm sorry if I've been rude.

JAL. No hard feelings.

GORDON. None. Goodbye.

(*He takes her hand again. Then he takes her in his arms and kisses her. The dance music stops.*)

GORDON. Maybe we'll meet again.

JAL. Maybe.

GORDON. And still be friends?

JAL. Of course. You can thank me for that.

(*His eyes blaze with excitement. ALF hurries in.*)

ALF. I say, old boy, the Big Noise is looking for you. I think 'e's going to make a speech. You'd better come along.

(*There is clapping off.*)

GORDON. You can tell Solberg from me to go to hell!

(*He rushes off. JAL stares after him.*)

ALF. Well, I mean to say – what's the big idea?

(*Enter DEIRDRE, BOB, MAYSIE, CHENEVIX, and a number of other guests.*)

DEIRDRE. My dear, I don't know what to do with Tony! He's sitting there in a corner pouring himself out imaginary drinks and then criticizing them!

BOB. I say, where's Gordon? Solberg is going to make a speech and he wants him to be there.

JAL. He's gone.

BOB. Gone? – But where?

JAL. Home to pack.

DEIRDRE. Why? What for?

JAL. He's going to Russia.

DEIRDRE. To Russia? And what about you?

(*In the next room the band breaks into a fanfare. The guests form into an excited laneway and the COMMISSIONAIRE enters*).

JAL. Me? Well, there's always Mr Solberg!

COMMISSIONAIRE. Ladies and Gentlemen – Mr Absalom Solberg!

(*The guests form an admiring lane, craning their necks to see*

241

off, and an excited murmur and a rattle of applause breaks from them. JAL, *with a laugh, drops into a low Court curtsy as Mr Solberg appears and the curtain falls. He is not at all as one would have expected. The band can still be heard after the curtain is down. That is the end of this play.*)

ST PETER'S PORT, 1934

THE CHARACTERS OF THE PLAY

GORDON KING is an untidy young man in the middle twenties with a mop of brown hair and a pugnacious face. His background is the English upper middle class but his outlook is one of youthful hostility to everything from which he has sprung. Having run away from a public school, he has found in films an outlet for his highly strung and nervous intelligence. Here is a new medium in which the field is still open to the pioneer. And so, before meeting Szilard, he flung himself with reckless enthusiasm into the task of conjuring meaning out of the uninspired work of second-rate directors by blending the strips of celluloid together into this or that order and combination. The world, as he knows it, leaves him in a state of perpetual irritation so that he is often deliberately rude to quite harmless and inoffensive people. Like many of his type he would probably call himself an anarchist, while meaning that he was a communist, though in fact he is neither, being an artist – which is the last thing that he would admit. For art and artists he associates with amateurs, gentility, suburbia and all the lumber that he has left behind. He admires Szilard with a fierce intensity as one who is in many ways his spiritual father, and having at last found in Szilard's work, material that is worthy of his effort, he dedicates it cheerfully to the accomplishment of all his theories and experiments, while quarrelling fiercely with Szilard for resenting this. Naturally quick-tempered, he flares up into a fury under the whip of his master's tongue, but his temper dies down again as quickly as it rises and work goes on as before.

BOB BRISTOW is an ex-officer of about thirty-six. An efficient chemist, now running to fat. He is all grin, good-nature and sentimentality. His guiding star is his fascinating little wife, Maysie, whom he worships like a dog, even to the extent of being ready to give her up whenever her soul tries to soar towards bigger, greater and more romantic things than Bulgy Bristow. Luckily he is amply repaid for his devotion, as her yearnings are only temporary and,

243

although in the meantime he may be put to a lot of trouble, he reaps his reward in her contrite arms sooner or later. A thorough-going lowbrow, there is nothing that moves him so deeply as a good dance band playing a torch song.

RAYMOND CHENEVIX is a man of about thirty. He is intelligent, but ineffective. He has the fatal ability of being talented in too many directions and like a kitten he always hesitates in his leap after any of them. Chock full of ideas, he has neither the concentration nor the application to carry any of them out. His ambition is to be a creative artist and to mix with and to be looked up to by intelligent and advanced people. Yet being devoid of any genuine personality of his own he adopts that of whoever he happens to admire at the moment. He is not really a fraud or a *poseur*. What appears to be his insincerity is really his frantic effort to be something that he is not – to convince himself that he has something he has not. When the play opens he is in his 'ruthless artist' phase, but before it is over he has taken Szilard as his model and is remodelling all his mannerisms to fit the new role. He dresses with a well-studied care-lessness in the earlier scenes.

ALF QUILT is an earnest and serious-minded Cockney – earnest and serious to the point at times of being sinister, as only a Cockney can be. He has a superstitious awe of the upper classes and of business success. Art he is prepared to treat with a friendly tolerance. In-tensely romantic in his ideas, his friendly nature is more easily offended by what he imagines to be a social slight than by any real injury or wrong. He probably went to a University on his Govern-ment grant for a few terms after the war and suffered intensely there on account of this. In the earlier scenes his costume bears witness to the fact that while he is an accountant on duty, and as such must wear a black coat, and a butterfly collar, he is never-theless at what he supposes to be the seaside and consequently is entitled to relax into grey flannel trousers, a brightly coloured tie and a string of sports medals across his waistcoat. His hair is clipped almost entirely away around the back of his head and above the ears. He clearly regards the Criochs as something on a par with Basutoland, but is always prepared to do his duty with a brave face.

DEIRDRE DOBBS is an enthusiastic amateur in the middle twenties. People call her an atrocious snob, but that is unfair. She genuinely likes nice people, well-bred people and intellectual people. She does not really look down on those who are not. She is genuinely sorry for them and never for a moment supposes that they are not sorry for themselves. She has excellent taste in clothes and can recognize and foretell a new fashion in intellectualism almost as readily as she can in clothes, without really understanding either. Hence her present interest in Film Art. She has this merit, that she does her best and puts all her goods – and a good many of other people's – into her shop window. In her heart, she would prefer to marry an intellectual than to marry money or a title. But she never will persuade one to do so and she will probably end by marrying Tony. And in all justice to her she will make a loyal, conscientious and well-studied wife – if you like that sort of thing.

JAL JOYCE is an impulsive, undisciplined girl in the early twenties. She is an untidy, outspoken, warm-hearted person. Her education has been sadly neglected entirely through her own fault, for she has run away from more than one school and her knowledge of the world is now largely bounded by the winds and tides of Calamore Bay where from an early age she has sailed all sorts of boats in all sorts of costumes and spends or loses most of her small income in fruitless and ill-considered ways at home. She has a ready tongue and a sharp incisive wit, living almost entirely on her emotions. For some years it has been assumed that she will eventually marry Martin Burke – the most eligible man of the ineligible lot in Tyrcluain. Not that she has given much thought to it herself. For as a woman she is yet largely undeveloped in spite of her age. But contact with the wider world represented by the film makers reveals in her new and unplumbed depths of feeling that have been as yet unsuspected. A disarming candour and trust, wedded to a fastidious pride, makes her a very vulnerable target for the blows of life.

SZILARD is a wiry, brown weather-beaten man in the middle fifties with wild white hair and an expression that changes from charm to ferocity with the greatest ease and frequency. Born in Budapest of humble parents, he emigrated to America at an early age, where he learnt his English. Here he worked for some years in a photographic studio before joining one of the early film companies as cameraman. These were the days when the industry was a somewhat contemptible adjunct of the amusement park, and this fact together with his undistinguished origin have developed in him a deep contempt for the new converts to 'Films as an Art' and

towards the crowd of enthusiastic upper-class *dilettanti* that have
come to flock around the modern studios. For years he has
struggled to improve pure camera work. Anything that can be
photographed is his enthusiasm. Angles – faces – distance – set-up,
these are the breath of life to him. The modern problems of cutting and montage he airily waves aside as mere theory. It is the
picture that matters to him more than the intellectual content of
the tale that is to be told. His innate restlessness and lack of dis-
cipline have, although a brilliant executant, lost him job after
job. He cannot work easily under direction though for years he
has been forced to do so. He hates all stars. And above all, he has
quarrelled fiercely with a long line of production chiefs whose concern has been more for the preparation of money-making pictures than with abstract problems of good camera work. Consequently he has in the end developed into a lone wolf, getting casual
employment from time to time in various parts of the world, from
occasional backers – for he has never accumulated any capital of
his own – where he makes documentary pictures of extraordinary
power and beauty, which his enemies – and they are many – dis-
miss as 'cameraman's pictures'. This life he finds to be exactly
fitted to his temperament. He is his own master and is in touch with
the simple primitive people whom he loves and understands, and
whom, as his enemies say, he can bully. For in a way he is a bully,
notwithstanding his charm and simplicity of manner. This is largely
due to the fact that he is entirely an emotional artist, being devoid
of all conscious intellectuality. He always feels himself at a disadvantage with highbrows or intellectuals with whom he is quite
unable to discuss his own work. Long ago he gave up trying to
solve the problem of life, and being of a humane and fundamentally
sensitive disposition he has taken to Work as the ultimate escape
from all the problems and contradictions of existence. And Work
he worships with a fierce energy that overrides everything, and
that gives him a black name in the lower ranks of the trade, where
the virtue of work is not so seriously regarded. Some people would
call him unintelligent – an unfair criticism when one takes into
account the intuitive rightness of everything he does in the way
of his own vocation – an asset much more valuable than any conscious intelligence. However, if he cannot adequately express his
aesthetic theories, he has on the other hand a shattering tongue, as
his enemies know full well. Not that he is ever deliberately offensive
to anybody. With the poor, the weak, the primitive he can be
gentle and considerate – although his affection is directed more

towards classes than to individuals. But with the rich he can be quite devoid of conscience or scruple, while normally full of courtesy and civility except when he loses his temper. Altogether he is the most lovable and charming of men though at times given to depression and despair, and he is often difficult to work with. In Gordon King he can see many of the qualities of brain and breeding that he himself lacks, wedded to a temperament that is not unlike his own, and in his heart he admires and respects him accordingly while fighting furiously with him over everyday things.

TONY, the Earl of Clanbrassil, is a sleepy good-humoured person of about twenty-eight. The ravages of port and lack of exercise are beginning to leave their mark upon him. He says little, but when he does his voice is liable to get out of control and to come out, quite unintentionally, with a loud bark or bellow.

MARTIN BURKE is a tired idealist – a high-minded and intelligent man for whom the cruelties and contradictions of life have been too much. Frustrated in the wider world of action, he has become the critic *in excelsis* and has retired to his small property in the west where he sharpens his keen and bitter wit on the small local society which looks up to him as a wit, and speaks of him with the awe and respect that he yearns for. It has been assumed for some time that at some future date, when it suits him, he will marry Jal Joyce.

THE ISLANDERS are a simple friendly folk, quite accustomed to visitors, whom they usually treat, not so much as equals as poor harmless lunatics. The men wear rough grey tweed trousers and waistcoats, blue jerseys, black tam-o'-shanters or ordinary cloth caps and cowhide slippers. The women wear voluminous blood-red skirts and bodices, shawls and the same type of cowhide slippers. They all talk with the meticulous care and precision of people who are speaking a foreign tongue. Their voices have a peculiarly soft and melodious quality that is most attractive.

There have, of course, been documentary pictures made in surroundings similar to those described in this play, to which the author is frankly indebted for most of the knowledge he possesses of the technique of film-making. Not, however, for his characters which are his own creations and are not intended to represent actual persons.

THE DREAMING DUST

A Play Designed for Performance or
Public Reading, not necessarily in a Theatre

PERIOD PIECE

With the exception of *The Moon in the Yellow River* all my plays included in the present collection are in various ways historical. That is to say, their very divergent plots have each got a factual basis. This detail is not offered as an alibi for any difficulties that you may experience in believing in some of them. The fact that it 'actually happened' is more likely to contribute to the badness of a play than to secure its success. Hollywood is often wise to enlarge on nature.

In the case of *The Dreaming Dust*, however, the hurdle that has taken some years of effort to surmount is not that of satisfying the customers in the auditorium with the truth of my tale. It has been the difficulty of ascertaining what the story actually is. For here, a formidable lobby of scholarship, entrenched for over two hundred years behind a barricade of print, insists on giving us, under the guise of biography, a story that is obviously fictitious.

Let me explain my point further. It would be comparatively easy to draw a stage portrait of the Dean of St Patrick's as a scatological problem-child with a hatred of the sex act and an obsession with lavatories, or as a tormentor of women who drove two of them into the grave, or simply as an unusually angry old man. One might also write quite an amusing satire on the subject of this 'heart burning with hatred against the human race' whose mightiest thunderbolt – *Gulliver's Travels* – was neatly caught by mankind, the target, and metamorphosed into a children's book.

Unfortunately the matter does not end here, as there are other characters to be considered as well as Swift, and if we stick honestly to the data in the case of these also, we soon find ourselves struggling in a Bedlam of eccentrics, from which nothing in the nature of an intelligible play could possibly emerge. What, for example, could any practical dramatist make of a heroine, generally supposed to be the hero's wife, but who is never acknowledged as such, and who never openly objects to this anomalous position, a

251

mettlesome and proud young woman who accepts the charity and support of a man whose relationship to her is questionable in the extreme, who acts as his hostess for over twenty-five years, and who never apparently has a show-down with him on the subject of matrimony?

A character in a play has to be explained sooner or later to the player who is expected to portray it, and this is no easy task if his or her behaviour bears no resemblance to any known pattern of human conduct, or even to some convention of the stage. Yet here we have a set of characters actually taken from life, the oddness of whose conduct is inescapable, whatever their real motives may have been.

So it will not be surprising when I say that the composition of this play has cost me more time and trouble than any other play that I have ever written, thanks to the peculiarity of the material. Its evolution from a frolic on the air into a serious attack on over a dozen authoritative biographies has been described already in the preface to an earlier English edition. Meanwhile the rough treatment of my solution – a roughness directed not so much at the solution itself as at my irritating insistence that it is right – has driven me, at last, to ventilate the whole matter in a biography of my own, entitled *In Search of Swift* – an enterprise that is wholly outside my province as a playwright, and ought to have been undertaken by somebody protected by a Ph.D.

In short, a speculative story invented to account for the peculiar behaviour of a given set of stage characters may perhaps turn out to be closer to the truth than was at first supposed. This may be accounted for by the fact that, while biographers can be intimidated by authorities, playwrights are even more intimidated by the need to make sense that can be explained to a cast.

After a moderately eventful life in various other shapes and sizes, and under at least one other title, the play has now assumed a format in which it may be performed with little in the way of alteration, either on a regularly equipped stage, with full orchestra and choral accompaniment, or as a simple reading without props or scenery, or as a radio play.

Theatrically, it has long since ceased to be as much concerned with the personal problems of Swift, as with the seven deadly sins, their relative deadlines, and the curious phenomenon that it is usually our own particular sin that we find really unbearable in other people. It is an exercise for actors and actresses with a flair for character, who seldom get enough opportunity to display their versatility in the course of one play. In spite of the fact that it is written with a particular eye to touring companies, it has until recently been performed more successfully on television than on the stage. What would probably be its ideal presentation – as an Interlude in St Patrick's Cathedral – is something that I am sure I shall never see.

The Dreaming Dust

This play was first produced in the Gaiety Theatre, Dublin, by Hilton Edwards and Micheál MacLiammóir on March 25th, 1940. In its next form, with a cast deliberately limited to eight or ten characters who appear and reappear in various guises, it was produced at the Provincetown Playhouse on Cape Cod, on July 19th, 1954, with the following cast:

The Dean – Dr Jonathan Swift (a leading man)	EMILE AUTOR
Stella – Moll (a leading woman)	VIRGINIA THOMS
Rev Mr Tisdall – John Gay (a character man)	FRED LEVY
Vanessa – A Trollop (an ingénue)	ANNE GERETY
Rebecca Dingley – Mrs Vanhomrigh (a character woman)	CATHERINE HUNTINGTON
Charles Ford – (a light comedian)	ROBERT BEATEY
Dr Berkeley – A Ballad Singer (a heavy)	THOMAS J. CLANCY
Brennan – The Sexton (a clown)	PATRICK CLANCY
Two extra Women	—

The production was directed by Tom Newton.

CHARACTERS AND SETTING

THE DEAN
PRIDE
ANGER
LUST
AVARICE
GLUTTONY
ENVY
SLOTH
THE SEXTON
TWO WOMEN CARRYING SKULLS

The action of the play opens in St Patrick's Cathedral, Dublin. In time it opens in the year 1835 but then ranges over many years during the first half of the eighteenth century.

While the stage directions here indicate its more elaborate method of presentation, this play is so constructed that it can be performed with a minimum of adaptation and scenery, either in a church, or in a hall equipped with ordinary stage lighting and with facilities for playing recorded music and effects. If an actual choir and organ are available, so much the better. Otherwise the number of recordings used, and the amount of scenery and properties that are employed, depend upon the taste of the producer and the facilities that are to hand.

With some minor cuts and alterations, it can be presented as a broadcast, lasting an hour and a half. If presented as a reading, without cuts or intervals, it should run for about an hour and three-quarters.

THE PLAY

*We are in a section of the south-east end of St Patrick's Cathedral, Dublin, looking across the nave. The area in front of us is divided by the central pillar of two Gothic arches, above which hang some tattered flags. Behind these arches is a side aisle, which in turn is backed by the south wall of the church. Through the western arch (*stage left*) we can see in this wall a large wooden double door which opens on to the street. Behind the eastern arch is a narrow stone opening through which a flight of steps leads up to the vestiaries. In this section of the wall is a niche containing Faulkiner's bust of the cathedral's most celebrated dean, and to the stage left of this are two plaques bearing respectively the epitaphs of Swift and of Stella. Swift's reads:*

HIC DEPOSITUM EST CORPUS
IONATHAN SWIFT S.T.D.
HUJUS ECCLESIAE CATHEDRALIS
DECANI,
UBI SAEVA INDIGNATIO
ULTERIUS
COR LACERARE NEQUIT.
ABI VIATOR
ET IMITARE, SI POTERIS,
STRENUUM PRO VIRILI
LIBERTATIS VINDICATOREM.
OBIIT 19 DIE MENSIS OCTOBRIS
A.D. 1745 ANNO AETATIS 78.

Directly in front of the central column a section of the floor has been taken up, leaving a hole. Beside the column, and also against the rear wall, are tables with hymn books and collecting-boxes. To right and left respectively of the open area in the centre are two lines of simple cathedral chairs, all facing stage right.

259

The organ is playing the introductory chorale to Bach's Passion of St John, and presently the choir enters down the steps from the vestiary, processes down centre, turns right and moves off up what is presumably the centre of the church. They are singing the opening chorus of the oratorio. As they go, two women and a man appear from the right, dressed in the fantastic costumes of some miracle play, and wearing masks, which each takes off as they speak. The organ continues softly in the distance.

PRIDE (*a Leading Woman*). Well, our little masque is over. (*Temptingly.*) I thought you were splendid, Anger.

ANGER (*an Ingénue*). Gluttony cut me out of two of my best speeches. Deliberately, I believe.

ENVY (*a Heavy*). There were no good speeches in that deplorable masque. More people should have been consulted about the script.

ANGER. I daresay that you, Envy, would have liked to have written in an extra Sin or two.

(*Two more men enter, also dressed for the performance, removing their masks as they speak.*)

SLOTH (*a Clown, yawning*). Seven sins are deadly enough for me. Well, now that we've finished our play-acting, perhaps we can all get home to bed.

GLUTTONY (*a Character Man*). Not before the party, Sloth. Isn't there going to be some sort of a party? I mean – after all the work we've had in staging this thing.

(*Another* MAN AND WOMAN PLAYER *follow, unmasking as before. Meanwhile* TWO WOMEN *have entered from the street door, each bearing a round object, wrapped in a cloth. One is a middle-aged woman. The other is a girl. They look around them, and are arrested by Swift's epitaph.*)

AVARICE (*a Character Woman*). A party? Is that all we're going to be given? I would much rather have my expenses.

SLOTH. Avarice has got her eye on the poor box. Better look out!

AVARICE. Don't be ridiculous, Sloth. Still, I do think . . .

LUST (*a Light Comedian*). You look charming, Pride, in that costume. May I help you with it?

PRIDE. No thank you, Lust. I can manage.

A WHISPER. I am that I am.

LUST (*turning*). What did you say?

ENVY. I said nothing.

LUST. I thought I heard a whisper.

PRIDE. So did I.

LUST. Curious. (*Pause.*) Well, let's all go up to the . . .

A VOICE (*with echo, sepulchrally*). I am that I am.

SLOTH. Jaysus! I'm getting out! (*He hurries off.*)

> (*The organ stops, and for a moment there is silence.*)

OLDER WOMAN. 'Saeva Indignatio'. There it is. This must be the place.

YOUNGER WOMAN. What a strange epitaph for a clergyman. What does it mean?

OLDER WOMAN. Don't ask me that. Nobody could understand such Latin. 'Virili.'

> (*She points at the plaque. The remaining* MASQUERS *have paused in their disrobing and have turned to the newcomers.*)

ENVY. That is Doctor Swift's epitaph, ma'am. It was you who spoke?

YOUNGER WOMAN. We're looking for his grave.

ENVY. He wrote that epitaph himself.

OLDER WOMAN. Then his Latin was more enigmatic than his English. Where are they laying down the floor?

GLUTTONY. Over here, madam. I'm afraid that you are late for our performance.

OLDER WOMAN. What performance?

GLUTTONY. 'The Masque of the Seven Deadly Sins'.

ENVY. They hope to make it an annual event.

ANGER. Not with me! I've had enough for two years.

AVARICE. What have you got there . . . in that bundle?

> (*The* OLDER WOMAN *is removing the wrapping, and there is a gasp of disgust as she exposes a skull.*)

A VOICE (*louder still*). Let the day perish wherein I was born.

> (*The* SINS *react more or less in unison.* PRIDE *turns away in silent distaste.*)

AVARICE. Oh, take it away!

ANGER. It's revolting.

LUST. A skull! Where did you get that thing?

ENVY. That voice again! Who is talking?

GLUTTONY. What a disgusting object!

OLDER WOMAN. (*Turning the skull around*). Dr Swift in person, I believe. To be returned again to his proper niche. Is this the hole from which they took it? (*She approaches the hole.*)

PRIDE. No wonder the Dean of St Patrick's is turning in his grave.

> (*From below, a dull thudding.*)

AVARICE. God preserve us! What's that?

GLUTTONY. Is there somebody down there?

(*A dirty head slowly emerges from the hole. It has the face of* SLOTH. AVARICE *and* ANGER *scream.*)

GLUTTONY (*making a closer inspection*). It's a Sexton cleaning out the water. Or – can it be one of us?

PRIDE. There's more than a Sexton in this grave.

SLOTH (*assuming the role of the Sexton*). I doubt it, ma'am. There's bones and there's water down here, and what more is a Sexton? What more is yourself, for the matter of that? Bones and water.

LUST (*with a nervous laugh*). Don't be alarmed ladies. It's only our old friend, Sloth, playing a better part than he had in that Masque.

ENVY. Then let him stop playing the fool. They don't pay you, fellow, for alarming the Friends of the Cathedral.

SEXTON. They pay me for digging, sir. Digging out this, and covering up that.

PRIDE. Then cover it up, whatever it is, and let's be off. I never liked this place.

(*The Older Woman hands the skull to the Sexton who lays it on the edge of the hole, facing the Audience.*)

OLDER WOMAN. They left it for me to bring back to where it belongs.

SEXTON. After passing it all around Dublin, I'll be bound.

OLDER WOMAN. Yes. It was examined by an eminent corps of phrenologists. (*Turning to the others.*) They were repairing the floor here, and somebody noticed the name on the coffin. Everybody was charmed at such a find . . . even if the verdict of the doctors was a little disappointing.

SEXTON. And what was that?

OLDER WOMAN. Anthropoid in shape, is the report. And sadly deficient in the bump of humour.

SEXTON. Bedad that may be. But he's smiling now.

GLUTTONY. That is in bad taste, sir. Swift has nothing to smile at now.

SEXTON. He has his dreams, your honour. Sure they all have them, down there.

ENVY. That's not a smile. Savage indignation is the phrase he coined, himself. About what, who knows?

(*There is a pause, and then the* YOUNGER WOMAN *uncovers another skull.*)

YOUNGER WOMAN. The report on the lady is much kinder. A charming skull, they say. A model of symmetry and proportion.

AVARICE. Oh not another one! I must go.

LUST. Is this Stella?

> (PRIDE *turns away, in profound emotion, separating herself from the others. The* OLDER WOMAN *shrugs her shoulders, as if to echo 'Who knows?'*)

LUST. Because if so, we must make sure that they are returned to the same grave.

ENVY. But that would be most improper. Stella was buried below the end of the buttress . . . over there. (*He points left.*)

ANGER. No, no. This is the woman's grave. He was buried further up the nave. (*She points right.*)

LUST. I don't agree. I am quite satisfied that they were buried together.

ANGER. Never! This is not his grave. It is hers.

LUST. After all, weren't they man and wife?

ENVY. Nonsense. They were never that.

AVARICE. Good heavens, what does it matter now? Does decency demand their separation in the earth?

ENVY. It isn't a question of decency. It's a question of fact. They were never married, and were buried ten feet apart.

ANGER. She here . . . he over there.

ENVY. No. Stella lies below the buttress . . . over there.

GLUTTONY. Wherever they lie, it is apart.

LUST. If he never married her, he must have been a monster.

ANGER. If he *did* marry her, he was a monster.

GLUTTONY. In short, he was a monster in any event – a fact that I have always maintained. So put them back anywhere and have done with it.

LUST. He was nothing of the kind. The people who knew him and were his friends insist that he was no monster.

> (*There is general outburst of argument, which is topped by an imperious gesture from* PRIDE.)

PRIDE. Oh, why can't you all be silent? Maybe then they could speak for themselves.

AVARICE. Speak for themselves?

PRIDE. Yes. We all heard that voice. Don't you feel that somebody else is here with us? Somebody very close . . . terribly close.

AVARICE (*after a short, pregnant silence*). Please don't say things like that.

THE SEXTON. Better be careful.

THE DEAN (*who has appeared and is listening*). What are you quarrelling about, my friends.

263

SEXTON. 'Tis about the bones of the dead, Mr Dean . . . a couple of old skulls the doctors have been measuring and taping. And now they're fighting over where they should be thrown.

DEAN (*picking up* SWIFT'S *skull*). I see. You should take better care of your charges, Maguire. These things are the bullion of the Church. Who permitted their removal?

ENVY. You hear what the Dean says. Man is endowed with more than bones and water, as this fellow would suggest.

DEAN. How true. How true Sir Envy. He is, for instance, the inheritor of seven of the most mysterious gifts of the spirit, his sins . . . those things that you ladies and gentlemen have been so ably depicting in your masque this evening. He is born with them. He spends his life trying to escape from them. But in the end one of them kills him. This skull is the symbol of that ritual. And now you are all arguing over where it should be laid to rest. But until you know for certain what was the sin that really killed this man, how can you solve the riddle of his life and death and burial?

GLUTTONY (*sententiously*). Indeed, who are we to judge anybody? We are all sinful.

DEAN. A worthy observation, sir. We are all sinful, as you say. But I have never noticed that a knowledge of that fact enables us to understand our neighbours.

GLUTTONY. I wouldn't presume to contradict you, Mr Dean.

DEAN. You are each, I can see, an authority on one of these human frailties. So let me ask you each in turn what was the sin that overcame this soul? Then, perhaps, we may be able to determine whether these poor relics should be laid together or apart. (*Pause.*) No answer. Perhaps you feel that they should tell their own story. They do, you know. Have you never sat below that column in the evening, and felt that some tormented spirit in this place had something that he longed to say? I have.

PRIDE. So have I.

AVARICE. I think . . . we should be going.

DEAN. One moment, madam. Bear with me, please, for just a moment. Under the pavement of this house of God a tragedy is buried that no masque of ours could ever match. If these skulls could speak, they might tell us what it is; but, as you see, they have no lips. But *you* have lips, my friends.

ENVY. What do you mean, sir?

DEAN. The past is closer than we think. Just four or five feet off, below the level of the floor. And closer still, now that this grave is opened. Lend it your lips, my friends, and let its tenants dream aloud. Listen.

A WHISPER. Yahoos! Yahoos!

(*They shudder, but remain silent. The organ is heard faintly in the distance as the scene begins to dissolve into a room at the deanery. The* DEAN *places the two skulls on the forestage.*)

PRIDE. Are you quite certain, Mr Dean, that you, yourself, will wish to hear this story?

DEAN (*momentarily taken aback*). What makes you ask that?

PRIDE. The dead are seldom as we would wish them to be. And once they start to speak we must listen till the end.

DEAN (*pulling himself together*). We will take our chance of that. So set the chairs and tables as in the deanery. I will assist in the performance, and we will begin a different masque.

(*The* PLAYERS *move, almost mechanically, to set the scene under his direction.*)

PRIDE. As you wish. But remember . . . to the end, Mr Dean.

DEAN (*to* AVARICE). Come, Madam Avarice, you shall be Mrs Dingley. Sit over there beside the fire and make yourself at home, while Brennan waits on you. (*He gestures to* SLOTH *with a chuckle.*) This will be good casting. (*Then turning to* GLUTTONY *while the* SEXTON *climbs out and covers the hole.*) And you, Gluttony can let us hear the charge that *you* prefer against this savage shade?

GLUTTONY. As I was saying, sir, it was the worst of sins . . . the sin that degrades the flesh to the level of the brute beast. *He* was the Yahoo . . . not man. An animal . . . a vicious pander to his own degraded appetites . . . a dirty, vulgar fellow.

DEAN. In short, the sin you represented in your masque. So come, Mr Tisdall, to the deanery, through the muddy liberties of St Patrick's. The flickering rushlights in the dingy houses. A stormy night, with the tower of the cathedral outlined against the scudding thunderclouds. That was the kind of night for you to call on Dr Swift.

(AVARICE *and* SLOTH *have assumed the guise of* DINGLEY *and* BRENNAN, *and now take their places in the scene. The* DEAN *assists* GLUTTONY *into the guise of* TISDALL *– an eighteenth-century clergyman. The organ music changes into a roll of thunder, which continues from time to time throughout the following scene. The other characters melt away to the sides of the stage, from which they watch.*)

265

DEAN. Now, Mr Tisdall, it is time for you to bang upon the great brass knocker of the deanery door.

(*The* DEAN *leaves the stage, as* TISDALL *batters an invisible knocker, which nevertheless resounds through the house.* SLOTH, *as* BRENNAN, *comes grumbling downstage to open an imaginary door. The two skulls remain on the forestage.*)

BRENNAN (*taking* TISDALL'S *cloak*). Ttt-ttt-ttt. He doesn't like water on the carpet.

TISDALL. A most unpleasant evening in the street.

BRENNAN. It'll be unpleasanter here when he gets home from the church.

TISDALL. Who is this lady by the fire?

DINGLEY (*stirring in her sleep*). Eh? What?

BRENNAN. That's only Mrs Dingley. Wake up, ma'am. We've got callers.

(*He takes* TISDALL'S *cloak and throws it on the floor in a corner.*)

DINGLEY (*opening her eyes*). Yes? What was that?

TISDALL. My humble apologies, ma'am. My name is Tisdall.

DINGLEY. Why, Mr Tisdall. I remember you.

TISDALL. Your health, I hope is good?

DINGLEY. As good as can be expected.

TISDALL. And Dr Swift?

DINGLEY. He does not see many visitors these days, but I am sure he will be glad to see *you*. Sometimes he is a little odd in his manner, but you musn't mind it. Hush! Here he comes. I always know his footsteps on the stairs.

(*The* DEAN *enters as* SWIFT).

SWIFT. Take my coat, fellow.

BRENNAN. Yes, Mr Dean.

(*He goes away with it.*)

DINGLEY. Jonathan, don't you see who has called? An old friend – the Reverend Mr Tisdall.

SWIFT. Why, so it is, begad! I thought the room seemed more crowded than usual.

TISDALL. Good evening, Mr Dean.

SWIFT. Good evening, Tisdall. What brings you here after all these years?

TISDALL. I have . . . um . . . been persuaded by my curate to ask a small favour of you on his behalf.

SWIFT. Ah!

DINGLEY. I am sure you would like him to stay to supper, Jonathan.

SWIFT. Let him stay if he wishes. We need some parson to drink the foul wine.

TISDALL. Wine? I never touch wine. At least only medicinally.

SWIFT. That is how this will taste.

TISDALL. I hope I was not mistaken in coming.

SWIFT. That depends on what it is you want for your curate.

TISDALL. My young friend is aspiring to climb the heights of Parnassus.

SWIFT. The heights of where?

TISDALL. He hopes some day to be considered, like yourself, as an author.

SWIFT. Like my friend Mr Congreve, I do not desire to be considered as an author, but as a gentleman. However, if you have brought some of his bum fodder for me to read I shall look it over after the meat. Meanwhile . . .

TISDALL. Sir, I have not brought any of his work.

SWIFT. Indeed? It might have proved an alternative to conversation.

TISDALL (*getting indignant*). You have always treated me with a certain strain of contempt. But . . .

SWIFT. Nonsense, Tisdall. You have misunderstood me. I never had any contempt for you.

TISDALL (*mollified*). Ah.

SWIFT. That is why I never troubled to make a bishop of you.

TISDALL (*indignantly*). To make a bishop of *me*. Let me tell you, sir . . .

(*Raised voices are heard outside.*)

SWIFT. What is all this noise outside in the street?

BRENNAN. Only a couple of beggers was asking after you at the door. I gave them the push.

SWIFT. Indeed! And since when have I given you permission to select my guests?

BRENNAN. Guests? Sure amn't I after telling you, 'tis only . . .

SWIFT. Go down at once and invite them in.

BRENNAN. Invite them in? An old trollop and a poxy ballad singer?

SWIFT. Both of them, sirrah – unless you wish to join them in the rain.

(BRENNAN *goes off grumbling.*)

DINGLEY. Jonathan, what is this latest nonsense?

SWIFT. Our traditional Irish hospitality, my dear Dingley. Tonight we keep open house. Can I receive one guest and turn away

267

another? Besides, my old friend must meet some of his successors in my affections.

DINGLEY. Inviting in all the rascality of the town. It's scandalous. But there's no use saying anything, I know.

(*A tittering* TROLLOP *appears – played by* ANGER *– and a* BALLAD SINGER *played by* ENVY.)

BRENNAN. Here's your fancy friends. And don't say you didn't send for them yourself, because the company heard you.

SWIFT. Ah, my dear friends. Welcome to the deanery.

(*They titter.*)

SWIFT. Tisdall, I want you to meet my sweetheart.

TROLLOP. God bless you, Mr Dean.

SWIFT. This is Pullagowna, one time my cook until she trapped this poor rogue into matrimony.

TROLLOP. I'm your bully woman, Mr Dean.

BALLAD SINGER. As cushy a mott as ever rattled a gut board on the flags.

SWIFT. A cunning trull for she takes in English, and she pays in French. How is your rascally spouse?

BALLAD SINGER. Poorly, your honour. Very poorly.

TROLLOP. We were thinking that maybe your honour . . .

SWIFT. Then let us hope this sickness will prove a blessing in disguise, and permit the hangman to devote himself to more profitable employments.

(*Raucous laughter.*)

SWIFT. But something tells me that there is a purpose in this visit. What do you want, my friends? A prayer, no doubt. Well, let us all kneel down together.

(*He proceeds to do so.*)

BALLAD SINGER. A prayer!

TROLLOP. What use is Protestant praying?

BALLAD SINGER. The weather's cold, but charity's colder.

TROLLOP. Sure, the Dane knows well what we're after. A few odd coppers, sir.

SWIFT (*rising*). Ah! You will have noted, Tisdall, the wisdom of my sweetheart. She does not look for pity or for pious edification. All that she wants is money, because she knows that without money she may be a pretty but never a proper woman.

TROLLOP. Them's my very words, Mr Dane.

SWIFT. But, madam, have you considered? If I give you money you will become like my poor friend here. (*Indicates* TISDALL.) He cannot sleep out under the hedges as you do, without the fear of having his pockets picked.

TROLLOP. Ah, go on owa that. As if we'd keep it overnight. (*Laughter*.)

SWIFT. An excellent answer, Pullagowna. You are not usurers to store it in your hose. With money well spent, barbarians are tamed and faithful friends are purchased every day.

(*He collects from* TISDALL, *and pours out the contents of his own purse*.)

SWIFT. Come, Dingley.

DINGLEY. Certainly not. These are most undeserving cases.

SWIFT. The more undeserving the greater the charity.

'Where is the man who can this truth deny,
A fishwife hath a fate, and so have I.'

DINGLEY. You can't change the habits of these people either by kindness or by persuasion?

SWIFT. No, Dingley. And even if I did, what would they get for the exchange?

TROLLOP. God will reward you, Mr Dane. For there's little enough we can give you in return.

SWIFT. You can leave me your pitch in Golden Lane.

TROLLOP. I will indeed, your honour. 'Twill be there in my will, settled and sealed by the scrivening bar attorneys.

SWIFT (*to the* BALLAD SINGER). And *you* can sing me the latest ballad on the Dean of St Patrick's. It is the hour of evensong.

TROLLOP. Go on, you scut. Sing when His Reverence tells you.

BALLAD SINGER (*singing*).

'Look down St Patrick, look, we pray
On thine own church and steeple
Convert thy dean on this great day
Or else God help thy people.

This place he got by wit and rhyme
And many ways most odd.
And might a bishop be in time
Did he believe in God.

But fearful as his wrath appears
We'll pray the Lord above
To still the sounds of women's tears
And save us from his love.'

(SWIFT'S *temper boils over*.)

SWIFT. Ungrateful rat. Is this the way you repay me?

BALLAD SINGER. I meant no harm, Mr Dane. I meant no harm.

SWIFT. 'Women's tears.' Out of my house, the pair of you. Out, out this instant.

TROLLOP. Holy Jezebel, he'll have us milled.

SWIFT (*driving them forth screeching*). Filthy, crapulous, cankered, mangy, verminous, off-scourings of the dunghill and the jakes.

TISDALL (*horrified*). Dr Swift.

SWIFT. Out, out to the middens that gave you life. Out, you poxy misbirths.

(*Their voices die away. Door slam.*)

TISDALL. Dr Swift, Dr Swift.

SWIFT. Well, sir? What is the matter with you, sir?

TISDALL. This language is outrageous in a priest. It was you who ordered him to sing.

SWIFT (*bitterly*). They call me a ribald priest, an apostate politician and a perjured lover – a heart burning with hatred against the human race. Tell me, sirrah, is that what you are saying of me?

TISDALL. I do not presume to pass judgment on my fellow-creatures, sir. Anything I say about you keeps strictly to the facts.

SWIFT. What facts, may I ask? The fact, I suppose, that I prevented your marriage to a lady you loved. Eh?

TISDALL. A lady whom you did not condescend to make happy yourself.

DINGLEY. Oh dear, oh dear!

SWIFT (*with icy calm*). So I prevented your marriage! But surely that was a service, my dear Tisdall, to save you from the disappointments of matrimony?

TISDALL. Some consider it a very honourable condition. My curate for instance, who for some reason that eludes me, wishes you to perform the ceremony.

SWIFT. So that is what you're after! I am to play Cupid for your factotum?

TISDALL. An odd way for a clergyman to describe one of his holy offices.

SWIFT. Marriage is an odd condition, my friend. They say, if you want to be blamed you must marry, and if you want to be praised you must die. But never fear, I shall perform the ceremony. Indeed I shall do more. I shall give him a poem for a wedding present. It is called 'Strephen and Chloe' and should be read by every bridegroom. Let me see. Where is it?

(He opens a drawer and takes out a paper. Dingley begins to get agitated.)

TISDALL. Dr Swift, if this is one of the poems of which I heard rumours . . .

SWIFT. It is purely instructional, Tisdall, and it may help your young friend. Take these lines, for instance . . .
> 'How great a change! How quickly made!
> They learn to call a spade a spade.
> They soon from all constraints are freed:
> Can see . . .'

(Dingley rises and starts to search a drawer.)

TISDALL. Sir, in deference to the presence of one of the gentler sex, I must insist – ahem – on reading this poem by myself.

SWIFT. Do, sir. Take it, and welcome.

TISDALL. There are certain subjects that are not . . . *(He looks at the poem.)* Dr Swift, your work revolts me. Be damned to my cloth, sir, it stinks. *You* stink, sir.

SWIFT. We all stink, Tisdall. It is the fate of the race of man to stink.

TISDALL. No good can come of continuing this visit. It was a mistake from the start. I shall take this poem with me, lest it fall into other hands.

SWIFT. Do, sir. I am sure it will compare favourably with some of the other squibs you keep locked in your drawers for private reading.

(TISDALL gives a cry of rage. DINGLEY's indignation has been rising. She has now found an envelope.)

DINGLEY. Jonathan.

SWIFT. Eh?

DINGLEY. Jonathan, I found an envelope today in one of the cupboards. I think it contains something that belongs to you.
(She gives him the envelope.)

SWIFT. What's this?

DINGLEY. I have not looked inside. But on the cover is written, 'Only a woman's hair'.

SWIFT *(sobering)*. Give it to me. *(He takes it and slams it in a drawer.)* You had no business to pry into my private letters. The visit is over, Tisdall. I hope I shall not look upon your face in this life again.
(SWIFT goes out, slamming the door.)

TISDALL. What a foul fellow.

(The thunder rolls, and cross-fades into the sound of the organ. The PLAYERS *relax into their original roles.)*

AVARICE. Oh dear! Hardly a fair picture. Swift's real fault was not in that lamentable incident. Mr Tisdall had private reasons for feeling resentful.

LUST *(appearing).* You mean this story about the Dean having prevented his marriage?

AVARICE. Yes, of course. All that Mr Tisdall remembers is a moment in his old age. The Dean was then an embittered man, and used to speak harshly about all the tender emotions. But that was only because he had lost, through his own fault, all chance of experiencing love himself.

LUST. It was Esther Johnson – Stella – of course, whom Mr Tisdall wanted to marry?

AVARICE. Yes, Hetty, Jonathan's ward. The very role for you Pride. Jonathan wanted to marry her himself, you see. And yet he could never bring himself to do so, because of his financial responsibilities. That was his only real fault. He was avaricious in money matters, and in the end this lost for both of them the happiness that they deserved. I have quite a different picture of him from that sour old demon.

LUST. Where would you place the next scene, madam?

AVARICE. In Laracor in the County Meath. Dr Swift was much younger then. A vicar with a country church, planted in a prim Dutch garden. Those were happier days, and he was much more his real self.

(Fade out organ and fade in the occasional twittering of birds. Hold these to background.)

AVARICE. One day Charles Ford came down with news from Dublin. He was the Doctor's closest friend . . . his closest male friend. Such a nice young man – and very popular too. It was a joke of the Doctor's that Charles never got married because he was always in love with somebody else before there was time to put up the banns.

LUST *(as* FORD*) (approaching).* A gross libel, Dingley. I never got married because you ladies were always too busy fussing over Jonathan to listen to my proposals.

DINGLEY. Flatterer!

FORD. Where is Hetty?

DINGLEY. In the garden – talking to Mr Tisdall.

FORD. Ah, I scent a nice bit of scandal here.

(A woman's cry of surprise is heard off.)

DINGLEY. Be quiet, Charles. They're coming.

PRIDE (*as* STELLA) (*approaching with* TISDALL). La, Mr Tisdall. I blush to hear such stories. Where do you learn these things?

TISDALL (*with some relish*). From my choir, Miss Hetty. I listen to their problems from the organ loft.

STELLA. What a world we live in. Why, Don Carlos, what brings you down to Laracor?

FORD. You, dear ladies. You, of course.

DINGLEY. Stuff and nonsense. He has a message for Jonathan from the Archbishop.

STELLA. Mr Tisdall – you know Mr Ford of Wood Park. Mrs Dingley always wrecks his prettiest compliments.

DINGLEY. Only when they are untrue. They want Jonathan to go to London on a political mission. It may mean advancement for him. Think of that, Hetty – advancement.

STELLA (*stiffening*). Indeed? How soon, pray?

FORD. At once.

STELLA. May we expect to lose Presto for some time.

FORD. Who knows? Maybe for months. God knows how long it will take to urge the rights of the Irish clergy upon the Queen.

TISDALL. I am sure that in Dr Swift's capable hands our interests . . .

STELLA. Mr Tisdall, will you and Mr Ford please go and look for the Doctor? I think he is over in the church.

TISDALL. A pleasure to oblige.

FORD (*agitated at such a prospect*). No, no, my dear. I am quite capable of finding Jonathan myself. Please don't interrupt your chat with Mr Tisdall.

STELLA. You will not be interrupting us, dear Carlos. We have finished for the moment and I know that you will enjoy hearing some of Mr Tisdall's views on the problems of his choir.

FORD (*grimly*). You are always so thoughtful for me, my dear Hetty. I must never be left out of anything. Come along, Tisdall. Abominable girl.

TISDALL (*going*). Yes, a delightful girl. What an ornament to any vicarage.

DINGLEY (*as Tisdall and Ford go away*). What *is* that man doing here? On such a day too.

STELLA. Mr Tisdall? He wishes me to marry him.

DINGLEY. To marry him! Oh I wonder what Jonathan will say to this.

STELLA (*sharply*). What has it got to do with Jonathan? Am I his property?

273

DINGLEY. Now, Hetty, don't get into one of your tantrums. Maybe this is just what is needed.

STELLA. To force Jonathan to ask me himself? I suppose that is what you mean?

DINGLEY. Well, after all, we've been living here in Ireland for more than eight years.

STELLA. Eight years, during which he has never once been with me, except in the presence of a third person.

DINGLEY. Yes, I've noticed that. His discretion is remarkable. Of course he is a clergyman.

STELLA (*indignantly*). And what am I? A trull – that I should compromise his reputation by being found alone with him?

DINGLEY. What a thing to say! I'm sure that's not the reason.

STELLA. Well, whatever the reason is, it doesn't seem to apply to – to other women.

DINGLEY. All I say is that if you don't know his intentions yet, it's high time that you did. And if he's going away to London, it's now or never.

STELLA. I would never condescend to ask him any such question.

DINGLEY. You don't have to ask him. All you have to do is to tell him that you're going to marry Tisdall. And if you won't tell him, I will.

STELLA. Ssssh! He's coming.

DINGLEY. I will not Sssh!

SWIFT (*approaching*). Well, my poppets. Have you heard the news? (SWIFT *is now a man in his early forties, affable and not unkind.*)

DINGLEY. Yes, I suppose you're going?

SWIFT. Of course I shall go. It will be amusing to bait these jacks-in-office.

DINGLEY. Then we must talk over several things before you leave. Come, Hetty. Speak up.

SWIFT. What is the matter with Dingley? I know that look in her eye. It is the eye of a conspirator.

DINGLEY. Never mind *my* eyes, Jonathan Swift. There are others you should be paying attention to.

SWIFT. She reminds me of my late but unlamented guardian, Uncle Godwin Swift – now in Hell.

DINGLEY. In Hell! Indeed, it would be better if you took after that estimable man.

SWIFT. I prefer to believe that I take after my mother – a very genteel lady – one of the Ericks of Leicestershire.

DINGLEY. Ericks of Leicestershire! I happen to know . . .

SWIFT (*with a flash of temper*). Aye, and if any of my poxy Swift relations told you otherwise they lied in their teeth.

DINGLEY. Why Jonathan . . .

SWIFT. A most ancient and respectable connection.

DINGLEY. Why, Jonathan, I was only going to say that Sir William Temple told me his father used to speak very highly of your mother.

SWIFT. That is quite enough on the subject.

(*Uncomfortable pause.*)

STELLA. When do you start for London?

SWIFT. As soon as we have arranged matters with the Archbishop. Charles Ford will come too.

DINGLEY. Mr Tisdall is here.

SWIFT. I know.

DINGLEY. Did you see him?

SWIFT. I had no time for him. What does he want?

STELLA. Now, Dingley!

DINGLEY. No, I will not be silent. He wants to marry Hetty.

SWIFT. The devil he does. Well, I hope you sent him about his business.

DINGLEY. Marriage is not an unnatural state for a woman.

SWIFT. For a woman, perhaps. But for Hetty – scarcely more than a child . . .

DINGLEY. A child . . . fiddlesticks. She's over twenty-six.

SWIFT (*surprised*). Twenty-six . . . Um . . . I suppose she is. Well, tell the fellow he's wasting his time, I wouldn't consider him for a moment.

STELLA. What right have you to talk like that, Jonathan?

SWIFT. Right! I am your guardian – charged with your protection.

STELLA. Jonathan you are not my guardian . . . and you know it.

SWIFT. Sir William Temple on his deathbed . . .

STELLA (*in a challenging tone*). My name is Esther *Johnson*. What has Sir William Temple to do with me?

SWIFT (*after a pause*). But, Hetty, my dear, you are surely not seriously considering Tisdall . . . that . . . that vulgar little . . .

STELLA. Mr Tisdall is not vulgar. He is always correcting vulgarity.

SWIFT. Always collecting it, you mean. His cupboards are stocked with the vulgarities of his parish, laid up in lavender to be brooded on, but never laughed at.

STELLA. He's a very decent man, whose public life is an example to his parish.

SWIFT. He is a self-indulgent sepulchre, preaching temperance to his flock, and eating and drinking in the privacy of his closet.

STELLA. What do you know about him?

SWIFT. I know that he's a hypocrite.

STELLA. At any rate, towards me his intentions are unambiguous.

DINGLEY. Which is more than can be said of some.

SWIFT. What do you mean by that?

STELLA. She means . . .

DINGLEY. He knows very well what I mean. We've known each other for twenty years, and we ought to be able to speak plainly. Hetty is a grown woman now, and it is time that she got married. If she is not to marry Mr Tisdall . . .

STELLA. Dingley, I forbid you.

DINGLEY. Very well, I shall say no more. But Jonathan understands.

SWIFT (*dully*). Yes, I understand. I should have foreseen this long ago. You wish to know whether I intend to marry her myself.

DINGLEY. Not an unreasonable question after all these years.

SWIFT. No. I suppose it's not. But, Poppet, these things are sometimes not very easy to explain.

STELLA. No explanations are necessary.

SWIFT. I am not the marrying sort, my dear. My circumstances – er – they hardly permit me to support a wife.

DINGLEY. Circumstances – fiddlesticks. You're as well off as any other parson. You're too mean – that's what you are.

STELLA. Don't listen to her Presto. I know the reason, and it is not that.

SWIFT (*startled*). You know the reason? What do you mean?

STELLA. Let's not talk about it any longer. It is entirely my own concern, and I shall marry whom I choose.

SWIFT. Hetty, I insist upon knowing what you meant by what you said.

STELLA. I have nothing more to say.

SWIFT. Hetty, come with me into the orchard. I must speak with you alone.

STELLA. It will make no difference, what you say.

SWIFT. Into the orchard, please, my dear. If I never make any other request, do this for me now.

STELLA. Very well, Presto. If you wish it. But there is nothing more that I want to hear.

SWIFT. We will see. We will see.

DINGLEY. You will see what? What else is there to see, except that we can't go on like this?

SWIFT. No. We can't go on like this.

(*He goes away with* STELLA, *and* AVARICE *reassumes her old role. Fade in organ.*)

AVARICE. But the strange thing is that that is just what they did do. What he said to her we shall never know. But she came back from the orchard with a smile on her calm, proud face, and never mentioned marriage again. No one ever dared to ask them another question. They were the strangest pair of lovers the world has ever known. And believe me, money must have been at the back of it.

LUST. I doubt that, ma'am. Swift loved women more than money. Indeed their company was something that he never could resist. To understand his sin, you must see him in London at the home of Mrs Vanhomrigh, an Irish widow with social ambitions and two lovely daughters. Esther and Moll, one of whom was the real key to his life. (*To* PRIDE.) Come. You must be Moll, my dear. With Gluttony as John Gay.

(*Cross-fade organ to an eighteenth-century string orchestra. The scene assumes the guise of a London drawing-room.* LUST *as* FORD – *is talking with* PRIDE *as* MOLL.)

VOICE (*off*). Sir Richard Steele. The Marquis and Marchioness of Wharton.

FORD. Wonders will never cease, Miss Moll. The Marquis with the Marchioness!

ANGER (*as* VANESSA) (*approaching*). Mr Ford, Where is your parson friend from Ireland?

FORD. Your servant, Miss Essie. I left Dr Swift paying his respects to your mother.

MOLL. A roomful of celebrities to choose from and Essie wants to know, 'Where is Parson Swift'.

VANESSA. Dr Swift has written a book. His conversation is very intellectual.

MOLL. Lord save us. Intellectual! Mr Ford will be wondering what the girls are coming to these days.

VOICE (*off*). Mr Joseph Addison. Mr John Gray.

(GLUTTONY *enters as* GAY.)

GAY. Gay, you fool. Not Gray! Now the imbecile has ruined my entrance. I shall have to make another.

FORD. Come over here, John, and stop playing the fool.

GAY. Charles Ford, the peripatetic Hibernian, on my life! And Miss Essie and Moll. How is your health, miss?

VANESSA. Pretty good, I thank you.

277

GAY. Pretty and good. There's two very rare things to match together.

VANESSA. You take me up before I am down, sir. Pray, let me rise by myself.

MOLL. Marry, you look as fine as fivepence, but I fear there is more cost than courtesy.

FORD. Moll remarks upon your new clothes, John. You have made an impression after all.

GAY. What? She likes them?

MOLL. Prodigious fine. It is a pity that the worst piece is in the middle.

(*Laughter. The orchestra has stopped.* SWIFT *is tiptoeing by.*)

GAY. Miss Moll, if you cannot be civil to me, I shall take myself home. Ah, here is a kindred spirit masquerading as a clergyman. I shall go and get drunk with him.

VANESSA. Dr Swift, you are not leaving?

SWIFT. Only to another room, miss. Your mother has decreed that one of the ladies is to sing a catch written by a certain Mr Gay. And I cannot abide music, least of all these bawdy ballads.

GAY. B'gad I take offence at that, sir. I am Mr Gay. I must have satisfaction. And do not think that you can shelter behind the breastplate of religion.

SWIFT. Your pardon, sir. Religion is not a breastplate. Religion is a pair of breeches – a necessary covering for nastiness and vice, which nevertheless is easily slipped down for the service of both.

GAY (*amid laughter*). Egad! The parson is a wit. His cloth becomes him as well as a saddle would a sow.

(*Applause off.*)

But listen. They are preparing for the massacre of my offspring. Let us all go and assist at the obsequies. (*Going.*) Come, Charles. Come, Moll.

FORD AND MOLL (*going*). We're coming.

(A WOMAN'S VOICE, *off, commences to sing 'Can love be controlled by advice' from* The Beggar's Opera.)

SWIFT. Now, miss, why do you remain here, when I have insulted all your closest friends?

VANESSA. You have not insulted them, sir. And if you had, it would be no more than they deserve.

SWIFT. You are a woman of discernment, eh? That is very ill done of you.

VANESSA. How is that?

SWIFT. In the economy of nature no woman should be fair as well as wise. How comes it you are not married, miss?

VANESSA. Maybe I shall be, one of these odd-come-shortlies.

SWIFT. And which of the sparks do you fancy?

VANESSA. An' I wed, it will be none of these fly-by-nights, be they ever so witty or so wealthy.

SWIFT. What do you look for in a husband?

VANESSA. I would have a man of genius.

SWIFT. Ah-ha!

VANESSA. Can you find one for me, Dr Swift?

SWIFT. A man of genius, eh? But that is not always a good thing for a young girl.

VANESSA. Why not, sir?

SWIFT. Because your man of genius is not always a man of character. To match happily with a man of genius is as rare as a widow of fifteen or a maid of five-and-twenty. You must walk warily, Miss Vanhomrigh, if that is your intention.

VANESSA. Mercy! You frighten me, Dr Swift. I shall need a friend to give me counsel.

SWIFT. True indeed. Perhaps you have some grave and suitable person in mind?

VANESSA. No indeed. Unless Dr Swift would condescend?

(*The singing is over. There is a patter of applause off.*)

SWIFT (*flattered*). My child, why do you waste your time on me when you have a roomful of wealth and influence next door? I am a poor parson, and have little to offer you, except my conversation.

VANESSA. You have always interested me. You don't seem to mind what the world says of you. You are not like the others – chasing the favour of the Ministers. You are a man of affairs, yet you have chosen Mr Harley as your friend – a mere nobody in the Commons – and you are seen about with Mrs Masham, who is little better than a waiting-maid to the Queen.

SWIFT. My dear young lady, my philosophy is to do what is right and be damned what the world says.

VANESSA. But how can I know what is right? That is what I wish to learn from my tutor. Will you accept the office, sir?

SWIFT. And the fee?

VANESSA. The fee . . . the fee, like the money in poets' pockets, will be invisible.

SWIFT. You are a diverting minx, and will meet with trouble if you are not protected. So if you wish it, you shall have your way.

279

When will we commence the first lesson?

VANESSA. Now, sir. At once.

SWIFT. Now? Here?

VANESSA. Last night I prayed for guidance. Prove to me now that prayer is always answered.

SWIFT. Then when you pray next, pray that you may serve Heaven – not that Heaven may serve you. If you would be my pupil you must learn neither to be a scold, a whore, nor a slut. And, mark you well, the worst of the three is the slut. Remember that however the world goes, a great torch may be lighted at a tiny candle, and a tinker may bring the plague into a city as readily as any member of the House of Peers.

VANESSA. Yes, yes! Go on.

SWIFT. As for ourselves, we cannot be people of consequence unless we have a sound body and live without care. So eat your best plums first and let the rest mend.

VANESSA (*joyfully*). Oh, what drolleries there are upon the earth. We shall laugh at them together, shall we not?

SWIFT. Yes, Miss Essie. We shall laugh at them together – you and I. Laughter is the best fee for your instruction.

VANESSA. Oh, the fee. We were forgetting the fee. What does my tutor need?

SWIFT. I have made it an inflexible rule – a rule I recommend to my pupil – never to require anything of any man.

VANESSA. Nor woman either?

SWIFT. Nor woman either. So set your mind at rest about the fee. No woman has anything to give me.

VANESSA. Not even this?

(*She kisses him impulsively.* FORD *has reappeared and sees this.*)

FORD. That was a hazardous kiss, young lady.

(*Swift's embarrassment suddenly turns to anger.*)

SWIFT (*furious*). Charles. What are you doing here?

VANESSA. Forgive me, Dr Swift. Please say that you forgive me.

SWIFT. The lesson is over.

FORD. The first lesson.

SWIFT. I asked you what you are doing here?

FORD. A messenger has arrived from Whitehall. The Lord Treasurer wishes to see you, Jonathan.

SWIFT (*surprised*). Godolphin. To see me?

FORD. Godolphin is no longer Lord Treasurer. The Whigs have fallen, and your good friend Mr Harley is in office. You had better go at once, Jonathan. (*Pause while* SWIFT *stares at* VANESSA.)

SWIFT. Forgive me, Miss Essie, if I go across to Whitehall.

(*Triumphant music from the orchestra.* SWIFT *stalks out, pausing for a moment beside her, for a moment it looks as if he might strike her, but as she cowers away, he relaxes slowly and then he gravely kisses her hand before leaving.*)

LUST. From that moment the vicar of Laracor became one of the most powerful men in England.

(*Fade out music: exeunt. Interval, after which* LUST *enters followed by* DR BERKELEY *and* GAY.)

LUST. You agree with me – er – oh, Dr Berkeley? You consider that I have described the position fairly.

BERKELEY. The British Constitution is a remarkable phenomenon, Mr Ford. I find no mention in it of the vicar of Laracor, yet the pivotal position of Dr Swift cannot be denied.

(AVARICE *enters as* MRS VANHOMRIGH, *followed by* SWIFT, VANESSA *and* MOLL, *played as before.*)

MRS VANHOMRIGH. Ah, gentlemen. I have just been congratulating Dr Swift upon his new deanery of St Patrick's.

SWIFT. Mrs Vanhomrigh is very condescending.

MRS VANHOMRIGH. They say it is a very excellent and profitable appointment.

SWIFT. They are misinformed, madam. I shall be the poorest gentleman in Ireland that eats upon gold plate, and the richest that lives without a coach.

MRS VANHOMRIGH. Still, Mr Dean, we all know that the air of Ireland is very excellent and healthy.

SWIFT. Then, for God's sake, madam, do not mention it here, for if you do they will assuredly tax it. Ah, Dr Berkeley, your servant. I understand that you are looking for a patron for your West Indian project?

BERKELEY. Indeed I had hoped to discuss the matter with you, Mr Dean.

SWIFT. Well, let me see now. Perhaps you will allow me to present Mr Gay.

BERKELEY. I have already met Mr Gay.

SWIFT. So much the better. Dr Berkeley is a philosopher. And do I hear you ask, what is the basis of his philosophy? Well, I shall tell you. He has satisfied himself, for all his imposing bulk, that matter does not exist at all.

BERKELEY. That is scarcely a correct analysis of . . .

SWIFT. He has also a project for a college in the West Indies, dedicated to the washing of Ethiopians – a college where sunbeams shall be extracted from cucumbers, and the natives will be instructed in the art of milking he-goats with a sieve. And you, my friend, I have selected as a proper person to assist in the furtherance of this excellent scheme.

GAY. Me?

SWIFT. Now do not be modest in your demands, Dr Berkeley. Mr Gay has a considerable fortune from his theatrical ventures, and you must not believe him if he tells you otherwise.

GAY. I thank you, for your good opinion of me, Mr Dean. But I really cannot see why I should be selected to assist Dr Berkeley.

SWIFT. Because, my friend, the Scriptures tell us that charity covereth a multitude of sins. Mr Gay is at your service, Dr Berkeley.

BERKELEY. Oh, thank you, Mr Gay. Your patronage is just what we need. But perhaps I may be permitted to correct some of the impressions about my college that Dr Swift may have –

(GAY *ad libs off, protesting, followed by* BERKELEY, *still talking.*)

MRS VANHOMRIGH. How is your chest, Moll? Are you properly wrapped up?

MOLL. Thank you. It is no worse, Mama.

MRS VANHOMRIGH. It is time for you to rest. Perhaps Mr Ford will be so kind as to assist you up the stairs. Not you, Essie. You must stay and entertain the Dean.

FORD. Your servant, ma'am.

MRS VANHOMRIGH. Then come along. Come along.

(*She hustles* FORD *and* MOLL *off, looking back significantly at* VANESSA.)

VANESSA (*laughing*). My dear tutor. You are so cruel to these gentlemen of quality.

SWIFT. Yes, Skinage, I treat them like dirt; for when their day comes I know they will treat me likewise.

VANESSA. Oh, what a glorious time we have had. Tell me that you have loved it too – tell me.

SWIFT. Of course I have.

VANESSA. We have found something together that we must never lose.

SWIFT. That is why I have taken some steps to perpetuate it. You see this paper?

VANESSA. Jonathan – when my mother dies, Moll and I will have an estate in Ireland.

SWIFT. Enough of these gloomy thoughts. Don't you wish to see what I have written?

VANESSA. A house at Celbridge, down beside the river.

SWIFT. I wrote it for you when we were at Windsor.

(*The orchestra starts to play in the distance.*)

VANESSA. Oh! A poem. And dedicated to me. 'Cadenus and Vanessa'. What does that mean? Cadenus?

SWIFT. 'Tis a play upon the word decanus – a dean.

VANESSA. And Vanessa. What a pretty name! Is it me?

SWIFT. Of course, my dear.

VANESSA. Cadenus and Vanessa. You and me.

> 'Vanessa not in years a score
> Dreams of a gown of forty-four,
> His conduct might have made him styled
> A father, and the nymph his child.'

Why, it is our history! Oh, read it to me yourself.

SWIFT. Tut. Not here.

VANESSA. But you must. Nobody will disturb us. Come! Governor Huff insists . . .

SWIFT. Well, you are a white witch and I suppose that Governor Huff must have her way. (*He takes back the m/s.*)

> 'Her knowledge with her fancy grew;
> She hourly pressed for something new;
> Ideas came into her mind
> So fast his lessons lagged behind.'

VANESSA (*taking the m/s*).

> 'I know by what you said and writ
> How dangerous things were men of wit.
> You cautioned me against their charms,
> But never gave me equal arms.
> Your lessons found the weakest part;
> Aimed at the head, but reached the heart.'

Oh, it is true, Cadenus. You never gave me equal arms. (*Suddenly afraid.*) Has your poem a happy ending?

SWIFT. That too is a secret. Will you hear it?

> 'But what success Vanessa yet;
> Is to the world a secret met,
> Whether the nymph to please her swain,
> Talks in a high romantic strain,
> Or whether he at last descends

To like with less seraphic ends;
Or, to compound the business, whether
They temper love and books together
Must never to mankind be told,
Nor shall the conscious muse unfold.'
(*The orchestra concludes.* FORD *reappears.*)

FORD. Charming. A new poem?

SWIFT (*irritably*). You again, Charles!

FORD. Yes, Jonathan, it is I. I have a letter for you from Dublin.

SWIFT. A letter? Give it to me. You may go, child, I shall follow presently.

VANESSA. You will not be long?

SWIFT. Not long.

VANESSA. I trust you, Mr Ford, not to keep him from me for more than five minutes.

FORD. I promise, Miss Essie.
(*She goes away.*)

FORD. What is the news?

SWIFT (*reading the letter*). Little enough. The ladies play at ombre in Donnybrook.

FORD. It is some time now since you wrote to them?

SWIFT (*irritably*). Since I have been in London, I have written nigh on a volume to the ladies. My journal used to go home to them every week.

FORD. But lately?

SWIFT. Lately there has been no news . . . to speak of. (*Pause.*) May I ask what you are hinting at?

FORD. You know quite well what is in my mind. (*Pause.*) This girl, Esther Vanhomrigh, is very young.

SWIFT (*his temper rising*). She is a grown woman and old enough to have a will of her own. I have asked for nothing that she has not freely offered, and I have promised her nothing in return.

FORD. Of course, Jonathan, I know that. But she is very charming and very tender.

SWIFT. There has been little enough of tenderness in my life.

FORD. Jonathan, I don't profess to understand your life, but surely there is tenderness waiting for you if you desire it?

SWIFT. Charles, you have been a good friend to me, but you have one irritating peculiarity. You will allow nobody to talk to a woman except yourself.

FORD (*his voice rising*). I don't deny that you can downface me,

284

Jonathan. But perhaps you will find it harder to answer your
conscience if you choose to listen to that.

SWIFT. What do you mean, sir?

FORD. I mean that this girl, Vanhomrigh, loves you. And before
long, she will expect you to marry her. Do you intend to marry
her?

SWIFT (*furious*). Marry her? (*Pause.*) Marry her! (*Pause.*) Con-
found you, sir. Can't you mind your own business?

> (*He walks off as a bell starts to toll . . . Hold to background . . .*
> ANGER *and* PRIDE *reappear.*)

LUST. Deaf, you see . . . deaf to the voice of reason wherever a
pretty face was concerned. There was no mystery about his vice.
It was a lusty one that might be forgiven in you or me, but was
fatal in a man of God.

PRIDE. At any rate he had to listen to that bell – tolling for the
death of the Queen, and the ruin of all his friends in office.

LUST. Yes, it was that bell that drove him back to Ireland – back
to his new deanery, to hide himself not only from the spite of
the Whigs, but also from love. Poor Swift, he might have survived the Whigs, but he could not survive the Vanhomrighs.

ANGER. Survive indeed! Who was it that survived – Swift or the
Vanhomrighs?

LUST. Why, madam, you seem angry?

ANGER. I am angry! You know quite well that he didn't escape
either from love or the Vanhomrighs by going back to Ireland.

LUST. Too true, I'm afraid. The flesh is very weak and she could
never be persuaded to give him up.

ANGER. Persuaded to give *him* up, forsooth – this shrinking violet,
who couldn't escape from the advances of a girl in her twenties!
If he had wanted to end the situation, all he had to say was 'I am
married to Esther Johnson'.

PRIDE. But what if he wasn't married?

ANGER. If he wasn't married, then he was doubly damned. He was
torturing two women, instead of one. Anything he suffered he
richly deserved.

LUST. I thought you liked the Dean, young lady?

ANGER. Like him? I hate him, and everything about him. He was a
bully and a tormentor. It wasn't the weakness of the flesh that
troubled him, but anger and resentment against a world he
loathed, and a sex he was determined to humiliate. Love was a
sentiment quite foreign to his stony heart.

LUST. Oh, ridiculous!

ANGER. It is not ridiculous. How else could he have behaved the way he did towards both of them? A refinement of torture, I tell you, dressed up in guise of affection. It is in Celbridge that you see the real Swift . . . in Celbridge with Vanessa.

(*Fade out bell.* LUST *vanishes as* ANGER *sits at a desk and commences to go through papers, while* PRIDE, *as* MOLL, *reclines in a chair as if mutely awaiting the approach of death.*)

ANGER (*as* VANESSA). Oh, these papers! These awful papers!

MOLL (*very weak and tired*). After all, it is our mother's estate, Essie. Tell them we can't spend all our days in paying off the debts of the dead. Life is short enough as it is.

VANESSA. Was that a horse?

MOLL (*hardly listening*). No, dear Essie. It was not a horse.

VANESSA. I am sorry, Moll. What were you saying?

MOLL. Shall we stop talking business?

VANESSA. No, no. What shall I say to the attorneys?

MOLL (*with a little twisted smile*). Maybe it was a horse.

VANESSA (*eagerly*). A horse. No, you are laughing at me.

MOLL. Will you see him when he comes?

VANESSA. No. I will not see him. I shall send him away. He hasn't written to me for nearly a month. Oh, Moll, why hasn't he written? Do you think that he loves me?

MOLL. Do you care whether he does or not?

VANESSA. No, I don't care. He is a beast. I hate him!

MOLL (*cynically*). Good.

VANESSA. But if he loves me why doesn't he come?

MOLL. And if he does *not* love you why *does* he come?

VANESSA. Yes, he wouldn't come at all if he didn't love me, would he? Would he, Moll?

MOLL. I suppose not.

VANESSA. Oh, if only I *knew.* (*Pause.*) Moll.

MOLL. Yes, Essie.

VANESSA. This other woman. What do you think she is to him?

MOLL (*not really caring*). Why don't you ask him, Essie?

VANESSA. Nothing would induce me to ask him anything about Mrs Johnson. Never, never, never. Unless of course he chooses to tell me himself.

MOLL. Which he ought to have done long ago. (*Rallying.*) Oh, my dear, dear Essie, can't you be sensible and put him from your mind? Let him go. No man is worth all these heartburnings.

VANESSA. Yes, Mollkins, I can . . . I *will* be sensible. I don't care if he never comes again. He has treated me shamefully. I don't ever want to see him again. If he tries to see me I shall ... listen, was that a horse? Yes. Yes. It is he! Oh, Mollkins, he has come. Perhaps he has been ill.

MOLL (*shaking her head*). Poor Essie. Poor Essie.

VANESSA. He looks pale. He's coming in.

MOLL. Oh, very well, I shall leave you. It's hopeless to reason with you.

VANESSA (*rushing to the mirror*). I shall be wise and sensible. I promise I shan't pester him with any questions. Oh, I'm so happy. Are my eyes red? How is my hair?

MOLL (*going*). Poor Essie. Poor Essie.

(*She goes, as* SWIFT *enters in a dusty riding habit.*)

VANESSA. Cadenus.

(*She rushes to his arms.*)

SWIFT. My dear.

VANESSA. It's been so long. You look tired. Aren't you well?

SWIFT. It's a wearisome journey on horseback at this time of year.

VANESSA. Give me your coat. Sit down, and let me make you comfortable.

SWIFT. Thank you, my dear. There is a quiet in this house – when Governor Huff isn't on the march. (*He sits.*) I like to talk to you and to recall old times. There's little else in this land of slaves to remind me of those days in London.

VANESSA. Yes, yes.

SWIFT. Harley impeached and imprisoned by the Whigs, the other Ministers fled to the Pretender, and I ... in exile here – hooted at in the streets by the rabble, insulted by every ignorant buck who chooses to do so.

VANESSA. Forget it all for a little while, Cadenus.

SWIFT. Was it to see me in my degradation that you followed me to Ireland?

VANESSA. Cadenus, I had to come. We had nowhere else to go after our mother died. But let me give you a glass of wine after your long ride from Dublin.

SWIFT. Thank you, my dear. It would be very welcome.

VANESSA. This is the claret that Harley used to like. Do you remember those receptions at my mama's?

SWIFT. I do.

VANESSA (*playing the footman*). 'The Marquis and Marchioness of Wharton.' 'Mr John Gray.' 'Mr Joseph Addison.'
'Pray sir, will you dance with me?' (*She hums a tune.*)

'Why, Dr Swift, you are very civil to have come to my little reception.'

SWIFT (*amused*). Your servant, madam. And may I ask who you are now?

VANESSA. Don't you recognize the classical profile of my poor mama? 'We all know, Mr Dean, that the air of Ireland is very excellent.' Go on, sir. Answer me.

SWIFT. What did I say then?

VANESSA. You said, 'For God's sake, madam, do not mention it here or they'll certainly tax it.'

(*She shouts with laughter. He smiles wanly.*)

SWIFT. Oh, we had an abundance of wit, and you were very much in my good graces. I wrote a million fine things upon it though I would let nobody read a word of them but myself.

VANESSA. I have here something else that you wrote. Something that nobody has seen but ourselves, though it is the finest poem you have ever penned.

(*She produces a paper.*)

SWIFT. Cadenus and Vanessa. God grant that nobody ever does see it.

(*He reads.*)

> 'Tis an old maxim in the schools,
> That vanity's the food of fools,
> Yet now and then your men of wit
> Will condescend to take a bit.'

That was nearer to the bone than I imagined. 'Vanity's the food of fools.' Yes, I had some genius when I wrote this poem. And what vanity!

VANESSA. Had! I won't allow you to talk so. You still have all your genius.

SWIFT. And all my vanity too?

VANESSA. You will write poems even finer than this one.

SWIFT. I wonder.

VANESSA. Though none of them will mean quite as much to me. This is our own story, Cadenus – our secret – set down in verse. Do you remember Spring Gardens in the summer?

SWIFT. What a foolish thing is time, and how foolish is man who would be as angry if time stopped as if it passed. Poor Vanessa, you could make use of no other black art besides your ink. It is a pity that your eyes aren't black or I would say the same of them. But you're a white witch, and can do no mischief.

(*She starts to weep.*)

288

SWIFT. Why are you weeping?

VANESSA. Do you love me still?

SWIFT. Of course I love you. Nobody in this world loves and values
you more than your friend Cadenus.

VANESSA (*agitated*). My friend?

SWIFT. Yes, your friend. That is what I said.

VANESSA (*emotionally*). Cadenus – is that all? Just your friend?

SWIFT. Remember, my dear. You have promised that there shall
be no more of those scenes.

VANESSA. I can't help it. I do my best to be calm, but I can't help it.

SWIFT. Then I must go away. (*She pulls him back as he tries to rise.*)

VANESSA. No, no. I can't bear to be neglected by you.

SWIFT. Vanessa, I cannot tolerate these scenes! If you cannot control yourself . . .

VANESSA. I love you. And you say that you love me. Is there somebody else you love more than me?

SWIFT. No, no! What I've told you is the truth.

VANESSA. Then I can't understand. What is it that keeps you from
me? Tell me, Cadenus.

SWIFT. I'm going. (*He struggles to his feet.*)

VANESSA. Cadenus! I must know. I can't bear it any longer. What
is this Mrs Johnson to you?

SWIFT. Vanessa, I have warned you.

VANESSA. I don't care. I must know.

SWIFT (*his fury rising*). Mrs Johnson is a friend. Do not mention
her name.

VANESSA. Why shouldn't I mention her name? Amn't I good
enough?

SWIFT. Be silent, I say.

VANESSA. I will not be silent any longer. Who is she that I mayn't
mention her name?

SWIFT. I have told you that . . .

VANESSA. Who is she that she should have a paid chaperone, while
my reputation can be flung to the winds?

SWIFT. I will not . . .

VANESSA. What is she to you? Is she your wife?

SWIFT (*thundering*). My wife?

VANESSA. Is that why you won't marry me?

SWIFT (*grimly, after a terrible pause*). Goodbye.

VANESSA. Answer me. For God's sake answer me.

SWIFT. You have disobeyed me. I have told you to be silent. Let me
go.

VANESSA. Cadenus, answer me. Oh, Cadenus, Cadenus.

SWIFT. Let me go.

(*He goes out, slamming the door.*)

VANESSA. Cadenus – what is she? Oh, God, I'm going mad! I must know. I shall demand to be told. I shall write a letter.

(*She staggers to the desk, and opens a drawer from which she takes a sheet of paper. Mumbling and coughing she writes.*)

To Mrs Esther Johnson, Ormond Quay...

(*Organ, as the lights fade. When they rise again she is gone and* ENVY *is talking to* SLOTH.)

ENVY. Personally, I feel that you are all flattering the Dean. He was not a big man at all, even in his vices. Quite petty, in fact. If he had been a bigger man, he would have made better friends, and might have attained the pinnacle of a bishopric. But he was always criticizing and offending his superiors. He was jealous of everyone who was more successful than himself. That was his trouble.

SLOTH. Mind your foot in the dirt.

ENVY (*moving his foot*). Take Dr Berkeley for instance . . . a man whose writings are still highly esteemed by thoughtful people – much more esteemed than anything the Dean ever wrote.

SLOTH. Why don't you slip over to the deanery like a good man, and go on with your talking there?

ENVY. That is just what Dr Berkeley did do, once or twice in the Dean's later years. His experiences were hardly the same as Mr Tisdall's and they throw some light on the point I want to make.

(*Organ out . . . the scene becomes the deanery.*)

ENVY (*as* BERKELEY). Yes I am Dr Berkeley, my good man. Dr Swift has invited me to supper.

BRENNAN. They'll all be in before long. I'll open a bottle now and have it ready. You take a drop, sir?

BERKELEY. Not in excess.

BRENNAN. Not in excess. Now that's very wise. They put the pledge on you, no doubt.

(*He draws a cork.*)

I never touch it myself.

(*He takes a swig from the bottle.*)

Here's some of them now.

(FORD, DINGLEY *and* STELLA *enter.*)

FORD. Welcome to the deanery, Dr Berkeley. You have met the ladies?

BRENNAN (*going*). I gave him a sup to go on with.

    (*He goes out.*)

BERKELEY. No, Mr Ford. I have not yet had that pleasure.

FORD. Mrs Johnson – Dr Berkeley – Mrs Dingley.

BERKELEY. Your most humble servant, ladies.

STELLA. We have all heard of Dr Berkeley.

DINGLEY. Hetty, is this the man who disbelieves in his own existence and wants us all to live on tar water?

STELLA. Dingley. Don't be ridiculous.

DINGLEY. That's what Jonathan says.

FORD (*hastily*). Mrs Johnson has received a new poem from the Dean. We were just about to hear it.

BERKELEY. Indeed.

STELLA. He always sends one on my birthday.

BERKELEY. Pray read it, madam.

STELLA. With your permission, sir.

        'Thou, Stella, wert no longer young
        When first for thee my harp I strung.
        Without one word of Cupid's darts,
        Of killing eyes or . . .'

    (BRENNAN *dashes in followed by* SWIFT *who is striking him with a cane.*)

SWIFT (*passing by*). There, sir. Take that, sir. And that. And that. And that.

BRENNAN. Oh, God. Oh, saints protect us. Oh, God.

    (*They disappear.*)

STELLA.

        '. . . of killing eyes or bleeding hearts.'

BERKELEY. Dear me.

STELLA. Did you speak, Dr Berkeley?

BERKELEY. What, madam?

STELLA. You said something, Dr Berkeley?

BERKELEY. Forgive me, madam. I did not intend to interrupt. Was that Dr Swift who passed by just now?

STELLA. Yes. That was the Dean.

FORD. He was only chasing his servant.

BERKELEY. Chasing his servant. I see. Ahem.

    (*He coughs.*)

STELLA. He will be back presently.

FORD. Don't you take any exercise Dr Berkeley?

BERKELEY. Oh yes, indeed, Mr Ford. But er . . .

FORD. But you do not chase your servants?

BERKELEY. Well, scarcely, Mr Ford. But then I'm not so . . . er . . .
remarkable a man as the Dean of St Patrick's. Pray proceed
madam.

STELLA.

> 'Of killing eyes or bleeding hearts.
> With friendship and esteem possesst
> I ne'er admitted love a guest.
> In all the habitudes of life . . .'

(SWIFT *and* BRENNAN *re-enter. The latter cowers panting in
a corner.*)

SWIFT. Now, sirrah, why have you not cleaned my boots?

BRENNAN. Ah, what's the use? What's the use? Sure, they'll only be
dirty again by morning.

SWIFT. Ah, an excellent reason. What splendid foresight. Well, my
good rogue, I here leave directions that you go to bed tonight
without your supper.

BRENNAN. What. No supper?

SWIFT. That is what I said. Why should we waste our good food
on you when you will only be hungry again by morning?

(BRENNAN *cries out and the company laugh.*)

Is that Berkeley whom I see?

BERKELEY. I am delighted to meet you once again, Mr Dean, in the
quiet of your home.

SWIFT. Why bless my soul. The whole company is gathered. That
means it is time for the victuals. Where is my honest cook?
Fetch her, Brennan. Fetch her. We must not keep our guests
from the food, or they will assuredly drink us out of the house.

BRENNAN. Yes, Mr Dean! . . . I . . .

SWIFT (*shouting*). Cook!

BRENNAN (*shouting*). Cook!

(ANGER *enters as the* TROLLOP.)

TROLLOP. Here I am. Here I am! What is it now?

SWIFT. We are ready to dine, my good woman. Serve the victuals.
But first of all, draw for the guests.

BRENNAN. Ah. Draw!

SWIFT. Not you, Brennan.

BERKELEY. I thank you, sir. I do not drink.

(*The* TROLLOP *pours out assisted by* BRENNAN.)

SWIFT. Then fill up your pipe.

BERKELEY. Nor do I smoke.

SWIFT. No bottle? No pipe? Egad, sir, what a poor education you
must have had. When I was at Trinity College, drinking and

smoking were the first rudiments of learning taught there, and indeed the only ones to survive into later life.

DINGLEY. I think I smell burning.

STELLA. Yes, I smell it too. It is coming from the kitchen.

DINGLEY. Cook!

TROLLOP. Yes, ma'am?

DINGLEY. What is burning in the kitchen?

TROLLOP. I don't know, ma'am, I'm sure. I wonder would it be the matches?

STELLA. Well, I always heard that matches were made in Heaven. But this smells more of the brimstone.

TROLLOP. God save us! It is the meat. The meat for the supper.
(*She hurries off, ad libbing.*)

SWIFT. The meat again. Brennan! Come here. Let me take you by the ear, sir.
(BRENNAN *protests faintly.*)

SWIFT. How fortunate we are to be able to sit here in comfort and luxury while so admirable a staff exerts itself on our behalf. At what hour did you rise this morning, sirrah?

BRENNAN. At six o'clock sharp, your honour.

SWIFT. At six o'clock sharp you interrupted your simple pleasures on my account. If true – which I doubt – that was very civil of you. Remember, Richard, if you ever hope to become a bishop you must rise early enough to cozen the devil.

BRENNAN. Yes, your honour. I'll remember that.

SWIFT. Alas, you will not. For the worse your sty, the longer you lie. Pass round the wine, you rascal. Dingley, were you in church this evening.
(BRENNAN *passes round the wine.*)

DINGLEY. No, Jonathan. I had other things to attend to.

SWIFT. Dingley, I fear you are a godless hussy. Have you never read of the lilies of the field?

DINGLEY. You're no lily, Jonathan Swift, and don't you forget it.

SWIFT. Tut, tut! I am this woman's spiritual adviser, Dr Berkeley, and she rewards me by turning my cathedral into a dormitory for the living as well as for the dead.

DINGLEY. Anyhow, I don't write improper verses about my archbishop. Marry, but I don't. Or have my unfortunate printers prosecuted by the Government.

SWIFT. Doctor, can I not persuade you to join me in an assault upon this iniquitous Government?

BERKELEY. Well, sir, I confess I agree with you in some respects,

293

about the Government. But is the moment opportune to . . . er . . . attack . . .

SWIFT. Maybe not, my dear Doctor. Perhaps it could better be launched from the eminence of a bishopric, later on? Eh?

BERKELEY. That would certainly carry more weight – not that I expect promotion, of course.

SWIFT. I understand. Well, when you get your mitre perhaps you will join me then?

BERKELEY. Maybe so, Mr Dean.

SWIFT. We will see. Take what you can, Dr Berkeley, for Fortune is a drunken whore, stone blind, who sees neither whom she raises up nor whom she casts down. But ho, my friend Brennan! What did I see just now in the pier glass?

BRENNAN. Nothing, your honour, nothing. I was pouring out the wine for the company.

SWIFT. Come, sir. Don't attempt to darn your cobwebs. You were pouring it down your own gullet. Dare you deny it?

BRENNAN. Now, Mr Dean, you know that I never . . .

SWIFT. No, no. I withdraw my question. One commandant is quite enough for any man to break at a time.

STELLA .Come, Presto. Let poor Richard go, and allow us to enjoy ourselves.

BRENNAN. Oh, thank you, ma'am.

SWIFT. Very well, sirrah. I am asked to forgive you, so I forgive you.

BRENNAN. Your honour's most humble servant.

SWIFT. I will merely stop two shillings out of your board wages to pay for your refreshments.

BRENNAN. Two shillings. Oh, merciful Providence, do you hear him? Two shillings.

SWIFT. 'Tis only what you owe me for the drink. You won't deny the tavern keeper his humble score?

BRENNAN. But sir . . . your honour . . . oh, speak to him, you, sir. Two shillings! Oh, I can't pay it, sir. I can't.

BERKELEY. Dr Swift, if I may intervene, to punish the fellow is one thing, but to stop two shillings out of his board wages for twopence worth of wine – surely, sir, that is . . .

SWIFT. Sir, I scorn to be outdone . . . even in cheating. Two shillings it shall be. Be off now, and bring up the food. But not until you have washed yourself. Even though you be a beggar, water is not so scarce that you may not have the use of it on special occasions.

TROLLOP (*entering with a smoking dish*). Oh, the meat is burnt, Mr Dean. 'Tis burnt.

DINGLEY. Oh, what a stench.

SWIFT. Begad, so it is. Then take it downstairs and do it less.

TROLLOP. Do it less? Do it less? I can't do it less, and well you know it.

SWIFT. Then what a stupid trollop you are, to commit a fault that cannot be remedied.

(BRENNAN *joins in with him from 'to commit a fault'*.)

BRENNAN. I know that one myself.

SWIFT. Into the dining-room instantly, sirrah.

(*The* TROLLOP *hurries off protesting*.)

SWIFT. She is a woman of great intelligence, and I hope by this means to teach her in a year or two not to burn the meat.

BRENNAN. Excuse me, sir, that was the doorbell I heard.

(*He hurries off*.)

DINGLEY. If you did not interfere so much in the running of the household, things would go much more smoothly. I have given most careful instructions to all your servants, myself.

SWIFT. Which they do not carry out.

DINGLEY. At any rate, they are proper instructions. You have no experience in these matters.

SWIFT. Forgive me, but I have. When I was chaplain to the Lord Lieutenant, I was so poor that I was obliged to keep a coffee house, and all the nobility resorted there to talk treason.

BERKELEY. The Duke of Grafton wished to make me his chaplain when he was Lord Lieutenant. A damned patronizing fellow he was, but I would not accept an appointment from such a man.

SWIFT. I' faith, I never liked him much myself, but when they asked him how he governed Ireland, he used to answer 'I pleased Dr Swift.' Would you care to see all the money that I made when I was advising the Queen's Ministers, Dr Berkeley? Being a thrifty man I have saved the whole of it.

(*He opens a drawer*.)

BERKELEY. But there is nothing here, Mr Dean.

SWIFT. Dingley, see that Dr Berkeley does not steal any of it. Like the money in poets' pockets, it is invisible. Now who used to say that, I wonder?

BRENNAN (*entering*). A letter for Mrs Johnson. 'Twas left in at the door.

STELLA. Forgive me, gentlemen. The handwriting is unfamiliar, and my curiosity overcomes me.

(She tears it open. BRENNAN *goes off.)*

BERKELEY. When the Duke approached me, I said to his emissary, 'Sir,' I said, 'I will not accept the patronage of any bastard. What if his father was a king,' I said, 'his mother was a harlot.'

STELLA *(reading the letter).* Oh!

BERKELEY. Did I speak well?

SWIFT. Sir, you spoke it in a manner worthy of the House of Peers. Is there anything the matter, Stella?

(PRIDE *walks down to the forestage, and stands there for a moment in silence.)*

DEAN *(following her, in some surprise).* What is wrong? Why are you stopping the scene?

PRIDE. The rest of the scene makes no sense.

DEAN. Stella . . .

PRIDE. I'm not Stella.

DEAN *(relaxing into* THE DEAN). Maybe not – but for the purposes of our . . .

PRIDE. I am not Stella in any sense of the word. I'm not even a credible woman. What woman in her senses would behave like this?

DEAN *(nervously).* Your behaviour is perfectly reasonable. A very wonderful woman.

PRIDE. Perfectly reasonable!

DEAN. It has satisfied generations of biographers.

PRIDE *(scornfully).* Swift's biographers – not hers. It's enough for *his* story that she should be content to live her life as his unacknowledged mistress.

DEAN. No! As his secret wife.

PRIDE. That is worse! If I am your wife, why shouldn't I be recognized? Am I something to be ashamed of? The hostess of your deanery for fifteen years . . . accepting your protection and your money, and yet not good enough to . . .

AVARICE. Oh, no, Hetty, no! We have our own money.

PRIDE. He pretends that it's our own money, but the little we possess doesn't provide half of what we get from him.

AVARICE. Oh, I can't believe that. I can't.

PRIDE. Well, I know it. And the gossips and scandalmongers know it, now that we are dead.

(GLUTTONY *rises from where he has been listening at the side of the stage and approaches.)*

GLUTTONY. Dead? Now look . . . please . . .

296

PRIDE. If it was justified by marriage or by any other reason, then in justice to me that reason should be known.

GLUTTONY. Look – please, don't let us get confused. We are all becoming a little too involved in . . .

DEAN. Of course there was a reason. We know that, Stella. But it is nobody's business but our own. I don't care what they think of me.

PRIDE. But I care what they think of me.

GLUTTONY. After all, you're not really Swift and Stella. Let's not forget that.

PRIDE. Who can say whom we are, now that this grave is open?

AVARICE (*with a shiver*). What a disturbing idea!

PRIDE. If I am Stella, I must be a real woman – not a wraith invented by some biographer to explain *his* behaviour.

DEAN (*sulkily*). The facts are true as we have shown them. You accepted them, and asked for nothing more.

PRIDE (*emotionally*). But that was before they knew so much about this other woman. She was just a silly girl, pursuing an older man. Now they know too much, and yet not enough. What does that terrible scene at Celbridge make of me? . . . a wife who stood silently by, and watched you drive another woman into the grave?

DEAN. There was a reason. What of it?

PRIDE. Yes . . . a reason, which you are still too proud to admit. But what about my pride? Am I just part of the scenery of your life, Jonathan Swift, dying quietly in my lodgings – happy in the role of being your unacknowledged wife? No, no. That is not good enough for me. Stella was not that kind of nonentity.

DEAN (*darkly, after a pause*). What is it that you want?

PRIDE. Before we go on any further with this scene of Dr Berkeley's, we must go back to the garden at Laracor. There was something that was said there that Dingley didn't hear.

AVARICE. Yes, I remember. The conversation that had such surprising results. I could never understand what happened between you then.

PRIDE. There is something missing from the picture . . . something that these graves have never yet disclosed. Without it everything that follows is unintelligible. So come, Presto. I warned you. We must let them have their say. Now that we have begun, we must hear it all.

DEAN (*after a strangled pause*). Very well. Have it your own way.

(*The other characters withdraw into the background, where*

297

they listen with rapt attention. Once again, we hear the twittering of birds, and the lights on the forestage change.)

PRIDE. I am young again, and it is just before you went to London. (*They reassume the roles of* SWIFT *and* STELLA *as younger people.*)

STELLA. Come, Presto. You want to know what I meant when I said that I knew why we could never be married. Come – we are in the orchard – out of Dingley's hearing.

SWIFT (*reluctantly*). Yes. That's what I asked you.

STELLA. First, I have a question for you, Presto.

SWIFT. What is it?

STELLA. Are you married already?

DEAN. Of course not.

STELLA. That is all that I wanted to know.

DEAN. There could be other impediments besides that.

STELLA. I realize that. Let us not talk about it any longer.

DEAN. What do you mean? Tell me at once.

STELLA. Very well. Since you insist. You know that Sir William Temple was my father. The vicar of Laracor could never condescend to marry a bastard.

DEAN. That is not the reason.

STELLA. Please don't try to make it any easier for me. It's best to face it.

DEAN (*thundering*). That has nothing whatever to do with it. I swear it. At least . . . not in the way that you imagine.

STELLA. Oh why can't you be honest, Jonathan? I understand, and I would never reproach you, if only you would be honest.

SWIFT. That is *not* the reason.

STELLA. Please, Jonathan, I am sorry for allowing the matter to be discussed at all. I don't know what came over me.

(*She turns to go.*)

SWIFT. Stop! Don't go.

STELLA. I can't stay here any longer. I am too humiliated.

SWIFT, I command you to stay. I will not permit you to think such things of me.

STELLA. Please let my arm go. You know you have no right to command me.

SWIFT. I have every right. For the selfsame reason that we can never marry . . .

STELLA. It's not true.

SWIFT. You fling your birth in my face. Very well. My own birth was no better than yours.

298

STELLA. *Your* birth?

SWIFT. Yes, mine. If you were more than a servant at Moor Park I was more than a secretary.

STELLA. Jonathan!

SWIFT. You have heard me speak of my mother and her ancient lineage in Leicestershire. Well, the truth is, she was a butcher's daughter with a post in the household of Sir William Temple's father.

STELLA. You mean to say that Sir William . . .

SWIFT. I was more than his secretary. I was his brother . . . the by-blow of an older generation.

STELLA. You . . . too?

SWIFT. What have I got to complain of? They treat their indiscretions well . . . these gentle Temples. The best school in Ireland, Dublin College and then Oxford. Oh, I was a very lucky fellow.

STELLA. Oh, Presto. You should have told me. Did you imagine that I would love you any the less for this?

SWIFT. But you must not love me, Poppet. Never, never. Not in that way.

STELLA. Never?

SWIFT. Don't you understand? I am your blood relation.

STELLA. You mean . . . it is a sin for me to love you?

SWIFT. More than a sin, Hetty. It is a crime . . . a crime against Church and State. Do you realize what this means in a world that is filled with bitter enemies? Above our heads hangs the unspeakable charge of incest.

STELLA. Oh, Presto, but why? Are you sure? Does anybody else . . . Who knows this, Presto?

SWIFT. I can never be certain of that. It happened so long ago . . . before the Revolution, and the Wars in Ireland.

STELLA. Then perhaps nobody . . .

SWIFT. But for all we can tell, there may still be somebody – some servant . . . some mean little attorney's clerk with a long memory . . . who can prove something – who is still waiting his chance. That is why we must never be found alone together so long as we both shall live. That is why we must always keep Dingley with us. Any other course would hand us over to the threat of blackmail until the day of our death.

(*She broods on this for a while.*)

STELLA. Then there is only one thing for me to do.

SWIFT. Yes?

STELLA. I must marry Mr Tisdall at once.

SWIFT. Oh no. Why that? Why that, Hetty?

STELLA. It will make our position clear. Nobody can ever accuse us of these things, once I am another man's wife.

SWIFT. But, Hetty, if you do this I shall lose you.

STELLA. You need never lose anything that you have now, Presto. You will never lose my love. And we can still see each other and be together, can't we?

SWIFT. But consider, my dear, how can we continue to see each other if you do this? I am a priest of the Church, and you will be another man's wife?.

STELLA. Oh!

(*Then quizzically.*)

Then perhaps you would prefer me not to marry?

SWIFT. I have no right to ask it of you. But . . . oh, my God! the very thought of you married to Tisdall!

STELLA. Presto, if you would rather that I didn't marry, I won't do so.

SWIFT (*surprised*). You mean . . . you would be content to be . . . just my friend? To remain as we are?

STELLA. If you wish it.

SWIFT (*deeply flattered*). You would rather be the friend of Jonathan Swift than the wife of any other man?

STELLA. Long ago when I was a little girl I made a promise to myself. I said that no man would ever marry me except Presto, my dear tutor. I am ready to keep that promise if you want me to.

SWIFT (*exalted*). Esther . . . my star . . . my dear, dear Stella. You are honouring me more than any man has ever been honoured, I am more deeply moved than I can say.

STELLA. Silly. How could I live with any other man after having known you? There is only one thing that troubles me. Suppose some day *you* wish to marry.

SWIFT. Nonsense. What could any other woman mean to me?

STELLA. You are a man, Jonathan, and men sometimes need a love that I will not be able to give you.

SWIFT. I am *more* than a man. I am Jonathan Swift, and I want nothing from any human being that I cannot get from you.

STELLA. Oh, I wonder.

SWIFT. Then stop wondering. I have spoken and there is nothing more to be said. What have we two to do with kisses? Our love is above such cheap embellishments. Come, give me your hand. We will go and look for Mr Tisdall.

STELLA (*going*). You called me Stella. That is a pretty name.
(*Fade out birds into a roll of thunder. The lights change to those of the deanery.* SWIFT *and* STELLA *return upstage.*)

PRIDE. And now, Dr Berkeley, before I so rudely interrupted, you were saying something about somebody's mother being a harlot weren't you?

ENVY (*confused*). Ahem! I feel, perhaps, that my account had better end at this point.

DEAN (*a little sarcastically*). As you wish, sir. Mrs Johnson may prefer to continue with the story herself, now that she has intervened so effectively. I think I replied that you had spoken in a manner worthy of the House of Peers. Well, Stella? You were reading that letter. Is there anything the matter?

STELLA (*upset*). Nothing, I thank you.

SWIFT. Charles, will you be so good as to take Dr Berkeley and Mrs Dingley in to supper? Mrs Johnson and I will follow presently.
(DINGLEY, BERKELEY *and* FORD *go off.*)

SWIFT. What is the matter, Stella?

STELLA. This letter is from Mrs Vanhomrigh.

SWIFT. She has written to you! How dare she!

STELLA. She demands that I tell her whether I am your wife.

SWIFT (*furious*). Give it to me at once. (*He takes the letter and reads it.*)

STELLA. What is this woman to you that she has the right to ask such a question of me?

SWIFT. Nothing. She has no right.

STELLA. Is that the truth, Presto?

SWIFT (*after a strangled pause*). No. It is not the truth.

STELLA. Thank you, Presto. It is best that I should know.

SWIFT. What are you going to do?

STELLA. What do you wish me to do?

SWIFT. Tell her that . . . No, you must not do that. Tell her . . . I cannot think!

STELLA. Am I to tell her that I am your wife?

SWIFT. No, no. You must never do that. Never.

STELLA. But why, Presto? What harm can come of it now?

SWIFT. Disaster can come of it. The most unspeakable of charges to overwhelm us both. Both of us . . . don't you understand?

STELLA. But surely that fear must have left you long ago, Presto? It is now almost sixty years since – since those things happened.

SWIFT. That fear will never leave me. It is the torture of all my waking hours. It is right that our friends should suspect our marriage. But for us to confirm it in any way, or to be found alone together . . . no, no! Never.

STELLA. Very well, Presto. I shall tell her then, that we are not married.

SWIFT. Yes . . . No . . . I don't know.

STELLA. If I do so, will she expect you to marry her?

SWIFT (*dully*). I suppose she will.

STELLA. Well? Do you wish to marry her?

SWIFT. I cannot marry her.

STELLA. You mean because of me?

SWIFT. Yes.

STELLA (*very proud*). Do not think, Presto, that I am going to stand in your way. If you love her and wish to marry her I shall not embarrass you in any way.

SWIFT (*eagerly*). Do you mean that it need not make any difference to our relationship?

STELLA (*with a touch of sarcasm*). That I shall remain the hostess of your deanery?

SWIFT. Will you still live near me and accept my protection?

STELLA. You would not have stayed with me if I had married Mr Tisdall. No, Presto. That is too much to ask of me.

SWIFT. Stella, for the love you bear me . . .

STELLA (*bitterly and with great firmness*). Yes, I love you. I always have and I always will love you. That is why I made the choice that I did.

SWIFT (*stricken*). It was I who asked you to make it. I should never have done so. That was my most terrible mistake.

STELLA. You are very cruel, Presto. Has it meant so little to you all these years? Are you sorry now that I decided as I did?

SWIFT. No, no! I am not sorry. You have meant everything to me. You have always been my greatest comfort, my dearest friend.

STELLA. Yet you love her.

SWIFT. That is different. I love you both, miserable man that I am. Can't a man love two women, each in their own way?

STELLA. Love two? Oh no, Presto, no! How can you ask such a question? You must have known how this would end. Why did you ever allow it to begin?

SWIFT. Because I wanted her.

STELLA. What do you mean, Presto? You once told me you would never want anything from any woman that I couldn't give you.

SWIFT. Yes, yes, that was true at the time. It's still true in the sense I meant it, then. But there is something else in me that needs her

... as a man needs a woman. Another kind of love. Oh, God, why must I be shut out from that for ever?

STELLA (*painfully*). Presto, are you ... after all ... are you only ...

SWIFT (*stung to the quick*). Yes, I'm only a man – just like other men! Why not? Time and again I asked myself, what before God, is the impediment? Have I wife of my own, that I must fly from her? Am I to chase after trulls and trollops all my life to keep my thoughts from honest women?

STELLA. Oh, my poor, poor Presto. You must marry her at once if this is how you feel. Believe me, there is no impediment. None whatsoever.

SWIFT. How can I marry her if it means that I must leave you?

STELLA. You will have to leave one of us, Presto.

SWIFT. Yes, one or the other. I can see that now. Somebody's heart must crack ... O God, forgive me.

STELLA (*tight-lipped again*). Please don't be concerned for me. I have my little fortune and my friends, and I shall never reproach you.

SWIFT (*brightening for a moment*). Oh, Stella. Do you mean ... ?

STELLA. It is my fault too. I should have known better than to hope.
(*This combination of pity and affectionate superiority completely baffles* SWIFT.)

SWIFT. ... I ... I ... don't know what to say.

STELLA. There is only one thing that I ask of you. It is my only right, Presto.

SWIFT. What is that?

STELLA. If you marry her, I want you to tell the world the truth of what lies between us two.

SWIFT. But, Stella ...

STELLA (*firmly*). I know what it will mean to both of us. But do you realize, Presto, the things that will be whispered of me, when once you marry her? It's a small request, and my only one. That is all I have to say.

SWIFT (*after a pause*). It's true, Stella. We can never part now and remain silent. We must tell our secret to the world if ever I marry.
(*Pause.*)
Then I will never marry. No woman on earth shall make me scandalize my mother's name and make a mockery of my best and dearest friend. I shall take this letter back to her, and I shall say ... I shall say ...

(*The organ fades in with agitated music.* STELLA *vanishes, and* VANESSA *appears in a spotlight.*)

VANESSA. Is he coming? Down the turnpike I hear the hoofbeats of his horse. He will be very angry because of my letter but I shall be calm. I know what I am going to say and I have my answers ready.

(*Through the music comes the beat of horse's hooves.*)

SWIFT (*in another spotlight, cloaked and wearing a hat*). By Kilmainham, by Palmerston, by Lucan, I ride to Celbridge. She knows what she will say to me, but what shall I say to her? Poor child. I must be kind. I shall pledge her to secrecy and then I shall tell her everything. She will understand. I shall say, here is my secret. Now you will understand why we can never marry.

VANESSA. He is mine and I am his. I will never give him up. Never. Never. Never. If he is married I shall kill myself. But no, he could never be such a monster, as to have kept that from me.

SWIFT. I shall say to her, 'Pray you, be my friend. I am doing you this wrong, but pray forgive and keep my secret safe. Think of my reputation and of Stella's.' And she will answer . . . she will answer . . . what will she answer? Trust her, Cadenus, for the love she bears you . . . this love you will not have! God! There is laughter in the skies . . . vile, bawdy, villainous laughter. It is ringing in my ears. It is tearing me to pieces. I shall say . . . I shall say . . .

(*The organ music stops and the horse clatters to a halt.*)

VANESSA. Listen! I hear him on the stairway. At the door. I'm not afraid. I am ready with an answer for anything he may say.

(*They meet in the centre of the frontstage. For a moment he stares at her in baffled torment.*)

Cadenus. Oh, Cadenus.

(*Pause.*)

Speak to me. Haven't you got anything to say?

(*He throws down the letter and vanishes out of the light.*)

VANESSA (*picking it up and recognizing it with a cry of despair*). Cadenus! My letter. Don't leave me here to die without a word, Cadenus!

(*Fade out on her sobbing and coughing into the sighing of the wind. Hold this to background. A spotlight rises on* SWIFT, *upstage, reading the Bible.*)

SWIFT. 'These things have I spoken unto you, that my joy might remain in you and that your joy might be full. This is my commandment, that ye love one another – love one another.'

304

(He pauses and listens to the wind.)

Oh God, her cry is always in my ears, and there is no escape. What is my sin that I must bear this burden all my life? It is love! this cursed noose that binds men and women together, until they strangle by each other's weight – this harlot rising from the bowels' ooze. I should have shut my ears against her cries, and driven her from my side. But I could not. Because of love! Love! Love! Cursed be love! Cursed be my covinous heart! Cursed be this thing called pity that has damned my soul to all eternity! 'Let the day perish wherein, I was born...'

(Take out wind effect.)

STELLA *(a ghostly voice)*. No, Jonathan. Neither pity nor love. But pride. Love is no sin, and pity brings no punishment. But pride is the sin of Lucifer himself, that loosed all other sins upon creation ... the sin that cannot bring itself to pray for pardon, and is the most deadly of the seven. That was the thing that destroyed you, Jonathan.

SWIFT. '... and the night which said, "There is a man child conceived". Let that day be darkness.'

(The light widens to disclose the deanery. FORD *enters.)*

FORD. Jonathan.

SWIFT. Do not interrupt me at my devotions.

FORD. I must speak to you about Miss Vanhomrigh.

SWIFT *(dully)*. Miss Vanhomrigh is dead.

FORD. Yes, and you mustn't close your eyes to the fact that she died your enemy.

SWIFT. A little transient fluttering of heartbeats that was a woman.

FORD. Jonathan, I do not presume to instruct you, but her will proves that she hated you.

SWIFT. Vanessa is what I used to call her.

FORD. I know, Jonathan. She has made Dr Berkeley her executor, and has encouraged him to publish all her private papers. This poem 'Cadenus and Vanessa' is already the talk of the town. For your own sake you must tell me whether you have written anything else that may compromise you.

SWIFT. Once I thought every day of death, but now every minute. Yet, I suppose I shall not all die, for half my body is already spent. I shall wither like a blasted elm from the top downwards. But first I shall finish my book. I have a legacy of my own to leave the human race. I shall lash them with scorpions, and dying, leave behind a memorial of my scorn that will last for all time.

FORD. Be careful, Jonathan. The human race is a prodigious enemy for one man to challenge. Who knows how it may treat your book?

SWIFT. I shall not care if it burns every copy. That will prove that my thunderbolt has struck home.

FORD. Maybe it will defend itself by subtler means.

SWIFT. No, no! There will be no parrying this blow. There will be no escape from what I say of them here. They shall understand my purpose well enough.

(BRENNAN *enters with* BERKELEY.)

BRENNAN. The Lord Bishop of Cloyne.

(BRENNAN *goes off.*)

BERKELEY. Dr Swift.

SWIFT. Ah, Dr Berkeley. So you have obtained your mitre at last?

BERKELEY. Yes, Mr Dean. Unworthy as I am. But I have called . . .

SWIFT. Accept my congratulations, my lord. And when your lordship has taken your seat in the House of Peers, may we expect that you will at last employ your considerable eloquence in the service of our own country?

BERKELEY. In good time, Dr Swift. My position is not yet as influential as it might be.

SWIFT. I see. Then when your lordship has obtained an even better bishopric you will perhaps become an honest man?

BERKELEY. Most assuredly, Mr Dean. Our mutual friend Mr . . . (*He realizes that he has been insulted.*) What was that, sirrah?

SWIFT. Till then, my lord, farewell.

(*He goes away.*)

BERKELEY. Why, what a scurrilous tongue! What impertinence! What a way to speak of me – who have come here in a spirit of good will! I am highly offended. I shall return home at once.

(*He turns to go.*)

FORD. No, no Dr Berkeley. Don't be offended by Dr Swift. He is a sick and tormented man.

BERKELEY. His troubles are entirely of his own making.

FORD. Maybe so, my lord. But much as we may sympathize with the troubles of the innocent, surely the sufferings of the guilty are fifty times more terrible?

BERKELEY. There can be no excuse for violence and cruelty.

FORD. True, Dr Berkeley, the Dean is a violent and bitter man. But whatever his sins may be, they need no punishment from us. He has full measure.

BERKELEY. This doesn't explain why you wish to see me now.

FORD. My lord, you are Miss Vanhomrigh's executor.

BERKELEY. That is true. She has left her fortune to my West Indian project.

FORD. But is it necessary that you publish all her private papers?

BERKELEY. But, Mr Ford, she intended me to do so. In particular this poem, 'Cadenus and Vanessa', which through no fault of mine has gone to the printer.

FORD. Your lordship realizes that this publication was designed by Miss Vanhomrigh with the object of injuring the Dean?

BERKELEY. It seemed to me that they were very excellent and well-written pieces, worthy of notice on their own merits. Otherwise I would never have allowed any of them to leave my hands.

FORD. Your lordship also realizes that these papers will cause – indeed have caused – a great deal of pain to persons other than Dr Swift. To Mrs Johnson, for instance?

BERKELEY. Bless my soul, that side of the matter had not occurred to me. I confess I am nonplussed. Mrs Johnson . . . She must indeed be very upset about it all! How is her health?

FORD. None too good, Dr Berkeley. We fear she has not long to live.

BERKELEY. Too bad. Too bad.

(STELLA *appears, leaning on* DINGLEY'S *arm.*)

FORD. Why, Hetty my dear, let me take your arm.

STELLA. Thank you, Don Carlos. You are very kind.

DINGLEY. She has taken her medicine, and it won't be long now before we have her back at the top of the ladder.

FORD. Of course.

STELLA. I fear I shall be out of breath before I reach the top. Is that Dr Berkeley?

BERKELEY. Your servant, madam. I have come to express my deep regret at . . . er . . . some embarrassment I seem to have caused you unwittingly.

STELLA. You mean . . . the Dean's poem?

BERKELEY. Yes, madam. I had no idea . . .

STELLA. It is a very fine poem. It would have been a great pity if it had been lost to posterity.

BERKELEY (*warming*). Quite so, madam. A most remarkable poem. Indeed, I feel it must have been inspired by a very remarkable person.

STELLA. Maybe so, my lord. On the other hand, the Dean has written very finely on the subject of 'A Broomstick'. You are smiling, Don Carlos. Hetty is herself again, you see.

DINGLEY. Come, my dear. You must lie down and rest for a little.

SWIFT (*entering*). Stella, what are you doing here? Give her to me.

BERKELEY (*trying to get between them*). No, no! Leave her to me, sir. I shall attend to Mrs Johnson's comfort.

SWIFT. Go away, sir.

STELLA (*politely disengaging herself from* BERKELEY *and giving her arm to* SWIFT). I thank you, my lord Bishop, for your kind intentions. I shall be quite happy with the Dean. He is very good to me. Forgive us if we leave you for a little while.

SWIFT (*going*). And do not disturb us. Come, my dear.

(SWIFT *and* STELLA *go off.*)

BERKELEY. Did you hear? What charity! What magnanimity! It is a lesson in the power of love.

FORD. And yet you remember that poem she read to us?
'With friendship and esteem possessed
They ne'er admitted love a guest.'

BERKELEY. Well, if it is not love, she must be a saint.

DINGLEY. A saint indeed! Hetty's no saint.

BERKELEY. Then the whole affair passes my comprehension.

DINGLEY. Twenty years ago I gave up trying to understand these two. I used to think that I knew something about men and women. But I know nothing. Not a thing! Now I ask no questions and am told no lies. And, Ford, I insist upon my cup of tea.

FORD (*going*). It's in the next room. Let us go.

BERKELEY. I will follow you in a moment.

(FORD *and* DINGLEY *go off.* BERKELEY *hesitates centre and then tiptoes in the direction taken by* SWIFT *and* STELLA.)

BERKELEY. It is inexcusable, I know. But . . . really I must . . .

SWIFT (*off*). Very well, my dear. If you wish it, it shall be owned. Let us tell them the truth, I am willing.

STELLA (*off*). No, Presto. Not now. It is too late.

BERKELEY. Most extraordinary. Oh, my goodness!

(*He hastily conceals himself as* SWIFT *enters in some agitation and kneels centre.*)

SWIFT. O merciful Father, take pity, we beseech thee, upon this Thy poor afflicted servant languishing under the weight of Thy hand. Give her a sincere repentance for all her transgressions . . .

BERKELEY (*indignantly*). Oh!

SWIFT. Accept and impute all . . . Who is there? Charles? Charles

– she must not die in the deanery. That would be a most improper thing.

BERKELEY (*appearing*). Die in the deanery! Improper! Is that all you can think about at this moment, you foul fellow?

SWIFT. Dr Berkeley!

BERKELEY. The effrontery – to offer your blasphemous prayers on her behalf. You are her only affliction – not God. How dare you speak like this, most of all in prayer to your Maker? Better ask forgiveness for your own sins.

SWIFT (*calling out in anguish*). Brennan! Dingley!

BERKELEY. This gentle lady, so loving, so lovely, so unhappy, whose tragedy we watch and mourn over, whose grief and sweet martyrdom is your work and yours alone . . .

SWIFT (*collapses, stricken*). No . . . no . . .

BERKELEY. What right have you to pray for her, you wretch, you fiend . . . here on the threshold of the second grave you have dug with your own infamous hands? Wretch! Have you no fear of God's judgment?

SWIFT. Stella!

STELLA (*entering*). Leave him alone. Leave him alone.

BERKELEY. Mrs Johnson!

STELLA. Leave him alone, I say. He is my friend.

BERKELEY. But he has wronged you grievously.

STELLA. He has not wronged me. He is my best and dearest friend. And when I die there will be no reproaches on my lips or in my heart. None whatsoever.

BERKELEY. But surely . . .

STELLA. That should be enough for you. Now leave us, please.
    (BERKELEY *rushes off. The organ and choir are heard faintly in Psalm 10.*)

SWIFT. Oh, Stella! Is it true that I have not wronged you? Did you really mean what you said?

STELLA. Of course, Presto.

SWIFT. If only I had done . . . if only I could do some little thing to repay you for the lifetime of devotion you have given me.

STELLA.
            'You taught how I might youth prolong.
            By knowing what was right and wrong,
            How from my heart to bring supplies
            Of lustre to my fading eyes.'

SWIFT. That is the poem you wrote for me on my birthday. You are a better poet than ever Presto was.

STELLA.

> 'Such is the fate of female race,
> With no endowments but a face;
> Before the thirtieth year of life
> A maid forlorn or hated wife.
> Stella to you, her tutor, owes
> That she has ne'er resembled those;
> Nor was a burthen to mankind
> With half her course of years behind.'

SWIFT. Stella, Stella. No, no! Stella! Open your eyes!

(The Psalm swells up and then fades out with the lights. When they rise again, all the characters, with the exception of SWIFT, *are grouped around the grave.)*

SEXTON. Well? Where am I to put back the skulls? Together or apart?

AVARICE. Does it matter – now?

SEXTON. Ne'er a bit. I'll get a box for them both and put in a note to say how they lived in arguments and were buried in arguments, and that I was the last to see them. *(He digs.)* Then I'll close up the floor, please God for the last time, and let them rest there till the Great Day.

ENVY. A brief memorandum of the seven deadly sins.

SEXTON. Sins, moryah! What do any of youse know about his sins, except maybe the one that happens to be your own? That's the only one that nobody can forgive.

LUST. How true. We have each accused him of being ourselves.

PRIDE. Even Stella?

LUST. Stella most of all. He used to say that he scorned to be outdone in anything. But she outdid even him in her pride. That is why they should rest together. They were of the same blood in more ways than one.

SLOTH. If you ask me, there's no man knows a man better than his own man. It was Brennan that did him his last service.

LUST. Brennan! We were almost forgetting you. How would Brennan remember him?

SLOTH. As a lazy, slothful old divil, sitting there in his chair day after day, and not a move or a word out of him, except maybe a curse, or a blow for them that's only trying their best to help him.

(Doorbell.)

Excuse me. That was the doorbell.

(All the characters slip away except SLOTH *and* AVARICE.)*

310

SLOTH (*as* BRENNAN). Good evening, Mrs Dingley, ma'am. So you've come to see the Dean.

DINGLEY. How is he tonight?

BRENNAN. Aw, not a word the wiser. Just sitting there in the old dressing-gown like a man that's dead the week before last. I can do nothing with him at all.

(*He brings her upstage. The light rises on* SWIFT – *an aged imbecile in his chair.* BRENNAN *slips away.*)

DINGLEY. Good evening, Jonathan. (*Pause.*) Good evening, Jonathan – don't you know me? It's your old friend Beccy Dingley come to read to you. Oh, ttttt-tttt. That is no sort of a face to make. There are a lot of people outside, Jonathan. They have come to pay their respects. It's your birthday. You know that, don't you? Your book about Captain Gulliver is still being a great success, I hear. I thought it a little exaggerated in parts – only in parts of course. But they tell me the children love it. In fact, it has become a classic of the nursery. I never would have expected you to write a children's book, Jonathan. Now, now, you mustn't get excited. What would you like me to read today? The Bible? I know that you like the Book of Job best, but I don't think too much of that is good for you. Now here's something nice that we had in church last Sunday.

(SWIFT *grunts.*)

'And Moses said unto God, Behold, when I come unto the Children of Israel, and shall say unto them, The God of your Fathers hath sent me unto you; and they shall say to me, what is his name? What shall I say unto them? And God said unto Moses, I am that I am. I Am hath sent me unto you.' You're not paying attention, Jonathan. Are you taking this in?

(SWIFT *hands her a paper.*)

SWIFT. Read.

DINGLEY. Read this? Why, it's some of your verse. Yes, that ought to be nicer.

> 'He gave the little wealth he had
> To build a house for fools and mad,
> And showed by one satiric touch
> No nation wanted it so much.
> Yet thus, methinks, I hear 'em speak,
> See how the Dean begins to break.'

(*She pauses.*)

Oh, do you think this is a good choice either?

SWIFT. Read.

DINGLEY (*with a break in her voice*).
> 'My female friends, whose tender hearts,
> Have better learned to act their parts,
> Receive the news with doleful dumps.'
> (*She pauses.*)
> ' "The Dean is Dead; (and what is trumps?)
> Then Lord have mercy on his soul.
> (Ladies I'll venture for the vole.)"
> "Six deans they say, must bear the pall
> (I wish I knew what King to call)" '
> (*With rising emotion.*)
> ' "Madam, your husband will attend
> The funeral of so good a friend?"
> "No Madam, 'tis a shocking sight;
> And he's engaged tomorrow night ..." '

(*She bursts into tears and hurries away. The choir can now be heard, at first very faintly in the final chorus of the Passion.* BRENNAN *leads on the others as a group of Dublin rabble.*)

BRENNAN (*whispering*). Whisht, now, all of ye. Be easy and I'll let yez see him. A silver sixpence and yez may have a look at the ould mad Dean. The great Draper on his birthday. There he is now ... the mad Dean of St Patrick's.

WHISPERINGS.
> Oh glory be to God, wouldn't it scarify you?
> Holy Jezebel, it's like looking into the clay face of death itself.
> Ah, harness your tongue and let me see.
> Well, his dancing days are dimmin'.
> Who said he was asleep?
> He's looking at us.
> He's awake. Oh Saint Larry O'Toole, he's getting up.
> (SWIFT *struggles slowly to his feet.*)

VOICE. He's going to speak.

SWIFT (*with quiet intensity*). I am that I am.
> (*There is puzzled silence.*)

VOICE. But them's the words of the Lord.

SWIFT (*louder*). I am that I am.
> (SWIFT *picks up the great Bible.*)

VOICES. It's blasphemy! Blasphemy!

SWIFT. Yahoos! Yahoos!

> (*He flings the Bible at them. There is a crash of glass and everybody runs screaming from the scene, leaving only the sobbing of one woman –* ANGER *– who is lost somewhere*

312

in the shadows. The voices of the choir grow louder as they approach down the aisle.)

SWIFT. I am ... that I am.

(*He sinks back into his chair. The choir appears, passing in front of* SWIFT'S *chair, where they pause and turn stage right.*)

A VOICE (*chanting off*). May the words of our lips and the meditation of our hearts be always acceptable in thy sight, O Lord, our strength and our redeemer. The Lord be with you.

CHOIR. And with thy spirit.

(*They turn left again, file upstage and pass through the door of the vestiary and disappear.* SWIFT *has vanished too. The organ concludes alone. That is the end of this play.*)

'STRANGE OCCURRENCE ON IRELAND'S EYE'

A Play about a Murder Trial

THE SCALES OF SOLOMON

The last play in this volume is about a murder trial, and concerns itself with the perennial question of whether a wrongful conviction is at all likely under the present system of British criminal procedure, and if so, how might it come about, without any particular malice or ill-will on the parts of the courts.

I have referred to British procedure deliberately, because – although my trial is an Irish one – the basic conceptions of criminal justice are the same on both sides of the Channel. In the United States, on the other hand, the Common Law, though apparently the same, is actually approached in quite a different spirit. Here its interpretation is not a magical one, but is a pragmatic process. In other words, to the American lawyer, the Law is something that a court is *likely* to decide – not what a court *ought* to decide, and this fundamental difference lies at the root of some of the difficulties that each country experiences in understanding the legal philosophy of the other. The same might be said of the language, which although ostensibly the same on both sides of the Atlantic, is all the more deceptive on that account.

On the Stage, any person on trial is usually the centre of the picture, and is generally required to be innocent. With one or two notable exceptions, trial plays culminate either in a triumphal acquittal or in a wrongful conviction – a practice that has placed judges and prosecuting counsel in the unfair position of being, as a rule, character villains.

In actual fact, the ends of justice are much more often defeated by the machinations of defending counsel – a state of affairs that has been sometimes countered in the United States by the practice of obtaining convictions under the heading 'B' in cases where everybody is aware of the fact that the actual crime is 'A'. We all know how Al Capone went to jail as an Income Tax defaulter because the legal process made it more likely that there would be a verdict of guilty under this category than under any other.

Once these roundabout tricks take a firm hold of legal thinking, it is only a short step to other departures from older principles, such as ex-post-facto punishment (as in the case of political undesirables), and the use of the courts, not as instruments of investigation, but as part of a ritual of public revenge (as in the case of the war criminals). One can see Mary Magdalene being triumphantly committed for contempt of court, had she shown any natural reluctance to answer the question, 'Are you prepared to state that you are not, and never have been, a whore?'

However, leaving aside these special cases (which make just as bad law as hard cases), the criminal courts on both sides of the Atlantic do not often break down at the expense of the individual; and whenever they do, the cause of the trouble is not usually malice, corruption, or any active ill-will on the part of the State. It is much more likely to be brought about by what might be described as the common-sense short cut, and the professionalism that springs not from hard-heartedness, but from long experience.

One of the prices that we have to pay for our traditional safeguards is the fact that we have to allow a considerable number of criminals the benefit of the doubt, and unfortunately clever rogues are much more skilful at taking advantage of this loophole than are stupid fools. In the course of time these cumulative escapes can inspire a certain impatience among those burdened with the enforcement of law. The thing becomes a game, with the cards stacked in favour of the smart crook, who, in spite of the fact that he is much more dangerous to society than the lesser one, is much more likely to get off. And so a dualism springs up in the attitude of the prosecutor towards matters of fact. There is what he can prove in accordance with the law of evidence. There is also what he knows to be true. And as an understandable reaction to all the play-acting that he has to put up with in court, he occasionally forgets that sometimes it is not play-acting at all, and he will snatch at a victory for what he believes to be common sense. As one of the characters in *Strange Occurrence* says:

'There are so many shady characters – always getting off on one excuse or another – why you and Mr Brownrigg must see it happening every day. So naturally you get cynical, and you want to play hard for your side. I can understand that. But that's just where the danger lies.'

In 1936 I wrote what was originally intended to be a radio play on some of these aspects of the criminal courts. I took as my subject a well-known Irish murder trial of 1852, where an innocent man was convicted, largely on the ground that he was a morally obnoxious character, and was clearly guilty of something or other. As with Dreyfus, it is highly irritating to all concerned, when a suspected person who has all the outward lineaments of a villain of romance turns out to be nothing of the kind. Kirwan was a victim of this hostility to such an extravagant degree that I soon realized that I would have to modify the actual facts of the story if my play was ever going to be believed. So, without changing the names of the characters or altering the locale, I transferred the action to the present century, and provided a gimmick from the modern law of evidence on which the denouement would turn, in preference to a conviction rooted in hysteria and stupidity, as had actually been the case.

The play was never performed at the time, as I shortly afterwards joined the staff of the B.B.C., and wrote a different trial play based, instead, on a rightful conviction for a wrong reason – the Glass Murder. The Kirwan script lay in my drawer for a while, and some months later I used the same gimmick as the climax of a rewrite of a Toller play, that he had persuaded me to disembowel. So, it will be noticed by anybody acquainted with this supposed collaboration, entitled *Blind Man's Buff*, that while the crime and the characters are entirely different, the feature of the trial which forms the middle act of both *Buff* and *Strange Occurrence* is basically the same. The reason for this similarity lies in the fact that *Buff* was the result of an attempt to combine an existing situation of Toller's with an existing trial of my own – an experiment doomed to failure in the end, since his heroes were my villains and vice versa, and no play can survive that has its stars in the wrong parts. *Strange Occurrence*, therefore, is a rewrite, not of *Blind Man's Buff*, but of an older radio play of my own, which is here presented in stage form.

William Burke Kirwan, the star of the original story (though not a star part in my play), was an artist of very moderate ability, who for ten years maintained two independent households in Dublin. In one of these lived his legitimate wife, and in the other he kept a mistress and – ultimately – no less than seven children. It might be wondered how he managed to preserve the secret of so spectacular a double life over so long a period. The answer, of course, is that he didn't. Indeed, he made so little effort to hush the situation up that he actually appears in the Dublic Directory for the year of the trial under his own name at both addresses.

Although it is no crime at law for a man to have as many con-
cubines as he can persuade to live with him, provided he marries
only one, and although he is perfectly at liberty to father an
indefinite number of children, legitimate and illegitimate, provided
that certain formalities are observed with regard to support, this
was clearly a situation that mid-Victorian Dublin could not be
expected to view with any calm – particularly as none of the parties
showed any disposition to bring it to an end. So, when the wife died
on Ireland's Eye under mysterious circumstances, it was natural
enough to leap to the conclusion that some dirty work had been
afoot.

From the statements sworn by the mistress, Teresa Kenny, it
appears that very great pressure was brought to bear upon her to
allege that she had gone through the ceremony of matrimony with
Kirwan. But this she resolutely refused to do, although driven from
every lodging that she fled to, threatened with larceny charges, and
even terrorized by the threat of the removal of her unfortunate
children to the Poor House. So, having failed to saddle Kirwan with
a bigamy charge, the Crown changed its tune and successfully
convicted him of murder. In this, the prosecution was greatly helped
by Kirwan's own behaviour, and particularly by his aggressiveness
towards every witness who might possibly have put in a good word
for him. He flouted his landlady, underpaid his boatmen, and in-
furiated the parish priest of Howth. At this distance, all of these
items can be seen to be better proof of his innocence than of his
guilt. Nor can one see why, after ten years of fruitful duality, he
should take it upon himself to murder a wife who had accepted
the situation, throughout, with the utmost complaisance. Yet none
of these aspects of the case was ever mentioned at the trial.

His sentence, of course, was commuted. Not even Kirwan's
spectacular unpopularity could justify the Crown in hanging him
on such evidence. But he was not released. The wretched man
served the standard term for a life sentence on Spike Island, from
which he emerged during the memory of some who are still alive,
and ended his days in Australia. From this, it will be seen why it
was necessary for me to soften down the plot of my play with
generous injections of synthetic credibility – otherwise it would
never be believed.

Let us not flatter ourselves, however, with the easy alibi that
such things could not possibly happen today. During the greater
part of the last century there was a much deeper regard for the
niceties of criminal procedure than is the case today. For one

thing, the trial as I have depicted it could never have had quite the same outcome, because Kirwan would not have been allowed to open his mouth in his own defence. We imagine that this recent development in criminal procedure was introduced for the greater security of the accused. Actually, the reverse is the case, and the present rule more frequently operates to facilitate convictions than to protect the prisoner.

It is true, of course, that in the great majority of cases the criminal courts manage to reach substantially just conclusions, and that wrongful convictions, especially on capital charges, are few and far between. It is equally important to mention that, even when these lapses do occur, there are sometimes one or two people like Brownrigg with sufficient regard for the system that they administer, to cry halt and to set it right, even at some danger to themselves. Man errs, but he also repairs.

'Strange Occurrence on Ireland's Eye'

This play was first produced by the Abbey Theatre Company in Dublin on August 20th, 1956, with the following cast:

Chief Superintendent Brownrigg	RAY MCANALLY
Sergeant Fell	PATRICK LAYDE
Sergeant Sherwood	MICHEÁL O'BRIAIN
Mrs Margaret Campbell	MAIRE KEAN
Patrick Nangle	BILL FOLEY
William Kenmis	PHILIP O'FLYNN
Brendan Brew	VINCENT DOWLING
Moira Brew	DOREEN MADDEN
Dr Teresa Mary Kenny	MAIRE NI DHOMHNAILL
William Burke Kirwan	SEATHRUN O GOILI
John Penefeather	PEADAR O LUAIN
Mrs Adelaide Crowe	EILEEN CROWE
John George Smyly, S.C.	T. P. MCKENNA
Mr Justice Crampton	HARRY BROGAN
Isaac Butt, S.C.	EDWARD GOLDEN
R. A. Walker	TOMAS MAC ANNA
George Hatchell	MICHEÁL O HAONGHUSA
Foreman of the Jury	DAIRE DE PAOR
Tipstaff	PADRAIG MAC GABHANN
Others in Court	PADRAIG O LUING
	EITHNE NI LIODAIN
	TRAOLACH O HAONGHUSA
	ROIBEARD MAC COMAIDH
	RUAIRU MAC GIOLLA COILLE

Production by Ria Mooney; settings designed by Tomas Mac Anna.

CHARACTERS

CHIEF SUPERINTENDENT HENRY J.
BROWNRIGG
SERGEANT FELL   } of the Garda Siochana
SERGEANT SHERWOOD

MRS MARGARET CAMPBELL, lodging-house keeper

PATRICK NANGLE, a boatman

WILLIAM KENMIS, State Solicitor

BRENDAN BREW, a golfer

MOIRA BREW, his wife

TERESA MARY KENNY, a dispensary doctor

WILLIAM BURKE KIRWAN, an artist

JOHN PENEFEATHER, barrister-at-law

MRS. ADELAIDE CROWE, an old lady

JOHN GEORGE SMYLY, senior counsel

MR JUSTICE CRAMPTON, a judge

ISAAC BUTT, senior counsel

R. A. WALKER, court registrar

GEORGE HATCHELL, Assistant State Pathologist

The enigmatic events upon which this play is based actually occurred on Ireland's Eye in the early 1850s. All the characters are real people, appearing under their actual names, in so far as these can now be fully ascertained. For the purposes of the theatre, however, the circumstances are re-dressed in modern trappings, and the trial is transferred to the year 1937.

ACT ONE   Scene 1 The office of the chief superintendent, Dublin Castle. Tuesday, October 5th
             Scene 2 The same. A day later
             Scene 3 The same. Monday, October 11th
             Scene 4 The same. Monday, December 6th
ACT TWO   The Central Criminal Court, Green Street, Dublin. Thursday, December 9th
ACT THREE   Scene 1 As in Act One. Friday, December 31st
             Scene 2 The same. Later on the same evening

326

ACT ONE

Scene 1

The office of the chief superintendent of the Civic Guard, Dublin Castle. It is a large, old-fashioned room full of modern filing-cabinets and Victorian glass-fronted bookcases. BROWNRIGG *is a good-looking middle-aged man, wearing a blue uniform, lighter in shade than that of the British police. He is working at a large centre table, and as the Curtain rises a telephone rings beside him. At a side table, near the door, a sergeant of the police is also at work.*

BROWNRIGG (*into the phone*). Superintendent Brownrigg speaking. Yes Canon, I've heard of the place. It's a properly licensed dance hall – quite in order. There are such things in Bray, you know. Wait a minute please, till I transfer you to the man who deals with these matters. (*He rattles the receiver.*) O'Reilly, will you please make a note of this complaint. Excuse me, Canon. Here's your man now. (*He hangs up, and sighs.*) Now Sergeant, is this the last of the Inspection Minutes?

FELL. Yes, Super. The sergeant from Howth is outside.

BROWNRIGG. What does he want?

FELL. Just a routine check, sir. His super is away on leave.

BROWNRIGG (*picking up a file of papers*). As yes. I remember. An elderly man. Likes a quiet time, unless I'm mistaken.

FELL. Sergeant Sherwood, sir. A very decent man.

BROWNRIGG. Fetch him in.

(FELL *goes to the door and speaks off. After* SHERWOOD *has come in,* FELL *goes to his own table and works there.*)

FELL. Come in, Sergeant. The super will see you now.

(SERGEANT SHERWOOD *enters – an elderly, tired-looking policeman – an old D.M.P. type who has obviously survived the Troubles by looking in the opposite direction, whenever this has been possible. Unlike the other two, he has his cap, and salutes.*)

BROWNRIGG (*not paying much attention*). Well Sergeant, how's Howth? Nothing bothering you, I hope?

SHERWOOD. Ah no, sir. Nothing out of the ordinary. But I thought I'd better check with you, sir, while Superintendent Percy is away.

BROWNRIGG (*selecting a file*). Howth. As yes. I think I've been through all your 'C Ones'. (*He looks through the papers.*) No, you seem to have no particular troubles on your hands at present. Doing all right out there – eh – on your own?

SHERWOOD. Yes, thank you, sir. I . . . er . . .

BROWNRIGG. By the way, here's something that caught my eye. A charge of obstructing a funeral. Rather an odd thing to do, isn't it?

SHERWOOD. Yes, sir. A couple of boatmen called Nangle. I wasn't going to press it, sir.

BROWNRIGG (*incredulous*). Boatmen? Obstructing a funeral?

SHERWOOD. Ah sure, 'twas only a bit of trouble over money, Super. This man Kirwan's wife was drowned and she swimming out on Ireland's Eye. He only gave the boatmen a couple of pounds for all their trouble in helping to find her and to bring her ashore.

BROWNRIGG. I see. Still, that's hardly an excuse for trying to stop the hearse, is it?

SHERWOOD. Ah well now, sir, they hardly went as far as that. Maybe if Father Hall hadn't been down there it would never have happened. I wouldn't want to press the charge, sir.

BROWNRIGG. Well, that's for you to decide. (*The telephone rings and he picks it up irritably.*) Excuse me. Superintendent Brownrigg speaking. Yes ma'am, I can hear you. Ah, so you think your lodger has murdered his wife! May I ask your name? Campbell. Mrs Margaret Campbell. (*He makes a note.* SHERWOOD *shows signs of agitation.*) And the local guards refuse to do anything about it. Well, isn't that very remiss of them! In league with the murderer, no doubt. May I ask where these lamentable events took place? Howth. Oh! (*He looks at* SHERWOOD *who shakes his head significantly.*) Well ma'am, I'm afraid you'll have to go back and see them again about it at the barracks. No, I can't see you here, even if you do come up to town. We have some very efficient policemen out in Howth, and you'll really have to let them deal with it. (*He bows to* SHERWOOD *with a slight smile of raillery.*) Very well, ma'am,

328

write to the Minister if you like. Goodbye. Goodbye. (*He hangs up.*) One of your clientele, eh, Sherwood?

SHERWOOD. Oh a very troublesome woman.

BROWNRIGG. You know her? Mrs . . . er . . . Campbell?

SHERWOOD. I do indeed, sir. Always lodging complaints and having complaints lodged about her.

BROWNRIGG. This is rather more than a complaint, Sergeant. A murder charge is a very serious matter.

SHERWOOD. I know, Super, but sure there's nothing to it at all. It's all over this couple, Kirwan, was stopping in her house for the summer.

BROWNRIGG. Kirwan? Didn't I hear that name before? Wasn't it in connection with that funeral the boatmen tried to stop?

SHERWOOD. Yes, Super. It's this same woman was drowned swimming off Ireland's Eye. Sure she's buried nearly a month now.

BROWNRIGG. Buried? Without an inquest?

SHERWOOD. Certainly there was an inquest. Wasn't I at it myself! On the seventh of September last it was.

BROWNRIGG (*to* FELL). Sergeant, get me the newspaper file covering the eighth of last month.

FELL (*going to fetch it*). Yes, sir.

SHERWOOD. A fit in the water she had. The verdict was 'found drowned'.

BROWNRIGG. Well, if that's the case, you'd better see this woman, and remind her that it's a very serious matter to throw charges of this sort around. You can tell her, too, that the guards don't like it being said that they're refusing to carry out their duties.

SHERWOOD (*uncomfortably*). She's a woman I don't like having any words with at all, sir. A very troublesome woman.

BROWNRIGG. Then tell her to stop being troublesome, or I'll have to go out and talk to her myself.

SHERWOOD. Sure, isn't that what she wants.

FELL (*laying a newspaper file before* BROWNRIGG). Here's the papers, Super. There's a report of the inquest on page four of the *Times*. There, sir.

BROWNRIGG. Is this it? 'Strange Occurrence on Ireland's Eye'. What's strange about it? The verdict seems to be quite definite. Then why was there this trouble at the funeral? Was it really just over money, Sherwood?

SHERWOOD. Well sir . . . mm (*He hesitates*).

BROWNRIGG. Come on. Tell me more about these boatmen, and what exactly happened.

SHERWOOD. Patrick and Michael Nangle, sir. Two very respectable
men. At ten in the morning they ferried them all out to the
island – this man Kirwan and his poor wife, and another couple
that was spending the day there too. And at six in the evening
they went out again to ferry them back. But by that time the
unfortunate woman was drowned, and they found her stretched
in the Long Hole where the tide had left her.

BROWNRIGG. Did I understand you to say that there was another
couple on the island with the Kirwans?

SHERWOOD. There was indeed, sir. A Mr and Mrs Brew and their
child along with them.

BROWNRIGG. Friends of the Kirwans?

SHERWOOD. No, sir. Just sharing the boat. Oh a very nice quiet pair.

BROWNRIGG. I see. Independent witnesses – no connection at all.
And the coroner's finding amounted to accidental drowning. It
all seems quite straightforward. But I'm still bothered about
this trouble at the funeral.

SHERWOOD. Ah sure, he's a mean sort of man, that same Kirwan.
Not likeable at all. Father Hall, the parish priest, was down
there speaking against him too.

BROWNRIGG. Ah, the parish priest! No wonder there was trouble.
But even if he is a mean sort of a man that's no reason for
accusing him of murder.

SHERWOOD. Ah well now, that Mrs Campbell is worse than himself.
I wouldn't believe a word out of that one, and he having fallen
foul of her.

BROWNRIGG. How did he fall foul of her?

SHERWOOD. Nothing would satisfy him but he must accuse her of
taking a ring of his wife that was missing from the digs. Ringing
up the barracks he was and wanting to have her arrested. I told
him at the time she'd only come back with worse charges against
himself. And I was right.

BROWNRIGG. Has he pressed this charge?

SHERWOOD. He has not, sir. For his poor wife was drowned in the
meantime. And isn't it best left the way it is, in the presence of
the dead? What use is all this charging and counter-charging
over nothing but bad feeling? Sure, it only causes trouble, and is
best forgotten.

BROWNRIGG. Well, I think I've got to the bottom of this at last. But
if this woman is going to write letters to the Minister, making
murder charges, it's something that can't be forgotten as easily
as that. You'd better bring her up to see me, Sherwood.

SHERWOOD (*reluctantly*). Yes, Super.

BROWNRIGG. And bring those boatmen along too. A thing like this must be dealt with one way or the other. In future Mrs Campbell either provides some basis for this sort of scandal, or she takes the consequences.

SHERWOOD. Yes, sir. Whatever you say, sir.

BROWNRIGG (*closing the file*). Yes, I'll see them, Sherwood. To-morrow if possible.

BLACK OUT

Scene 2

When the lights rise, it is the next day, and MRS CAMPBELL *is alone with* BROWNRIGG. *She is an embittered-looking, middle-aged lodging-house keeper with a strident voice.*

MRS CAMPBELL. Threatening me! Threatening me – that's what you are. But don't think you can stop my mouth. I'll speak my mind, and no threats can muzzle me.

BROWNRIGG. If you like to regard my warning as a threat, Mrs Campbell, go ahead and do so. But you'd better remember that there's a law in this country against making reckless accusations.

MRS CAMPBELL. A low, loose-living immoralist – that's what he is – breaking the law of God and man, carrying on with another woman and he a married man, that's what he is. Father Hall will bear me out.

BROWNRIGG. All this may be so, but you're accusing him of committing a crime.

MRS CAMPBELL. And isn't it a crime to do what he did with that other one? And then making it worse by taking her to have something done to her that no lips of mine will put a name to.

BROWNRIGG. What do you mean?

MRS CAMPBELL. You know well what I mean. He got her into trouble, that's what he did. And then he got her out of it by a sin against nature that's worse.

BROWNRIGG (*after a slight pause*). If there's anything in what you

331

say, Mrs Campbell, that certainly is a crime. But you're accusing him of murdering his wife.

MRS CAMPBELL. And why wouldn't he murder her, with that black sin on his soul? I tell you, his wife had learnt the truth. With my own ears I heard them arguing about it. And if you don't believe me, ask him for the letters he had in the drawer of the desk, and read them for yourself.

BROWNRIGG. How do you know what letters he had in a drawer?

MRS CAMPBELL. That's my business. It's your business to take them from him and show the truth of what I'm saying.

BROWNRIGG. What you're saying, my good woman, is based on the simple fact that he was going to charge you with stealing a ring. Isn't that so?

MRS CAMPBELL. It's a lie – a dirty lie. I never stole no ring and if he says so I'll have the law on him for that too. I'm telling you he took her to the island the day after she'd found out about his carryings on, and there he stopped her mouth. But nobody will stop mine.

BROWNRIGG. The woman was drowned after having a stroke while bathing.

MRS CAMPBELL. She was never drowned. She was stabbed with a knife – Nangle, the boatman's knife.

BROWNRIGG (*sarcastically*). In the presence, no doubt, of two independent witnesses and a child, who were on the island with them at the same time.

MRS CAMPBELL. If it's the Brews, you mean, they were nowhere near the island at the time. The Nangles brought them back at two o'clock. Mrs Kirwan wanted to come back too, but the fly-by-night wouldn't let her go. He wanted to have her alone for the rest of the day.

BROWNRIGG. Oh! I didn't know that the other people came back. Is this the truth?

MRS CAMPBELL. It's a truth you can find out for yourself – like a lot more truths you know nothing about. Have you ever asked Nangle about his knife?

BROWNRIG. If necessary I'll ask the boatman about several matters. And in any event, a woman can hardly be stabbed without leaving a wound.

MRS CAMPBELL. He stood over the women who laid her out to stop them from seeing it.

BROWNRIGG (*irritably*). Ah, don't talk nonsense, woman. There was an inquest, and the body was examined then.

MRS CAMPBELL. An inquest, moryah! And whose word did the coroner take that there was no wound?

BROWNRIGG. I presume he had some medical evidence.

MRS CAMPBELL. He had that all right – from Kenny, the woman doctor from Baldoyle, who pushed her way in when she heard who was dead. And do you know who she is?

BROWNRIGG. No. Who is she?

MRS CAMPBELL. The other woman in the case, you gawm! The strap he's been carrying-on with.

BROWNRIGG (*surprised*). Indeed!

MRS CAMPBELL. I told you you should read them letters. They'd open your eyes for you. And if you won't read them maybe there's others that will.

BROWNRIGG. I see. (*Pause.*) Well, maybe there are some more inquiries that ought to be made.

MRS CAMPBELL. Maybe there are. Maybe there's some of the Guards that ought to learn their job before coming and threatening me.

BROWNRIGG (*rising*). Well, that's all I'll bother you with now, Mrs Campbell. Thank you for coming.

MRS CAMPBELL (*as he shows her to the door*). Am I to write to the Minister, or am I not?

BROWNRIGG. Just as you please, ma'am. In any event I know what my duties are. Goodbye.

MRS CAMPBELL (*triumphantly*). You'd better do something! Make no mistake of that. I'll see that justice is done.

(*She goes off with a spate of querulous ad libs.* BROWNRIGG *speaks off.*)

BROWNRIGG. Are you the boatman? Will you come in, please.

(NANGLE *enters. He is a middle-aged fisherman. His manner, to begin with, is furtive and defensive, but he soon loosens up.*)

BROWNRIGG. Take a seat, Nangle. Isn't that your name?

NANGLE (*sitting down*). Yes, sir. The sergeant told me himself there'd be no charge.

BROWNRIGG. Charge? Oh yes, of course. Obstructing a funeral. What made you do that?

NANGLE. 'Twasn't on account of the money at all. If he says so it's a lie. Are you charging me or are you not?

BROWNRIGG. That depends on how ready you are to help us. Eh?

NANGLE. Oh, if that's the way of it I'll help you all you want.

Father Hall says if the guards had done their duty the woman wouldn't have been buried then at all.

BROWNRIGG. Look here, better tell me the whole story from the start. Who is this man, Kirwan? And what happened on the day you took him and his wife out to the island?

NANGLE. An artist he is, painting pictures on the pier, or maybe an odd time up on the hill. A dry sort of a man that nobody cared for.

BROWNRIGG. How long had he and his wife been in Howth?

NANGLE. All the summer – the pair of them. And never once seen at mass of a Sunday.

BROWNRIGG. Well what of it? Perhaps they're Protestants.

NANGLE. That's not what Mrs Campbell says.

BROWNRIGG. Never mind her! Did you often take him out to the island?

NANGLE. Not once, sir, until Monday the sixth last. I'll remember that date till my dying day. For I see now why he took her.

BROWNRIGG. At what time did you ferry them out to the island?

NANGLE. At ten in the morning. And this Mr and Mrs Brew and their child along with them.

BROWNRIGG. These Brews were summer visitors too?

NANGLE. No, sir. Only down from Dublin for the day. Oh, a very nice couple – not like the others – not that I'd say a word against the dead, R.I.P. But they paid what they were asked, and no arguments about it. And with the price of petrol what it is . . .

BROWNRIGG. We'll come to that in a moment. Did they bring anything with them?

NANGLE. Lunch-baskets – they were carrying. And Mrs Kirwan had a towel and her bathing suit. And the little lad had a bucket and spade. And Mr Brew had his bag of golf clubs.

BROWNRIGG. Surely there's not a golf links out there?

NANGLE. No, sir. It was for to practise his golfing strokes on the beach. I seen him at it myself on our way back in the boat. And then your man had his painting box and some class of a stand for to hold the pictures when he'd be at them.

BROWNRIGG. Is it true that you took the Brews back first?

NANGLE. It is, sir. At two o'clock, nearly an hour after high water – that's when we were told to go back to pick them up.

BROWNRIGG. Where were they all when you arrived to collect them?

NANGLE. The Brews were packing up the basket and your man was painting away at his picture fornenst the martello tower. Come

334

back about six, says he. So then his wife says she'll go up the island and take a swim. And Mr and Mrs Brew calls for the child, and we took the three of them ashore.

BROWNRIGG. Was anybody else left on the island with the Kirwans?

NANGLE. Not a living soul, sir. By the time September comes around there's not many would be out there of a Monday afternoon. And seeing what he meant to do, he must have known that well.

BROWNRIGG. You seem to be quite certain what he meant to do?

NANGLE. Well, didn't he borrow me knife? I thought it was for something to do with his painting. Little did I know what he had in his mind. It was a good knife, sir – a fisherman's clasp knife with a spike for splicing rope on the back side.

BROWNRIGG. Did he borrow it from you when you left with the Brews?

NANGLE. No, sir. It was when we were on the way out the first time. And that was the last I ever saw of it. Lost, is all he would say when I asked for it back. Oh, a very ignorant sort of a man, as we soon found out. Well, just before six o'clock when the cousin and I were on the pier, getting ready to go back in the boat, didn't we hear a wild scream from over the water.

BROWNRIGG. What sort of a scream?

NANGLE. Like a wail it was – like someone in mortal agony. I remarked on it to Michael at the time. Like mortal agony is the very words I used.

BROWNRIGG. Shortly before six. And then you went straight out in the boat?

NANGLE. Soon after. And there was your man still painting away at the martello tower as if butter wouldn't melt in his mouth, and only we asked him where was Mrs Kirwan he'd have got in the boat and come ashore without another word about her.

BROWNRIGG. That's strange behaviour.

NANGLE. Where's your wife? says I. On the beach, says he. She is not, says I, for there was no one on the beach and we coming by. So he lets out a few roars and there's no answer. So then he goes and looks at the beach, and comes back and says we've got to help him to search the island before it's dark. So we tied up the boat and went off after him. It was half seven and getting dark before we found her on a rock in the Long Hole. (BROWNRIGG *rises and goes to inspect a map on the wall.*)

BROWNRIGG. Where's that?

335

NANGLE. At the other end of the island from the tower. On the far side.

BROWNRIGG. Was she in the water?

NANGLE. She was not. The tide by then was a good two feet lower than the rock she was stretched on. Oh, Mary, Mary, says he, letting on to be surprised. And then he runs and lifts the body up, and sends the two of us to look for her clothes.

BROWNRIGG. She wasn't dressed?

NANGLE. She was, sir, in the bathing suit. But he must have known where the clothes were for he pointed where to look. So then we covered up the poor soul and brought her ashore in the boat. It was half nine before we had her up at the house, and it was after that he give us the two pounds. Two pounds for two trips to the island, searching for nearly an hour and a half, and for carrying the woman up to the house. That's the sort of a man he is!

BROWNRIGG. Were there any signs of violence on the body?

NANGLE. Ah, sure there was little enough we could see in the dark. But I remember remarking that there was blood on the towel that was covering her head. That's when I asked about my knife, and he said it was lost. And ne'er a sign of it have I seen since, though I've been back to look.

BROWNRIGG. I see. And it was after this that you kicked up a scene at the funeral?

NANGLE. The next day, sir – after the inquest. When Father Hall came down with Mrs Campbell, and said that Kirwan was a scandal to a Christian country, and the woman shouldn't be taken to Glasnevin till the truth was known about her death. That's when we tried to stop the hearse. Were we right or were we wrong?

BROWNRIGG (*coming to the telephone*). If all you say is true, Nangle, there may have been some excuse for what you did.

NANGLE (*rising*). Every word of it is true, sir. So what about . . . ?

BROWNRIGG. There'll be no charge against either of you for the present. Thank you very much for your co-operation. That'll be all, Nangle.

(*He lifts the telephone.*)

BROWNRIGG. Get me the State Solicitor.

NANGLE (*going to the door*). Thank you, sir. I'll be off now.

BROWNRIGG. Good afternoon. Thank you.

NANGLE (*as he goes*). Thank *you*, sir.

BROWNRIGG. Hello. Is that Mr Kenmis? Chief Superintendent

speaking. I want an order for the exhumation of a body buried
in Glasnevin on the ninth of last month. A woman called Sarah
Mary Kirwan with an address in Upper Merrion Street. Yes,
it's urgent and important. A possible murder charge.

BLACK OUT

Scene 3

It is Monday, five days later, in the afternoon. BROWNRIGG *is alone
at his desk, but rises when* KENMIS *enters, with some papers in his
hands.* KENMIS *is a poker-faced, legal civil servant in the forties,
dressed in professional clothes.*

KENMIS. Well, Brownrigg.

BROWNRIGG. Oh, Mr Kenmis. It's good of you to come over. Won't
you take a seat?

KENMIS (*doing so*). Thanks. I just thought you'd better be warned
that the chief pathologist is still in Majorca. So we're having
this damn post mortem you asked for carried out by one of his
assistants.

BROWNRIGG. Well, there's no trouble about that, is there?

KENMIS. None – except that it looks like taking about twice as long
as usual. New brooms, you know. We've only had an interim
report so far.

BROWNRIGG. And what does he say?

KENMIS (*looking at his papers*). Oh, a lot of damn generalities about
deputy coroners and woman doctors. Takes every chance he
can to show off, and slap them down. A prize bore, if you ask
me.

(*He hands a sheet to* BROWNRIGG, *who looks through it
eagerly.*)

BROWNRIGG. But what about the body?

KENMIS. See for yourself. As far as I can make out, it's in no condition now to be examined at all. What would you expect after
a month in the ground? But you'll see where he says there
definitely are some marks on the face and head – particularly
in one ear.

337

BROWNRIGG. Ah! No mention of this was made at the inquest. (*He reads on.*) Not that a wound in the ear signifies much. What we're really looking for is the mark of a stab.

KENMIS. That's just the point. This fellow has some theory that a stab through the ear with some sort of a pointed instrument could penetrate the brain. Sounds like Edgar Wallace to me.

BROWNRIGG. A pointed instrument! My God, maybe he's got something there.

KENMIS. I'd hate to think so. He's tiresome enough as it is, without turning out to be right.

BROWNRIGG. No wonder there was blood on the towel! No wonder he hid the thing afterwards!

KENMIS. Hid what?

BROWNRIGG. The boatman's knife. That had a spike on it, and Kirwan wouldn't give it back. I see it all now. He was afraid there might be traces on it of what he'd done. Mr Kenmis, we've got to arrest this man.

KENMIS. Arrest him? Not on this evidence, you don't.

BROWNRIGG. Not good enough, eh?

KENMIS. Good enough! It's non-existent. Why, we'd never get a remand, much less a conviction.

BROWNRIGG. Mr Kenmis, I'd like you to stay and meet two people I've got coming here this afternoon. In fact they're due now.

KENMIS. I haven't much time. Who are they?

BROWNRIGG. The Brews. You know – the other couple that was out on the island with the Kirwans. I don't know what they'll have to say, but it might be illuminating.

KENMIS. My dear Superintendent, I don't care what they say. I still see no reason for throwing overboard a perfectly good inquest.

BROWNRIGG (*with some excitement*). Maybe I'll have something to show you about that too. Mr Kenmis, I think you ought to know that this morning I applied for and got a search warrant. Some of my men ought to be back any minute now with whatever they've found. And if it's what I expect . . .

KENMIS. A search warrant? Against whom?

BROWNRIGG. This man Kirwan. I have good reason to believe that he has a bundle of letters in his house that may throw a lot of light on that inquest.

KENMIS. In what way?

BROWNRIGG. I believe they'll show not only a motive, but also the

338

fact that this Dr Teresa Kenny, who held a bogus post mortem the day after the death, was Kirwan's mistress.

KENMIS. His mistress! Look here, Brownrigg, isn't your thirst for the dramatic running away with you?

BROWNRIGG. That remains to be seen. (*There is a knock on the door.*) Come in.

(SERGEANT FELL *looks in.*)

FELL. A Mr and Mrs Brew to see you Super. They say they have an appointment.

BROWNRIGG. Send them in, Sergeant. (FELL *disappears.*) Here they are, Mr Kenmis. I hope you've got a few minutes to spare. Maybe there's nothing in it, but there's quite a scandal brewing up in Howth, and there'll be trouble if it isn't ventilated.

KENMIS. There'll be worse trouble if you arrest a man for murder, and then get laughed out of court.

BROWNRIGG. I'll have to take my chance at that. The parish priest is on the warpath.

KENMIS (*reluctantly impressed*). Oh God – not the parish priest! Why can't people leave my office in peace? We have enough on our hands, as it is, without a lot of damn nonsense too. However, I suppose I'll have to wait.

(FELL *enters with* BRENDAN *and* MOIRA BREW – *a young married couple with pleasant suburban accents. He has a club tie and wears sports clothes.*)

FELL. This way please.

(FELL *goes.*)

BROWNRIGG (*crossing to greet them*). Come in, Mr and Mrs Brew, and let me introduce myself. I'm Superintendent Brownrigg.

MRS BREW. How do you do.

BREW. Delighted to meet you, Super.

BROWNRIGG. And this is the State Solicitor, Mr Kenmis.

MRS BREW. How do you do.

BREW. Well, I must say you have us both shaking with terror – wondering which of our many offences we've been caught out in. (*He laughs heartily.*)

BROWNRIGG. None whatever, Mr Brew. We just thought you might be able to help us in a little matter. Won't you sit down?

BREW (*doing so*). Well now, that's a great relief. Moira thought it must be my tail light, but I said no. It's probably for reading the English Sunday papers. (*He laughs.*)

MRS BREW. Now Brendan, behave yourself.

BROWNRIGG (*smiling*). Nothing so serious as that, I assure you. Cigarette?

BREW (*taking one*). Thanks muchly.

BROWNRIGG. It's really very good of you both to come, and I'll promise not to keep you long. You're a golfer, I see.

BREW. Well, I used to play a pretty fair game at the Grange, though maybe I shouldn't say so, myself. But once the winter comes round and the old bones start to creak – well one has to cut down a bit. Indeed the last time I had the old clubs out was that day we went to Ireland's Eye, wasn't it Moira?

BROWNRIGG. As a matter of fact that's just what I wanted to talk to you about.

MRS BREW. There now, Brendan, didn't I tell you? It'll be something about that poor woman, I said.

BREW. That's exactly what she said! A woman's intuition. (*He laughs.*) Yes, Superintendent, that's the last time I had the clubs out. I remember I got in a bit of practice on the beach while the women gossiped. Not much of a one for picnics, you know. (*He laughs.*)

MRS BREW. It was the last day of Declan's holidays so . . .

BROWNRIGG. Declan is your little boy?

MRS BREW. Yes. Nine years old and at school with the nuns in Rathgar.

BREW. Little devil. (*He laughs.*) He's a one.

MRS BREW. So my husband gave up his round to take us on our little excursion.

BREW. Well – got to think of the nipper, you know. Only young once.

BROWNRIGG. Quite so. But this is hardly what we wanted to bother you about. Might I ask if you'd ever met this Mr and Mrs Kirwan before?

BREW. Never seen them before or since. Not, of course, that we could have seen her. (*He laughs and then coughs embarrassedly as* MRS BREW *reproves him.*) Yes – terrible tragedy, wasn't it?

MRS BREW. And to think that we were out there with them just before it happened.

BROWNRIGG. Did they appear to be on good terms?

BREW. Oh perfectly. We all had our sandwiches together. A nice fresh day, with a bit of a breeze.

MRS BREW. Ah now, Brendan, I don't think that's quite what the superintendent means. They didn't talk much – now did they? Not to each other anyway. He just went on with his painting, while she chatted with me, and Brendan got in his golf strokes.

BREW. Maybe they weren't speaking. You never can tell with these artist fellows. Never very chatty in my experience. I often try various topics, but there's no blotting it out. They never have anything to talk about. Just close up whenever I start. I daresay it's what they call the artistic temperament. (*He laughs.*)

MRS BREW (*rather primly*). The only time I remember him raising his voice was with Declan once.

BREW. Ah well now, you can hardly blame him for that. The kid was playing with his brushes, and getting in his way. You can hardly blame him for that.

MRS BREW. All the same I thought he was a bit sharp. I'd have cared more for her.

BREW. Ah well, that's the woman's point of view. (*He laughs.*)

BROWNRIGG. Tell me this. When you left in the boat soon after two, do you remember whether Mrs Kirwan wanted to come back too?

MRS BREW. No, I don't remember that. I just remember her getting her bathing things ready.

BROWNRIGG. Some people seem to think that she wanted to go back to Howth along with you, but that Mr Kirwan persuaded her to stay?

BREW. Well the fact of the matter is . . .

(*There is a knock, and the door opens, admitting* FELL.)

BROWNRIGG. What is it, Sergeant?

FELL. Sorry for interrupting, sir, but there's somebody here wants to see Mr Kenmis.

(KENMIS, *who has been showing growing impatience with the* BREWS, *rises.*)

KENMIS. Who is it?

FELL. Dr Teresa Kenny, sir, from Baldoyle. She's outside, and says it's urgent.

KENMIS (*to* BROWNRIGG). Is this . . . ?

BROWNRIGG (*nodding*). Yes. The post mortem.

KENMIS. Then I wonder whether we need bother Mr and Mrs Brew any longer, Brownrigg? I'm sure they've been a great help.

BROWNRIGG. Yes. Maybe that's all we have to ask them. It was very good of you both to come along. All right, Sergeant – in a moment.

(FELL *nods and goes out, closing the door.*)

BREW. Always ready to oblige. But what's it all about?

MRS BREW. We wouldn't like to find ourselves mixed up in anything nasty, you know.

BROWNRIGG (*encouraging them towards the door*). Don't worry about that, Mrs Brew. It may not be a matter of any importance at all. But we're very grateful for your help. Goodbye. No – the other door, please.

BREW. I was just going to say that Moira was packing up the basket at the time, and I was looking for the golf bag and that young rascal of a Declan. So if the boatmen say that she wanted to come back . . .

KENMIS (*impatiently*). We quite understand that there's very little more that you can say. Goodbye.

BROWNRIGG. Thank you very much.

BREW. Oh not at all, not at all. Always glad to keep on the right side of the Guards, you know. (*He laughs.*) You never can tell when . . . ha, ha, ha . . .

MRS BREW. I hope it's nothing serious, because I'd hate to find myself mixed up in anything . . .

BROWNRIGG. Goodbye.

BREW (*going*). Oh, that's all right, Moira. Didn't you hear the super say . . .

MRS BREW (*going*). It'd be a terrible thing to find ourselves called on to come out in public and have to . . .

(*They ad lib off, and a side door closes upon their voices.*)

BROWNRIGG. I suppose Dr Kenny's heard about the exhumation.

KENMIS. And wants to kick up a row about it. I know. I'm not surprised. Well, aren't you going to get her in?

(BROWNRIGG *opens the other door.*)

BROWNRIGG. Come in, please.

(TERESA KENNY *enters – an attractive woman in the late twenties, dressed with sensible good taste. They all look at each other.*)

KENMIS. Won't you take a chair, Doctor?

TERESA. They told me I must see the State Solicitor. Are you Mr Kenmis?

KENMIS. I am. And this is Chief Superintendent Brownrigg.

TERESA (*swiftly dismissing the preliminaries*). How do you do. I hear that a woman on whom I performed a post mortem has been exhumed in Glasnevin on your order.

KENMIS (*coolly*). Not exactly on my order, Doctor. I can't order such things. At my request, perhaps. The court does the ordering.

342

TERESA. Mr Kenmis, is there something wrong? Because if so I want to know about it.

KENMIS. That's just our position, too. In a nutshell.

TERESA. Mr Kenmis . . .

BROWNRIGG. Let me speak to her. Doctor, we're not entirely satisfied with the findings at that inquest. You certified a case of drowning, without any reference to certain signs of violence that were apparent on the body.

TERESA. There were no signs of violence on the body.

BROWNRIGG. I'm afraid our information is rather different. The head was injured in several places, and there was a deep wound in one of the ears. We find it hard to believe that you didn't see this when you made your examination.

TERESA. I did see some scars on the head. But they weren't caused by violence – I'm sure of that. At least not what you mean by violence.

BROWNRIGG. Then what kind of violence do you mean?

TERESA. I don't know for sure. It's all very horrible, but . . . (*She pauses.*)

BROWNRIGG. But what?

TERESA. Those rocks are infested with small green crabs. It's revolting what they can do in the course of a few hours to something that was once a human being.

KENMIS. So that's your answer – crabs.

BROWNRIGG. I'm afraid that's nonsense, Doctor, because – crabs or not – they didn't have a few hours. Only the time it took for the motor-boat to go out from the harbour to the island, and for the men to find the body. What is more, at six o'clock, when she died, the rock on which she was found was already high and dry. So it's strange that you should have come to the conclusion that she was drowned at all.

TERESA. Six? She must have died long before six.

BROWNRIGG. No. She was heard to cry out about six by the boatmen on the harbour wall.

TERESA. But that's absurd! At that distance they could never have heard anybody crying out from the Long Hole. It's on the other side of the island.

(KENMIS *rises and studies the map on the wall.*)

BROWNRIGG (*calmly*). Then she can't have been in the Long Hole when she cried out.

TERESA. But she was found there.

BROWNRIGG. Exactly. It's all very strange, isn't it?

(*Significant pause.*)

KENMIS. Dr Kenny, did you know the Kirwans personally?

TERESA (*after a considerable pause*). I used to know Mr Kirwan. But I'd never met his wife.

BROWNRIGG. Do you think, in the circumstances, it was a good idea for you to have taken part in this inquest?

TERESA. Why not? I don't understand.

BROWNRIGG. Don't you? Are you quite sure?

TERESA. For one thing I didn't realize I'd ever met either of them, until I'd nearly finished the post mortem.

BROWNRIGG. Whatever way you did find out, isn't it a little odd that you didn't retire from the proceedings as soon as you discovered who the deceased was?

TERESA (*confused*). I don't see why. How could I? It would have suggested that there was some reason . . . some objection to my being there.

BROWNRIGG. And was there none?

TERESA (*after another pause*). I don't know what you mean.

(*In response to their continued silence she then goes on a little hysterically.*)

TERESA. If you've got anything to say, why keep on beating about the bush? Why can't you say what you've got in your minds? I hate hinting and suggestions!

(*The door crashes open and* KIRWAN *enters, pursued by the* SERGEANT. *He is an aggressive, rather eccentric-looking man in his thirties.*)

KIRWAN. Tessa, what are you doing here?

TERESA. Bill!

FELL (*struggling with him*). Come out of that. You can't go in there.

KIRWAN. Take your hands off me.

BROWNRIGG. Wait a minute, Fell. Who is this man?

KIRWAN. My name is Kirwan.

KENMIS. Ah, Mr Kirwan. A very opportune arrival. Maybe this will shorten things considerably.

BROWNRIGG. Let him in, Sergeant.

FELL. Very good sir. The detective sergeant is back sir, from that job you sent him on.

BROWNRIGG. Fine. (*Then to* KENMIS.) Shall I go and see what's he's got?

KENMIS. Do.

(FELL *and* BROWNRIGG *go out.*)

KIRWAN. What is the meaning of this, sir? Some of your police have been to my house. They forced their way in, opened my desk and took away some of my private papers.

KENMIS. Yes, Mr Kirwan. They were acting under a search warrant. Quite within the law.

KIRWAN. Oh, they were, were they. Then let me tell you sir, that this is robbery and I'm going to sue you for this. You're a blackguard, sir, and if I don't get them back this instant, I'm going straight to my solicitor.

KENMIS. I think, Mr Kirwan, you may have to see your solicitor anyhow.

TERESA. Bill, be careful what you say. I'm afraid there's going to be a terrible mistake.

KIRWAN. Yes, they're making a hell of a mistake in interfering with my private affairs. A hell of a mistake. And if I don't . . .

(BROWNRIGG *enters with a package of letters in his hand.*)

BROWNRIGG. There you are, Mr Kenmis. They seem to be exactly what was alleged.

(*He gives them to* KENMIS. KIRWAN *tries to seize them.*)

KIRWAN. Those are my letters! Give them back at once.

BROWNRIGG. Stand back, Kirwan. Don't try any of your violence here. We want to talk to you. But first let me warn you that you don't have to answer, but that anything you do say may be used in evidence. Is that understood?

KIRWAN (*surprised*). Are you trying to imply that I'm under arrest?

BROWNRIGG. That depends to some extent upon yourself. Are you prepared to answer a few questions?

KIRWAN. I am not. You have no right to ask me any questions.

TERESA. Oh Bill, be careful! Don't talk like that!

KIRWAN. I'll answer no questions, and don't you answer any either. That's the way they try to get you – these fellows. They ask you questions and then try to twist your answers against you. They're a lot of crooks and robbers. But there's still a law in this country. If you answer no questions they can do nothing.

BROWNRIGG (*calmly*). Well, Mr Kenmis? Do you agree now to the next step?

KENMIS (*going through the letters*). Yes, Superintendent. I've taken a look through these letters and I agree.

BROWNRIGG. William Burke Kirwan, I arrest you on the charge that

345

on the ninth day of September last at Ireland's Eye in the County of Dublin with malice aforethought you did feloniously kill and slay your wife, Sarah Mary Kirwan.

TERESA (*horror-struck*). Oh!

Scene 4

It is eight weeks later, in the afternoon. BROWNRIGG *is concluding a conversation with* MRS CROWE, *a distinguished old lady in the seventies, of formidable spirit, although somewhat vague in her manner.*

MRS CROWE. Inspector, I am still not at all clear why I have been sent this little piece of paper.

BROWNRIGG (*patiently*). We want you to give evidence, ma'am, about your daughter's state of health.

MRS CROWE. Evidence?

BROWNIGG. You remember my coming to discuss it with you. You told me that your daughter, Mrs Kirwan, never . . .

MRS CROWE. Evidence? Is this some sort of a lawsuit?

BROWNRIGG. Yes ma'am. I'm afraid it's a murder charge. I hope that doesn't upset you.

MRS CROWE. Upset me? Why should it? The country's full of murderers. Has been for years. Who's been murdered now?

BROWNRIGG. Your daughter, ma'am, I'm afraid. Didn't you know that she was dead?

MRS CROWE. Of course I know she's dead. Somebody has been interfering with the little railing that I put around her plot in Glasnevin. But I didn't hear that she was murdered.

(KENMIS *enters with* JOHN PENEFEATHER, *barrister-at-law – a fussy little man with a black brief-bag out of which he soon takes piles of papers.*)

KENMIS. Are we too early?

BROWNRIGG. Not at all, Mr Kenmis. I've just been checking over Mrs Crowe's statement.

PENEFEATHER. Smyly will be here in a moment. He couldn't get away from the Supreme Court.

MRS CROWE. Who are these men?

BROWNRIGG. This is Mr Kenmis, the State Solicitor. And Mr Penefeather, our junior counsel in the case.

MRS CROWE. How do you do. I am Mrs Crowe from Kingstown.

KENMIS. From where?

MRS CROWE (*firmly*). From Kingstown.

BROWNRIGG. The mother of the deceased woman.

KENMIS (*sitting down*). Evidently a breath from the past.

PENEFEATHER. Ah yes. A very important witness.

MRS CROWE. The inspector tells me that my daughter has been murdered.

PENEFEATHER. You seem surprised, madam.

MRS CROWE. Not at all. Why should I be, these days? Who did it?

PENEFEATHER. We say it was her husband. But surely you . . .

MRS CROWE. Her husband. Really? I never liked that man. Have you met him?

BROWNRIGG (*with a smile at the others*). Yes, ma'am; we certainly have met him.

MRS CROWE. Not at all a man for poor May.

KENMIS. Apparently not.

MRS CROWE. How did he do it? Poison?

PENEFEATHER (*agitated*). No, no! We allege that he stabbed her. He alleges that she had a fit while she was out swimming.

MRS CROWE. A fit indeed!

PENEFEATHER. . . . and was drowned as a result. Why hasn't all this been made clear to you?

MRS CROWE. Just like him to say a thing like that.

BROWNRIGG. That's all that you're likely to be asked, Mrs Crowe – to say whether your daughter would be likely to have a fit. We won't bother you with anything else.

MRS CROWE. Absolute rubbish. May couldn't possibly have had a fit.

PENEFEATHER. Ah, good! You'll be ready to swear to that?

MRS CROWE. Certainly, I shall swear to it. Is that all you want me for?

BROWNRIGG. Yes, Mrs Crowe. And now I'm afraid I must ask you to leave. We're having a consultation with counsel.

MRS CROWE (*rising*). And this is where I have to come on Thursday?

BROWNRIGG (*helplessly*). No, ma'am. Not here. Green Street Courthouse. At half past ten.

(*Voices are heard off.*)

PENEFEATHER. Ah, here's Smyly now.

MRS CROWE. Green Street. Can I get there direct from Kingstown?

KENMIS (*shouting irritably*). Madam, there is no such place as Kingstown. It is now called Dun Laoghaire.

(JOHN SMYLY *enters. He is a big bluff senior counsel of great assurance.*)

SMYLY. Who's annoying the State Solicitor?

MRS CROWE. That's what they keep telling me on the trams. No such place as Kingstown. However I just get off, and wait for the next.

SMYLY. It must take you rather a long time to get home?

MRS CROWE. Yes, but it's so cheap. I never seem to have to pay any fares. Well, goodbye till Thursday. (*To herself.*) Do I know that man?

BROWNRIGG. Goodbye!

(MRS CROWE *trots off.*)

SMYLY. Charming. And who might that be, pray?

KENMIS. One of your star witnesses, Smyly.

SMYLY. A touch of lavender in Green Street. Just what we need.

KENMIS. You'll find that one is more like a gooseberry bush. We're sorry for dragging you all the way over here from the Supreme Court, but it seemed the most convenient place to meet.

SMYLY. Don't apologize, my dear fellow. It's always a pleasure to be taken away from the lucubrations of my brethren of the bar. Particularly in the Supreme Court.

(*He settles down in the principal chair, and opens his brief.*)

PENEFEATHER. This is a highly important case, Smyly. I've been through all the . . .

SMYLY. All cases are highly important, Penefeather. Just sit down over there and keep quiet.

PENEFEATHER. To shorten things for you I've made this summary of some of the salient points in the brief . . .

SMYLY. My dear fellow, I am quite capable of reading the brief myself, and ascertaining which are the salient points. Now just let me see. All the usual, I suppose. Letters, statements, photostats. Easy to see that somebody is being paid by the folio, eh?

KENMIS. It's easy to be flippant, Smyly. But how are we to know beforehand what eminent senior counsel are going to ask for in a case like this?

SMYLY. I tell you what I *would* like. A model of the motor-boat. I sometimes get pressed by my younger son to find him a . . .

348

KENMIS (*wearily*). Why not go straight to the pathologist's statement?

SMYLY. What? Do you mean this thing? Um. What's the name of this fellow, anyway? I can't make head or tail of it.

KENMIS. He's only an assistant, but they say he's pretty good.

SMYLY. Good! He's miraculous. I see that he pronounces that the woman was killed by a stab through the ear. How in hell does he know that?

BROWNRIGG. Isn't that his business?

SMYLY. His business is to ascertain the cause of death. The fact that she had a wound in the ear from which she died doesn't necessarily mean that somebody killed her. The defence will have a good laugh at this. Who's on the other side, by the way?

KENMIS. Butt is leading young Curran, I believe.

SMYLY. Butt. That's not too good. No sluicing out of that old hogshead. And the judge – Crampton. You know, Kenmis, there's going to be an acquittal in this case.

(BROWNRIGG *and* PENEFEATHER *react adversely.*)

BROWNRIGG. What?

PENEFEATHER. Really Smyly – with all these exhibits.

SMYLY. I don't care if there's half a hundred exhibits. Kenmis knows what I mean.

KENMIS. Yes. I know what he means.

BROWNRIGG. I don't understand. Surely it must be obvious that . . .

SMYLY. It's not a question of the obvious, my dear Superintendent. It is a question of the evidence. This isn't a piece of literary research. It's a murder trial, where the question is not what we think, but what we can prove by evidence. And what *is* the admissible evidence? A woman dies on Ireland's Eye. We say it was at six o'clock when somebody heard a scream. The other side say that it was earlier when the tide was in. And nobody knows for sure. We think she was stabbed in the ear with a spike that we haven't got. The other side says she drowned after throwing a fit, and that the injury to her ear was caused by crabs. And all we have to contradict them is this pompous young official who examined the body after it had been buried for a month, and who produces a report that will be laughed out of court. This is the case on which I am going to have to ask a jury to hang a man.

BROWNRIGG. Then you don't believe that he did it?

SMYLY. Murder his wife? Of course I believe he did it. I have a wife of my own.

KENMIS. Ah, cut out the jokes for heaven's sake!

SMYLY. Why should I? I'm not presuming to blame the wretched fellow. He may have ample excuse for killing half a dozen wives for all I know. All I do say is this: if we're going to ask the jury for a conviction, we're going to have to give them a motive in return – a reasonable motive.

BROWNRIGG. A motive! And the fellow living in adultery with another woman – a woman who has faked up an inquest for him?

SMYLY. What evidence is there that the inquest was faked? If Kenny says that the woman was drowned, and that the rest of the damage was done by crabs, do you suppose they'll be so anxious to hang the man, that they'll listen to O'Thingummy in preference to her? (*With a change of tone.*) Is she good-looking?

KENMIS. Very.

SMYLY. There you are.

BROWNRIGG. But when they know the relationship...

SMYLY. The jury won't hear about the relationship.

BROWNRIGG. Of course they will. Mrs Campbell swears in her deposition that the wife had only just found out that Kenny had been pregnant by her husband.

SMYLY. Exactly. A bad character produces evidence about another bad character. Who's going to listen to that? My dear fellow, that sort of evidence won't be admitted. It's just spite and speculation.

BROWNRIGG. But isn't it all confirmed by what's in the letters – the letters we got from his house?

SMYLY. Stale dirt, my dear chap. What's the good of that? The man was involved in procuring an illegal operation on Kenny almost two years ago. O.K. That's one charge. But what's it got to do with his murdering his wife last September? I tell you, Brownrigg, those letters will be ruled out.

BROWNRIGG. But don't they show the circumstances? Surely that makes them relevant?

SMYLY. They show some circumstances a couple of years ago. And you know the line that old Crampton will take with that. Oh, I'll do my best to get them in, of course. But if Crampton can keep anything from the jury, he'll keep it. He assumes that all juries are composed of idiots. And he's usually right, of course, but that's no good to us. Now, if we could show that Kenny and Kirwan were still billing and cooing it might be a different matter. Then we'd have reason for getting this sort of stuff in as part of the present case. How about that?

BROWNRIGG. No. We've made inquiries, but I'm afraid there's nothing to show that anything is still going on between them.

KENMIS. We can't even show that she knew whose inquest it was when she went to Howth.

BROWNRIGG. Of course she knew.

KENMIS. I daresay she did. But we can't prove a state of mind.

SMYLY. There you are. Just what I say. Campbell's no good to us. As a matter of fact you ought to be prosecuting her, too.

BROWNRIGG. Most of the information we get comes from people whom we ought to be prosecuting. But that doesn't mean that it's no use.

SMYLY. Oh it'd be useful all right, if we ever got it to the jury. There's nothing they like better than a nice bit of dirt. But believe me, they'll never hear a word of it, if I know Crampton.

BROWNRIGG. Well, it's a damned scandal! If a man like this can get off on a mere point of evidence – is that justice?

SMYLY. No, my dear fellow. It's law – not justice. There's a subtle distinction. Justice is something that is properly reserved for the Deity. We're not so presumptuous as to aspire to that. All we can do is to play a game called law, according to certain rules, and hope for the best. If it means that a good many rascals get off from time to time, that's the penalty we have to pay for making sure that the opposite doesn't happen and that a lot of people don't go to jail for things they haven't done.

PENEFEATHER. Ttt-ttt-ttt.

SMYLY. And Penefeather, will you kindly refrain from making those irritating noises.

BROWNRIGG. I see what you mean. But if it's a game, aren't there any rules that might help our side? If it's fair to take advantage of the rules one way, surely it's equally fair on the other?

SMYLY. Oh, yes. We needn't give up hope, just because we're a couple of suits short in the deal.

KENMIS. Suppose they attack Mrs Campbell's character in cross-examination?

SMYLY. Oh, of course; then we'll have them on toast.

PENEFEATHER. On what?

SMYLY. There's a well-established rule of law, Penefeather, that I'm surprised you don't know about. The previous bad character of any accused person is irrelevant in any trial . . .

PENEFEATHER. I am perfectly well acquainted with that rule.

SMYLY (*louder*). Nevertheless I will continue. If the defence chooses to attack the character of any of the prosecution's witnesses . . .

PENEFEATHER. I tell you I know this.

SMYLY (*shouting him down*). Then evidence of the accused's bad character may also be admitted. So you see, if they attack our disreputable witness, Mrs Campbell, we may then say what we like about Kirwan. But there isn't a chance of that. They'll leave Campbell alone.

KENMIS. It'll be rather tempting. After all, if she hadn't pinched that ring, the case against Kirwan would never have arisen at all.

SMYLY. Oh, I'll try and goad Butt into it, of course, by cracking her up. But for all his damned long-windedness, Butt's a good lawyer and he'll be too smart to fall for that. It'll be an amusing bit of strategy all round. But if you can't give me any better ammunition than this, I say there'll be an acquittal.

PENEFEATHER. There's just one other thing. About this knife . . .

SMYLY. Which reminds me that it's dinner time. Let's all go home to some knives and forks of our own. Time enough to bother about Nangle's knife on Thursday.

(*They all rise.*)

CURTAIN

ACT TWO

Thursday, three days later. The Central Criminal Court, Green Street, Dublin. SERGEANT SHERWOOD *is in the witness's chair, undergoing examination by* PENEFEATHER. *The audience is in the direction that would be occupied by the jury.*

SHERWOOD (*sententiously*). On the date aforesaid the tide was full at one five p.m. with approximately eight foot of water over the rock on which the body was subsequently found.

CRAMPTON (*the judge*). Not too fast, Sergeant, please. I must get these figures down.

SHERWOOD. Beg pardon, melud.

PENEFEATHER. According to your observations, Sergeant, what depth of water would you say was over this rock at about four thirty?

SHERWOOD (*referring to his notes*). At four thirty? Approximately three foot six inches, sir.

PENEFEATHER. And at six?

SHERWOOD. Oh, at six o'clock it would be well dry.

CRAMPTON (*writing*). Six o'clock – dry. Mr Penefeather, do you attach much significance to these varying depths of water?

PENEFEATHER. Yes, melud. If I may advert for a moment to . . .

BUTT, S.C. (*without rising*). All these measurements are admitted.

PENEFEATHER. But melud . . .

CRAMPTON. One moment, Mr Penefeather, please. If the measurements are admitted and no further significance is to be attached . . .

SMYLY (*rising*). None whatever, melud, apart from the agreed fact that when the body was found at about half past seven, the water was at least two feet below the top of the rock.

PENEFEATHER. On the other hand . . .

CRAMPTON. Mr Penefeather, I think that disposes of this part of the sergeant's evidence. We have no need to lengthen the case unduly.

SMYLY. Your Lordship is very considerate. And so also is my learned friend, Mr Butt.

(*He sits down.*)

BUTT (*not interested*). Thank you, my dear fellow.

CRAMPTON. Now, Sergeant, briefly, is there anything else that you wish to put in?

SHERWOOD. I produce a towel alleged to have covered the head of the deceased while being brought ashore . . . a set of fingerprints taken from the accused . . . and a bundle of six letters found in a drawer in the accused's house, No 11 Merrion Street Upper on Monday the eleventh of October last under a search warrant.

CRAMPTON. See that they're all marked, Mr Walker.

(*The* REGISTRAR *takes all these exhibits and proceeds to mark them for identification.*)

BUTT (*rising*). Melud.

CRAMPTON. Yes, Mr Butt?

BUTT. Melud, this packet of letters is quite irrelevant to the present charge. I must respectfully object to its admission.

PENEFEATHER (*who is still on his feet*). If I might be allowed to say a word . . .

SMYLY (*rising*). I think the relevance of these letters will become much clearer after I have called the landlady, Mrs Campbell.

BUTT. It will become nothing of the sort. My friend knows perfectly well that I object to a large part of Mrs Campbell's deposition.

CRAMPTON (*confused*). Gentleman, what is all this about?

BUTT. Melud, before the matter is discussed at all I would suggest that the members of the jury and all witnesses on both sides be required to leave the court.

CRAMPTON (*delighted*). That's usually a good idea. Do you agree, Mr Smyly?

SMYLY. I am in Your Lordship's hands. Personally I don't care in the slightest whether they're here or not.

CRAMPTON. In that case, the jury and the witnesses will kindly withdraw.

(*There is an outburst of annoyed whispering, as the* TIPSTAFF *urges these witnesses out. The* REGISTRAR *responds with a vigorous, Sssh! and then waves the audience on its way. The* TIPSTAFF *also ascertains that all have gone.*)

CRAMPTON. The tipstaff will see that you are all comfortably accommodated.

REGISTRAR. Silence. Silence there.

CRAMPTON. Now, Mr Butt, while these ladies and gentlemen are retiring, what were you about to say?

BUTT (*as* PENEFEATHER *indignantly sits down*). What I wanted to make clear to Your Lordship was the fact that on the remand I strenuously objected to a certain part of this Mrs Campbell's evidence. The section marked 'X', melud, which you will see is before you.

SMYLY (*very offhand*). The district justice let it in, subject to Your Lordship's ruling.

BUTT. The district justice should never have let it in. The whole thing should have been struck out.

CRAMPTON. One moment, Mr Butt, while I finish my reading. (*Pause.*) Well, now that I have finished, I think I see the basis of your objection to its being brought to the notice of the jury.

SMYLY (*rising*). I am surprised that my learned friend imagines that I had intended to do anything improper without Your Lordship's permission.

BUTT. I never suggested that.

CRAMPTON. Indeed, I am sure that Mr Smyly wouldn't dream of doing anything improper even with my permission.

(*Laughter in court, in which* LEARNED COUNSEL *join without much enthusiasm.*)

CRAMPTON. I think we had better leave this troublesome matter over until this lady is called as a witness. I presume that you intend to call her, Mr Smyly?

SMYLY. Of course, melud. And I think Your Lordship's solution is an excellent one. I wish I had thought of it myself.

BUTT (*sitting down*). I agree. Forgive my interruption.

SMYLY (*following suit*). I don't mind being interrupted in the slightest

CRAMPTON. As a matter of fact, it is Mr Penefeather who has been interrupted. Well, now that all this is agreed, bring back the jury, Mr Walker.

REGISTRAR. Fetch the jury.

(*The* TIPSTAFF *comes downstage and beckons the audience to come back. Nobody does the same for the witnesses.*)

CRAMPTON. Now where were we? Have you finished your examination of the sergeant, Mr Penefeather?

PENEFEATHER (*annoyed*). Melud, I do not intend to say anything more.

CRAMPTON. Good. And you, Mr Butt? Do you wish to cross-examine the sergeant?

BUTT (*not rising*). No, melud. No further questions.

CRAMPTON. Thank you, Sergeant. Now, who is your next witness, Mr Smyly?

(*The* SERGEANT *leaves the chair, and his place is taken by* GEORGE HATCHELL *a precise-looking young civil servant with glasses and a hard collar. In his lapel is a fainne.*)

SMYLY. Shershee er . . . The State Pathologist, melud.

REGISTRAR. Seoirse O'Tabhairmach.

CRAMPTON. Ah, so this is your expert witness. (*To the audience.*) This should be interesting, gentlemen. I hope we're all paying proper attention.

REGISTRAR (*gabbling*). Raise the book in your right hand, please. I swear by Almighty God.

HATCHELL. I swear by Almighty God.

REGISTRAR. That the evidence I shall give to the court and jury in this case.

HATCHELL. That the evidence I shall give to the court and jury in this case.

REGISTRAR. Shall be the truth the whole truth and nothing but the truth.

HATCHELL. Shall be the truth the whole truth and nothing but the truth.

RIGISTRAR. What's your name?

HATCHELL. Seoirse O'Tabhairmach.

CRAMPTON. What was that?

REGISTRAR. George Hatchell, melud.

CRAMPTON. Ah yes, of course.

SMYLY. You are the State Pathologist.

HATCHELL. I am an assistant state pathologist. M.B., B.Ch., N.U.I.

SMYLY. Exactly. And I believe that in this capacity you examined the body of Mrs Sarah Mary Kirwan?

HATCHELL. After the exhumation, yes.

CRAMPTON (*making notes*). What date was this?

HATCHELL. I began my post mortem on the eighth of October, My Lord.

SMYLY. And are you able to tell us anything about the cause of death?

HATCHELL (*producing some elaborate notes*). In spite of the advanced stage of necrosis I was able to form a clear opinion on that point – an opinion which I am afraid is at variance with the findings at the inquest. If I may refer to this written report which I made at the time . . .

CRAMPTON. What report is this?

HATCHELL. I have a copy My Lord, and one for the jury as well.
(*He hands them around. A copy is eagerly seized on by*
BUTT.)

CRAMPTON (*offended*). Mr Smyly, how can this piece of paper be
regarded as evidence here?

SMYLY (*embarrassed*). I think, melud, that this witness is merely
producing it as a note or memorandum made at the time. He
will, of course, give his evidence in full.

BUTT (*rising*). Melud – forgive my further interruption . . .

SMYLY (*sitting down*). It's always a pleasure. Any time you like.

BUTT. Melud, I take very great exception to this document.

CRAMPTON. Indeed, I am not surprised.

BUTT. Not only on the grounds of its admissibility, melud, but also
because it shows that this alleged expert has grossly exceeded
his duties as a State expert. (*A general stir in the court.*) It is
not this gentleman's business to determine the issues arising in
this case. That is the duty of the court. Yet I notice that in this
document he has taken it upon himself to state, not only the
cause of death, but also that the woman was 'killed by a stab' –
as he puts it.

SMYLY (*good humouredly, knowing that he is in the wrong*). Melud,
whatever my learned friend is choosing to object to, I must
object to his language. He has referred to the Assistant State
Pathologist as an 'alleged expert', and I must really ask him to
withdraw that expression.

BUTT. Please sit down, Mr Smyly.

SMYLY. I will do nothing of the sort. My witness is entitled to the
protection of the court.

BUTT. On the contrary, your witness is in contempt.

SMYLY (*enjoying his red herring*). Really, I cannot allow this to
pass.

CRAMPTON. Now gentlemen, gentlemen, this has been a most
amicable trial up to the present. I hope it will remain so.

SMYLY. I assure Your Lordship, nobody has enjoyed it more than I
have. But my friend goes too far.

CRAMPTON. Now, Mr Smyly, I am sure it's not the witness himself
whom Mr Butt is attacking, but only his memorandum. And
you must admit that there is something to be said for his
objection.

SMYLY. If these notes are in any way at fault, my witness ought to
have a chance to explain himself further without being abused

like this. To call him an 'alleged expert' . . . !

CRAMPTON. Yes, yes, I'm sure that remark was intemperate and inadvisable. Both sides are at fault.

BUTT. Well, I shall take back my remark, if you take back your expert.

SMYLY. I tell you what I'll do – if only for the sake of peace. You withdraw what you said, and I'll agree to strike out the word 'killed' from my witness's memorandum.

CRAMPTON. There now, Mr Butt. That seems to be a very reasonable solution.

BUTT. Melud, there is no one better able than Mr Smyly to get out of a difficulty of his own making, and then make the act seem like a kindness to the other side. I don't care what he strikes out of an inadmissible document. I still have the right to cross-examine this man.

SMYLY. My dear Mr Butt, you may not only cross-examine him. You may cross-examine him at once. I merely reserve my right to re-examine. (*He sits down.*)

BUTT (*after a moment's surprise*). Well, sir. What have you got to say about all of this?

HATCHELL (*shaking with fury*). If my notes contain any mistake in legal terminology His Lordship will correct me. But so far as medical matters are concerned I go back on nothing that is in them.

BUTT. Even this word 'killed'.

HATCHELL (*doggedly*). Yes.

BUTT. Don't talk nonsense, man. How can it be a matter of medical observation that Mr Kirwan killed his wife?

HATCHELL. Let me see what I wrote, please. (*He looks at the paper.*) Ah, as I thought. Where do I say that Mr Kirwan killed her? I merely say that the woman was killed.

BUTT. In other words, what you're now saying is that there are clues by which you can state scientifically that Mrs Kirwan was actually killed by somebody.

HATCHELL. I would say so.

BUTT. Mention one.

HATCHELL. Well . . . there are various signs. None of which was ever brought out at the inquest.

BUTT. Never mind about the inquest. Just tell me one of these signs.

HATCHELL. Well . . . for example, the woman had a deep incised wound in one of the ears. No mention was ever made of that.

BUTT. Might not that have been made by a crab?

HATCHELL. It was not made by a crab.

BUTT. How do you know?

HATCHELL (*irritably*). I can tell. It's not an easy thing to explain these details to a layman.

BUTT. And that is all you have to say?

HATCHELL. On that point, yes.

BUTT. Unerring science has spoken. You claim that this clinches the matter?

HATCHELL. I claim the right to use my professional knowledge, and my eyes.

BUTT. And to deliver a final word on crab bites – a matter too complicated to explain to us simple laymen . . .

HATCHELL. It's not merely a matter of crab bites. The whole condition of the body is involved.

BUTT. . . . but in your own view good enough to hang a man.

HATCHELL. I object to that remark. I have no wish to hang anyone. When you imply that I can't tell . . .

BUTT (*sitting down*). Thank you, Mr Hatchell. That is all we wish to know.

HATCHELL. But I haven't finished.

BUTT. The jury will draw its own conclusions.

SMYLY. Let him finish, please.

HATCHELL. Am I not going to be allowed to say what I have to say, My Lord? A question has been put to me . . .

CRAMPTON. Eh? What question? I didn't catch what the question was.

SMYLY. If your Lordship will allow me, I'm sure that the witness can clear the whole matter up in re-examination.

CRAMPTON. I hope so, Mr Smyly. I am not at all clear about this.

SMYLY (*feeling his way*). Arising out of my friend's cross-examination, I take it that crab bites, severe enough to amount to what you describe as a deep incised wound, would take a considerable time to inflict?

HATCHELL. Certainly they would.

SMYLY. Three or four hours at least?

BUTT. Don't lead the witness, please.

SMYLY. All right. How long would even a battalion of crabs take to make a scar like the one you have described.

HATCHELL. At least four or five hours.

BUTT (*softly*). Congratulations.

SMYLY. So that if Mrs Kirwan was alive as late as six o'clock, there would have been no time for such injuries to have been inflicted.

HATCHELL. I am certain of that.

BUTT. There is no proof that she was alive at six o'clock.

SMYLY. On the contrary. Both boatmen have sworn that they heard her cry out just before they left for the island at six.

BUTT. That is not admitted.

SMYLY. Nor is it contradicted. Mr Butt, am I or are you addressing the court?

CRAMPTON. Yes, Mr Butt. You must allow Mr Smyly to examine his witness in peace.

BUTT. Your Lordship pleases.

SMYLY. Now, sir, I take it that a wound of this kind, if it was not inflicted by crabs, but by the insertion of some sharp instrument into the ear, could have caused death?

HATCHELL. In my opinion, it could. Without leaving any other scars.

SMYLY. In fact, you believe that it did?

BUTT (*loud and deliberate*). Mr Smyly, do not lead the witness.

CRAMPTON. Yes, Mr Smyly, we must be careful. This is all very important.

SMYLY. Nothing would be easier, melud, than to rephrase that question. Do you believe, sir, that such a stab did cause death?

HATCHELL. Yes.

SMYLY. Does that satisfy you, Mr Butt?

BUTT. Ask him why.

SMYLY. With pleasure. Why do you believe this?

HATCHELL. Because the woman did die, and the only alternative is that she was drowned.

SMYLY. Well?

HATCHELL. Well, how could she have been drowned in less than a foot of water in the Long Hole? If she was drowned it must have been on the beach, and Kirwan must then have carried her to the Long Hole in full view of the boat coming out.

BUTT. I object. What sort of scientific evidence is this?

CRAMPTON. Mr Hatchell, I am afraid I must rule out that answer. After all, you are here in the capacity of a medical man – not as a detective.

(*Laughter in court.*)

HATCHELL (*upset*). I'm sorry, My Lord. I'm only giving you my conclusions.

SMYLY. Come now, haven't you got any conclusions based upon your own examination? Your professional conclusions?

HATCHELL. What do you mean?

SMYLY (*helping him*). The general condition of the body, for example. You mentioned that. What did you mean by your reference to the condition of the body? Was there anything about that that would rule out death by drowning?

HATCHELL (*suddenly enlightened*). Why yes, of course. Asphyxia. There were no traces of asphyxia.

SMYLY. From which you conclude that she did not drown.

HATCHELL (*with relief*). And if she didn't drown it follows that she must have died from this wound in the ear, that I alone appear to have observed.

SMYLY. From which you not unreasonably assume that she must have been killed by someone.

HATCHELL. Exactly.

SMYLY. Thank you sir. That is all.

BUTT. Wait a minute. What does he mean by . . .

SMYLY. Pardon me, Mr Butt. Your cross-examination is over.

CRAMPTON. Yes, Mr Butt. Everybody has had quite enough latitude. Much too much, in my opinion.

BUTT (*sulky*). Your Lordship pleases.

SMYLY. Call Margaret Campbell.

REGISTRAR. Margaret Campbell. (*He rises and indicates the audience to the* JUDGE). Melud – the foreman. He wishes to say something.

CRAMPTON. Yes, yes. What is it? I can't hear a word.

REGISTRAR. He says, melud, that the jury are a little confused about all this.

CRAMPTON (*to the audience*). The jury are not alone in that condition, Mr Foreman. We can only trust that learned counsel will come to our assistance before long. Who did you say your next witness is, Mr Smyly?

SMYLY. Mrs Campbell, melud. The boarding-house keeper.

CRAMPTON. Ah, yes.

RIGISTRAR. Take off your glove, and raise the book in your right hand . . . no, your right hand. Now repeat after me. (*She is duly sworn.*) What's your name?

MRS CAMPBELL (*very hangdog*). Margaret Campbell.

SMYLY. Don't drop your voice. His Lordship and the jury will want to hear you. When did the accused and his wife come to stay with you last summer?

MRS CAMPBELL. Towards the end of June, sir.

SMYLY. Do you remember the morning of the sixth of September last, when they went for a picnic to Ireland's Eye?

MRS CAMPBELL. Yes, sir. I remember it well because it was the day after the row I heard between them the night before, when she discovered . . .

BUTT. Objection.

CRAMPTON. What's that, Mr Butt?

BUTT. Melúd, this is the woman who is causing the trouble already referred to. I take it that my friend will be careful not to ask her any question connected with the section of her deposition marked 'X' until Your Lordship has decided whether or not it is to be admitted?

CRAMPTON. Ah yes. I remember. The section marked 'X'.

BUTT. I'm quite prepared to argue this matter now, unless my learned friend would rather let us have the rest of her evidence before we touch on the disputed part?

SMYLY. I am entirely in His Lordship's hands.

REGISTRAR (*rising and pointing at the audience*). Melud – the foreman again.

CRAMPTON. Yes. What is it? Ttt-ttt – I still can't hear a word.

REGISTRAR. He says, melud, that the jury would like to see this section marked 'X'.

CRAMPTON. Not at all. Not at all. Not until I have decided whether you may have it. What's that? Can't you speak up?

REGISTRAR. He says that the jury are upset over the fact that everybody seems to have seen it, except them.

CRAMPTON. That will do, my man.

REGISTRAR (*towards the audience*). That will do, my man.

CRAMPTON. Kindly tell him to stop interrupting and to sit down. (*The* REGISTRAR *gestures sternly at the audience.*) Now, Mr Smyly, I think you had better finish with the undisputed part first of all. Once we have got rid of that we can go on and consider the other matter.

SMYLY. Very good, melud. Now, Mrs Campbell, tell me this. When the body was brought back that evening, did you notice any signs of violence upon it?

MRS CAMPBELL. I saw blood on the towel that was over the head. But neither me nor the women that laid it out had any chance to examine the body at all. No more than when it was up before that she-doctor from Baldoyle, who insisted on doing the certifying as soon as she heard who it was.

BUTT. Objection.

SMYLY. Now, Mrs Campbell, I must warn you only to answer exactly the questions that I put to you.

MRS CAMPBELL. I came here to tell the truth.

CRAMPTON. Yes, my good woman. But I am the judge of how much of what you may have to say is relevant in the present case. You will be punished very severely if you attempt to disregard my ruling.

MRS CAMPBELL (*sulkily*). The truth! Can I not tell that?

CRAMPTON. A very proper ambition, I'm sure. But only so far as it concerns us now. Please remember that.

MRS CAMPBELL (*pursing her lips*). Mmm.

SMYLY. Now, Mrs Campbell, it was thanks to your public-spirited action that information was first lodged with the police in this matter?

MRS CAMPBELL. That's right.

SMYLY. In fact, but for you, the fact that this inquest may have been in error, might never have come to the notice of the authorities at all?

MRS CAMPBELL. That's right. I want to see justice done.

CRAMPTON. Very commendable, Mrs Campbell. Very commendable. I am sure that is what we all want.

MRS CAMPBELL. Thank you, My Lord.

SMYLY. I am sure it is recognized by everybody that Mrs Campbell's action in the matter reflects the greatest credit on her. Eh? (*Pause.*) No response from my learned friend. Well, let us proceed. There was something, I suppose, that originally aroused your suspicions? Just answer yes or no.

MRS CAMPBELL. Yes. I overheard them quarrelling the night before he took her to the island.

SMYLY. That's enough. And now, melud, before asking this witness what it was that she overheard, I propose to apply for Your Lordship's permission to introduce the portion of her deposition marked 'X'. On the authority of Dowling versus Dowling ten Irish Common Law Reports at page 236 I am entitled to call evidence showing the circumstances and position of the parties involved in the alleged offence, which is precisely what the disputed portion amounts to. What is more, it is corroborated by the bundle of letters which I also tender to the court and jury for the same reason.

CRAMPTON (*enjoying himself*). I presume that you press your objection, Mr Butt?

BUTT. Most strenuously, melud. These stale disclosures of events almost two years old have no relevance whatever to the situation of the parties at the time of the offence.

SMYLY. They have great relevance to the inquest.

BUTT. None whatever. Our contention is that there was nothing wrong with the inquest, either in its conduct or in its findings.

SMYLY (*contemptuously*). Ha!

BUTT. In short, it is mere evidence of the accused's previous character.

CRAMPTON. Now, Mr Smyly, it may well be that certain evidence given at the inquest came from an unfortunate source. But this does not necessarily mean that the findings were incorrect. And I cannot see how we can decide that they were, without also deciding this case at the same time.

BUTT. The whole subject is a red herring, and has been introduced with the object of prejudicing the issue.

SMYLY. I wonder what my friend means by 'prejudicing the issue'? Is he suggesting that Mrs Campbell had some ulterior motive for doing what she did, or that her deposition is untrue?

BUTT. Far from it. I'm sure Mrs Campbell is a highly respectable lady. Nothing whatever is suggested against her.

CRAMPTON. Of course, Mr Butt. I can't see any reason why Mrs Campbell should have made a charge of this sort except from the highest of motives.

BUTT. My client has nothing against Mrs Campbell. All we say is that the portion marked 'X', whether true or false, has nothing to do with the present case. My learned friend is the only person who is trying to make improper use of it.

SMYLY (*disappointed*). Ah! Pity.

CRAMPTON. Of course, Mr Smyly, I can see your point. There is – ahem – one serious difficulty in the presentation of your case, so far.

SMYLY. I know what Your Lordship is referring to. Motive.

CRAMPTON. Precisely. And you feel that evidence of this kind might assist you in that connection. Well, let me tell you what I feel about it. If you are going to be able to show the court that this – er – unfortunate event is part of a pattern of conduct that culminated in the death of Mrs Kirwan, I am prepared to hear you on its admissibility. On the other hand, if it is merely an isolated incident taking place about two years ago, I cannot see its relevance . . . at the moment.

SMYLY. I had expected a difficulty of this kind, melud, and I – er – well, I have to agree that there is at present no further evidence of *res gestae*. All I can do is to offer this evidence as it stands, and accept Your Lordship's decision.

CRAMPTON. I see. Well, if that is the case, I must rule out these letters, and also the section of this witness's deposition marked 'X'. As at present offered, it is mere evidence of character, which of course, you are not entitled to bring.

SMYLY. Will you kindly not pull at my gown, Penefeather. If so, melud, I have no further questions for Mrs Campbell.

(*He sits down.*)

CRAMPTON. And what about you, Mr Butt?

BUTT. Nor I, melud. I don't want to ask her anything.

SMYLY (*half rising*). Then that completes the State's case. You may go now, my good woman.

MRS CAMPBELL (*indignantly*). Go? But I haven't said . . .

CRAMPTON. Silence, woman. Be off when you are told to go. You have no right to address the court.

(MRS CAMPBELL *comes muttering out of the witness's chair, as the* REGISTRAR *rises again.*)

REGISTRAR. The foreman, again, melud.

CRAMPTON. What is it now? What is the fellow saying?

REGISTRAR. He is saying, melud, that the jury feels upset at not being allowed to see these letters.

CRAMPTON. Mr Foreman, the jury must not be allowed to confuse itself over matters that do not concern it. Eh? What?

REGISTRAR. He says they're confused already sir. They were turned out of court, and they don't see why they should be the only ones to be kept in the dark. If they are to decide the case at all, they must know . . .

CRAMPTON. Oh do be quiet. They must take my direction on such matters. Has he sat down?

REGISTRAR. Yes, melud.

CRAMPTON. Very well. See that he stops there. Now, Mr Butt, we are all waiting for you to open the defence.

BUTT (*rising with a new air of confidence*). Bring in Dr Kenny, please. (*Somebody fetches* TERESA, *who enters during his speech to the audience*). May it please Your Lordship, gentlemen of the jury, your very natural reaction to my learned friend's case against Mr Kirwan has been, 'What on earth is all this about?' Well, gentlemen, let me set your minds at rest by telling you what it is all about. In the words of the Immortal Bard, it is Much Ado About Nothing. In the course of my entire career in the criminal courts, I have never had to meet so flimsy and ridiculous a charge. What, gentlemen, are you being asked to believe? That Mr Kirwan – a happily married man, enjoying

his summer holiday with his well-loved wife, has taken her out
to Ireland's Eye, on a bogus picnic, accompanied – mark you –
by three complete strangers, and there stabbed her to death
with a weapon which he has openly borrowed from the boatmen. And upon what evidence? Upon a supposed quarrel overheard by his landlady, upon the allegations of two fishermen
who think that they heard a cry from the island about six,
which they manifestly could not have heard if it had come from
the Long Hole, and finally upon the opinion of a junior assistant pathologist who examined the body more than a month
after the accident, and who gave an opinion that left the court
rocking with laughter.

I shan't keep you long, gentlemen, as I'm sure you all want to
get away to other matters that will not be such a waste of your
valuable time. All I want to say is this – that even if the State's
case against Mr Kirwan were three times as convincing, there
would still be no reason for his ever having committed so
atrocious a crime. There is not one tittle of evidence as to why
such a thing should ever have occurred. Indeed, I would go so
far as to say that if it is possible for a respectable man to be
charged with an offence like this, simply because he has suffered
the loss of his wife in a bathing fatality when nobody else
happens to be present – if this is possible at all, gentlemen,
which one of us can ever go in safety on a picnic without bringing along independent witnesses to protect us against such
appalling eventualities? And now, before calling the accused
himself to tell the Court what really happened, I shall offer you
the evidence of the expert witness who made everything perfectly clear at the inquest – Dr Teresa Kenny.

(TERESA *is now in the chair*.)

REGISTRAR. Raise the book in your right hand please.

(*She is sworn*.)

BUTT. Are you the dispensary doctor in Baldoyle?

TERESA. I am.

BUTT. And in this capacity, did you examine the body of Mrs
Sarah Mary Kirwan on a date early in last September.

TERESA. Yes. On the seventh.

BUTT. In your opinion, what was the cause of death?

TERESA. In my opinion, death was caused by drowning.

BUTT. You have no doubts on that point?

TERESA. None whatever.

BUTT. Did you notice any signs of violence upon the body?

TERESA. No. At least, that depends upon what you mean by violence. Not human violence.

BUTT. Explain further please.

TERESA. There were certain marks and scratches on the face and head – particularly on one ear, which had been partially eaten away.

BUTT. To what did you attribute these marks?

TERESA. To the work of small crabs after death.

BUTT. How long do you suppose these crabs would have taken to inflict this damage to the body?

TERESA. At least three or four hours.

BUTT. So that according to your observations, if the woman was found at half past seven, she must have been dead from about three or four o'clock.

TERESA. So I would say.

BUTT. Thank you, Doctor. That is all.

(*He sits down, and* SMYLY *rises.*)

SMYLY. Dr Kenny, you made no reference to these supposed crab-marks in the evidence you gave before the deputy coroner.

TERESA. No. I didn't.

SMYLY. Why not?

TERESA. I was describing what I considered to be the cause of death. In my opinion these were not the cause of death, but occurred afterwards.

SMYLY. You don't think you ought to have mentioned them?

TERESA. I don't see how they mattered if they came later.

SMYLY. In the light of what the State Pathologist subsequently found, do you think now that it would have been better if you had mentioned them?

TERESA. I don't know what the State Pathologist can possibly have based his opinion on, thirty-one days after the death.

SMYLY. What was your own opinion based on, Doctor? Did you make a thorough examination?

TERESA. Reasonably so.

SMYLY. On what evidence did you base your conclusions that the woman had been drowned?

TERESA. On the general appearance of the body.

SMYLY. Did you trouble to find out whether there was any sea water in the stomach?

TERESA. No.

SMYLY. I put it to you, Doctor, that you made a very superficial and perfunctory examination?

TERESA. Maybe I should have taken more time over it. But it was perfectly obvious that she had been drowned.

SMYLY (*with menace*). Why did you skimp this examination, Doctor?

TERESA. I . . . I don't think it could be described as skimped.

SMYLY. I put it to you, that it was because you knew the deceased?

TERESA. I . . . I didn't know her.

SMYLY. At least you knew who she was?

TERESA (*rather hysterically*). Yes, I knew who she was, but I didn't find out until I was half-way through the post-mortem. And then . . . maybe I *was* upset. Then this Mrs Campbell turned up and made a statement that upset me even more.

SMYLY. I put it to you that you knew who she was from the start – from the time that you offered to conduct this post mortem?

TERESA. I didn't 'offer' – as you put it – to conduct the post mortem.

SMYLY. Mrs Campbell swears in the open part of her deposition that you admitted in her presence that you offered to conduct the post mortem because you knew who the deceased was.

TERESA. I don't know how she can say that. It's the coroner who appoints some qualified person to –

SMYLY. Is it true? Or is Mrs Campbell a liar?

TERESA. A liar? No. I know I . . . mustn't call her that.

SMYLY. Then what she says is true?

TERESA (*after a pause*). I don't know what to say.

SMYLY. Come now. Is it your evidence that Mrs Campbell is perjuring herself in making this statement?

TERESA (*doggedly*). I have nothing to say against Mrs Campbell.

SMYLY (*sarcastically*). Really?

CRAMPTON. Dr Kenny, whether or not you volunteered your services, don't you think in the light of – ahem – certain matters, that it was a very unfortunate thing for you to have given evidence at this inquest at all?

TERESA. I don't see why, My Lord. I'm a local dispensary doctor.

CRAMPTON. You don't see why! Well, other people may see why. Indeed, it appears to me to have been unprofessional in the extreme, and I trust that the matter will be reported to the proper quarter. That is all I have to say.

SMYLY. And is that all you have to say, Doctor?

TERESA. What more can I say?

SMYLY. Mmm.

BUTT. You can leave the box, Doctor. Call the prisoner. William Burke Kirwan.

REGISTRAR. William Burke Kirwan.

(*There is a buzz of excitement as the murmur of the oath is heard.* KIRWAN *is shaking with indignation.*)

BUTT. William Burke Kirwan, did you murder your wife?

KIRWAN. I did not.

BUTT. When did you last see her alive?

KIRWAN. At about half past two on the day of her death.

BUTT. In other words, when Mr and Mrs Brew left for Howth in the boat, and your wife went away for her swim?

KIRWAN. That is right.

BUTT. What did you do for the rest of the afternoon?

KIRWAN. I stayed where I was – painting.

BUTT. Until the boat came back after six o'clock?

KIRWAN. Until then. I never moved at all from the spot where I was working.

BUTT. Did you hear any cry during that time?

KIRWAN. No.

BUTT. Was there anything unusual in your wife spending an afternoon in the water while you painted?

KIRWAN. Nothing whatever. She was very fond of swimming.

BUTT. Were you on good terms?

KIRWAN. Excellent terms.

BUTT. There was in fact no quarrel on the previous evening?

KIRWAN. There was not. We had a discussion. And I'm not responsible for what an eavesdropper thinks she hears.

BUTT. That's all right, Mr Kirwan. We'll leave it at that. Your witness, Mr Smyly.

(*He sits down and* SMYLY *rises.*)

SMYLY. Was your wife a good swimmer?

KIRWAN. Very good.

SMYLY. An athletic type. You never saw her having a fit, I suppose?

KIRWAN. No. I can't say that I ever did.

SMYLY. And what have you got to say about this quarrel that Mrs Campbell swears that she heard on the previous evening?

KIRWAN. Nothing – except that I would attach no importance whatever to anything that Mrs Campbell might swear.

SMYLY. You're not suggesting, are you, that Mrs Campbell is telling lies?

KIRWAN. She most certainly is telling lies. What's more. Mrs Campbell is not only a liar, but a thief.

BUTT. Now be careful, Kirwan.

KIRWAN (*venomously*). I will not 'be careful' as you call it! This woman is making all sorts of lying charges against me, and it's only fair that the jury know why. Why shouldn't they hear the truth about her?

REGISTRAR (*to the audience*). Sssh!

CRAMPTON. Now, Mr Kirwan, we all enjoy the experience of buying a dog and then doing the barking ourselves. But I am sure you would be wiser to leave the conduct of your case to your counsel, and only answer whatever you are asked.

KIRWAN. My Lord, not five minutes ago I swore to tell the whole truth. Am I supposed to do so, or am I not?

CRAMPTON. You are indeed, Mr Kirwan. Nobody has got any right to dictate what your evidence shall be. That is entirely a matter for yourself . . . and I may add, your own responsibility.

BUTT (*rising in some agitation*). Melud, I have had a word with my client about this situation, but I don't think he fully understands . . .

KIRWAN. I understand well enough that I'm supposed to take part in some sort of a conspiracy to whitewash Mrs Campbell. I'm supposed to sit mum while everybody, including my own counsel, presents her with bouquets as a respectable woman who has started these proceedings out of a noble sense of public spirit. Even Dr Kenny has to be abused by Your Lordship for the sake of this woman.

BUTT. Melud, I must ask you to . . .

SMYLY. Don't interrupt, Mr Butt.

CRAMPTON. Now, Mr Butt, I'm afraid you can't be allowed to prompt your client. It is clear that you have done your duty in advising him.

BUTT. But melud . . .

CRAMPTON. And having done so, there your duties end. He is now in Mr Smyly's hands.

BUTT (*sitting down*). I bow to Your Lordship's ruling.

SMYLY. Well, Mr Kirwan, what is this very serious charge that you want to bring against Mrs Campbell?

KIRWAN. She's a thief and a pilferer. She stole a ring from my wife. And when I took the matter to the guards in Howth, she tried to get her own back by trumping up this charge against me. That's what's at the back of this whole case.

(*Pause.*)

SMYLY. I see. Well, Mr Kirwan, you may be sure that what you have said will be conveyed to the Attorney General. And I have no doubt that when the necessary information has been sworn, a warrant will be issued for Mrs Campbell's arrest.

CRAMPTON. If that is what Mr Kirwan wants.

KIRWAN. Yes. I want it.

SMYLY. Then it will be seen to. In the meantime, let us return to our immediate concern. Mr Kirwan having made the gravest of charges against the character of one of the State's witnesses, I am now entitled under Section I(f) of the Criminal Justice Evidence Act 1924 to introduce the subject of his own character. After cross-examining him on this point, I then propose with Your Lordship's permission to re-examine Margaret Campbell on the portion of her deposition marked 'X', and also on the letters that she alleges she found in the accused's drawer.

CRAMPTON. That seems to be an unanswerable proposition, Mr Butt.

BUTT. Melud, the matter has passed out of my hands.

CRAMPTON. Mr Smyly, your application is granted. You may recall Margaret Campbell, after you have finished your cross-examination of the accused.

SMYLY (*triumphantly*). William Kirwan, is it a fact that you have been living in adultery with Dr Teresa Kenny, and that some months before she gave evidence at the inquest on your wife, you assisted her to procure an abortion?

(*Black out.*)

CURTAIN

ACT THREE

Scene 1

It is the late afternoon of Friday, December 31st, and we are back in the chief superintendent's office. BROWNRIGG *is working at his desk, with* SERGEANT FELL *in attendance, as before. The telephone rings.*

BROWNRIGG. Superintendent Brownrigg speaking. No ma'am – not unless they're causing an obstruction. The fact that the occupants of the car are of opposite sexes does not necessarily amount to an offence. I'll transfer you to the proper officer. (*He rattles the receiver.*) O'Reilly, take a note of this complaint please. (*He hangs up.*) Now, Sergeant, is that the end of the 'C Ones'?

FELL. Yes, Super. There's someone outside wants to see you.

BROWNRIGG. I'm very busy. Who is it?

FELL. That Dr Kenny, sir. The one was in the Kirwan case.

BROWNRIGG. Dr Kenny? Is she still around? How tiresome! Old Mrs Crowe is coming to see me about something, and I don't suppose they'll want to meet. Tell the doctor I can give her a few minutes, and don't let the old lady in until I send for her. Just give me a buzz to let me know when she's arrived.

FELL. Very good sir. (*He opens the door.*) Come in, miss. The superintendent can give you a couple of minutes now.

(TERESA KENNY *enters in a state of defiant agitation.*)

TERESA. Mr Brownrigg, I've got to see you.

BROWNRIGG (*closing the door behind* FELL.) One moment, Doctor. (*He offers her a chair.*) Now what can I do for you?

TERESA. What can you do for Bill Kirwan? That's what I want to know.

BROWNRIGG. I'm not aware that there is anything more to be done for Kirwan. He got a very good run for his money.

372

TERESA. A run for his money! Is that how you describe that dreadful trial?

BROWNRIGG. What was wrong with the trial? It was a perfectly fair one.

TERESA. Fair! How can you possibly call it that? With that result?

BROWNRIGG. Perfectly fair. And what's wrong with the result? His idea was to have Mrs Campbell arrested. Our purpose was to jail him. Now all our dreams have come true. What's unfair about that?

TERESA. The law was used to trick him.

BROWNRIGG. Not at all. It was *his* counsel who was very skilfully using the law to trick us. However – 'set a thief'. Truth has a way of winning out.

TERESA. I wish I knew whether you are incredibly callous or just very obtuse.

BROWNRIGG. Why should I be either?

TERESA. With people like you it doesn't seem to be a matter of finding out the truth. To you this whole horrible business of a criminal trial is just some sort of a game – a game that has nothing to do with guilt or innocence. It all depends on who has the best set of tricks. Bill Kirwan hasn't been convicted because he's guilty, but because he didn't play the rules as smartly as you people did.

BROWNRIGG (*stung*). Now, don't be melodramatic, Doctor.

TERESA. It's true, isn't it?

BROWNRIGG. It's nothing of the sort. Since you force me, I'll tell you the basis of my attitude towards the whole thing. It's a perfectly straightforward one. I believe that Kirwan killed his wife. I don't care whether he is punished or not. That's not my concern. All I say is, he killed his wife. And any trial that ends in a statement of that truth is, to me, an honest one.

TERESA. But how can you be so certain of anything as that? Do you imagine that you're infallible?

BROWNRIGG. No. But I do claim the right to use my brains in this peculiar job of mine. Maybe it's dangerous for a policeman to exercise some intelligence in carrying out his duties. Perhaps it makes him a little hard on the guilty. At the same time it means that I'm just as ready to take a sensible line with the innocent and the irresponsible, whenever they cross my path.

TERESA. All except Bill.

BROWNRIGG (*shaking his head*). He doesn't come under either heading.

TERESA. Yes, you *are* infallible.

BROWNRIGG. I am nothing of the sort. I know it's never wise to discuss these things out of court, but you've annoyed me, Dr Kenny, with your persistence. So I'm going to tell you two things that have satisfied me about Kirwan's guilt. First of all, his concealment of the boatman's knife.

TERESA. What's in that? Just because a knife is lost . . .

BROWNRIGG. Not lost, Doctor. Hidden . . . or thrown away. There's always some reason for concealment, and there was something about the condition of that knife that might have convicted Kirwan. So he got rid of it. Secondly, there is the line taken by all the independent witnesses towards the surrounding circumstances – something that isn't conclusive, but that I always find to be a damned good lead. Why are they all so hostile to Kirwan, if there isn't something behind it all? Something that's known, but isn't put into words.

TERESA. Oh, those boatmen and the women! Surely it's obvious what they've got against him. Bill was a fool. They think he cheated them out of some money, and maybe he did. But do you suppose that a man who had just killed his wife would pick on such a moment to have a quarrel with his boatmen over two pounds?

BROWNRIGG (*after a pause*). I admit that's a fair point. But I think there's more in their attitude than that. I think that they knew he was lying about having broken it off with you, and about your part in the inquest. Indeed I think that you're still lying about this yourself, Doctor.

TERESA. Oh, no. No!

BROWNRIGG. So long as you keep up this pretence, it's very hard to believe anything else that you say. Weren't you the cause of a quarrel with his wife, the night before he took her to the island? Does that suggest that it was all over?

TERESA. But that's absurd. She knew about me all along – from the time that it happened. All her family knew. If she didn't leave him two years ago, why would she wait to have a row about it last September?

(*The buzzer goes off.*)

BROWNRIGG. You say, her family knew?

TERESA. Of course they did. How could there be any secret about such a thing inside the family circle?

BROWNRIGG. Dr Kenny, you realize that these matters can be checked? Old Mrs Crowe is outside.

TERESA. Then ask her. She knows about it better than anybody.

BROWNRIGG. It may not help you at all if I do, Doctor. You realize that, I hope?

TERESA. Realize what?

BROWNRIGG. You must understand that ever since Kirwan's trial there has been a great deal of pressure on the Attorney General to have you prosecuted, too. Not for the murder, of course, but for another earlier offence which some quarters regard as just as serious as murder.

TERESA. Well? (*Pause.*) Why haven't you started? I'm here, aren't I?

BROWNRIGG. It's a matter of evidence. Those letters by themselves are rather ambiguous. They might be interpreted in more ways than one, and without some clear information as to what they do refer to, they're hardly proof of . . . what they presumably mean.

TERESA. You could make me admit it, couldn't you? That shouldn't be hard.

BROWNRIGG (*offended*). Doctor, under our conception of justice, the law does not force people to provide evidence against themselves. To be perfectly frank, the Attorney was giving you the benefit of the doubt, after what you've been through already.

TERESA (*bitterly*). How kind.

BROWNRIGG. We rather imagined that you would have the sense to take the hint and quietly disappear.

TERESA. Run away, in other words.

BROWNRIGG. If you like to put it that way – yes. We don't enjoy prosecuting people, Dr Kenny. But if I start asking questions now to Mrs Crowe, and she gives me the kind of answers that you say she will – direct evidence of an abortion having been procured a couple of years ago – this information may have to be used against you. You realize that?

TERESA. I can't help that. A man has been condemned to death.

BROWNRIGG. It may not affect his position.

TERESA. It'll tell the truth about one thing anyhow. I don't believe he ever had any quarrel with his wife over me. If he wouldn't quarrel with her when I needed him so badly, why would he do it last September?

BROWNRIGG. I don't see how this necessarily affects the verdict. But I'll ask Mrs Crowe about it if you want me to.

TERESA. Yes, I want you to.

BROWNRIGG. Dr Kenny, you are either a very rash woman, or a very foolish one.

TERESA (*almost in tears*). Maybe I'm a truthful one. You don't seem to have thought of that.

BROWNRIGG. Well, let's see – if you insist. If you'll wait in the next room, I'll talk to Mrs Crowe now. She's outside.

TERESA. Ask her anything you like. All I want is for you to get the truth.

BROWNRIGG. I'll do my best. Let's hope for your sake that we don't always get what we want.

(*He sees her off by a side door, and then admits* MRS CROWE *by the other.*)

BROWNRIGG. I'm sorry for keeping you, Mrs Crowe. Will you come in, please.

MRS CROWE. Inspector, I have come to see you about my daughter's grave. You know that I put a little railing around it?

BROWNRIGG. Yes, Mrs Crowe, I know all about that.

MRS CROWE. Well, judge of my surprise when I found the whole place dug up and the little railing completely ruined. May I ask who's going to pay for this damage?

BROWNRIGG. It was done by order of the Minister, Mrs Crowe. We had to find out whether your daughter really died as a result of a fit.

MRS CROWE. Perfectly outrageous! The next thing, I suppose, they'll dig up my late husband's grave simply because he died of a fit.

BROWNRIGG. I don't think that's likely, ma'am. But did your late husband die of a fit?

MRS CROWE (*nodding*). In Irishtown in 1917. I suppose this means that not even his grave is safe from this iniquitous Government?

BROWNRIGG. Was your husband subject to fits, ma'am?

MRS CROWE. The lieutenant was a martyr to epilepsy. But is that any reason why he shouldn't be allowed to rest peacefully in his grave?

BROWNRIGG. Yet, you say your daughter never suffered from anything of the kind?

MRS CROWE. I'm sure I never said that. As a little girl she used to have them, of course. But then she got this bottle which was absolutely infallible. She couldn't have them after that – never again.

BROWNRIGG. Mrs Crowe, are you telling me now, that your daugh-

376

ter used to take some form of medicine to arrest a tendency to epilepsy?

MRS CROWE. Of course. And it completely cured her, thank God.

BROWNRIGG. Don't you think you might have mentioned this before?

MRS CROWE. But I *am* mentioning it. I always said that it was ridiculous to say that she had fits. Never since she was quite small.

BROWNRIGG. But Mrs Crowe, if your daughter was ever subject to epilepsy, what makes you so certain that she was murdered?

MRS CROWE. Now don't be aggressive, Inspector. You're not cross-examining me, you know. I was told quite definitely that she was murdered.

BROWNRIGG. Who told you that?

MRS CROWE. Who told me? Why, you did, of course.

BROWNRIGG. I did? (*Pause.*) Mrs Crowe, may I ask you another question?

MRS CROWE. Certainly. I only hope it's not a silly one.

BROWNRIGG. Did anybody ever ask you whether you or your daughter knew of her husband's association with Dr Kenny?

MRS CROWE. I don't remember anybody asking me that. And I'm very glad they didn't.

BROWNRIGG. Why?

MRS CROWE. Because it is a subject that I prefer not to discuss.

BROWNRIGG. You mean that you *did* know?

MRS CROWE. It was all very disagreeable. Everybody agreed to forget about it afterwards.

BROWNRIGG. Everybody agreed to forget what? This is important, Mrs Crowe. Do you mean to say that you all knew about something that took place two years ago? Please apply your mind to this.

MRS CROWE. I shall do nothing of the sort, Inspector. It would just end in my having to say nasty things about my daughter. If she were still alive I might. But dead, no.

BROWNRIGG (*surprised*). About your daughter? Nasty things about what? Mrs Crowe, I must know.

MRS CROWE (*firmly*). Well, I have no intention of going into it.

BROWNRIGG. All right, Mrs Crowe. Don't go into it. But whatever event took place two years ago, am I right in supposing that youg daughter knew about it?

MRS CROWE. I'm sorry to say that it was she who insisted on it. I said at the time that no good could come of such wickedness.

Everybody concerned should have faced up to the situation, and taken the consequences.

BROWNRIGG (*in a deathly calm*). Mrs Crowe, didn't you hear the prosecution making it an important part of their case that your daughter only discovered about her husband and Dr Kenny last September?

MRS CROWE. I heard nothing of the sort. I was very rudely put out of the court half-way through the case, and kept in a draughty little room.

BROWNRIGG. At any rate, do you now tell me that the prosecution was wrong in making such a point?

MRS CROWE. I really don't know what my daughter could have discovered about that man that we didn't know long ago. We had trouble enough in 1935, and if there was anything more this year I don't want to hear anything about it.

BROWNRIGG. I see. Well, thank you, Mrs Crowe. That's all I . . . have to ask you.

MRS CROWE. Now about this little railing, Inspector. Who is going to . . . ?

BROWNRIGG. I'll take up the matter with the Department, and let you know what can be done.

MRS CROWE. I hope so, Inspector. It's all very upsetting. Good afternoon.

BROWNRIGG. Good afternoon, ma'am. Not that way. The other door, please.

(MRS CROWE *goes out by the way she came in.* BROWNRIGG *lifts the telephone.*)

BROWNRIGG. Sergeant, give a ring to the State Solicitor's office, and ask whether it would be convenient for me to go over and have a word with him. Also . . . wait a minute; I'm not finished . . . find out for me, too, whether any date has been fixed yet for Kirwan's execution.

(*He replaces the telephone, and goes to the side door and admits* TERESA KENNY.)

BROWNRIGG (*motioning her to a chair*). Will you come back, Doctor, please.

TERESA (*sitting down*). Well? What did she say?

BROWNRIGG. She wouldn't say what it was that she knew. But it's reasonably clear that she did know something.

TERESA. Oh thank God!

BROWNRIGG. In fact, I gathered from what little could be made of

378

Mrs Crowe's remarks, that the dead woman was the principal promoter of this other . . . felony. Is this so?

TERESA. Of course she was. Doesn't that show that there was nothing whatever for her to discover last September? And if not, why should they quarrel?

BROWNRIGG (*thoughtfully*). They might have quarrelled about many things – you included.

TERESA. No, no! Not about me. You know that I never saw him again.

BROWNRIGG. At any rate, there's no evidence that you did.

TERESA. Then you're satisfied! You'll tell them what Mrs Crowe said – that her daughter knew all about that operation from the very start?

BROWNRIGG. Mrs Crowe never mentioned any operation. In fact, there's still nothing except surmise to indicate what she was talking about.

TERESA. Then I'll have to make it clear what she was talking about.

BROWNRIGG. You mean, you'll make a statement?

TERESA. I'll make any statement that's needed. I'll describe the whole disgusting business, and the part that Mrs Kirwan played in it. Will that satisfy you.

BROWNRIGG. I've already told you that we have no wish to press you to incriminate yourself.

TERESA. You're not pressing me. I'm offering it. Will it satisfy the Attorney General that there was no motive, if I make a statement?

BROWNRIGG. I dare say it will satisfy him that the motive offered by the State at the trial was a wrong one. But that won't prove Kirwan innocent.

TERESA. It might help?

BROWNRIGG. It might raise some doubts about one aspect of the trial. I can't say more than that.

TERESA. Then I'll make it.

BROWNRIGG. If you do, it must be on the distinct understanding that I'm offering you no inducements and making no promises.

TERESA. Write it out yourself, and put that in. I'll sign it.

BROWNRIGG (*staring at her*). Why?

TERESA. A man has been convicted of something he didn't do. If you don't know why I should want to rectify that, there's no good my trying to explain.

BROWNRIGG. Oh, very well. (*He takes out a sheet of paper and starts*

379

to write.) This Kirwan seems to be a very remarkable man. First of all he manages to persuade a woman like you to have an affair with him. And now he inspires you to run the risk of going to jail in order to get him out of trouble. I suppose you're still deeply attached to him?

TERESA. I'd rather not discuss my feelings for Bill Kirwan.

BROWNRIGG. Nevertheless, an outsider may perhaps wonder how you ever got involved with him. To most people he seems rather an unattractive type.

TERESA (*emotionally*). You wouldn't understand if I told you. People are only black or white to you. A man is an unattractive type – so he can be hanged for something he didn't do.

BROWNRIGG (*finishing his writing*). That remark is hardly worthy of you, Doctor. Kirwan is not in any danger of hanging because of his lack of charm.

TERESA. Are you quite sure?

BROWNRIGG (*after a pause*). It's usually the privilege of the police to do the questioning. So perhaps you'll allow me to leave yours unanswered, and offer you my query instead. (*He hands her the paper.*) Is that statement correct? Don't answer if you'd rather not.

(*She reads it.*)

TERESA (*quietly*). Yes. It's correct.

BROWNRIGG. If you sign this thing voluntarily, all I can undertake is to offer it to the Attorney General as new evidence, showing that the motive attributed to Kirwan by the State may have been wrong.

TERESA. I understand.

BROWNRIGG. On the other hand, as it's an admission of a felony on your own part, I'm afraid I shall also have to ask the authorities to decide what course they intend to adopt towards you.

TERESA. May I borrow your pen, please?

BROWNRIGG. Certainly.

(*He gives her one, and as she signs,* KENMIS *enters.*)

KENMIS. What is it, Brownrigg? I was on my way out for something to eat when I heard that you wanted to see me.

BROWNRIGG. You remember Dr Kenny. Mr Kenmis, the State Solicitor.

KENMIS (*bowing stiffly*). Of course.

TERESA (*rising*). How do you do. Well there you are. Now I expect you'll both want to be alone. I'll be waiting – whenever you want me.

380

BROWNRIGG (*speaking out of the door*). Sergeant, look after Dr Kenny, please.

(*She goes out, and* BROWNRIGG *stares after her in some perplexity.*)

KENMIS. Well – fraternizing with the enemy, I see. Or is it just that you can't give up a good case that involves a pretty face?

BROWNRIGG. I wonder what she sees in that fellow?

KENMIS. Is that what you want to discuss with me?

BROWNRIGG (*looking at the statement in his hand*). I don't believe they ever broke it off. They couldn't have. Not if she's still in love with him as much as this.

KENMIS. Listen my friend, I've got a full night's work of arrears waiting on my desk, and only half an hour in which to snatch a meal. So if you'll excuse me . . .

BROWNRIGG. Mr Kenmis, there are two things about the Kirwan case that I think you ought to know. The first is that whatever they quarrelled about that night, it was not over the fact that the deceased had just found out about her husband's relations with another woman.

KENMIS. Indeed.

BROWNRIGG. I've just discovered that both Mrs Kirwan and her relatives knew all about this affair with Kenny from the start. In fact, it was Mrs Kirwan who suggested the abortion.

KENMIS. So what does this amount to?

BROWNRIGG. It amounts to the fact that the motive we gave to the jury was a wrong one.

KENMIS. Very well, it was a wrong one. That doesn't affect the case. Motive is only a tit-bit to please the laymen. The man was convicted for what he did. Not because of his reasons.

BROWNRIGG. He might never have been convicted at all if this evidence had come out.

KENMIS. In other words, there might been a grave miscarriage of justice. You're not suggesting, are you, that he didn't kill the woman?

BROWNRIGG. No, I still think he must have done it. At the same time, I've also found out that the dead woman was subject to epilepsy. Nobody knew about that.

KENMIS. What are you up to, Brownrigg? Trying to land us with a new trial?

BROWNRIGG. No. But I've promised to bring this paper to the attention of the Attorney General.

KENMIS. Bring what? (BROWNRIGG *holds out the statement.*) No, don't show it to me. I've got a feeling I'd rather not have seen it.

BROWNRIGG. It's a statement by Dr Kenny on the whole circumstances of that illegal operation. It confirms and explains what Mrs Crowe has just said to me – that the dead woman knew all about it at the time, and indeed was the first person to urge it.

KENMIS. Good God, Brownrigg. Have you got that wretched girl to sign a statement like that?

BROWNRIGG. She insisted on signing it. I warned her, but she's convinced that it will help Kirwan.

KENMIS. Well it won't help Kirwan, and you damn well know it. Now that there's been a verdict, it will take more than a few doubts about his motive to upset it. All that it will do is force us to prosecute Kenny, which I suppose is what you're after, though why I can't imagine. I would have thought you'd caused enough trouble already for that unfortunate woman.

BROWNRIGG (*indignantly*). I'm not after any such thing. I'm only trying to carry out my duty.

KENMIS. God preserve me from all idiots who 'only want to do their duty'. However, if you want to put the girl in jail, go ahead. I can't stop you taking that damn thing to the Attorney.

BROWNRIGG. What alternative have I?

KENMIS. You can be a sensible man and forget about it. I always thought you were sensible. But in this case common sense seems to be in short supply. I suppose you resent her still standing up for the fellow. Want her yourself, perhaps. Oh to hell with it all and a Happy New Year!

(*He leaves the office as* SERGEANT FELL *enters.*)

FELL. January the fifteenth, sir.

BROWNRIGG (*deep in thought*). Eh? What's that?

FELL. The date of the execution, Super. You asked for it.

BROWNRIGG. Oh yes, of course. Er – I hope you won't repeat that scandalous remark of the State Solicitor.

FELL. I heard nothing, Super. January the fifteenth is all I came to say. That's unless they reprieve him in the meantime.

BROWNRIGG. You think that's a possibility?

FELL. Well, you never can tell, sir. It's a difficult case, full of things I find it hard to believe. Though I dare say he's guilty all right.

BROWNRIGG. So you feel that way yourself, do you? What sort of things?

FELL. Well, sir, it's none of my business to express an opinion, but

I know Howth well, and I always found it hard to believe that it happened at six o'clock . . . leastways not in the Long Hole.

BROWNRIGG. Why not?

FELL. Sure you'd never hear a scream from there, and you on the harbour wall. It's too far.

BROWNRIGG. Two people swore they heard it.

FELL. Well, whatever it was, it wasn't from the Long Hole. Or else it wasn't a scream.

BROWNRIGG (*after a thoughtful pause*). Fell, I've got to get to the bottom of this somehow. Things have been said to me this evening that shake my belief in myself. Tell the orderly to fetch my car. I'm going to take a run out to Howth.

FELL. Yes, Super. And will I give a ring to Sergeant Sherwood, and tell him to meet you there?

BROWNRIGG. Do, please. Down at the harbour.

FELL. Will he want to bring any papers?

BROWNRIGG. No. Only his vocal chords. I've taken other people's word for this long enough. Now we're going to do some shouting for ourselves.

BLACK OUT

Scene 2

It is late in the same evening in the same place. TERESA KENNY *is sitting half asleep in one of the chairs, when* BROWNRIGG *comes in wearing his greatcoat, which he takes off and hangs up. He is followed by* MR BREW, *who is dressed for a festive occasion.*

BROWNRIGG. Good heavens, Dr Kenny, what are you doing here?

TERESA (*waking up*). I thought you told me to wait.

BROWNRIGG. Wait? What for?

TERESA. While you found out what they intend to do about me.

BROWNRIGG. Oh, absurd! I didn't mean you to do that. I'm so sorry. By the way, you know Mr Brew, I suppose.

TERESA. Yes, I remember Mr Brew.

BREW (*genially*). Compliments of the season.

BROWNRIGG (*picking up the phone*). Excuse me while I make a call.

TERESA. If you don't want me, I'll go home.

383

BROWNRIGG. No, no. Wait a minute, and I'll see that you're brought home by car. I'm so sorry.

TERESA. Please don't bother. I . . .

BROWNRIGG. Just a minute, please. There's something I want to . . . Hello, is the State Solicitor still there? Oh so it's you, Mr Kenmis. I'm sorry to bother you at this hour, but if you could possibly come over again for a few minutes . . . I'd come to you, but I have a number of other people here . . . O.K. I thought you'd be charmed.

(*He hangs up with a wry smile.*)

BREW (*to* TERESA). Funny running into the Super on my way up to Christchurch Place. I never thought the Guards had to work such late hours on New Year's Eve. It'd never be allowed in my business. (*He laughs.*)

BROWNRIGG. Sit down, please. I'm very glad you're both here to confirm some things I have to lay before Mr Kenmis. For one thing, I've just been out to Howth, and I'd like your opinion, Mr Brew, on a certain problem.

BREW. Ah, Howth – the old spot! Can't keep away from the scene of the crime – eh! Am I right? (*He laughs.*)

BROWNRIGG. I sent a sergeant out to the island to try an experiment. It's been tried before, but I find it's always a mistake to take anyone else's word on these things.

BREW. True enough, Super. You had him shouting, I suppose.

BROWNRIGG. Yes, it's an exceptionally calm evening tonight. Hardly any wind at all, and . . .

BREW. And you didn't hear him, I suppose.

BROWNRIGG. How did you guess that? I just managed to hear him from the beach. From the Long Hole I could hear nothing.

BREW. Mmm. I'm not really surprised.

BROWNRIGG. I think you said there was quite a lot of wind on the day in question?

BREW. There was. In fact, I'll tell you no lie, Super. I never could understand that yarn about the boatmen hearing a cry at six o'clock. I wanted to say so at the trial, but the wife kept telling me not to stick my nose into things I wasn't asked. So I didn't.

BROWNRIGG. So you think the boatmen must have been wrong?

BREW. I wouldn't like to say a word against the boatmen, Super. Very decent fellows all of them. But if you ask me, I always thought it must have been seagulls.

BROWNRIGG (*quietly*). Seagulls. You thought that all along, eh?

384

BREW (*awkwardly*). Well yes. But then of course, it's none of my business to express an opinion is it?

BROWNRIGG. It's everybody's business to help us to get at the truth, Mr Brew.

BREW. Aw, game ball. There's no getting away from that. All the same, I hope I'm the kind of fellow that always plays fair for my side. I wouldn't let you down, you know, by saying a thing like that in court.

BROWNRIGG. There's no question of letting us down, Mr Brew. A trial isn't a sporting event (*with a look at* TERESA), in spite of what some people think.

BREW. Well of course if that's the line you take, it throws quite a different light on it all. I'm sorry Moira's not along with me to hear you say that. She always says, 'Keep your mouth shut, Brendan, or they'll say you've some reason for trying to get the man off.' (*He laughs nervously.*)

TERESA. I know what you mean, Mr Brew. We're not the sort of people you want to be mixed up with.

BREW. Ah well now, I wouldn't say that. I can be as broadminded as anyone. All the same . . . the course of justice . . . you know, even if it's not quite right in all the facts, you know. We mustn't obstruct the course of justice must we?

TERESA. You mean that there are some other facts besides the scream that you think are wrong?

BREW (*very uncomfortably*). Well . . . yes. As a matter of fact . . . yes.

TERESA. What are they?

BREW. Aw, I wouldn't say that without the Super's permission. (*To* BROWNRIGG.) As a matter of fact, I was going to come and see you when I found it. But the wife said, no. 'What's done's done,' she said. 'So don't be causing trouble for everybody.'

BROWNRIGG. You have my permission, Mr Brew, to tell me every-thing you know about this case . . . whether it's likely to cause trouble or not. In fact, it's your duty.

BREW. Well if you put it that way I suppose I've no choice in the matter. Only don't tell Moira I did anything more than what you asked me.

BROWNRIGG (*impatiently*). All right. All right. What is it?

BREW. Ah, it's just a small point. Makes no difference to the fact that he killed the poor woman. I'm not denying that. But I don't think it was with the boatman's knife.

BROWNRIGG. Why not?

BREW. Well . . . em . . . I got the old golf clubs out again a couple of days ago. First time since . . . well, that very day.

BROWNRIGG. Yes. Go on.

BREW. Well . . . em . . . about that knife. I had a sort of feeling that little rascal of mine had his eye on it when we were out there on the island. In fact we took a look in his pockets on the way home. But as it wasn't there I thought no more about it. But do you know what he must have done?

(*He gives a nervous laugh.*)

TERESA. What?

BREW. Why, hid it in the bottom of my golf bag! I thought I felt something hard down there when I was playing a round on Wednesday, and by jiminy, when I turned the bag out, there it was at the bottom.

BROWNRIGG. You're sure it's the same knife?

BREW. Absolutely, old man. Couldn't be mistaken. I have it at home now.

BROWNRIGG. And you found this two days ago?

BREW (*laughing nervously*). Yes, Super. Hope it doesn't get the little beggar into trouble. I was for ringing you up at once, but the wife said, 'What difference does it make?'

BROWNRIGG. Only this difference; as you say yourself, if the knife came back in the boat with you in the early afternoon, Kirwan could not have used it to stab his wife.

BREW. Yes, that's what I thought too. I wonder what he did use?

(KENMIS *enters in a rage.*)

KENMIS. Look here, Brownrigg, if you think you're going to . . . Who's this?

BROWNRIGG. Mr Brew of Ranelagh. One of the witnesses.

KENMIS. Ah, yes. I remember.

BROWNRIGG. And of course, Dr Kenny. Well thank you, Mr Brew, for your information. I won't keep you any longer.

BREW. Right. I'll be trotting along. Just got time to get up to the cathedral for the fun. Happy New Year all.

(*He mops his forehead and laughs his way off.*)

KENMIS. Brownrigg, if this is anything more about Dr Kenny, I've already told you I don't want to hear it now. This is no time . . .

BROWNRIGG. It's not about Dr Kenny. It's about Kirwan. Mr Kenmis, I'm afraid I'm going to have to ask you to get the verdict set aside.

KENMIS (*dumbfounded*). What?

BROWNRIGG. He didn't do it.

TERESA (*rising*). Oh!

KENMIS. What do you mean – he didn't do it?

BROWNRIGG. Nangle's knife has just been found. Kirwan couldn't have used it, because it left the island at half past two in the bottom of Brew's golf bag.

KENMIS (*shaken*). A nice time to discover this.

BROWNRIGG. What's more, I've been carrying out some experiments for myself in Howth. On a day with any sea running, those boatmen could never have heard that scream. It was seagulls. I'm certain of that.

KENMIS (*sitting down wearily*). Indeed. Well I'm not. Listen Brownrigg, it was you who promoted this prosecution. It would never have started but for your damned investigations. And if you're going to begin having doubts, you ought to have had them long ago.

BROWNRIGG. Maybe I should. Maybe we all should. But we didn't.

KENMIS. Well, it's too late now. There's been an appeal and the verdict has been upheld.

BROWNRIGG. It's never too late to save a man's life.

KENMIS. Ah, don't be so damned melodramatic. If it turns out that there are any serious doubts, the death sentence will be commuted.

BROWNRIGG. To life imprisonment?

TERESA. That's no way out! If he didn't do it, he's entitled to be found not guilty. It's no answer to put him in jail for life.

BROWNRIGG. She's right. If there are any serious doubts, the man is entitled to be acquitted.

KENMIS. Listen, Brownrigg. I don't give a damn what he stabbed her with or when either. I have expert evidence that she wasn't drowned, but died of a stab, and so far as I'm concerned that stands. I don't hire a dog and bark myself, as Crampton said. I leave that to Kirwan.

BROWNRIGG. But surely . . .

KENMIS. I know what you're going to say. He had no motive. And now you're proposing to produce Dr Kenny and old Mrs Crowe to prove your point, all of which is going to end in Dr Kenny going to jail, too. Very well. If that's what you want, give me her statement, and I'll start the machinery working.

BROWNRIGG (*blandly*). I'm afraid I don't know what you mean.

KENMIS. Come on. Give me her statement. You began this, so we may as well go through with it.

BROWNRIGG. There must be some misunderstanding, Mr Kenmis. I haven't got any statement from Dr Kenny.

KENMIS (*with menace*). Did you or did you not tell me earlier in the evening that Dr Kenny had signed a statement admitting a very serious offence?

BROWNRIGG. No, Mr Kenmis, I didn't.

KENMJS. And that Mrs Crowe had confirmed it?

BROWNRIGG. I'm afraid I can't remember Mrs Crowe saying anything of the sort.

(TERESA *collapses into a chair.*)

KENMIS. So that's the latest. Your memory's beginning to fail.

BROWNRIGG (*with a half-smile*). Well, as somebody said to me recently, sensible men don't always have very good memories.

KENMIS. Forgetfulness, if carried too far, sometimes leads to retirement.

BROWNRIGG. Anyhow, I hope I shall have long enough to clear this matter up.

KENMIS. You fool! How are you going to upset the verdict so long as the motive stands?

BROWNRIGG. I'm going to try and do without the motive, Mr Kenmis. You said yourself that motive is only a tit-bit to please laymen. I'm going to show that six o'clock is a washout for the time of the supposed crime; and I'm going to ask Hatchell to admit that the woman might have drowned in a few feet of water in the course of an epileptic fit. No verdict can stand up against that.

KENMIS. To go back on his evidence at this stage! You're crazy if you think Hatchell will ever do that.

BROWNRIGG. Well, anyhow, I'm going to try. I've asked him to come down tonight, and that's why I wanted you here, too.

KENMIS. Brownrigg, are you off your head?

BROWNRIGG. The man is innocent.

KENMIS. Whatever he is, he's not innocent. If it's not one crime it's another.

TERESA. Whatever he did, he didn't kill his wife. Why should he hang for that?

KENMIS. He won't hang for that, you tiresome woman . . . not if there's any doubt. He won't even get a life sentence. If there's any substance in what you're saying, the sentence can be commuted after a couple of years. He can come out after serving not a day longer than he would have got for assisting in an abortion.

388

TERESA. If he didn't kill his wife, he shouldn't go to jail for killing his wife.

KENMIS. Look. You keep out of this. We're not done with you yet.

TERESA (*to* BROWNRIGG). How can this man be such a monster? As if it didn't matter what Bill's convicted of!

KENMIS. Nice language, I must say.

BROWNRIGG. She has a right to be upset. Why are you against any review of this case, Mr Kenmis?

KENMIS. I'll tell you why. Not because I'm a monster, but because there are other considerations besides Kirwan's reputation – which is far from spotless anyhow. You know as well as I do, that if the Department releases Kirwan, and there's no prosecution for anything else, there'll be a public outcry.

TERESA. Is that . . . ?

(*She is silenced by both of the men.*)

KENMIS. On the other hand, if there has to be a new trial, it's going to amount to an open declaration that it's possible for an innocent man to be convicted after a perfectly fair hearing.

BROWNRIGG. Well . . . apparently it *is* possible.

KENMIS. All right . . . supposing it is . . . in this particular case! Is that any reason for making a fool out of the system – the system that you and I are supposed to be operating? Are you prepared to shake public confidence in the whole administration of justice because this fellow happens to be in jail for 'B' instead of for 'A'?

BROWNRIGG. I don't want to make a fool out of the system. I believe in the system. I admire it. That's why, if there's been any mistake I want it to be my mistake – our mistake, if you like – but not the mistake of the law. That may shake public confidence in you and me, but not in the law.

KENMIS. Thank you very much. It's nice to know that I'm being sacrificed to your deep regard for the law. I notice all the same that your high-flown sentiments don't drive you into doing your duty as regards Dr Kenny. When a good-looking woman comes in by the door, all high-faluting principles go up the chimney.

BROWNRIGG. Mr Kenmis, this lady at very great risk to herself has had the courage to downface me in my office and show me that an injustice has been done. I'd think very poorly of myself if I allowed her to go to jail for doing that.

KENMIS. Don't talk rubbish. You're in love with the woman. I ought to have known it from the start.

BROWNRIGG (*furious*). I am *not* in love with the woman! Can't a man have some regard for the truth without being accused of melodramatic nonsense?

KENMIS. What's more, you're jealous of the fact that she's still in love with Kirwan.

TERESA. Look here, who said I was . . . ?

BROWNRIGG. It's a damned lie. I'm not in the slightest jealous of Kirwan.

KENMIS. Oh, yes you are. And being a bloody fool in the way you show it.

(FELL *enters*.)

FELL. Excuse me, Super, but Mr Hatchell is here now.

KENMIS. Hah! Imagining that you're going to get Hatchell to go back on what he's sworn in open court! Crazy isn't the word for it.

BROWNRIGG. If he does take it back, will you agree to reopen the whole case with the Attorney General?

KENMIS. If he doesn't, will you hand me over that confession of Dr Kenny's?

BROWNRIGG (*hesitating*). Well . . .

KENMIS. I thought not. It's just as I said.

TERESA. Yes he will. If he won't, I'll give you another one myself.

KENMIS. It's a deal. But remember this, Brownrigg, if somebody gets up in the Dail and says that the Department of Justice is not capable of getting a conviction when a conviction is clearly called for, you're going to be a very unpopular policeman. Somebody's going to be blamed for that, and it's not going to be the Minister. However – perhaps you're got another job in mind.

BROWNRIGG. Show Mr Hatchell in please, Sergeant.

FELL. Yes, sir.

(FELL *goes out and returns with* HATCHELL.)

HATCHELL. *Conus ata tu?*

BROWNRIGG. Ah Mr O'Tabhairmach. It was very kind of you to come – especially on such a night.

HATCHELL. *Go raibh maith agat. Abair do ghno me se do thoil e.*

BROWNRIGG. I dare say you speak English, Mr O'Tabhairmach?

HATCHELL. Certainly, Superintendent, whenever appropriate. I would have hoped that between two officials . . . However, if you have not the national language . . .

BROWNRIGG. At the moment I'm not interested in politics. I want to talk to you as a pathologist. And in that field I'm afraid I shall have to ask you to use the vulgar tongue. Cigarette?

HATCHELL. No thank you. I prefer my own. Well, what is it?

BROWNRIGG. It's about the Kirwan case. You remember it?

HATCHELL. Ah yes. A very unsavoury case. A very bad character altogether.

BROWNRIGG. Probably so. But it was your expert evidence that made it possible to get a conviction.

HATCHELL. Well, I'm glad to have been some help to you. That's your job isn't it – getting convictions?

BROWNRIGG. No, Mr O'Tabhairmach, strangely enough it's not. When you were in the box you stated that in your opinion the woman could not have died from drowning.

HATCHELL. That's right. It was a clear case. There were no signs of asphyxia.

BROWNRIGG. So you said. But when exactly did that aspect of your evidence occur to you?

HATCHELL (*stiffening*). I don't follow.

BROWNRIGG. Was that opinion really a result of your examination, or was it something that Smyly had just put into your head?

HATCHELL. I take a very poor view of that insinuation.

BROWNRIGG. I'm sorry. But it's something we've got to know.

HATCHELL. You have no right to talk to me like that. I have nothing further to add to my evidence. *Slan agat.*

BROWNRIGG. Wait a minute please. It now appears that Kirwan couldn't have used the boatman's knife. Nor is it likely that she died at the time we first thought. What's more, she was liable to epilepsy ever since childhood – a thing we didn't know before.

HATCHELL. So far as I'm concerned none of that has any significance.

BROWNRIGG. No significance! My God, don't you see that it means that if there is any doubt about your evidence that she couldn't have been drowned, the trial will have to be set aside.

HATCHELL. Why should there be any doubt about my evidence?

BROWNRIGG. Why should there be any doubt about mine either? Because we both made mistakes, man, that's why.

HATCHELL. Mr Kenmis, are you a party to this attack on my qualifications?

KENMIS. No. I'm only the man waiting with the meat-chopper.

TERESA. Mr Hatchell, it isn't a question of qualifications. The greatest experts can make mistakes. In fact they're the only ones

391

who ever admit it. The superintendent agrees that he was wrong himself.

HATCHELL (*suspiciously*). What's that got to do with me?

BROWNRIGG. I'll tell you . . .

TERESA. No. Please let me talk to him. Mr Hatchell, would you mind telling us what it was about the woman that convinced you that she didn't drown?

HATCHELL. I've been through all that a dozen times. It was perfectly clear from the start that the evidence at the inquest had been most superficial.

TERESA. I know, I know. My post mortem was hopeless. I didn't even examine the stomach for sea water. But did you?

HATCHELL. Me? For sea water . . . almost a month later? Ridiculous!

TERESA. Then you didn't examine it any more than I did?

HATCHELL. Why should I? It was perfectly clear what had happened. (*Turning to* KENMIS). That post mortem was carried out by a woman assistant at the request of a deputy coroner who obviously . . .

TERESA. Yes, yes. I admit all that. But it doesn't answer the question.

BROWNRIGG. Let's agree the inquest was a farce, and that nobody examined the stomach. By what tests did you determine that the woman didn't drown?

HATCHELL. By several tests.

BROWNRIGG. Tell us one of them.

HATCHELL. Well . . . by the absence of any signs of asphyxia.

BROWNRIGG. Where would you expect to find such signs?

HATCHELL. Oh, in various organs. The lungs, for example.

BROWNRIGG. Did you look in the lungs? (*Pause. Then louder.*) Did you look in the lungs?

HATCHELL. Superintendent Brownrigg, you have no right to bally-rag me. I warn you, I will not be ballyragged. There was a wound in her ear . . .

BROWNRIGG. . . . on the basis of which you stated she had been killed. That's the sole basis to your evidence, eh?

HATCHELL. I'll see that·you hear more of this, sir. You have no jurisdiction over me – no authority to make this scandalous attack on my professional qualifications.

BROWNRIGG. To hell with your professional qualifications! I'm asking you . . .

TERESA. Oh, please, please don't let's get angry. Mr Hatchell, the superintendent's professional reputation is in much greater danger than yours.

HATCHELL. In what way?

TERESA. In going on with these inquiries he's doing something . . .

BROWNRIGG. Anything I'm doing is my own business. Dr Kenny is the one who's in danger. You ought to know that she's taken a line for the sake of the truth that is liable to put her in jail herself. What's anybody's reputation compared to that?

HATCHELL (*turning to* KENMIS). What are they talking about?

KENMIS. Don't ask me. All I know is that if somebody doesn't go to jail for something, there's going to be a vacancy in the police force.

HATCHELL. Then why are they trying to upset the case?

KENMIS. They're both in search of a miasma that they're pleased to call the truth . . . a dangerous luxury for a public servant to get addicted to. I trust you're not afflicted in the same way, Hatchell?

HATCHELL. I've as much regard for the truth as any man. Who says I haven't?

TERESA. Nobody, Mr Hatchell . . . unless you want to deny it yourself.

HATCHELL (*upset*). He was a very disreputable character all round.

TERESA. Of course he was, Mr Hatchell. So am I, God help me.

BROWNRIGG. Who isn't, I'd like to know?

TERESA. But isn't that just where you people have got to be so careful? There are so many disreputable characters – always getting off on one excuse or another – why, you and Mr Brownrigg must see it happening every day. So naturally you get tough, and you want to play hard for your side. I can understand that. But that's just where the danger lies.

BROWNRIGG. She's right, Hatchell. We see so many smart scoundrels using the rules to wriggle out of what they deserve, that we forget what we owe to the fools who are their own worst enemies. It's not the upright man who needs the law's protection. It's the disreputable characters.

KENMIS. This is becoming an annual convention of guardian angels.

BROWNRIGG. Shut up, Kenmis!

TERESA. The superintendent isn't claiming any jurisdiction over you, Mr Hatchell. Neither of you are servants of the other, but of something far bigger – science and justice. And how long will either of you think that science or justice are worth serving,

if you ever start prostituting them to your professional reputa-
tions?

HATCHELL (*shaken*). I'm sure you mean well, Doctor, but . . .

TERESA. Of course I do. And so do you. That's why I think you
ought to answer the superintendent's question.

HATCHELL (*dully*). What question?

BROWNRIGG. Are you honestly and scientifically certain that Mrs
Kirwan could not possibly have died from drowning?

HATCHELL (*suddenly shouting after a lengthy pause*). No, sir. I'm
not. Damn you!

BROWNRIGG. Thank you, Seoirse.

(KENMIS *rises and grimly gathers up his papers.*)

KENMIS. Well, I suppose I'll have to go now and ring up the
Attorney General. It may not be to wish him a Happy New
Year, but at least he'll be pleased to have a few more vacancies
to give to party hacks. Good evening.

TERESA. Thank you, Mr Kenmis.

KENMIS. For nothing, ma'am.

(*He goes out followed by* HATCHELL. BROWNRIGG *returns to
his desk.*)

TERESA. Bill Kirwan will get off now, won't he?

BROWNRIGG. He's bound to. There's nothing left to support the
verdict.

(*He starts to work.*)

TERESA. Thank you for . . . everything.

BROWNRIGG (*writing*). No need to thank me for carrying out my
duties. (*Pause.*) Or at any rate, some of them.

TERESA. Some of them. Yes . . . I know what you mean. (*Pause.*)
Still, you'll never get any thanks from anybody else. Least of all
from Bill. He's not the grateful type.

BROWNRIGG. To be thanked by Bill Kirwan would be a very second-
rate experience. However . . . give him my congratulations, for
what they're worth.

TERESA. Congratulations? On getting off?

BROWNRIGG. No. On his wedding. You'll marry him now, I
suppose?

TERESA (*bursting into laughter*). Marry Bill! Oh, you really are
absurd! I knew you never believed me when I said that I'd had
quite enough of Bill long ago.

BROWNRIGG (*surprised*). Then why did you do it? I can scarcely
imagine your doing what you did without intending to marry
him.

TERESA. What romantic nonsense you men can talk! Why, you're just as bad as Kenmis with his silly old Love Motive.

BROWNRIGG. Then you didn't run yourself into all that danger because you were . . . still attached to him?

TERESA. Attached! Why I've loathed him . . . that cheap Narcissus . . . loathed him ever since I found him out two years ago. I *had* to take the line that I did. I couldn't bear the thought of feeling sorry for him.

BROWNRIGG (*relaxing*). Well I'll be damned.

TERESA. How could you think anything else? You're risking just as much as I am. More now. And you're not in love with me.

BROWNRIGG. No.

TERESA. Or are you?

BROWNRIGG. No. Don't worry. I did it for myself – I suppose. Yes. I'd have had a poor view of myself if I hadn't. So, I suppose, would Hatchell.

TERESA. You'll have a poorer view if you lose your job.

BROWNRIGG. Don't worry. Kenmis's bark is worse than his bite.

(*The church bells are heard.*)

TERESA. There's the New Year.

BROWNRIGG (*rising and going to a cupboard*). Yes. I – er – suppose it would be a mistake to have a small drink before I send you home in the black maria? (*He produces a bottle.*) I feel in no condition to face a New Year. Should we . . . do you suppose?

TERESA (*smiling*). No. I don't think we should. I'm not really a very nice character, and it would look bad if your sergeant came in.

BROWNRIGG. Yes. Very bad. He'd almost certainly expect to join us. However . . . (*He pours out.*) . . . even if we can't have the Love Motive, we can still have a curtain line that Hatchell would approve of. (*He holds out a glass.*) *Slainte.*

TERESA (*taking it*). *Slainte.*

(*That is the end of this play.*)